Mediterranean Europe

phrasebooks

Mediterranean Europe phrasebook
2nd edition – February 2007

Published by
Lonely Planet Publications Pty Ltd ABN 36 005 607 983
90 Maribyrnong St, Footscray, Victoria 3011, Australia

Lonely Planet Offices
Australia Locked Bag 1, Footscray, Victoria 3011
USA 150 Linden St, Oakland CA 94607
UK 72–82 Rosebery Ave, London, EC1R 4RW

Cover illustration
Europa by Yukiyoshi Kamimura

ISBN 978 1 74104 076 6

10 9 8 7 6 5 4 3 2

Printed by C&C Offset Printing Co Ltd, China

acknowledgments

This book is based on existing editions of Lonely Planet's phrasebooks as well as new content. It was developed with the help of the following people:

- Anila Mayhew for the Albanian chapter
- Gordana Ivetac and Ivan Ivetac for the Croatian chapter
- Michael Janes for the French chapter
- Thanasis Spilias for the Greek chapter
- Karina Coates, Pietro Iagnocco and Susie Walker for the Italian chapter
- Liljana Mitkovska for the Macedonian chapter
- Robert Landon and Anabela de Azevedo Teixeira Sobrinho for the Portuguese chapter
- Urška Pajer for the Slovene chapter
- Marta López for the Spanish chapter
- Arzu Kürklü for the Turkish chapter

Editor Branislava Vladisavljevic would also like to thank Floriana Badalotti (Italian), Gina Tsarouhas (Greek), Gus Balbontin (Spanish), Jean-Pierre Masclef (French), William Gourlay (Turkish) and Yukiyoshi Kamimura (Portuguese) for additional language expertise.

Lonely Planet Language Products

Publishing Manager: Chris Rennie
Commissioning Editor: Karin Vidstrup Monk
Editor: Branislava Vladisavljevic
Assisting Editors: Vanessa Battersby & Francesca Coles
Managing Editor: Annelies Mertens
Project Manager: Adam McCrow

Layout Designers: Jacqui Saunders, Laura Jane & David Kemp
Managing Layout Designer: Sally Darmody
Cartographer: Wayne Murphy
Series Designer & Illustrations: Yukiyoshi Kamimura
Production Manager: Jennifer Bilos

contents

CONTENTS

4

Mediterranean Europe

Spanish
Turkish

Note: Language areas are approximate only.
For more details see the relevant introduction.

EUROPE

mediterranean europe – at a glance

One of the most rewarding things about travelling around Mediterranean Europe is the rich variety of cuisine, customs, architecture and history. The flipside of course is that you'll encounter a number of very different languages. Most languages spoken in Mediterranean Europe belong to what's known as the Indo-European language family, believed to have originally developed from one language spoken thousands of years ago. Luckily for English speakers, most of these languages also use Roman script.

The Romance languages (French, Italian, Spanish and Portuguese) all developed from Vulgar Latin, which spread through Western Europe during the rule of the Roman Empire. The freedom with which English has borrowed Latin-based vocabulary means you'll quickly recognise many words from these languages. The Slavic languages are a branch of the Indo-European language family and share a large amount of basic vocabulary. Macedonian and Serbian which were traditionally associated with the Orthodox Church use the Cyrillic alphabet, while Croatian and Slovene, which were influenced by the Catholic Church, use the Roman alphabet. Albanian and Greek both form single branches of the Indo-European language family. Finally, Turkish is part of the Ural-Altaic language family, which includes languages spoken from the Balkan Peninsula to northeast Asia. Arabic script was replaced by Roman script for Turkish in the early 20th century.

did you know?

- The European Union (EU) was established by the Maastricht Treaty in 1992. It developed from the European Economic Community, founded by the Treaty of Rome in 1957. Since the 2004 enlargement, it has 25 member states and 20 official languages.
- The EU flag is a circle of 12 gold stars on a blue background – the number 12 representing wholeness.
- The EU anthem is the 'Ode to Joy' from Beethoven's Ninth Symphony.
- Europe Day, 9 May, commemorates the 1950 declaration by French Foreign Minister Robert Schuman, which marks the creation of the European Union.
- The euro has been in circulation since E-Day, 1 January 2002. The euro's symbol (€) was inspired by the Greek letter epsilon (ε) – Greece being the cradle of European civilisation and ε being the first letter of the word 'Europe'.
- The Eurovision Song Contest, held each May, has been running since 1956. For the larger part of the competition's history, the performers were only allowed to sing in their country's national language, but that's no longer the case.

Albanian

albanian alphabet

A a a	B b b	C c ts	Ç ç ch	D d d	Dh dh dh
E e e	Ë ë uh	F f f	G g g	Gj gj dy	H h h
I i ee	J j y	K k k	L l l	Ll ll ll	M m m
N n n	Nj nj ny	O o o	P p p	Q q ty	R r r
Rr rr rr	S s s	Sh sh sh	T t t	Th th th	U u oo
V v v	X x dz	Xh xh j	Y y ew	Z z z	Zh zh zh

■ albanian

GJUHA SHQIPE

introduction

Albanian (*gjuha shqipe* dyoo-ha *shtyee*-pe) is one of the oldest Indo-European languages, generally considered the only descendant of Illyrian, the language of the ancient inhabitants of the Balkans. With no close relatives and constituting a branch of its own, it's a proud survivor of the Roman, Slavic and Ottoman influxes and a European linguistic oddity on a par with Basque.

Albanian's position on the edge of the turbulent and multilingual Balkans means that it's been influenced by many languages. Some similarities with Romanian, for example, suggest that the two languages were closely related and that their speakers interacted even in pre-Roman times. The Romans, who established control over the present-day Albania by 167 BC and ruled for the next five centuries, left their mark on the vocabulary and structure of the language. After the division of the Roman Empire in AD 395, Albanians fell within the realm of Byzantium and Greek Orthodox culture. The interaction with Bulgarian and Serbian began after the arrival of the Slavs to the Balkans in the 6th century. With the Ottoman conquest in 1479 Turkish and Arabic influences were added to the mix.

There are two main dialects of Albanian – Tosk (with about 3 million speakers in southern Albania, Greece, Italy and Turkey) and Gheg (spoken by about 2.8 million people in northern Albania, Kosovo and the surrounding areas of Serbia, Montenegro and Macedonia). Tosk is the official language of Albania and is also the variety used in this phrasebook.

Not surprisingly, Albanian has been written in various alphabets since the earliest written records from the 15th century. A single-sentence baptismal formula dating from 1462 and a Catholic prayer book from 1555 were both written in the Roman alphabet, which was mainly used for the Gheg dialect during the 17th and 18th centuries. The Tosk dialect, on the other hand, was originally written in the Greek alphabet. However, during the Ottoman rule, texts in both varieties were often in Arabic script (also used for Turkish). Even Cyrillic script was occasionally in use. This orthographic confusion was finally settled by the Manastir Congress in 1908, which adopted a modified Roman alphabet as the standard written form of Albanian.

Even though many Albanians speak English, you'll find attempts to communicate in Albanian are welcomed. Discovering some of the mysteries of this intriguing language will be rewarding – try learning a few of the 27 words Albanian has for 'moustache' or the other 27 used for 'eyebrows'!

pronunciation

vowel sounds

The Albanian vowel system is relatively easy to master, as the sounds mostly have equivalents in English.

symbol	english equivalent	albanian example	transliteration
a	father	*pak*	pak
ai	aisle	*çaj*	chai
e	bet	*pse*	pse
ee	see	*klima*	*klee*-ma
ew	ee pronounced with rounded lips	*dy*	dew
ia	tiara	*djali*	*dia*-lee
o	pot	*mosha*	*mo*-sha
oo	zoo	*jug*	yoog
uh	ago	*vëlla*	vuh-*lla*

word stress

For the vast majority of words in Albanian, the main stress falls on the last syllable of a word (or the last stem of a compound word). In a sentence, the main stress generally falls on the last word of a phrase. In our coloured pronunciation guides, the stressed syllable is always in italics.

consonant sounds

The Albanian consonant sounds shouldn't present many problems for English speakers. Note that 'rr' and 'll' are pronounced stronger than when they're written as single letters.

symbol	english equivalent	albanian example	transliteration
b	bed	*bukë*	*boo*-kuh
ch	cheat	*çaj, qen*	chai, chen
d	dog	*disa*	dee-*sa*
dh	that	*bardhë*	*bar*-dhuh
dy	joke	*gjalpë, xhami*	*dyal*-puh, *dya*-mee
dz	adds	*nxehtë*	n-*dzeh*-tuh
f	fat	*frenat*	*fre*-nat
g	go	*gisht*	geesht
h	hat	*hundë*	*hoon*-duh
k	kit	*raki*	ra-*kee*
l	lot	*omletë*	om-*le*-tuh
ll	strong l	*llum*	lloom
m	man	*muze*	moo-*ze*
n	not	*sapun*	sa-*poon*
ny	canyon	*një*	nyuh
p	pet	*po*	po
r	run	*ari*	a-*ree*
rr	strong r	*rrotë*	*rro*-tuh
s	sun	*sot*	sot
sh	shot	*shesh*	shesh
t	top	*tani*	ta-*nee*
th	thin	*uthull*	*oo*-thooll
ts	hats	*cili*	*tsee*-lee
v	very	*veri*	ve-*ree*
y	yes	*jo*	yo
z	zero	*zarf*	zarf
zh	pleasure	*bizhuteri*	bee-zhoo-te-*ree*

pronunciation – ALBANIAN

13

tools

language difficulties

Do you speak English?
A flisni anglisht?   a *flees*·nee ang·*leesht*

Do you understand?
A kuptoni?   a koop·*to*·nee

I (don't) understand.
Unë (nuk) kuptoj.   *oo*·nuh (nook) koop·*toy*

What does (*vrapoj*) mean?
Ç'do të thotë fjala (vrapoj)?   chdo tuh *tho*·tuh *fya*·la (vra·*poy*)

How do you ...?   *Si ...?*   see ...
  pronounce this   *shqiptohet kjo*   shcheep·*to*·het kyo
  write (*atje*)   *shkruhet fjala (atje)*   *shkroo*·het *fya*·la (at·*ye*)

Could you please ...?   *..., ju lutem.*   ... yoo *loo*·tem
  repeat that   *Përsëriteni*   puhr·suh·*ree*·te·nee
  speak more slowly   *Flisni më*   *flees*·nee muh
    ngadalë   nga·*da*·luh
  write it down   *Shkruajeni*   shkroo·*a*·ye·nee

---

essentials

Yes.	*Po.*	po
No.	*Jo.*	yo
Please.	*Ju lutem.*	yoo *loo*·tem
Thank you	*Faleminderit*	fa·le·meen·*de*·reet
(very much).	(*shumë*).	(*shoo*·muh)
You're welcome.	*S'ka përse.*	ska puhr·*se*
Excuse me.	*Më falni.*	muh *fal*·nee
Sorry.	*Më vjen keq.*	muh vyen kech

numbers

0	zero	ze·ro	17	shtatëmbëdhjetë	shta·tuhm·buh·dhye·tuh
1	një	nyuh	18	tetëmbëdhjetë	te·tuhm·buh·dhye·tuh
2	dy	dew	19	nëntëmbëdhjetë	nuhn·tuhm·buh·dhye·tuh
3	tre/tri m/f	tre/tree	20	njëzet	nyuh·zet
4	katër	ka·tuhr	21	njëzet e një	nyuh·zet e nyuh
5	pesë	pe·suh	30	tridhjetë	tree·dhye·tuh
6	gjashtë	dyash·tuh	40	dyzet	dew·zet
7	shtatë	shta·tuh	50	pesëdhjetë	pe·suh·dhye·tuh
8	tetë	te·tuh	60	gjashtëdhjetë	dyash·tuh·dhye·tuh
9	nëntë	nuhn·tuh	70	shtatëdhjetë	shta·tuh·dhye·tuh
10	dhjetë	dhye·tuh	80	tetëdhjetë	te·tuh·dhye·tuh
11	njëmbëdhjetë	nyuhm·buh·dhye·tuh	90	nëntëdhjetë	nuhn·tuh·dhye·tuh
12	dymbëdhjetë	dewm·buh·dhye·tuh	100	njëqind	nyuh·cheend
13	trembëdhjetë	trem·buh·dhye·tuh	1000	një mijë	nyuh mee·yuh
14	katërmbëdhjetë	ka·tuhrm·buh·dhye·tuh			
15	pesëmbëdhjetë	pe·suhm·buh·dhye·tuh			
16	gjashtëmbëdhjetë	dyash·tuhm·buh·dhye·tuh			

time & dates

What time is it?	Sa është ora?	sa uhsh·tuh o·ra
It's one o'clock.	Ora është një.	o·ra uhsh·tuh nyuh
It's (two) o'clock.	Ora është (dy).	o·ra uhsh·tuh (dew)
Quarter past (one).	(Një) e një çerek.	(nyuh) e nyuh che·rek
Half past (one).	(Një) e gjysmë.	(nyuh) e dyews·muh
Quarter to (eight).	(Tetë) pa një çerek.	(te·tuh) pa nyuh che·rek
At what time ...?	Në çfarë ore ...?	nuh chfa·ruh o·re ...
At ...	Në ...	nüh ...
am	paradite	pa·ra·dee·te
pm	mbasdite	mbas·dee·te

Monday	*e hënë*	e *huh*·nuh
Tuesday	*e martë*	e *mar*·tuh
Wednesday	*e mërkurë*	e muhr·*koo*·ruh
Thursday	*e enjte*	e *eny*·te
Friday	*e premte*	e *prem*·te
Saturday	*e shtunë*	e *shtoo*·nuh
Sunday	*e diel*	e *dee*·el

January	*janar*	ya·*nar*
February	*shkurt*	shkoort
March	*mars*	mars
April	*prill*	preell
May	*maj*	mai
June	*qershor*	cher·*shor*
July	*korrik*	ko·*rreek*
August	*gusht*	goosht
September	*shtator*	shta·*tor*
October	*tetor*	te·*tor*
November	*nëntor*	nuhn·*tor*
December	*dhjetor*	dhye·*tor*

| What date is it today? | *Sa është data sot?* | sa *uhsh*·tuh *da*·ta sot |
| It's (10 October). | *Është (dhjetë tetor).* | *uhsh*·tuh (*dhye*·tuh te·*tor*) |

| since (May) | *që në (maj)* | chuh nuh (mai) |
| until (June) | *deri në (qershor)* | *de*·ree nuh (cher·*shor*) |

next week	*javën e ardhshme*	*ya*·vuhn e *ardh*·shme
next month	*muajin e ardhshëm*	*moo*·a·yeen e *ardh*·shuhm
next year	*vitin e ardhshëm*	*vee*·teen e *ardh*·shuhm

last ...	... *e kaluar*	... e ka·*loo*·ar
night	*mbrëmjen*	*mbruhm*·yen
week	*javën*	*ya*·vuhn
month	*muajin*	*moo*·a·yeen
year	*vitin*	*vee*·teen

yesterday/tomorrow ...	*dje/nesër ...*	dee·*e*/ne·suhr ...
morning	*në mëngjes*	nuh muhn·*dyes*
afternoon	*mbasdite*	mbas·*dee*·te
evening	*në mbrëmje*	nuh *mbruhm*·ye

16

weather

What's the weather like?	*Si është koha?*	see uhsh·tuh *ko·*ha
It's ...	*Koha është ...*	ko·ha uhsh·tuh ...
cold	*e ftohtë*	e ftoh·tuh
hot	*e nxehtë*	e ndzeh·tuh
raining	*me shi*	me shee
snowing	*me borë*	me bo·ruh
sunny	*me diell*	me dee·ell
warm	*e ngrohtë*	e ngroh·tuh
windy	*me erë*	me e·ruh
spring	*pranverë* f	pran·ve·ruh
summer	*verë* f	ve·ruh
autumn	*vjeshtë* f	vyesh·tuh
winter	*dimër* m	dee·muhr

border crossing

I'm here ...	*Jam këtu ...*	yam kuh·too ...
on business	*me punë*	me poo·nuh
on holiday	*me pushime*	me poo·shee·me
I'm here for ...	*Do të qëndroj për ...*	do tuh chuhn·droy puhr ...
(10) days	*(dhjetë) ditë*	(dhye·tuh) dee·tuh
(two) months	*(dy) muaj*	(dew) moo·ai
(three) weeks	*(tri) javë*	(tree) ya·vuh

I'm going to (Tirana).
Do të shkoj në (Tiranë).   do tuh shkoy nuh (tee·ra·nuh)

I'm staying at the (Hotel Tirana).
Po qëndroj te (hotel Tirana).   po chuhn·droy te (ho·tel tee·ra·na)

I have nothing to declare.
S'kam asgjë për të deklaruar.   skam as·dyuh puhr tuh de·kla·roo·ar

I have something to declare.
Dua të deklaroj diçka.   doo·a tuh de·kla·roy deech·ka

That's (not) mine.
(Nuk) Është e imja.   (nook) uhsh·tuh e eem·ya

transport

tickets & luggage

Where can I buy a ticket?
  Ku mund të blej një biletë?   koo moond tuh bley nyuh bee-*le*-tuh

Do I need to book a seat?
  A duhet të bëj rezervim?   a *doo*-het tuh buhy re-zer-*veem*

One ... ticket	*Një biletë ...*	nyuh bee-*le*-tuh ...
(to Shkodër),	*(për në Shkodër),*	(puhr nuh *shko*-duhr)
please.	*ju lutem.*	yoo *loo*-tem
one-way	*për vajtje*	puhr *vai*-tye
return	*kthimi*	*kthee*-mee

I'd like to ... my	*Dua ta ... biletën*	*doo*-a ta ... bee-*le*-tuhn
ticket, please.	*time, ju lutem.*	*tee*-me yoo *loo*-tem
cancel	*anuloj*	a-noo-*loy*
change	*ndryshoj*	ndrew-*shoy*
collect	*marr*	marr
confirm	*konfirmoj*	kon-feer-*moy*

I'd like a ... seat,	*Dua një vend ...,*	*doo*-a nyuh vend ...
please.	*ju lutem.*	yoo *loo*-tem
nonsmoking	*ku s'pihet duhan*	koo *spee*-het doo-*han*
smoking	*ku pihet duhan*	koo *pee*-het doo-*han*

How much is it?
  Sa kushton?   sa koosh-*ton*

Is there air conditioning?
  A ka ajër të kondicionuar?   a ka *a*-yuhr tuh kon-*dee*-tsee-o-noo-ar

Is there a toilet?
  A ka banjë?   a ka *ba*-nyuh

How long does the trip take?
  Sa zgjat udhëtimi?   sa zdyat oo-dhuh-*tee*-mee

Is it a direct route?
  A është linjë direkte?   a *uhsh*-tuh *lee*-nyuh dee-*rek*-te

I'd like a luggage locker.
  Dua një kyç për valixhet.   *doo*-a nyuh kewch puhr va-*lee*-dyet

My luggage has been ...	*Valixhe e mia ...*	va-*lee*-dyet e *mee*-a ...
damaged	*janë dëmtuar*	ya-nuh duhm-*too*-ar
lost	*kanë humbur*	ka-nuh hoom-boor
stolen	*i kanë vjedhur*	ee ka-nuh *vye*-dhoor

getting around

Where does flight (728) arrive/depart?
Ku mbërrin/niset linja — koo mbuh-rreen/*nee*-set *lee*-nya
(728)? — (shta-tuh-*cheend* e *nyuh*-zet e *te*-tuh)

Where's (the) ...?	*Ku është ...?*	koo *uhsh*-tuh ...
arrivals hall	*salla e mbërritjes*	sa-lla e mbuh-*rree*-tyes
departures hall	*salla e nisjes*	sa-lla e *nee*-syes
duty-free shop	*dyqani pa taksa*	dew-*cha*-nee pa *tak*-sa
gate (12)	*hyrja*	*hew*-rya
	(dymbëdhjetë)	(dewm-buh-*dhye*-tuh)

Is this the ... to	*Është ... për në*	*uhsh*-tuh ... puhr nuh
(Durrës)?	*(Durrës)?*	(*doo*-rruhs)
boat	*kjo anija*	kyo a-*nee*-ya
bus	*ky autobusi*	kew a-oo-to-*boo*-see
plane	*ky aeroplani*	kew a-e-ro-*pla*-nee
train	*ky treni*	kew *tre*-nee

What time's	*Në ç'orë vjen*	nuh *cho*-ruh vyen
the ... bus?	*autobusi ...?*	a-oo-to-*boo*-see ...
first	*i parë*	e *pa*-ruh
last	*i fundit*	e *foon*-deet
next	*tjetër*	*tye*-tuhr

At what time does it arrive/leave?
Në ç'orë arrin/niset? — nuh *cho*-ruh a-*rreen*/*nee*-set

How long will it be delayed?
Sa do të vonohet? — sa do tuh vo-*no*-het

What station/stop is this?
Cili stacion është ky? — *tsee*-lee sta-tsee-*on* uhsh-tuh kew

What's the next station/stop?
Cili është stacioni tjetër? — *tsee*-lee *uhsh*-tuh sta-tsee-*o*-nee *tye*-tuhr

Does it stop at (Vora)?
A ndalon në (Vorë)? — a nda-*lon* nuh (*vo*-ruh)

transport – ALBANIAN

19

Please tell me when we get to (Kruja).
Ju lutem më tregoni kur të arrijmë në (Krujë).
yoo *loo*·tem muh tre·*go*·nee koor tuh a·*rrey*·muh nuh (*kroo*·yuh)

How long do we stop here?
Për sa kohë do ndalojmë këtu?
puhr sa *ko*·huh do nda·*loy*·muh kuh·*too*

Is this seat available?
I lirë është ky vendi?
ee *lee*·ruh *uhsh*·tuh kew *ven*·dee

That's my seat.
Ky është vendi im.
kew *uhsh*·tuh *ven*·dee eem

I'd like a taxi ...	*Dua një taksi ...*	doo·a nyuh tak·*see* ...
at (9am)	*në orën (nëntë paradite)*	nuh o·ruhn (*nuhn*·tuh pa·ra·*dee*·te)
now	*tani*	ta·*nee*
tomorrow	*nesër*	*ne*·suhr

Is this taxi available?
Është bosh kjo taksia?
uhsh·tuh bosh kyo tak·*see*·a

How much is it to ...?
Sa kushton për të vajtur në ...?
sa koosh·*ton* puhr tuh *vai*·toor nuh ...

Please put the meter on.
Ju lutem ndizeni matësin e kilometrave.
yoo *loo*·tem *ndee*·ze·nee *ma*·tuh·seen e kee·lo·*me*·tra·ve

Please take me to (this address).
Ju lutem më çoni te (kjo adresë).
yoo *loo*·tem muh *cho*·nee te (kyo a·*dre*·suh)

Please ...	*Ju lutem ...*	yoo *loo*·tem ...
slow down	*uleni shpejtësinë*	*oo*·le·nee shpey·tuh·*see*·nuh
stop here	*ndaloni këtu*	nda·*lo*·nee kuh·*too*
wait here	*prisni këtu*	*prees*·nee kuh·*too*

car, motorbike & bicycle hire

I'd like to hire a ...	*Dua të marr me qira një ...*	doo·a tuh marr me chee·*ra* nyuh ...
bicycle	*biçikletë*	bee·chee·*kle*·tuh
car	*makinë*	ma·*kee*·nuh
motorbike	*motor*	mo·*tor*

with ...	me ...	me ...
a driver	shofer	sho-*fer*
air conditioning	ajër të	*a*-yuhr tuh
	kondicionuar	kon-*dee*-tsee-o-*noo*-ar
antifreeze	kundërngrirës	koon-duhr-*ngree*-ruhs
snow chains	zinxhira për borë	zeen-*dyee*-ra puhr *bo*-ruh

How much for	Sa kushton	sa koosh-*ton*
... hire?	për një ...?	puhr nyuh ...
hourly	orë	*o*-ruh
daily	ditë	*dee*-tuh
weekly	javë	*ya*-vuh

air	ajër m	*a*-yuhr
oil	vaj m	vai
petrol	benzinë f	ben-*zee*-nuh
tyres	goma f	*go*-ma

I need a mechanic.
Më duhet një mekanik.   muh *doo*-het nyuh me-ka-*neek*

I've run out of petrol.
Më ka mbaruar benzina.   muh ka mba-*roo*-ar ben-*zee*-na

I have a flat tyre.
Më ka rënë goma.   muh ka *ruh*-nuh *go*-ma

directions

Where's the ...?	Ku është ...?	koo *uhsh*-tuh ...
bank	banka	*ban*-ka
city centre	qendra e qytetit	*chen*-dra e chew-*te*-teet
hotel	hoteli	ho-*te*-lee
market	tregu	*tre*-goo
police station	rajoni i policisë	ra-*yo*-nee ee po-lee-*tsee*-suh
post office	posta	*pos*-ta
public toilet	banja publike	*ba*-nya poo-*blee*-ke
tourist office	zyra turistike	*zew*-ra too-rees-*tee*-ke

Is this the road to (Berat)?
A është kjo rruga për në (Berat)?   a *uhsh*-tuh kyo *rroo*-ga puhr nuh (be-*rat*)

Can you show me (on the map)?
A mund të ma tregoni (në hartë)?   a moond tuh ma tre-*go*-nee (nuh *har*-tuh)

What's the address?
Cila është adresa?   tsee·la *uhsh*·tuh a·*dre*·sa

How far is it?
Sa larg është?   sa larg *uhsh*·tuh

How do I get there?
Si mund të shkoj atje?   see moond tuh shkoy at·*ye*

Turn ...	*Kthehuni ...*	*kthe*·hoo·nee ...
at the corner	*te qoshja e rrugës*	te *chosh*·ya e *rroo*·guhs
at the traffic lights	*te semafori*	te se·ma·*fo*·ree
left/right	*majtas/djathtas*	*mai*·tas/*diath*·tas

It's ...	*Është ...*	*uhsh*·tuh ...
behind ...	*prapa ...*	*pra*·pa ...
far away	*larg*	larg
here	*këtu*	kuh·*too*
in front of ...	*përpara ...*	puhr·*pa*·ra ...
left	*majtas*	*mai*·tas
near (to ...)	*afër ...*	a·*fuhr* ...
next to ...	*ngjitur me ...*	*ndyee*·toor me ...
on the corner	*te qoshja*	te *chosh*·ya
opposite ...	*përballë ...*	puhr·*ba*·lluh ...
right	*djathtas*	*diath*·tas
straight ahead	*drejt*	dreyt
there	*atje*	at·*ye*

by bus	*me autobus*	me a·oo·to·*boos*
by taxi	*me taksi*	me tak·*see*
by train	*me tren*	me tren
on foot	*në këmbë*	nuh *kuhm*·buh

north	*veri*	ve·*ree*
south	*jug*	yoog
east	*lindje*	*leen*·dye
west	*perëndim*	pe·ruhn·*deem*

Hyrje/Dalje	*hewr*-ye/*dal*-ye	**Entrance/Exit**
Hapur/Mbyllur	*ha*-poor/*mbew*-lloor	**Open/Closed**
Ka vende	ka *ven*-de	**Rooms Available**
Nuk ka vende	nook ka *ven*-de	**No Vacancies**
Informacion	een-for-ma-tsee-*on*	**Information**
Rajoni i policisë	ra-*yo*-nee ee po-lee-*tsee*-suh	**Police Station**
E ndaluar	e nda-*loo*-ar	**Prohibited**
Banjat	*ba*-nyat	**Toilets**
Burra	*boo*-rra	**Men**
Gra	gra	**Women**
Nxehtë/Ftohtë	ndzeh-tuh/*ftoh*-tuh	**Hot/Cold**

accommodation

finding accommodation

Where's a ...?	*Ku ka një ...?*	koo ka nyuh ...
camping ground	*vend kampimi*	vend kam-*pee*-mee
guesthouse	*bujtinë*	booy-*tee*-nuh
hotel	*hotel*	ho-*tel*
youth hostel	*fjetore për të rinj*	fye-*to*-re puhr tuh reeny
Can you	*A mund të më*	a moond tuh muh
recommend	*rekomandoni*	re-ko-man-*do*-nee
somewhere ...?	*një vend ...?*	nyuh vend ...
cheap	*të lirë*	tuh *lee*-ruh
good	*të mirë*	tuh *mee*-ruh
nearby	*këtu afër*	kuh-*too* a-*fuhr*

I'd like to book a room, please.
Dua të rezervoj një dhomë,   doo-a tuh re-zer-*voy* nyuh *dho*-muh
ju lutem.   yoo *loo*-tem

I have a reservation.
Kam bërë rezervim.   kam *buh*-ruh re-zer-*veem*

My name is ...
Unë quhem ...   oo-nuh *choo*-hem ...

Do you have a ... room?	A keni një dhomë ...?	a ke·nee nyuh dho·muh ...
single	teke	te·ke
double	dopjo	dop·yo
twin	dyshe	dew·she

How much is it per ...?	Sa kushton për një ...?	sa koosh·ton puhr nyuh ...
night	natë	na·tuh
person	njeri	nye·ree

Can I pay ...?	A mund të paguaj me ...?	a moond tuh pa·goo·ai me ...
by credit card	kartë krediti	kar·tuh kre·dee·tee
with a travellers cheque	çek udhëtimi	chek oo·dhuh·tee·mee

I'd like to stay for (two) nights.
Dua të qëndroj (dy) net.
doo·a tuh chuhn·droy (dew) net

From (2 July) to (6 July).
Nga (dy korriku) deri më (gjashtë korrik).
nga (dew kor·ree·koo) de·ree muh (dyash·tuh ko·rreek)

Can I see it?
A mund ta shoh?
a moond ta shoh

Am I allowed to camp here?
A mund të bëj kampim këtu?
a moond tuh buhy kam·peem kuh·too

Is there a camp site nearby?
A ka vend kampimi këtu afër?
a ka vend kam·pee·mee kuh·too a·fuhr

requests & queries

When/Where is breakfast served?
Kur/Ku shërbehet mëngjesi?
koor/koo shuhr·be·het muhn·dye·see

Please wake me at (seven).
Më zgjoni në orën (shtatë), ju lutem.
muh zdyo·nee nuh o·ruhn (shta·tuh) yoo loo·tem

Could I have my key, please?
Dua çelësin, ju lutem.
doo·a che·luh·seen yoo loo·tem

Can I get another (blanket)?
A mund të më jepni një (batanije) tjetër?
a moond tuh muh yep·nee nyuh (ba·ta·nee·ye) tye·tuhr

Is there a/an ...?	A ka ...?	a ka ...
elevator	ashensor	a-shen-sor
safe	kasafortë	ka-sa-for-tuh

The room is too ...	Dhoma është shumë e ...	dho-ma uhsh-tuh shoo-muh e ...
expensive	shtrenjtë	shtreny-tuh
noisy	zhurmshme	zhoorm-shme
small	vogël	vo-guhl

The ... doesn't work.	Është prishur ...	uhsh-tuh pree-shoor ...
air conditioning	ajri i kondicionuar	ai-ree ee kon-dee-tsee-o-noo-ar
fan	ventilatori	ven-tee-la-to-ree
toilet	banja	ba-nya

This ... isn't clean.	Ky ... nuk është i pastër.	kew ... nook uhsh-tuh ee pas-tuhr
pillow	jastëk	yas-tuhk
sheet	çarçaf	char-chaf
towel	peshqir	pesh-cheer

checking out

What time is checkout?
Në çfarë ore është çrregjistrimi?
nuh chfa-ruh o-re uhsh-tuh
chrre-dyees-tree-mee

Can I leave my luggage here?
A mund t'i lë valixhet këtu?
a moond tee luh va-lee-dyet kuh-too

Could I have my ..., please?	A mund të më jepni ..., ju lutem?	a moond tuh muh yep-nee ... yoo loo-tem
deposit	paratë e depozituara	pa-ra-tuh e de-po-zee-too-a-ra
passport	pasaportën	pa-sa-por-tuhn
valuables	gjërat e mia	dyuh-rat e mee-a

communications & banking

the internet

Where's the local Internet café?
Ku është qendra lokale   koo *uhsh*·tuh *chen*·dra lo·*ka*·le
e internetit?   e een·*ter*·ne·teet

How much is it per hour?
Sa kushton për një orë?   sa koosh·*ton* puhr nyuh *o*·ruh

I'd like to ...	*Dua të ...*	doo·a tuh ...
check my email	*kontrolloj postën*	kon·tro·*lloy pos*·tuhn
	time elektronike	tee·me e·lek·tro·*nee*·ke
get Internet access	*futem në internet*	foo·tem nuh een·*ter*·net
use a printer	*përdor një printer*	puhr·*dor* nyuh *preen*·ter
use a scanner	*përdor një skaner*	puhr·*dor* nyuh *ska*·ner

mobile/cell phone

I'd like a mobile/cell phone for hire.
Dua të marr me qira një   doo·a tuh marr me qee·*ra* nyuh
telefon celular.   te·le·*fon* tse·loo·*lar*

I'd like a SIM card for your network.
Dua të blej një kartë SIM   doo·a tuh bley nyuh *kar*·tuh seem
për rrjetin tuaj.   puhr *rrye*·teen *too*·ai

What are the rates?
Sa është tarifa?   sa *uhsh*·tuh ta·*ree*·fa

telephone

What's your phone number?
Sa e ke numrin e telefonit?   sa e ke *noom*·reen e te·le·*fo*·neet

The number is ...
Numri është ...   *noom*·ree *uhsh*·tuh ...

Where's the nearest public phone?
Ku ka telefon publik këtu afër?   koo ka te·le·*fon* poob·*leek* kuh·*too* a·*fuhr*

I'd like to buy a phonecard.
Dua të blej një kartë telefonike.   doo·a tuh bley nyuh *kar*·tuh te·le·fo·*nee*·ke

I want to ...	Dua të ...	doo-a tuh ...
call (Singapore)	telefonoj (Singaporin)	te-le-fo-noy (seen-ga-po-reen)
make a local call	bëj një telefonatë lokale	buhy nyuh te-le-fo-na-tuh lo-ka-le
reverse the charges	anuloj tarifat	a-noo-loy ta-ree-fat

How much does a (three)-minute call cost?
Sa kushtojnë (tri) minuta   sa koosh-toy-nuh (tree) mee-noo-ta
në telefon?   nuh te-le-fon

How much does each extra minute cost?
Sa kushton çdo minutë shtesë?   sa koosh-ton chdo mee-noo-tuh shte-suh

(100) lek per minute.
(Njëqind) lekë minuta.   (nya-cheend) le-kuh mee-noo-ta

post office

I want to send a ...	Dua të dërgoj një ...	doo-a tuh duhr-goy nyuh ...
fax	faks	faks
letter	letër	le-tuhr
parcel	pako	pa-ko
postcard	kartolinë	kar-to-lee-nuh

I want to buy a/an ...	Dua të blej një ...	doo-a tuh bley nyuh ...
envelope	zarf	zarf
stamp	pullë	poo-lluh

Please send it (to Australia) by ...	Ju lutem dërgojeni (në Australi) me ...	yoo loo-tem duhr-go-ye-nee (nuh a-oos-tra-lee) me ...
airmail	postë ajrore	pos-tuh ai-ro-re
express mail	postë ekspres	pos-tuh eks-pres
registered mail	letër rekomande	le-tuhr re-ko-man-de
surface mail	postë të rregullt	pos-tuh tuh rre-goollt

Is there any mail for me?
A më ka ardhur ndonjë letër?   a muh ka ar-dhoor ndo-nyuh le-tuhr

bank

Where's a/an ...?	Ku ka një ...?	koo ka nyuh ...
automated teller machine	makinë automatike për të holla	ma-kee-nuh a-oo-to-ma-tee-ke puhr tuh ho-lla
foreign exchange office	zyrë për këmbim valute	zew-ruh puhr kuhm-beem va-loo-te

I'd like to ...	Dua të ...	doo-a tuh ...
Where can I ...?	Ku mund të ...?	koo moond tuh ...
arrange a transfer	të bëj një transferim	tuh buhy nyuh trans-fe-reem
cash a cheque	thyej një çek	thew-ey nyuh chek
change a travellers cheque	thyej një çek udhëtimi	thew-ey nyuh chek oo-dhuh-tee-mee
change money	këmbej valutën	kuhm-bey va-loo-tuhn
get a cash advance	marr para në avancë	marr pa-ra nuh a-van-tsuh
withdraw money	bëj tërheqje parash	buhy tuhr-hech-ye pa-rash

What's the ...?	Sa është ...?	sa uhsh-tuh ...
charge for that	tarifa për këtë	ta-ree-fa puhr kuh-tuh
commission	komisioni	ko-mee-see-o-nee
exchange rate	kursi i këmbimit	koor-see ee kuhm-bee-meet

It's ...	Është ...	uhsh-tuh ...
(12) lek	(dymbëdhjetë) lekë	(dewm-buh-dhye-tuh) le-kuh
free	falas	fa-las

What time does the bank open?
Në ç'orë hapet banka? — nuh cho-ruh ha-pet ban-ka

Has my money arrived yet?
A kanë mbërritur paratë e mia? — a ka-nuh mbuh-rree-toor pa-ra-tuh e mee-a

sightseeing

getting in

What time does it open/close?
Në ç' orë hapet/mbyllet?   nuh *cho*-ruh *ha*-pet/*mbew*-llet

What's the admission charge?
Sa kushton bileta e hyrjes?   sa koosh-*ton* bee-*le*-ta e *hewr*-yes

Is there a discount for students/children?
A bëni zbritje për   a *buh*-nee *zbree*-tye puhr
studentët/fëmijët?   stoo-*den*-tuht/fuh-*mee*-yuht

I'd like a . . .	*Desha një . . .*	*de*-sha nyuh . . .
catalogue	*broshurë*	bro-*shoo*-ruh
guide	*manual*	ma-*noo*-al
local map	*hartë lokale*	*har*-tuh lo-*ka*-le

I'd like to see . . .	*Dua të shikoj . . .*	*doo*-a tuh shee-*koy* . . .
What's that?	*Ç'është ajo?*	chuhsh-tuh *a*-yo
Can I take a photo?	*A mund të bëj*	a moond tuh buhy
	fotografi?	fo-to-gra-*fee*

tours

When's the next . . . ?	*Kur është . . . ?*	koor *uhsh*-tuh . . .
day trip	*udhëtimi tjetër*	oo-dhuh-*tee*-mee *tye*-tuhr
	ditor	dee-*tor*
tour	*udhëtimi tjetër*	oo-dhuh-*tee*-mee *tye*-tuhr
	turistik	too-rees-*teek*

Is . . . included?	*A përfshihet . . . ?*	a puhr-*fshee*-het . . .
accommodation	*fjetja*	*fye*-tya
the admission	*tarifa e*	ta-*ree*-fa e
charge	*regjistrimit*	re-dyees-*tree*-meet
food	*ushqimi*	oosh-*chee*-mee
transport	*transporti*	trans-*por*-tee

How long is the tour?
Sa zgjat udhëtimi turistik?   sa zdyat oo-dhuh-*tee*-mee too-rees-*teek*

What time should we be back?
Në ç'orë duhet të kthehemi?   nuh *cho*-ruh *doo*-het tuh *kthe*-he-mee

sightseeing

castle	*kështjellë* f	kuhsh-*tye*-lluh
church	*kishë* f	*kee*-shuh
main square	*shesh kryesor* m	shesh krew-e-*sor*
monastery	*manastir* m	ma-nas-*teer*
monument	*monument* m	mo-noo-*ment*
mosque	*xhami* f	dya-*mee*
museum	*muze* m	moo-*ze*
old city	*qytet i vjetër* m	chew-*tet* ee *vye*-tuhr
ruins	*rrënoja* f	rruh-*no*-ya
stadium	*stadium* m	sta-dee-*oom*
statue	*statujë* f	sta-*too*-yuh

shopping

enquiries

Where's a ... ?	*Ku është ...?*	koo *uhsh*-tuh ...
bank	*banka*	*ban*-ka
bookshop	*libraria*	lee-bra-*ree*-a
camera shop	*dyqani i aparatëve fotografikë*	dew-*cha*-nee e a-pa-*ra*-tuh-ve fo-to-gra-*fee*-kuh
department store	*dyqani i veshjeve*	dew-*cha*-nee ee *vesh*-ye-ve
grocery store	*ushqimorja*	oosh-chee-*mor*-ya
market	*tregu*	*tre*-goo
newsagency	*agjencia e lajmeve*	a-dyen-*tsee*-a e *lai*-me-ve
supermarket	*supermarketi*	soo-per-*mar*-ke-tee

Where can I buy (a padlock)?
Ku mund të blej (një dry)?   koo moond tuh bley (nyuh drew)

I'm looking for ...
Po kërkoj për ...   po kuhr-*koy* puhr ...

Can I look at it?
Ta shikoj pak?   ta shee-*koy* pak

Do you have any others?
A keni të tjera?   a *ke*-nee tuh *tye*-ra

Does it have a guarantee?
A ka garanci? — a ka ga·ran·*tsee*

Can I have it sent abroad?
A mund ta dërgoj jashtë shtetit? — a moond ta duhr·*goy* yash·tuh *shte*·teet

Can I have my ... repaired?
A mund të ma riparoni ...? — a moond tuh ma ree·pa·*ro*·nee ...

It's faulty.
Është prishur. — uhsh·tuh *pree*·shoor

I'd like ..., please.	*Desha ..., ju lutem.*	de·sha ... yoo *loo*·tem
a bag	*një çantë*	nyuh *chan*·tuh
a refund	*kthim të parave*	ktheem tuh pa·*ra*·ve
to return this	*ta kthej këtë*	ta kthey kuh·*tuh*

paying

How much is it?
Sa kushton? — sa koosh·*ton*

Can you write down the price?
A mund ta shkruani çmimin? — a moond ta *shkroo*·a·nee *chmee*·meen

That's too expensive.
Është shumë shtrenjtë. — uhsh·tuh *shoo*·muh *shtreny*·tuh

What's your lowest price?
*Cili është çmimi më i
ulët që ofroni?* — *tsee*·lee uhsh·tuh *chmee*·mee muh ee
oo·luht chuh o·*fro*·nee

I'll give you (five) lek.
Do t'ju jap (pesë) lekë. — do tyoo yap (*pe*·suh) *le*·kuh

There's a mistake in the bill.
Është gabim fatura. — uhsh·tuh ga·*beem* fa·*too*·ra

Do you accept ...?	*A pranoni ...?*	a pra·*no*·nee ...
credit cards	*karta krediti*	*kar*·ta kre·*dee*·tee
debit cards	*karta debitore*	*kar*·ta de·bee·*to*·re
travellers cheques	*çeqe udhëtimi*	*che*·che oo·dhuh·*tee*·mee

I'd like ..., please.	*Dua ..., ju lutem.*	*doo*·a ... yoo *loo*·tem
a receipt	*një faturë*	nyuh fa·*too*·ruh
my change	*kusurin*	koo·*soo*·reen

clothes & shoes

Can I try it on?	*A mund ta provoj?*	a moond ta pro·*voy*
My size is (40).	*Numri im është (dyzet).*	*noom*·ree eem *uhsh*·tuh (dew·*zet*)
It doesn't fit.	*Nuk më nxë.*	nook muh ndzuh
small	*e vogël*	e *vo*·guhl
medium	*mesatare*	me·sa·*ta*·re
large	*e madh*	e *ma*·dhe

books & music

I'd like a ...	*Dua një ...*	*doo*·a nyuh ...
newspaper	*gazetë*	ga·*ze*·tuh
(in English)	*(në anglisht)*	(nuh an·*gleesht*)
pen	*stilolaps*	stee·lo·*laps*

Is there an English-language bookshop?
A ka ndonjë librari të — a ka *ndo*·nyuh lee·bra·*ree* tuh
gjuhës angleze? — *dyoo*·huhs an·*gle*·ze

Can I listen to this?
A mund ta dëgjoj këtë? — a moond ta duh·*dyoy* kuh·tuh

photography

Can you ...?	*A mund ...?*	a moond ...
burn a CD from	*të djeg një*	tuh *dee*·eg nyuh
my memory card	*CD nga karta*	tsuh duh nga *kar*·ta
	ime e memorjes	*ee*·me e me·mor·*yes*
develop this film	*ta laj këtë film*	ta lai kuh·*tuh* feelm
load my film	*fus filmin*	foos *feel*·meen
I need a ... film	*Më duhet një film ...*	muh *doo*·het nyuh feelm ...
for this camera.	*për këtë aparat*	puhr kuh·*tuh* a·pa·*rat*
	fotografik.	fo·to·gra·*feek*
colour	*me ngjyra*	me *ndyew*·ra
slide	*diapozitiv*	dee·a·po·zee·*teev*
(200) speed	*me shpejtësi*	me shpey·tuh·*see*
	(dyqind)	(dew·cheend)

When will it be ready? *Kur do të jetë gati?* — koor do tuh *ye*·tuh *ga*·tee

meeting people

greetings, goodbyes & introductions

Hello.	Tungjatjeta.	toon-dya-tye-ta
Hi.	Ç'kemi.	chke-mee
Good night.	Natën e mirë.	na-tuhn e mee-ruh
Goodbye/Bye.	Mirupafshim.	mee-roo-paf-sheem
See you later.	Shihemi më vonë.	shee-he-mee muh vo-nuh
Mr	Zotëri	zo-tuh-ree
Mrs	Zonjë	zo-nyuh
Miss	Zonjushë	zo-nyoo-shuh
How are you?	Si jeni/je? pol/inf	see ye-nee/ye
Fine, thanks.	Mirë, faleminderit.	mee-ruh fa-le-meen-de-reet
And you?	Po ju/ti? pol/inf	po yoo/tee
What's your name?	Si quheni?	see choo-he-nee
My name is ...	Unë quhem ...	oo-nuh choo-hem ...
I'm pleased to meet you.	Gëzohem që u njohëm.	guh-zo-hem chuh oo nyo-huhm
This is my ...	Ky është ...	kew uhsh-tuh ...
boyfriend	i dashuri im	ee da-shoo-ree eem
brother	vëllai im	vuh-lla-ee eem
daughter	vajza ime	vai-za ee-me
father	babai im	ba-ba-ee eem
friend	shoku im m	sho-koo eem
	shoqja ime f	sho-chya ee-me
girlfriend	e dashura ime	e da-shoo-ra ee-me
husband	burri im	boo-rree eem
mother	nëna ime	nuh-na ee-me
partner (intimate)	partneri im m	part-ne-ree eem
	partnerja ime f	part-ne-rya ee-me
sister	motra ime	mot-ra ee-me
son	djali im	dia-lee eem
wife	gruaja ime	groo-a-ya ee-me
Here's my ...	Ja ...	ya ...
address	adresa ime	ad-re-sa ee-me
email address	adresa ime e emailit	ad-re-sa ee-me e ee-mey-leet

What's your ...?	Cila është ...?	tsee·la uhsh·tuh ...
address	adresa juaj	ad·re·sa yoo·ai
email address	adresa juaj e emailit	ad·re·sa yoo·ai e ee·mey·leet
Here's my ...	Ja ...	ya ...
fax number	numri im i faksit	noom·ree eem ee fak·seet
phone number	numri im i	noom·ree eem ee
	telefonit	te·le·fo·neet
What's your ...?	Cili është ...?	tsee·lee uhsh·tuh ...
fax number	numri juaj i faksit	noom·ree yoo·ai ee fak·seet
phone number	numri juaj i	noom·ree yoo·ai ee
	telefonit	te·le·fo·neet

occupations

What's your occupation?	Ç'punë bëni?	chpoo·nuh buh·nee
I'm a/an ...	Jam ...	yam ...
artist	artist/artiste m/f	ar·teest/ar·tees·te
businessperson	biznesmen m	beez·nes·men
	biznesmene f	beez·nes·me·ne
manual worker	punëtor/punëtore m/f	poo·nuh·tor/poo·nuh·to·re
office worker	nëpunës m	nuh·poo·nuhs
	nëpunëse f	nuh·poo·nuh·se
student	student/studente m/f	stoo·dent/stoo·den·te
tradesperson	tregtar/tregtare m/f	treg·tar/treg·ta·re

background

Where are you from?	Nga jeni?	nga ye·nee
I'm from ...	Jam nga ...	yam nga ...
Australia	Australia	a·oos·tra·lee·a
Canada	Kanadaja	ka·na·da·ya
England	Anglia	an·glee·a
New Zealand	Zelanda e Re	ze·lan·da e re
the USA	Shtetet e Bashkuara	shte·tet e bash·koo·a·ra
Are you married?	A jeni i martuar? m	a ye·nee ee mar·too·ar
	A je e martuar? f	a ye e mar·too·ar
I'm married.	Jam i/e martuar. m/f	yam ee/e mar·too·ar
I'm single.	Jam beqar/beqare. m/f	yam be·char/be·cha·re

age

How old ...?	Sa vjeç ...?	sa vyech ...
are you	jeni/je pol/inf	ye·nee/ye
is your daughter	është vajza	uhsh·tuh vai·za
	juaj/jote pol/inf	yoo·ai/yo·te
is your son	djali juaj/yt pol/inf	dia·lee yoo·ai/ewt

I'm ... years old.
Jam ... vjeç.   yam ... vyech

He/She is ... years old.
Ai/Ajo është ... vjeç.   a·ee/a·yo uhsh·tuh ... vyech

feelings

I'm (not) ...	(Nuk) Kam ...	(nook) kam ...
Are you ...?	Po ju a keni ...?	po yoo a ke·nee ...
cold	ftohtë	ftoh·tuh
hot	vapë	va·puh
hungry	uri	oo·ree
thirsty	etje	et·ye

I'm (not) ...	(Nuk) Jam ...	(nook) yam ...
Are you ...?	Po ju a jeni ...?	po yoo a ye·nee ...
happy	i/e gëzuar m/f	ee/e guh·zoo·ar
OK	mirë	mee·ruh
sad	i/e mërzitur m/f	ee/e muhr·zee·toor
tired	i/e lodhur m/f	ee/e lo·dhoor

entertainment

going out

Where can I find ...?	Ku mund të gjej ...?	koo moond tuh dyey ...
clubs	një klub	nyuh kloob
gay venues	vendtakim për	vend·ta·keem puhr
	homoseksualë	ho·mo·sek·soo·a·luh
pubs	një bar	nyuh bar

I feel like going to a/the ...	Dua të shkoj në ...	doo-a tuh shkoy nuh ...
concert	koncert	kon-tsert
movies	kinema	kee-ne-ma
restaurant	restorant	res-to-rant
theatre	teatër	te-a-tuhr

interests

Do you like ...?	A ju pëlqen ...?	a yoo puhl-chen ...
I (don't) like ...	(Nuk) Më pëlqen ...	(nook) muh puhl-chen ...
art	arti	ar-tee
cooking	gatimi	ga-tee-mee
movies	kinemaja	kee-ne-ma-ya
reading	leximi	le-dzee-mee
sport	sporti	spor-tee
travelling	udhëtimi	oo-dhuh-tee-mee

Do you like to ...?	A ju pëlqen të ...?	a yoo puhl-chen tuh ...
dance	vallëzoni	va-lluh-zo-nee
go to concerts	shkoni në koncerte	shko-nee nuh kon-tser-te
listen to music	dëgjoni muzikë	duh-dyo-nee moo-zee-kuh

food & drink

finding a place to eat

Can you recommend a ...?	A mund të më rekomandoni një ...?	a moond tuh muh re-ko-man-do-nee nyuh ...
bar	bar	bar
café	kafene	ka-fe-ne
restaurant	restorant	res-to-rant

I'd like ..., please.	Dua ..., ju lutem.	doo-a ... yoo loo-tem
a table for (four)	një tavolinë për (katër veta)	nyuh ta-vo-lee-nuh puhr (ka-tuhr ve-ta)
the nonsmoking section	një vend ku ndalohet duhani	nyuh vend koo nda-lo-het doo-ha-nee
the smoking section	një vend ku lejohet duhani	nyuh vend koo le-yo-het doo-ha-nee

ordering food

breakfast	*mëngjes* m	muhn·*dyes*
lunch	*drekë* f	dre·kuh
dinner	*darkë* f	dar·kuh
snack	*zemër* f	ze·muhr

What would you recommend?	*Çfarë më rekomandoni?*	chfa·ruh muh re·ko·man·*do*·nee
I'd like (the) ..., please.	*Më sillni ..., ju lutem.*	muh *seell*·nee ... yoo *loo*·tem
bill	*faturën*	fa·*too*·ruhn
drink list	*listën e pijeve*	*lees*·tuhn e *pee*·ye·ve
menu	*menunë*	me·*noo*·nuh
that dish	*atë gjellën*	a·*tuh* dye·lluhn

drinks

(cup of) coffee/tea ...	*(filxhan) kafe/çaj ...*	(feel·*dyan*) ka·fe/chai ...
with milk	*me qumësht*	me *choo*·muhsht
without sugar	*pa sheqer*	pa she·*cher*
(orange) juice	*lëng (portokalli)* m	luhng (por·to·*ka*·llee)
soft drink	*pije joalkolike* f	*pee*·ye yo·al·koo·lee·ke
... water	*ujë ...*	*oo*·yuh ...
boiled	*i valuar*	ee va·*loo*·ar
mineral	*gline mineral*	*glee*·ne mee·ne·*ral*

in the bar

I'll have ...	*Dua ...*	*doo*·a ...
I'll buy you a drink.	*Do t'ju/të të qeras me një pije.* pol/inf	do tyoo/tuh tuh che·*ras* me nyuh *pee*·ye
What would you like?	*Çfarë dëshironi?*	chfa·ruh duh·shee·*ro*·nee
Cheers!	*Gëzuar!*	guh·*zoo*·ar
a bottle/glass of beer	*një shishe/gotë birrë*	nyuh *shee*·she/*go*·tuh *bee*·rruh
cocktail	*koktej* m	kok·*tey*
cognac	*konjak* m	ko·*nyak*
a shot of (whisky)	*një gllënjkë (uiski)*	nyuh *glluhny*·kuh (*oo*·ees·kee)

a bottle/glass	një shishe/gotë	nyuh *shee*·she/*go*·tuh
of … wine	verë …	*ve*·ruh …
red	të kuqe	tuh *koo*·che
sparkling	me shkumë	me *shkoo*·muh
white	të bardhë	tuh *bar*·dhuh

self-catering

What's the local speciality?
Cili është specialiteti vendas?   tsee·lee uhsh·tuh spe·tsee·a·lee·te·tee *ven*·das

How much is (a kilo of cheese)?
Sa kushton (një kilogram djathë)?   sa koosh·ton (nyuh kee·lo·gram dia·thuh)

I'd like …	Dua …	*doo*·a …
(100) grams	(njëqind) gram	(nyuh·*cheend*) gram
(two) kilos	(dy) kile	(dew) *kee*·le
(three) pieces	(tri) copa	(tree) *tso*·pa
(six) slices	(gjashtë) feta	(*dyash*·tuh) *fe*·ta

Less.	Më pak.	muh pak
Enough.	Mjaft.	myaft
More.	Më shumë.	muh *shoo*·muh

special diets & allergies

Is there a vegetarian restaurant near here?
A ka ndonjë restorant   a ka *ndo*·nyuh res·to·*rant*
vegjetarian këtu afër?   ve·dye·ta·ree·*an* kuh·*too* a·fuhr

Could you prepare	A mund të përgatisni	a moond tuh puhr·ga·*tees*·nee
a meal without …?	një gjellë pa …?	nyuh *dye*·lluh pa …
butter	gjalpë	*dyal*·puh
eggs	vezë	*ve*·zuh
meat stock	lëng mishi	luhng *mee*·shee

I'm allergic to …	Kam alergji ndaj …	kam a·ler·*dyee* ndai …
dairy produce	bulmetrave	bool·*me*·tra·ve
gluten	glutenit	gloo·*te*·neet
MSG	msg-së	muh·suh·guh·suh
nuts	arrave	a·rra·ve
seafood	prodhimeve të detit	pro·*dhee*·me·ve tuh *de*·teet

burani f	boo-ra-*nee*	dish of spinach, rice & other greens
byrek m	bew-*rek*	filo pastry stuffed with cheese or spinach
çomlek m	chom-*lek*	meat & onion stew
djathë i fërguar m	*dia*-thuh ee fuhr-*goo*-ar	fried cheese
dollma me lakër f	doll-*ma* me *la*-kuhr	stuffed cabbage leaves
fërgesë f	fuhr-*ge*-suh	rich beef stew with cheese
fërgesë Tirane f	fuhr-*ge*-suh tee-*ra*-ne	dish of offal, eggs & tomatoes
filetë peshku me arra f	fee-*le*-tuh *pesh*-koo me *a*-rra	fish fillet with nuts
gjel deti m	dyel *de*-tee	turkey
hallvë f	*hall*-vuh	dessert with fried almonds in syrup
jani me fasule f	ya-*nee* me fa-*soo*-le	thick bean soup
japrakë me mish m pl	ya-*pra*-kuh me meesh	vine leaves stuffed with meat & rice
kadaif m	ka-da-*eef*	pastry soaked in sugar syrup & flavoured with nuts
kukurec m	koo-koo-*rets*	roasted entrails of sheep or goat
kurabie f	koo-ra-*bee*-e	oval-shaped biscuits
lakror misri m	lak-*ror* mees-ree	corn pie
midhje në verë të bardhë f pl	mee-dhye nuh *ve*-ruh tuh *bar*-dhuh	mussels in white wine
mish qingji m	meesh *cheen*-dyee	fried veal with walnuts
musaka me patate f	moo-sa-*ka* me pa-*ta*-te	potato casserole
omëletë me djathë f	om-*le*-tuh me *dia*-thuh	cheese omelette
paidhaqe f	pai-*dha*-che	grilled lamb ribs
pastiço me djathë f	pas-*tee*-cho me *dia*-thuh	pie with noodles, cheese, eggs & meat

patate të skuqura f pl	pa-*ta*-te tuh skoo-choo-ra	*fried potatoes*
patëllxhane të mbushura m pl	pa-tuhll-*dya*-ne tuh mboo-shoo-ra	*stuffed eggplants*
peshk i pjekur m	peshk ee *pye*-koor	*grilled fish*
petulla me kos f pl	pe-too-lla me kos	*pancakes with yogurt*
pulë e pjekur me oriz f	*poo*-luh e *pye*-koor me o-*reez*	*fried chicken with rice*
pulë me arra f	*poo*-luh me *a*-rra	*fried chicken with walnuts*
qefull i furrës m	che-fooll ee *foo*-rruhs	*baked mullet*
qofte f	*chof*-te	*meatballs*
romstek m	rom-*stek*	*mincemeat patties*
rosto me salcë kosi f	*ras*-to me *sal*-tsuh ko-see	*roast beef with sour cream*
sallatë me fasule f	sa-*lla*-tuh me fa-*soo*-le	*bean salad*
shishqebap m	sheesh-che-*bap*	*grilled meat on a skewer*
speca të mbushur m pl	*spe*-tsa tuh mboo-shoor	*stuffed peppers*
spinaq me kos m	spee-*nach* me kos	*spinach with yogurt*
supë me barishte f	*soo*-puh me ba-*reesh*-te	*vegetable soup*
supë me patate e lakër f	*soo*-puh me pa-*ta*-te e *la*-kuhr	*potato & cabbage soup*
tarator m	ta-ra-*tor*	*yogurt & cucumber salad*
tavë Elbasani f	*ta*-vuh el-ba-*sa*-nee	*baked lamb with yogurt, eggs & rice*
tavë kosi f	*ta*-vuh ko-see	*baked lamb with yogurt*
tavë me peshk f	*ta*-vuh me peshk	*fish casserole*
tavë me presh f	*ta*-vuh me presh	*baked leeks with ground meat*
turli perimesh m pl	toor-*lee* pe-*ree*-mesh	*sautéed vegetables (potatoes, tomatoes, eggplant & peppers)*

emergencies

basics

Help!	*Ndihmë!*	ndeeh·muh
Stop!	*Ndal!*	ndal
Go away!	*Ik!*	eek
Thief!	*Hajdut!*	hai·*doot*
Fire!	*Zjarr!*	zyarr
Watch out!	*Kujdes!*	kooy·*des*
Call ...!	*Thirrni ...!*	theerr·nee ...
a doctor	*doktorin*	dok·*to*·reen
an ambulance	*ambulancën*	am·boo·*lan*·tsuhn
the police	*policinë*	po·lee·*tsee*·nuh

It's an emergency!
Është urgjente!   uhsh·tuh oor·*dyen*·te

Could you help me, please?
A mund të më ndihmoni, ju lutem?   a moond tuh muh ndeeh·*mo*·nee yoo *loo*·tem

I have to use the telephone.
Më duhet të përdor telefonin.   muh *doo*·het tuh puhr·*dor* te·le·*fo*·neen

I'm lost.
Kam humbur rrugën.   kam *hoom*·boor rroo·guhn

Where are the toilets?
Ku janë banjat?   koo *ya*·nuh *ba*·nyat

police

Where's the police station?
Ku është rajoni i policisë?   koo uhsh·tuh ra·*yo*·nee ee po·lee·*tsee*·suh

I want to report an offence.
Dua të bëj një denoncim.   doo·a tuh *buh*·ee nyuh de·non·*tseem*

I have insurance.
Kam sigurim.   kam see·goo·*reem*

I've been ...	*Më kanë ...*	muh *ka*·nuh ...
assaulted	*sulmuar*	sool·*moo*·ar
raped	*përdhunuar*	puhr·dhoo·*noo*·ar
robbed	*plaçkitur*	plach·*kee*·toor

I've lost my ...	Kam humbur ...	kam *hoom*·boor ...
My ... was/were stolen.	Ma/M'i vodhën ... sg/pl	ma/mee *vo*·dhuhn ...
backpack	çantën e shpinës sg	*chan*·tuhn e *shpee*·nuhs
bags	çantat pl	*chan*·tat
credit card	kartën e kreditit sg	*kar*·tuhn e kre·*dee*·teet
handbag	çantën e dorës sg	*chan*·tuhn e do·ruhs
jewellery	bizhuteritë pl	bee·zhoo·te·*ree*·tuh
money	paratë pl	pa·*ra*·tuh
passport	pasaportën sg	pa·sa·*por*·tuhn
travellers cheques	çeqet e udhëtimit pl	*che*·chet e oo·dhuh·*tee*·meet
wallet	kuletën sg	koo·*le*·tuhn
I want to contact my ...	Dua të lidhem me ... time.	*doo*·a tuh *lee*·dhem me ... *tee*·me
consulate	konsullatën	kon·soo·*lla*·tuhn
embassy	ambasadën	am·ba·*sa*·duhn

health

medical needs

Where's the nearest ...?	Ku është ... më i afërt?	koo *uhsh*·tuh ... muh ee *a*·fuhrt
dentist	dentisti	den·*tees*·tee
doctor	doktori	dok·*to*·ree
hospital	spitali	spee·*ta*·lee
(night) pharmacist	farmacisti (i natës)	far·ma·*tsees*·tee (ee *na*·tuhs)

I need a doctor (who speaks English).
Kam nevojë për një mjek (që flet anglisht).
kam ne·*vo*·yuh puhr nyuh myek (chuh flet an·*gleesht*)

Could I see a female doctor?
A mund të vizitohem te një mjeke?
a moond tuh vee·zee·*to*·hem te nyuh *mye*·ke

I've run out of my medication.
Më është mbaruar ilaçi.
muh *uhsh*·tuh mba·*roo*·ar ee·*la*·chee

symptoms, conditions & allergies

| I'm sick. | Jam i/e sëmurë. m/f | yam ee/e suh·moo·ruh |
| It hurts here. | Më dhemb këtu. | muh dhemb kuh·too |

I have a (a) ...

asthma	Jam me azëm.	yam me a·zuhm
bronchitis	Jam me bronkit.	yam me bron·keet
constipation	Jam bërë kaps.	yam buh·ruh kaps
cough	Jam me kollë.	yam me ko·lluh
diarrhoea	Më shkon bark.	muh shkon bark
fever	Kam temperaturë.	kam tem·pe·ra·too·ruh
headache	Kam dhimbje koke.	kam dheem·bye ko·ke
heart condition	Jam me zemër.	yam me ze·muhr
nausea	Më përzihet.	muh puhr·zee·het
pain	Kam dhimbje.	kam dheem·bye
sore throat	Më dhembin grykët.	muh dhem·been grew·kuht
toothache	Më dhemb dhëmbi.	muh dhemb dhuhm·bee

I'm allergic to ... | Kam alergji ndaj ... | kam a·ler·dyee ndai ...

antibiotics	antibiotikëve	an·tee·bee·o·tee·kuh·ve
anti-	ilaçeve	ee·la·che·ve
inflammatories	antipezmatuese	an·tee·pez·ma·too·e·se
aspirin	aspirinës	as·pee·ree·nuhs
bees	bletëve	ble·tuh·ve
codeine	kodinës	ko·dee·nuhs
penicillin	penicilinës	pe·nee·tsee·lee·nuhs

antiseptic	antiseptik m	an·tee·sep·teek
bandage	fasho f	fa·sho
condoms	prezervativ m	pre·zer·va·teev
contraceptives	kontraceptiv m	kon·tra·tsep·teev
diarrhoea medicine	ilaç për diarrenë m	ee·lach puhr dee·a·rre·nuh
insect repellent	ilaç insektlargues m	ee·lach een·sekt·lar·goo·es
laxatives	laksativ m	lak·sa·teev
painkillers	ilaç kundër	ee·lach koon·duhr
	dhimbjes m	dheem·byes
rehydration salts	kripëra	kree·puh·ra
	rihidruese f pl	ree·hee·droo·e·se
sleeping tablets	hape gjumi f pl	ha·pe dyoo·mee

english–albanian dictionary

Albanian nouns in this dictionary have their gender indicated by ⓜ (masculine) or ⓕ (feminine). If it's a plural noun, you'll also see pl. Adjectives are given in the masculine form only. Words are also marked as a (adjective), v (verb), sg (singular), pl (plural), inf (informal) or pol (polite) where necessary.

A

accident *aksident* ⓜ ak-see-dent
accommodation *vend për të fjetur* ⓜ
  vend puhr tuh *fye*-toor
adaptor *adaptor* ⓜ a-dap-*tor*
address *adresë* ⓕ ad-*re*-suh
after *pas* pas
air-conditioned *me ajër të kondicionuar*
  me *a*-yuhr tuh kon-dee-tsee-o-noo-ar
airplane *aeroplan* ⓜ a-e-ro-*plan*
airport *aeroport* ⓜ a-e-ro-*port*
Albania *Shqipëri* ⓕ shchee-puh-*ree*
Albanian (language) *gjuha shqipe* ⓜ dyoo-ha shchee-pe
Albanian a *shqip* shcheep
alcohol *alkool* ⓜ al-kol
all *gjithë* dyee-thuh
allergy *alergji* ⓕ a-ler-*dyee*
ambulance *ambulancë* ⓕ am-boo-*lan*-tsuh
and *dhe* dhe
ankle *thembër* ⓕ them-buhr
arm *krah* ⓜ krah
ashtray *tavëll duhani* ⓕ ta-vuhll doo-ha-nee
ATM *makinë automatike për të holla* ⓕ
  ma-kee-nuh a-oo-to-ma-tee-ke puhr tuh *ho*-lla

B

baby *bebe* ⓕ be-be
back (body) *shpinë* ⓕ shpee-nuh
backpack *çantë shpine* ⓕ chan-tuh shpee-ne
bad *keq* kech
bag *çantë* ⓕ chan-tuh
baggage claim *tërheqje e bagazhit* ⓕ
  tuhr-hech-ye e ba-ga-zheet
bank *bankë* ⓕ ban-kuh
bar *bar* ⓜ bar
bathroom *banjë* ⓕ ba-nyuh
battery *bateri* ⓕ ba-te-ree
beautiful *i bukur* ee boo-koor
bed *krevat* ⓜ kre-vat
beer *birrë* ⓕ bee-rruh

before *përpara* puhr-*pa*-ra
behind *mbrapa* mbra-pa
bicycle *biçikletë* ⓕ bee-chee-*kle*-tuh
big *i madh* ee madh
bill *faturë* ⓕ fa-*too*-ruh
black *i zi* ee zee
blanket *batanije* ⓕ ba-ta-nee-ye
blood group *grup gjaku* ⓜ groop *dya*-koo
blue *blu* bloo
boat *anije* ⓕ a-nee-ye
book (make a reservation) v *rezervoj* re-zer-*voy*
bottle *shishe* ⓕ shee-she
bottle opener *hapës shishesh* ⓜ ha-puhs shee-shesh
boy *djalë* ⓜ *dia*-luh
brakes (car) *frena* ⓜ pl *fre*-na
breakfast *mëngjes* ⓜ muhn-*dyes*
broken (faulty) *i prishur* ee pree-shoor
bus *autobus* ⓜ a-oo-to-*boos*
business *biznes* ⓜ beez-nes
buy *blej* bley

C

café *kafene* ⓕ ka-fe-*ne*
camera *aparat fotografik* ⓜ a-pa-*rat* fo-to-gra-*feek*
camp site *vend kampimi* ⓜ vend kam-pee-mee
cancel *anuloj* a-noo-loy
can opener *hapës konservash* ⓜ ha-puhs kon-ser-vash
car *makinë* ⓕ ma-kee-nuh
cash *të holla* ⓕ pl tuh ho-lla
cash (a cheque) v *thyej (një çek)* thew-ey (nyuh chek)
cell phone *telefon celular* ⓜ te-le-fon tse-loo-lar
centre *qendër* ⓕ chen-duhr
change (money) v *këmbej (para)* kuhm-bey (pa-ra)
cheap *i lirë* ee lee-ruh
check (bill) *faturë* ⓕ fa-*too*-ruh
check-in *registrohem* re-dyees-*tro*-hem
chest *kraharor* ⓜ kra-ha-ror
child *fëmijë* ⓕ fuh-mee-yuh
cigarette *cigare* ⓕ tsee-*ga*-re
city *qytet* ⓜ chew-tet
clean a *i pastër* ee pas-tuhr

closed *mbyllur* mbew-lloor
coffee *kafe* ① ka-fe
coins *monedha* ① pl mo-ne-dha
cold a *i ftohtë* ee ftoh-tuh
collect call *telefonatë e paguar nga marrësi* ①
    te-le-fo-na-tuh e pa-goo-ar nga ma-rruh-see
come *vij* veey
computer *kompjuter* ⓜ kom-pyoo-ter
condom *prezervativ* ⓜ pre-zer-va-tev
contact lenses *lente kontakti* ① pl len-te kon-tak-tee
cook v *gatuaj* ga-too-ai
cost *kosto* ⓜ kos-to
credit card *kartë krediti* ① kar-tuh kre-dee-tee
cup *gotë* ① go-tuh
currency exchange *këmbim valute* ⓜ
    kuhm-beem va-loo-te
customs (immigration) *doganë* ① do-ga-nuh

D

dangerous *i rrezikshëm* ee rre-zeek-shuhm
date (time) *datë* ① da-tuh
day *ditë* ① dee-tuh
delay *vonesë* ① vo-ne-suh
dentist *dentist* ⓜ den-teest
depart *nisem* nee-sem
diaper *pelenë* ① pe-le-nuh
dictionary *fjalor* ⓜ fya-lor
dinner *darkë* ① dar-kuh
direct *direkt* dee-rekt
dirty *i pistë* ee pees-tuh
disabled *invalid* een-va-leed
discount *zbritje* ① zbree-tye
doctor *doktor* ⓜ dok-tor
double bed *krevat dopjo* ⓜ kre-vat dop-yo
double room *dhomë dopjo* ① dho-muh dop-yo
drink *pije* ① pee-ye
drive v *i jap makinës* ee yap ma-kee-nuhs
drivers licence *patentë shoferi* ① pa-ten-tuh sho-fe-ree
drug (illicit) *drogë* ① dro-guh
dummy (pacifier) *biberon* ⓜ bee-be-ron

E

ear *vesh* ⓜ vesh
east *lindje* ① leen-dye
eat *ha* ha
economy class *klasë ekonomike* ①
    kla-suh e-ko-no-mee-ke
electricity *elektricitet* ⓜ e-lek-tree-tsee-tet
elevator *ashensor* ⓜ a-shen-sor

email *email* • *postë elektronike*
    ee-meyl • pos-tuh e-lek-tro-nee-ke
embassy *ambasadë* ① am-ba-sa-duh
emergency *urgjencë* ① oor-dyen-tsuh
English (language) *anglisht* ang-leesht
entrance *hyrje* ① hewr-ye
evening *mbrëmje* ① mbruhm-ye
exchange rate *kurs këmbimi* ⓜ koors kuhm-bee-mee
exit *dalje* ① dal-ye
expensive *i shtrenjtë* ee shtreny-tuh
express mail *postë ekspres* ① pos-tuh eks-pres
eye *sy* ⓜ sew

F

far *larg* larg
fast *shpejt* shpeyt
father *baba* ba-ba
film (camera) *film* ⓜ feelm
finger *gisht* ⓜ geesht
first-aid kit *kuti e ndihmës së shpejtë* ①
    koo-tee e ndeeh-muhs suh shpey-tuh
first class *klas i parë* ⓜ klas ee pa-ruh
fish *peshk* ⓜ peshk
food *ushqim* ⓜ oosh-cheem
foot *këmbë* ① kuhm-buh
fork *pirun* ⓜ pee-roon
free (of charge) *falas* fa-las
friend *shok/shoqe* ⓜ/① shok/sho-che
fruit *frutë* ① froo-tuh
full *plot* plot
funny *për të qeshur* puhr tuh che-shoor

G

gift *dhuratë* ① dhoo-ra-tuh
girl *vajzë* ① vai-zuh
glass (drinking) *gotë* ① go-tuh
glasses *syze* ① pl sew-ze
go *shkoj* shkoy
good *mirë* mee-ruh
green *jeshil* ye-sheel
guide *shoqërues* ⓜ sho-chuh-roo-es

H

half *gjysmë* ① dyews-muh
hand *dorë* ① do-ruh
handbag *çantë dore* ① chan-tuh do-re
happy *i gëzuar* ee guh-zoo-ar
have *kam* kam

he *ai* a-ee
head *kokë* ① ko-kuh
heart *zemër* ① ze-muhr
heat *nxehtësi* ① ndzeh-tuh-see
heavy *i rëndë* ee ruhn-duh
help v *ndihmoj* ndeeh-moy
here *këtu* kuh-too
high *lart* lart
highway *rrugë kryesore automobilistike* ①
  rroo-guh krew-e-so-re a-oo-to-mo-bee-lees-tee-ke
hike v *eci në natyrë* e-tsee nuh na-tew-ruh
holiday *pushime* pl poo-shee-me
homosexual *homoseksual* ho-mo-sek-soo-al
hospital *spital* ⑩ spee-tal
hot *i nxehtë* ee ndzeh-tuh
hotel *hotel* ⑩ ho-tel
hungry *i uritur* ee oo-ree-toor
husband *burrë* ⑩ boo-rruh

I

I *unë* oo-nuh
identification (card) *kartë identifikimi* ①
  kar-tuh ee-den-tee-fee-kee-mee
ill *i sëmurë* ee suh-moo-ruh
important *i rëndësishëm* ee ruhn-duh-see-shuhm
included *përfshihet* puhr-fshee-het
injury *lëndim* ⑩ luhn-deem
insurance *sigurim* ⑩ see-goo-reem
Internet *internet* ⑩ een-ter-net
interpreter *përkthyes* ⑩ puhr-kthew-es

J

jewellery *bizhuteri* ① pl bee-zhoo-te-ree
job *punë* ① poo-nuh

K

key *çelës* ⑩ che-luhs
kilogram *kilogram* ⑩ kee-lo-gram
kitchen *kuzhinë* ① koo-zhee-nuh
knife *thikë* ① thee-kuh
Kosovo *Kosovë* ① ko-so-vuh

L

laundry (place) *lavanteri* ① la-van-te-ree
lawyer *avokat* ⑩ a-vo-kat
left (direction) *majtas* mai-tas

left-luggage office *zyra për lënien e valixheve* ①
  zew-ra puhr luh-nee-en e va-lee-dye-ve
leg *këmbë* ① kuhm-buh
lesbian *lezbiane* lez-bee-a-ne
less *më pak* muh pak
letter (mail) *letër* ① le-tuhr
lift (elevator) *ashensor* ⑩ a-shen-sor
light *dritë* ① dree-tuh
like v *pëlqej* puhl-chey
lock *kyç* ⑩ kewch
long *i gjatë* ee dya-tuh
lost *i humbur* ee hoom-boor
lost-property office *zyra e sendeve të humbura* ①
  zew-ra e sen-de-ve tuh hoom-boo-ra
love v *dashuroj* da-shoo-roy
luggage *valixhe* ① va-lee-dye
lunch *drekë* ① dre-kuh

M

mail *postë* ① pos-tuh
man *burrë* ⑩ boo-rruh
map *hartë* ① har-tuh
market *treg* ⑩ treg
matches *shkrepëse* ① shkre-puh-se
meat *mish* ⑩ meesh
medicine *ilaç* ⑩ ee-lach
menu *menu* ① me-noo
message *mesazh* ⑩ me-sazh
milk *qumësht* ⑩ choo-muhsht
minute *minutë* ① mee-noo-tuh
mobile phone *telefon celular* ⑩ te-le-fon tse-loo-lar
money *para* ① pa-ra
month *muaj* ⑩ moo-ai
morning *mëngjes* ⑩ muhn-dyes
mother *nënë* ① nuh-nuh
motorcycle *motor* ⑩ mo-tor
motorway *autostradë* ① a-oo-tos-tra-duh
mouth *gojë* ① go-yuh
music *muzikë* ① moo-zee-kuh

N

name *emër* ⑩ e-muhr
napkin *pecetë* ① pe-tse-tuh
nappy *pelenë* ① pe-le-nuh
near *afër* a-fuhr
neck *qafë* ① cha-fuh
new *i ri* ee ree
news *lajm* ⑩ laim
newspaper *gazetë* ① ga-ze-tuh

night *natë* ① na-tuh
no *jo* yo
noisy *i zhurmshëm* ee zhoorm-shuhm
nonsmoking *ku ndalohet duhani*
  koo nda-lo-het doo-ha-nee
north *veri* ⑩ ve-ree
nose *hundë* ① hoon-duh
now *tani* ta-nee
number *numër* ⑩ noo-muhr

O

oil (engine) *vaj* ⑩ vai
old *i vjetër* ee vye-tuhr
one-way ticket *biletë vetëm për vajtje* ①
  bee-le-tuh ve-tuhm puhr vai-tye
open a *i hapur* ee ha-poor
outside *jashtë* yash-tuh

P

package *pako* ① pa-ko
paper *letër* ① le-tuhr
park (car) v *parkoj* par-koy
passport *pasaportë* ① pa-sa-por-tuh
pay *paguaj* pa-goo-ai
pen *stilolaps* ⑩ stee-lo-laps
petrol *benzinë* ① ben-zee-nuh
pharmacy *farmaci* ① far-ma-tsee
phonecard *kartë telefonike* ① kar-tuh te-le-fo-nee-ke
photo *fotografi* ① fo-to-gra-fee
plate *pjatë* ① pya-tuh
police *polici* ① po-lee-tsee
postcard *kartolinë* ① kar-to-lee-nuh
post office *postë* ① pos-tuh
pregnant *shtatzënë* shtat-zuh-nuh
price *çmim* ⑩ chmeem

Q

quiet *i qetë* i che-tuh

R

rain *shi* ⑩ shee
razor *brisk* ⑩ breesk
receipt *faturë* ① fa-too-ruh
red *i kuq* ee kooch
refund *kthim parash* ⑩ ktheem pa-rash
registered mail *letër rekomande* ①
  le-tuhr re-ko-man-de

rent v *marr me qira* marr me chee-ra
repair v *riparoj* ree-pa-roy
reservation *rezervim* ⑩ re-zer-veem
restaurant *restorant* ⑩ res-to-rant
return v *kthej* kthey
return ticket *biletë kthimi* ① bee-le-tuh kthee-mee
right (direction) *djathtas* diath-tas
road *rrugë* ① rroo-guh
room *dhomë* ① dho-muh

S

safe a *i sigurt* ee see-goort
sanitary napkin *pecetë higjienike* ①
  pe-tse-tuh hee-dyee-e-nee-ke
seat *vend* ⑩ vend
send *dërgoj* duhr-goy
service station *pikë karburanti* ①
  pee-kuh kar-boo-ran-tee
sex *seks* ⑩ seks
shampoo *shampo* ① sham-po
share (a dorm) *marr (dhomë) bashkë*
  marr (dho-muh) bash-kuh
shaving cream *pastë rroje* ① pas-tuh rro-ye
she *ajo* a-yo
sheet (bed) *çarçaf* ⑩ char-chaf
shirt *këmishë* ① kuh-mee-shuh
shoes *këpucë* ① kuh-poo-tsuh
shop *dyqan* ⑩ dew-chan
short *i shkurtër* ee shkoor-tuhr
shower *dush* ⑩ doosh
single room *dhomë teke* ① dho-muh te-ke
skin *lëkurë* ① luh-koo-ruh
skirt *fund* ⑩ foond
sleep v *fle* fle
slowly *me ngadalë* me nga-da-luh
small *i vogël* ee vo-guhl
smoke (cigarettes) v *pij cigare* peey tsee-ga-re
soap *sapun* ⑩ sa-poon
some *disa* dee-sa
soon *së shpejti* suh shpey-tee
south *jug* ⑩ yoog
souvenir shop *dyqan suveniresh* ⑩
  dew-chan soo-ve-nee-resh
speak v *flas* flas
spoon *lugë* ① loo-guh
stamp *pullë* ① poo-lluh
stand-by ticket *biletë rezervë* ① bee-le-tuh re-zer-vuh
station (train) *stacion (treni)* ⑩ sta-tsee-on (tre-nee)
stomach *stomak* ⑩ sto-mak
stop v *ndaloj* nda-loy

(bus) stop *stacion (autobusi)* ⓜ sta-tsee-*on* (a-oo-to-*boo*-see)
street *rrugë* ① *rroo*-guh
student *student/studente* ⓜ/① stoo-*dent*/stoo-*den*-te
sun *diell* ⓜ dee-*ell*
sunscreen *krem mbrojtës* ⓜ krem *mbroy*-tuhs
swim v *notoj* no-*toy*

T

tampons *tampona* ① pl tam-*po*-na
taxi *taksi* ① tak-*see*
teaspoon *lugë çaji* ① *loo*-guh *cha*-yee
teeth *dhëmbë* ⓜ pl *dhuhm*-buh
telephone *telefon* ⓜ te-le-*fon*
television *televizor* ⓜ te-le-vee-*zor*
temperature (weather) *temperaturë* ①
  tem-pe-ra-*too*-ruh
tent *çadër* ① *cha*-duhr
that (one) *atë* a-*tuh*
they *ata* a-*ta*
thirsty *i etur* ee e-*toor*
this (one) *këtë* kuh-*tuh*
throat *grykë* ① *grew*-kuh
ticket *biletë* ① bee-*le*-tuh
time *kohë* ① *ko*-huh
tired *i lodhur* ee *lo*-dhoor
tissues *shami letre* ① sha-mee *le*-tre
today *sot* sot
toilet *banjë* ① *ba*-nyuh
tomorrow *nesër* *ne*-suhr
tonight *sonte* *son*-te
toothbrush *furçë dhëmbësh* ① *foor*-chuh *dhuhm*-buhsh
toothpaste *pastë dhëmbësh* ① *pas*-tuh *dhuhm*-buhsh
torch (flashlight) *elektrik dore* ⓜ e-lek-*treek* do-re
tour *vizitë* ① vee-*zee*-tuh
tourist office *zyrë turistike* ① *zew*-ruh too-rees-*tee*-ke
towel *peshqir* ① pesh-*cheer*
train *tren* ⓜ tren
translate *përkthej* puhr-*kthey*
travel agency *agjenci udhëtimi* ①
  a-dyen-*tsee* oo-dhuh-*tee*-mee
travellers cheque *çek udhëtimi* ⓜ
  chek oo-dhuh-*tee*-mee
trousers *pantallona* ① pl pan-ta-*llo*-na
twin beds *krevatë dyshe* ⓜ pl kre-*va*-tuh *dew*-shuh
tyre *gomë* ① *go*-muh

U

underwear ① pl *mbathje* *mba*-thye
urgent *urgjent* oor-*dyent*

V

vacant *bosh* bosh
vacation *pushime* ⓜ pl poo-*shee*-me
vegetable *zarzavate* ① zar-za-*va*-te
vegetarian a *vegjetarian* ve-dye-ta-ree-*an*
visa *vizë* ① *vee*-zuh

W

waiter *kamarier* ka-ma-*ree*-er
walk v *eci* e-*tsee*
wallet *kuletë* ① koo-*le*-tuh
warm a *i ngrohtë* ee *ngroh*-tuh
wash (something) *laj* lai
watch *orë dore* ① *o*-ruh do-re
water *ujë* ⓜ *oo*-yuh
we *ne* ne
weekend *fundjavë* ① *foond*-ya-vuh
west *perëndim* pe-ruhn-*deem*
wheelchair *karrocë invalidi* ① ka-rro-tsuh een-va-*lee*-dee
when *kur* koor
where *ku* koo
white *i bardhë* ee bar-*dhuh*
who *kush* koosh
why *pse* pse
wife *grua* ① *groo*-a
window *dritare* ① dree-*ta*-re
wine *verë* ① *ve*-ruh
with *me* me
without *pa* pa
woman *grua* ① *groo*-a
write *shkruaj* shkroo-*ai*

Y

yellow *i verdhë* ee *ver*-dhuh
yes *po* po
yesterday *dje* dee-*e*
you sg inf *ti* tee
you sg pol & pl *ju* yoo

Croatian

croatian & serbian alphabets

croatian	serbian	croatian	serbian	croatian	serbian	croatian	serbian
A a a	А а	*E e* e	Е е	*Lj lj* l′	Љ љ	*Š š* sh	Ш ш
B b be	Б б	*F f* ef	Ф ф	*M m* em	М м	*T t* te	Т т
C c tse	Ц ц	*G g* ge	Г г	*N n* en	Н н	*U u* u	У у
Č č tch	Ч ч	*H h* ha	Х х	*Nj nj* n′	Њ њ	*V v* ve	В в
Ć ć ch	Ћ ћ	*I i* i	И и	*O o* o	О о	*Z z* zed	З з
D d de	Д д	*J j* y	Ј ј	*P p* pe	П п	*Ž ž* zh	Ж ж
Dž dž dzh	Џ џ	*K k* ka	К к	*R r* er	Р р		
Đ đ j	Ђ ђ	*L l* el	Л л	*S s* es	С с		

croatian/serbian

introduction

Did you know that the words *Dalmatian* and *cravat* come from Croatian (*hrvatski* hr-vat-ski), which is also referred to as Serbo-Croatian? Croatian isn't really a separate language from Serbian or Bosnian. Linguists commonly refer to the varieties spoken in Croatia, Bosnia-Hercegovina, Montenegro and Serbia with the umbrella term 'Serbo-Croatian' while acknowledging dialectical differences between them. Croats, Serbs and Bosnians themselves generally maintain that they speak different languages, however – a reflection of their desire to retain separate ethnic identities.

As the language of about 5 million people in one of the world's newest countries, Croatian has an intriguing, cosmopolitan and at times fraught history. Its linguistic ancestor was brought to the region in the sixth and seventh centuries AD by the South Slavs, who may have crossed the Danube from the area now known as Poland. This ancestral language split off into two branches: East South Slavic, which later evolved into Bulgarian and Macedonian, and West South Slavic, of which Slovene, Serbian and Croatian are all descendants.

Croatia may be a peaceful country today but the Balkan region to which it belongs has a long history of invasion and conflict. These upheavals have enriched and politicised the language. The invasion by Charlemagne's armies and the conversion of Croats to the Roman Church in AD 803 left its mark on Croatian in the form of words borrowed from Latin and the adoption of the Latin alphabet rather than the Cyrillic alphabet (with which Serbian is written). Subsequent invasions by the Hapsburg, Ottoman and Venetian empires added vibrancy to the language through an influx of German, Turkish and Venetian dialect words. Many words from the standard Italian of Croatia's neighbour Italy have also been absorbed.

The good news is that if you venture into Serbia or Montenegro, you'll be able to enrich your travel experience there by using this chapter. In case of the most common differences between Croatian and Serbian, both translations are given and indicated with ©/⑤. The Cyrillic alphabet (used alternatively with the Latin alphabet in Serbia and Montenegro) is also included on the page opposite. Croatian is a handy lingua franca in any of the other states that made up part of the former Yugoslavia, as it's an official language in Bosnia-Hercegovina (along with Serbian and Bosnian) and people in Macedonia and Slovenia, who speak closely related languages, generally understand Croatian. In other words (often heard throughout this region) – *nema problema* ne-ma pro-ble-ma (no problem)!

pronunciation

vowel sounds

In written Croatian, vowels that appear next to each other don't run together as in English. When you see two or more vowels written next to each other in a Croatian word, pronounce them separately.

symbol	english equivalent	croatian example	transliteration
a	father	*zdravo*	*zdra*-vo
ai	aisle	*ajvar*	*ai*-var
e	bet	*pet*	pet
i	hit	*sidro*	*si*-dro
o	pot	*brod*	brod
oy	toy	*tvoj*	tvoy
u	put	*skupo*	*sku*-po

word stress

As a general rule, in two-syllable words in Croatian stress usually falls on the first syllable. In words of three or more syllables, stress may fall on any syllable except the last. In our pronunciation guides, the stressed syllable is italicised.

Croatian also has what's known as 'pitch accent'. A stressed vowel may have either a rising or a falling pitch and be long or short. The combination of stress, pitch and vowel length in a given syllable occasionally affects the meaning of a word, but you don't need to worry about reproducing this feature of Croatian and we haven't indicated it in this book. In the few cases where it's important, it should be clear from the context what's meant. You may notice though that the speech of native speakers has an appealing musical lilt to it.

consonant sounds

Croatian consonant sounds all have close equivalents in English. The rolled r sound can be pronounced in combination with other consonants as a separate syllable – eg *Hrvat* hr·vat (Croat). If the syllables without vowels look a bit intimidating, try inserting a slight 'uh' sound before the r to help them run off your tongue more easily.

symbol	english equivalent	croatian example	transliteration
b	bed	*glazba*	*glaz*·ba
ch	cheat	*četiri, ćuk*	*che*·ti·ri, chuk
d	dog	*doručak*	*do*·ru·chak
f	fat	*fotograf*	fo·*to*·graf
g	go	*jagoda*	*ya*·go·da
h	hat	*hodnik*	*hod*·nik
j	joke	*džep, đak*	jep, jak
k	kit	*krov*	krov
l	lot	*lutka*	*lut*·ka
ly	million	*nedjelja*	ned·ye·*lya*
m	man	*mozak*	*mo*·zak
n	not	*nafta*	*naf*·ta
ny	canyon	*kuhinja*	ku·*hi*·nya
p	pet	*petak*	*pe*·tak
r	run (rolled)	*radnik*	*rad*·nik
s	sun	*sastanak*	*sas*·ta·nak
sh	shot	*košta*	*kosh*·ta
t	top	*sat*	sat
ts	hats	*prosinac*	pro·*si*·nats
v	very	*viza*	*vi*·za
y	yes	*svjetlost*	*svyet*·lost
z	zero	*zec*	zets
zh	pleasure	*koža*	*ko*·zha
'	a slight y sound	*kašalj, siječanj*	*ka*·shal', si·*ye*·chan'

tools

language difficulties

Do you speak English?
Govorite/Govoriš li engleski? pol/inf — go·vo·ri·te/go·vo·rish li en·gle·ski

Do you understand?
Da li razumijete/razumiješ? pol/inf — da li ra·zu·mi·ye·te/ra·zu·mi·yesh

I (don't) understand.
Ja (ne) razumijem. — ya (ne) ra·zu·mi·yem

What does (*dobro*) mean?
Što znači (dobro)? — shto zna·chi (do·bro)

How do you ...?	*Kako se ...?*	ka·ko se ...
pronounce this	*ovo izgovara*	o·vo iz·go·va·ra
write (*dobro*)	*piše (dobro)*	pi·she (do·bro)

Could you please ...?	*Možete li ...?* pol	mo·zhe·te li ...
	Možeš li ...? inf	mo·zhesh li ...
repeat that	*to ponoviti*	to po·no·vi·ti
speak more slowly	*govoriti sporije*	go·vo·ri·ti spo·ri·ye
write it down	*to napisati*	to na·pi·sa·ti

essentials

Yes.	*Da.*	da
No.	*Ne.*	ne
Please.	*Molim.*	mo·lim
Thank you (very much).	*Hvala vam/ti (puno).* pol/inf	hva·la vam/ti (pu·no)
You're welcome.	*Nema na čemu.*	ne·ma na che·mu
Excuse me.	*Oprostite.*	o·pro·sti·te
Sorry.	*Žao mi je.*	zha·o mi ye

numbers

0	*nula*	*nu*·la	14	*četrnaest*	*che*·*tr*·na·est
1	*jedan* m	*ye*·dan	15	*petnaest*	*pet*·na·est
	jedna f	*yed*·na	16	*šesnaest*	*shes*·na·est
	jedno n	*yed*·no	17	*sedamnaest*	se·*dam*·na·est
2	*dva* m&n	dva	18	*osamnaest*	o·*sam*·na·est
	dvije f	*dvi*·ye	19	*devetnaest*	de·*vet*·na·est
3	*tri*	tri	20	*dvadeset*	*dva*·de·set
4	*četiri*	*che*·ti·ri	21	*dvadeset jedan*	*dva*·de·set *ye*·dan
5	*pet*	pet	30	*trideset*	*tri*·de·set
6	*šest*	shest	40	*četrdeset*	*che*·*tr*·de·set
7	*sedam*	se·*dam*	50	*pedeset*	pe·*de*·set
8	*osam*	o·*sam*	60	*šezdeset*	shez·*de*·set
9	*devet*	de·*vet*	70	*sedamdeset*	se·dam·*de*·set
10	*deset*	de·*set*	80	*osamdeset*	o·sam·*de*·set
11	*jedanaest*	ye·*da*·na·est	90	*devedeset*	de·ve·*de*·set
12	*dvanaest*	*dva*·na·est	100	*sto*	sto
13	*trinaest*	*tri*·na·est	1000	*tisuću/hiljadu* ©/Ⓢ	*ti*·su·chu/*hi*·lya·du

time & dates

What time is it?	*Koliko je sati?*	ko·*li*·ko ye *sa*·ti
It's one o'clock.	*Jedan je sat.*	*ye*·dan ye *sa*·t
It's (10) o'clock.	*(Deset) je sati.*	(*de*·set) ye *sa*·ti
Quarter past (10).	*(Deset) i petnaest.*	(*de*·set) i *pet*·na·est
Half-past (10).	*(Deset) i po.*	(*de*·set) i *po*
Quarter to (10).	*Petnaest do (deset).*	*pet*·na·est do (*de*·set)
At what time?	*U koliko sati?*	u ko·*li*·ko *sa*·ti
At ...	*U ...*	u ...
am	*prijepodne*	*pri*·ye·*pod*·ne
pm	*popodne*	po·*pod*·ne
Monday	*ponedjeljak*	po·*ne*·dye·lyak
Tuesday	*utorak*	*u*·to·rak
Wednesday	*srijeda*	sri·*ye*·da
Thursday	*četvrtak*	chet·*vr*·tak
Friday	*petak*	*pe*·tak
Saturday	*subota*	*su*·bo·ta
Sunday	*nedjelja*	*ne*·dye·lya

January	siječanj	si·ye·chan'
February	veljača	ve·lya·cha
March	ožujak	o·zhu·yak
April	travanj	tra·van'
May	svibanj	svi·ban'
June	lipanj	li·pan'
July	srpanj	sr·pan'
August	kolovoz	ko·lo·voz
September	rujan	ru·yan
October	listopad	li·sto·pad
November	studeni	stu·de·ni
December	prosinac	pro·si·nats

What date is it today?	Koji je danas datum?	ko·yi ye da·nas da·tum
It's (18 October).	(Osamnaesti listopad).	(o·sam·na·e·sti li·sto·pad)
since (May)	od (svibnja)	od (svib·nya)
until (June)	do (lipnja)	do (lip·nya)
last night	sinoć	si·noch
last week	prošlog tjedna ⓒ	prosh·log tyed·na
	prošle nedelje ⓢ	prosh·le ne·de·lye
last month	prošlog mjeseca	prosh·log mye·se·tsa
last year	prošle godine	prosh·le go·di·ne
next week	idućeg tjedna ⓒ	i·du·cheg tyed·na
	iduće nedelje ⓢ	i·du·che ne·de·lye
next month	idućeg mjeseca	i·du·cheg mye·se·tsa
next year	iduće godine	i·du·che go·di·ne
yesterday/	jučer/	yu·cher/
tomorrow ...	sutra ...	su·tra ...
morning	ujutro	u·yu·tro
afternoon	popodne	po·pod·ne
evening	uvečer	u·ve·cher

weather

What's the weather like?	Kakvo je vrijeme?	kak·vo ye vri·ye·me
It's ...	... je.	... ye
cloudy	Oblačno	o·blach·no
cold	Hladno	hlad·no
hot	Vruće	vru·che
raining	Kišovito	ki·sho·vi·to
snowing	Snjegovito	snye·go·vi·to
sunny	Sunčano	sun·cha·no
warm	Toplo	to·plo
windy	Vjetrovito	vye·tro·vi·to
spring	proljeće n	pro·lye·che
summer	ljeto n	lye·to
autumn	jesen f	ye·sen
winter	zima f	zi·ma

border crossing

I'm here ...	Ja sam ovdje ...	ya sam ov·dye ...
in transit	u prolazu	u pro·la·zu
on business	poslovno	po·slov·no
on holiday	na odmoru	na od·mo·ru
I'm here for ...	Ostajem ovdje ...	o·sta·yem ov·dye ...
(10) days	(deset) dana	(de·set) da·na
(two) months	(dva) mjeseca	(dva) mye·se·tsa
(three) weeks	(tri) tjedna ©	(tri) tyed·na
	(tri) nedelje Ⓢ	(tri) ne·de·lye

I'm going to (Zagreb).
Ja idem u (Zagreb).   ya i·dem u (za·greb)

I'm staying at the (Intercontinental).
Odsjesti ću u (Interkontinentalu).   od·sye·sti chu u (in·ter·kon·ti·nen·ta·lu)

I have nothing to declare.
Nemam ništa za prijaviti.   ne·mam nish·ta za pri·ya·vi·ti

I have something to declare.
Imam nešto za prijaviti.   i·mam nesh·to za pri·ya·vi·ti

That's (not) mine.
To (ni)je moje.   to (ni·)ye mo·ye

transport

tickets & luggage

Where can I buy a ticket?
Gdje mogu kupiti kartu? — gdye mo·gu ku·pi·ti kar·tu

Do I need to book a seat?
Trebam li rezervirati mjesto? — tre·bam li re·zer·vi·ra·ti myes·to

One ... ticket	Jednu ... kartu	yed·nu ... kar·tu
(to Split), please.	(do Splita), molim.	(do spli·ta) mo·lim
one-way	jednosmjernu	yed·no·smyer·nu
return	povratnu	po·vrat·nu

I'd like to ... my	Želio/Željela bih ...	zhe·li·o/zhe·lye·la bih ...
ticket, please.	svoju kartu, molim. m/f	svoy·u kar·tu mo·lim
cancel	poništiti	po·ni·shti·ti
change	promijeniti	pro·mi·ye·ni·ti
collect	uzeti	u·ze·ti
confirm	potvrditi	pot·vr·di·ti

I'd like a ...	Želio/Željela bih ...	zhe·li·o/zhe·lye·la bih ...
seat, please.	sjedište, molim. m/f	sye·dish·te mo·lim
nonsmoking	nepušačko	ne·pu·shach·ko
smoking	pušačko	pu·shach·ko

How much is it?
Koliko stoji? — ko·li·ko stoy·i

Is there air conditioning?
Imate li klima-uređaj? — i·ma·te li kli·ma·u·re·jai

Is there a toilet?
Imate li zahod/toalet? ©/® — i·ma·te li za·hod/to·a·let

How long does the trip take?
Koliko traje putovanje? — ko·li·ko trai·e pu·to·va·nye

Is it a direct route?
Je li to direktan pravac? — ye li to di·rek·tan pra·vats

Where can I find a luggage locker?
Gdje se nalazi pretinac/sanduče — gdye se na·la·zi pre·ti·nats/san·du·che
za odlaganje prtljage? ©/® — za od·la·ga·nye prt·lya·ge

My luggage has been ...	Moja prtljaga je ...	moy·a prt·lya·ga ye ...
damaged	oštećena	osh·te·che·na
lost	izgubljena	iz·gub·lye·na
stolen	ukradena	u·kra·de·na

getting around

Where does flight (10) arrive?
Gdje stiže let (deset)?   gdye *sti*·zhe let (*de*·set)

Where does flight (10) depart?
Odakle kreće let (deset)?   o·*dak*·le *kre*·che let (*de*·set)

Where's (the) ...?	Gdje se nalazi ...?	gdye se *na*·la·zi ...
arrivals hall	dvorana za dolaske	dvo·*ra*·na za *do*·las·ke
departures hall	dvorana za odlaske	dvo·*ra*·na za *od*·las·ke
duty-free shop	duty-free	dyu·ti·fri
	prodavaonica	pro·da·va·o·ni·tsa
gate (12)	izlaz (dvanaest)	*iz*·laz (*dva*·na·est)

Which ... goes	Koji ... ide	*koy*·i ... *i*·de
to (Dubrovnik)?	za (Dubrovnik)?	za (*du*·brov·nik)
boat	brod	brod
bus	autobus	a·u·*to*·bus
plane	zrakoplov/avion ©/®	zra·ko·plov/a·*vi*·on
train	vlak/voz ©/®	vlak/voz

What time's the ... bus?	Kada ide ... autobus?	*ka*·da *i*·de ... a·u·*to*·bus
first	prvi	*pr*·vi
last	zadnji	*zad*·nyi
next	slijedeći	sli·*ye*·de·chi

At what time does it arrive/leave?
U koliko sati stiže/kreće?   u ko·*li*·ko *sa*·ti *sti*·zhe/*kre*·che

How long will it be delayed?
Koliko kasni?   ko·*li*·ko *kas*·ni

What station/stop is this?
Koja stanica je ovo?   *koy*·a *sta*·ni·tsa ye *o*·vo

What's the next station/stop?
Koja je slijedeća stanica?   *koy*·a ye sli·*ye*·de·cha *sta*·ni·tsa

Does it stop at (Zadar)?
Da li staje u (Zadru)?   da li *sta*·ye u (*zad*·ru)

transport – CROATIAN

59

Please tell me when we get to (Pula).
Molim vas recite mi — *mo*-lim vas *re*-tsi-te mi
kada stignemo u (Pulu). — *ka*-da *stig*-ne-mo u (*pu*-lu)

How long do we stop here?
Koliko dugo ostajemo ovdje? — ko-*li*-ko *du*-go o-*stai*-e-mo *ov*-dye

Is this seat available?
Da li je ovo sjedište slobodno? — da li ye *o*-vo sye-dish-te *slo*-bod-no

That's my seat.
Ovo je moje sjedište. — *o*-vo ye *moy*-e *sye*-dish-te

I'd like a taxi …	*Trebam taksi …*	*tre*-bam tak-si …
at (9am)	*u (devet prijepodne)*	u (*de*-vet *pri*-ye-*pod*-ne)
now	*sada*	*sa*-da
tomorrow	*sutra*	*su*-tra

Is this taxi available?
Da li je ovaj taksi slobodan? — da li ye *o*-vai tak-si *slo*-bo-dan

How much is it to …?
Koliko stoji prijevoz do …? — ko-*li*-ko *stoy*-i pri-*ye*-voz do …

Please put the meter on.
Molim uključite taksimetar. — *mo*-lim uk-*lyu*-chi-te *tak*-si-me-tar

Please take me to (this address).
Molim da me odvezete — *mo*-lim da me *od*-ve-ze-te
na (ovu adresu). — na (*o*-vu a-*dre*-su)

Please …	*Molim vas …*	*mo*-lim vas …
slow down	*usporite*	u-*spo*-ri-te
stop here	*stanite ovdje*	*sta*-ni-te *ov*-dye
wait here	*pričekajte ovdje*	*pri*-che-kai-te *ov*-dye

car, motorbike & bicycle hire

I'd like to	*Želio/Željela*	*zhe*-li-o/*zhe*-lye-la
hire a …	*bih iznajmiti … m/f*	bih iz-*nai*-mi-ti …
bicycle	*bicikl*	bi-*tsi*-kl
car	*automobil*	a-u-to-*mo*-bil
motorbike	*motocikl*	mo-to-*tsi*-kl

with …	*sa …*	sa …
a driver	*vozačem*	vo-*za*-chem
air conditioning	*klima-uređajem*	*kli*-ma-u-re-jai-em

How much for ... hire?	Koliko stoji najam po ...?	ko·*li*·ko *stoy*·i *nai*·am po ...
hourly	satu	*sa*·tu
daily	danu	*da*·nu
weekly	tjednu/nedelji ©/Ⓢ	*tyed*·nu/*ne*·de·lyi

air	zrak/vazduh m ©/Ⓢ	zrak/*vaz*·duh
oil	ulje n	*u*·lye
petrol	benzin m	*ben*·zin
tyres	gume f pl	*gu*·me

I need a mechanic.
Trebam automehaničara.   tre·bam *a*·u·to·me·*ha*·ni·cha·ra

I've run out of petrol.
Nestalo mi je benzina.   ne·sta·lo mi ye ben·*zi*·na

I have a flat tyre.
Imam probušenu gumu.   i·mam pro·bu·she·nu *gu*·mu

directions

Where's the ...?	Gdje je ...?	gdye ye ...
bank	banka	*ban*·ka
city centre	gradski centar	*grad*·ski *tsen*·tar
hotel	hotel	*ho*·tel
market	tržnica/pijaca ©/Ⓢ	*trzh*·ni·tsa/*pi*·ya·tsa
police station	policijska stanica	po·*li*·tsiy·ska *sta*·ni·tsa
post office	poštanski ured	po·shtan·ski *u*·red
public toilet	javni zahod/toalet ©/Ⓢ	*yav*·ni za·hod/to·a·*let*
tourist office	turistička agencija	tu·*ris*·tich·ka a·*gen*·tsi·ya

Is this the road to (Pazin)?
Je li ovo cesta/put za (Pazin)? ©/Ⓢ   ye li o·vo *tse*·sta/put za (*pa*·zin)

Can you show me (on the map)?
Možete li mi to   mo·zhe·te li mi to
pokazati (na karti)?   po·*ka*·za·ti (na *kar*·ti)

What's the address?
Koja je adresa?   koy·a ye a·*dre*·sa

How far is it?
Koliko je udaljeno?   ko·*li*·ko ye *u*·da·lye·no

How do I get there?
Kako mogu tamo stići?   ka·ko *mo*·gu ta·mo *sti*·chi

Turn ...	Skrenite ...	skre·ni·te ...
at the corner	na uglu	na u·glu
at the traffic lights	na semaforu	na se·ma·fo·ru
left/right	lijevo/desno	li·ye·vo/de·sno

It's ...	Nalazi se ...	na·la·zi se ...
behind ...	iza ...	i·za ...
far away	daleko	da·le·ko
here	ovdje	ov·dye
in front of ...	ispred ...	i·spred ...
left	lijevo	li·ye·vo
near ...	blizu ...	bli·zu ...
next to ...	pored ...	po·red ...
on the corner	na uglu	na u·glu
opposite ...	nasuprot ...	na·su·prot ...
right	desno	de·sno
straight ahead	ravno naprijed	rav·no na·pri·yed
there	tamo	ta·mo

by bus	autobusom	a·u·to·bu·som
by taxi	taksijem	tak·si·yem
by train	vlakom/vozom ©/⑤	vla·kom/vo·zom
on foot	pješke	pyesh·ke

north	sjever m	sye·ver
south	jug m	yug
east	istok m	is·tok
west	zapad m	za·pad

signs

Ulaz/Izlaz	u·laz/iz·laz	**Entrance/Exit**
Otvoreno/Zatvoreno	ot·vo·re·no/zat·vo·re·no	**Open/Closed**
Slobodna Mjesta	slo·bod·na mye·sta	**Rooms Available**
Bez Slobodnih Mjesta	bez slo·bod·nih mye·sta	**No Vacancies**
Informacije	in·for·ma·tsi·ye	**Information**
Policijska Stanica	po·li·tsiy·ska sta·ni·tsa	**Police Station**
Zabranjeno	za·bra·nye·no	**Prohibited**
WC	ve·tse	**Toilets**
Muški	mush·ki	**Men**
Ženski	zhen·ski	**Women**
Toplo/Hladno	to·plo/hlad·no	**Hot/Cold**

62

accommodation

finding accommodation

Where's a ...?	Gdje se nalazi ...?	gdye se na·la·zi ...
camping ground	kamp	kamp
guesthouse	privatni smještaj	pri·vat·ni smyesh·tai
	za najam	za nai·am
hotel	hotel	ho·tel
youth hostel	prenoćište za	pre·no·chish·te za
	mladež	mla·dezh

Can you recommend	Možete li	mo·zhe·te li
somewhere ...?	preporučiti negdje ...?	pre·po·ru·chi·ti neg·dye ...
cheap	jeftino	yef·ti·no
good	dobro	do·bro
nearby	blizu	bli·zu

I'd like to book a room, please.
Želio/Željela bih rezervirati zhe·li·o/zhe·lye·la bih re·zer·vi·ra·ti
sobu, molim. m/f so·bu mo·lim

I have a reservation.
Imam rezervaciju. i·mam re·zer·va·tsi·yu

My name's ...
Moje ime je ... moy·e i·me ye ...

Do you have a ...	Imate li ...?	i·ma·te li ...
room?		
single	jednokrevetnu sobu	yed·no·kre·vet·nu so·bu
double	sobu sa duplim	so·bu sa dup·lim
	krevetom	kre·ve·tom
twin	dvokrevetnu sobu	dvo·kre·vet·nu so·bu

How much is it per ...?	Koliko stoji po ...?	ko·li·ko sto·yi po ...
night	noći	no·chi
person	osobi	o·so·bi

Can I pay by ...?	Mogu li platiti sa ...?	mo·gu li pla·ti·ti sa ...
credit card	kreditnom	kre·dit·nom
	karticom	kar·ti·tsom
travellers cheque	putničkim čekom	put·nich·kim che·kom

For (three) nights.
Na (tri) noći.   na (tri) *no*-chi

From (2 July) to (6 July).
Od (drugog srpnja) do   od (*dru*-gog *srp*-nya) do
(šestog srpnja).   (*she*-stog *srp*-nya)

Can I see it?
Mogu li je vidjeti?   *mo*-gu li ye *vi*-dye-ti

Am I allowed to camp here?
Mogu li ovdje kampirati?   *mo*-gu li *ov*-dye kam-*pi*-ra-ti

Where can I find the nearest camp site?
Gdje se nalazi najbliže   gdye se *na*-la-zi *nai*-bli-zhe
mjesto za kampiranje?   *mye*-sto za kam-*pi*-ra-nye

requests & queries

When/Where is breakfast served?
Kada/Gdje služite doručak?   *ka*-da/gdye *slu*-zhi-te *do*-ru-chak

Please wake me at (seven).
Probudite me u (sedam), molim.   pro-*bu*-di-te me u (*se*-dam) *mo*-lim

Could I have my key, please?
Mogu li dobiti moj   *mo*-gu li *do*-bi-ti moy
ključ, molim?   klyuch *mo*-lim

Could I have another (blanket)?
Mogu li dobiti jednu dodatnu   *mo*-gu li *do*-bi-ti *yed*-nu *do*-dat-nu
(deku)?   (*de*-ku)

Is there a/an ...?	*Imate li ...?*	*i*-ma-te li ...
elevator	*dizalo/lift* ©/®	*di*-za-lo/lift
safe	*sef*	sef

The room is too ...	*Suviše je ...*	*su*-vi-she ye ...
expensive	*skupo*	*sku*-po
noisy	*bučno*	*buch*-no
small	*malo*	*ma*-lo

The ... doesn't work.	*... je neispravan.*	... ye *ne*-i-spra-van
air conditioning	*Klima-uređaj*	*kli*-ma-*u*-re-jai
fan	*Ventilator*	ven-ti-*la*-tor
toilet	*Zahod/Toalet* ©/®	*za*-hod/to-a-*let*

This ... isn't clean.	Ova ... nije čista.	o-va ... ni-ye chis-ta
blanket	deka	de-ka
sheet	plahta ©	plah-ta

This ... isn't clean.	Ovaj ... nije čist.	o-va ... ni-ye chist
sheet	čaršav ⑤	char-shav
towel	ručnik/peškir ©/⑤	ruch-nik/pesh-kir

checking out

What time is checkout?
U koliko sati treba napustiti sobu?   u ko-li-ko sa-ti tre-ba na-pu-sti-ti so-bu

Can I leave my luggage here?
Mogu li ovdje ostaviti svoje torbe?   mo-gu li ov-dye o-sta-vi-ti svoy-e tor-be

Could I have my ..., please?	Mogu li dobiti ..., molim?	mo-gu li do-bi-ti ... mo-lim
deposit	svoj depozit	svoy de-po-zit
passport	svoju putovnicu/ pasoš ©/⑤	svoy-u pu-tov-ni-tsu/ pa-sosh
valuables	svoje dragocjenosti	svo-ye dra-go-tsye-no-sti

communications & banking

the internet

Where's the local Internet café?
Gdje je mjesni internet kafić?   gdye ye mye-sni in-ter-net ka-fich

How much is it per hour?
Koja je cijena po satu?   koy-a ye tsi-ye-na po sa-tu

I'd like to ...	Želio/Željela bih ... m/f	zhe-li-o/zhe-lye-la bih ...
check my email	provjeriti svoj email	pro-vye-ri-ti svoy i-meyl
get Internet access	pristup internetu	pri-stup in-ter-ne-tu
use a printer	koristiti pisač/ štampač ©/⑤	ko-ri-sti-ti pi-sach/ shtam-pach
use a scanner	koristiti skener	ko-ri-sti-ti ske-ner

mobile/cell phone

I'd like a ...	*Trebao/Trebala*	*tre·ba·o/tre·ba·la*
	bih ... m/f	*bih ...*
mobile/cell phone for hire	*iznajmiti mobilni telefon*	*iz·nai·mi·ti mo·bil·ni te·le·fon*
SIM card for your network	*SIM karticu za vašu mrežu*	*sim kar·ti·tsu za va·shu mre·zhu*

What are the rates?
Koje su cijene telefoniranja? ko·ye su tsi·ye·ne te·le·fo·ni·ra·nya

telephone

What's your phone number?
Koji je vaš/tvoj broj telefona? pol/inf koy·i ye vash/tvoy broy te·le·fo·na

The number is ...
Broj je ... broy ye ...

Where's the nearest public phone?
Gdje je najbliži javni telefon? gdye ye nai·bli·zhi yav·ni te·le·fon

I'd like to buy a phonecard.
Želim kupiti telefonsku karticu. zhe·lim ku·pi·ti te·le·fon·sku kar·ti·tsu

I want to ...	*Želim ...*	*zhe·lim ...*
call (Singapore)	*nazvati (Singapur)*	*naz·va·ti (sin·ga·pur)*
make a (local) call	*obaviti (lokalni) poziv*	*o·ba·vi·ti (lo·kal·ni) po·ziv*
reverse the charges	*obaviti poziv na račun pozvanog*	*o·ba·vi·ti po·ziv na ra·chun poz·va·nog*

How much does ... cost?	*Koliko košta ...?*	*ko·li·ko kosh·ta ...*
a (three)-minute call	*poziv od (tri) minute*	*po·ziv od (tri) mi·nu·te*
each extra minute	*svaka naknadna minuta*	*sva·ka nak·nad·na mi·nu·ta*

| (3 kuna) per (30) seconds. | *(3 kune) po (30) sekundi.* | (tri *ku·*ne) po (*tri·*de·set) se·*kun·*di |

post office

I want to send a ...	Želim poslati ...	zhe·lim po·sla·ti ...
fax	telefaks	te·le·faks
letter	pismo	pi·smo
parcel	paket	pa·ket
postcard	dopisnicu	do·pi·sni·tsu

I want to buy a/an ...	Želim kupiti ...	zhe·lim ku·pi·ti ...
envelope	omotnicu/koverat ©/®	o·mot·ni·tsu/ko·ve·rat
stamp	poštansku marku	posh·tan·sku mar·ku

Please send it	Molim da pošaljete	mo·lim da po·sha·lye·te
by ... to (Australia).	to ... u (Australiju).	to ... u (a·u·stra·li·yu)
airmail	zračnom/vazdušnom	zrach·nom/vaz·dush·nom
	poštom ©/®	posh·tom
express mail	ekspres poštom	eks·pres posh·tom
registered mail	preporučenom	pre·po·ru·che·nom
	poštom	posh·tom
surface mail	običnom poštom	o·bich·nom posh·tom

Is there any mail for me?
Ima li bilo kakve pošte za mene?   i·ma li bi·lo kak·ve posh·te za me·ne

bank

Where's a/an ...?	Gdje se nalazi ...?	gdye se na·la·zi ...
ATM	bankovni automat	ban·kov·ni a·u·to·mat
foreign exchange	mjenjačnica za	mye·nyach·ni·tsa za
office	strane valute	stra·ne va·lu·te

Where can I ...?	Gdje mogu ...?	gdye mo·gu ...
I'd like to ...	Želio/Željela bih ... m/f	zhe·li·o/zhe·lye·la bih ...
arrange a transfer	obaviti prijenos	o·ba·vi·ti pri·ye·nos
	novca	nov·tsa
cash a cheque	unovčiti ček	u·nov·chi·ti chek
change a	zamijeniti	za·mi·ye·ni·ti
travellers cheque	putnički ček	put·nich·ki chek
change money	zamijeniti novac	za·mi·ye·ni·ti no·vats
get a cash	uzeti predujam/avans	u·ze·ti pre·du·yam/a·vans
advance	u gotovini ©/®	u go·to·vi·ni
withdraw money	podignuti novac	po·dig·nu·ti no·vats

What's the ...?	Koji/Kolika je ...? m/f	koy·i/ko·li·ka ye ...
charge for that	pristojba/tarifa	pri·stoy·ba/ta·ri·fa
	za to f ©/®	za to
exchange rate	tečaj/kurs	te·chai/kurs
	razmjene m ©/®	raz·mye·ne

It's ...	To je ...	to ye ...
(50) kuna	(pedeset) kuna	(pe·de·set) ku·na
free	besplatno	bes·plat·no

What time does the bank open?
U koliko sati se otvara banka?   u ko·li·ko sa·ti se ot·va·ra ban·ka

Has my money arrived yet?
Da li je moj novac stigao?   da li ye moy no·vats sti·ga·o

sightseeing

getting in

What time does it open/close?
U koliko sati se otvara/zatvara?   u ko·li·ko sa·ti se ot·va·ra/zat·va·ra

What's the admission charge?
Koliko stoji ulaznica?   ko·li·ko stoy·i u·laz·ni·tsa

Is there a discount for students/children?
Imate li popust za   i·ma·te li po·pust za
studente/djecu?   stu·den·te/dye·tsu

I'd like a ...	Želio/Željela bih ... m/f	zhe·li·o/zhe·lye·la bih ...
catalogue	katalog	ka·ta·log
guide	turistički vodič	tu·ri·stich·ki vo·dich
local map	kartu mjesta	kar·tu mye·sta

I'd like to see ...
Želio/Željela bih vidjeti ... m/f   zhe·li·o/zhe·lye·la bih vi·dye·ti ...

What's that?
Što je to?   shto ye to

Can I take a photo?
Mogu li slikati?   mo·gu li sli·ka·ti

tours

When's the next ...?	Kada je idući/ iduća ...? m/f	ka·da ye i·du·chi/ i·du·cha ...
day trip	dnevni izlet m	dnev·ni iz·let
tour	turistička ekskurzija f	tu·ri·stich·ka ek·skur·zi·ya
Is ... included?	Da li je ... uključen/ uključena? m/f	da li ye ... uk·lyu·chen/ uk·lyu·che·na
accommodation	smještaj m	smye·shtai
the admission charge	ulaznica	u·laz·ni·tsa
food	hrana f	hra·na
transport	prijevoz m	pri·ye·voz

How long is the tour?
Koliko traje ekskurzija?   ko·li·ko trai·e ek·skur·zi·ya

What time should we be back?
U koje bi se vrijeme   u koy·e bi se vri·ye·me
trebali vratiti?   tre·ba·li vra·ti·ti

sightseeing

castle	dvorac m	dwa·rats
cathedral	katedrala f	ka·te·dra·la
church	crkva f	tsr·kva
main square	glavni trg m	glav·ni trg
monastery	samostan/manastir m ©/®	sa·mo·stan/ma·nas·tir
monument	spomenik m	spo·me·nik
museum	muzej m	mu·zey
old city	stari grad m	sta·ri grad
palace	palača f	pa·la·cha
ruins	ruševine f pl	ru·she·vi·ne
stadium	stadion m	sta·di·on
statue	kip m	kip

shopping

enquiries

Where's a ...?	Gdje je ...?	gdye ye ...
bank	banka	ban·ka
bookshop	knjižara	knyi·zha·ra
camera shop	prodavaonica	pro·da·va·o·ni·tsa
	fotoaparata	fo·to·a·pa·ra·ta
department store	robna kuća	rob·na ku·cha
grocery store	prodavaonica	pro·da·va·o·ni·tsa
	namirnica	na·mir·ni·tsa
market	tržnica/pijaca	tr·zhni·tsa/pi·ya·tsa
newsagency	prodavaonica	pro·da·va·o·ni·tsa
	novina	no·vi·na
supermarket	supermarket	su·per·mar·ket

Where can I buy (a padlock)?
Gdje mogu kupiti (lokot)?   gdye mo·gu ku·pi·ti (lo·kot)

I'm looking for ...
Tražim ...   tra·zhim

Can I look at it?
Mogu li to pogledati?   mo·gu li to po·gle·da·ti

Do you have any others?
Imate li bilo kakve druge?   i·ma·te li bi·lo kak·ve dru·ge

Does it have a guarantee?
Ima li ovo garanciju?   i·ma li o·vo ga·ran·tsi·yu

Can I have it sent abroad?
Možete li mi to   mo·zhe·te li mi to
poslati u inozemstvo?   po·sla·ti u i·no·zemst·vo

Can I have my (backpack) repaired?
Mogu li popraviti svoj (ranac)?   mo·gu li po·pra·vi·ti svoy (ra·nats)

It's faulty.
Neispravno je.   ne·is·prav·no ye

I'd like ..., please.	Želio/Željela bih ... m/f	zhe·li·o/zhe·lye·la bih ...
a bag	vrećicu	vre·chi·tsu
a refund	povrat novca	pov·rat nov·tsa
to return this	ovo vratiti	o·vo vra·ti·ti

paying

How much is it?
Koliko stoji/košta? ©/®
ko·*li*·ko *sto*·yi/*kosh*·ta

Can you write down the price?
Možete li napisati cijenu?
mo·zhe·te li na·*pi*·sa·ti tsi·*ye*·nu

That's too expensive.
To je preskupo.
to ye *pre*·sku·po

Do you have something cheaper?
Imate li nešto jeftinije?
i·ma·te li *nesh*·to yef·*ti*·ni·ye

I'll give you (five kuna).
Dati ću vam (pet kuna).
da·ti chu vam (pet *ku*·na)

There's a mistake in the bill.
Ima jedna greška na računu.
i·ma *yed*·na *gresh*·ka na ra·*chu*·nu

Do you accept ...?	*Da li prihvaćate ...?*	da li *pri*·hva·cha·te ...
credit cards	*kreditne kartice*	*kre*·dit·ne *kar*·ti·tse
debit cards	*debitne kartice*	*de*·bit·ne *kar*·ti·tse
travellers cheques	*putničke čekove*	*put*·nich·ke *che*·ko·ve
I'd like ..., please.	*Želio/Željela bih ...* m/f	zhe·li·o/zhe·*lye*·la bih ...
a receipt	*račun*	*ra*·chun
my change	*moj ostatak novca*	moy o·*sta*·tak *nov*·tsa

clothes & shoes

Can I try it on?	*Mogu li to probati?*	*mo*·gu li to *pro*·ba·ti
My size is (40).	*Moja veličina je (četrdeset).*	*moy*·a ve·li·*chi*·na ye (che·tr·*de*·set)
It doesn't fit.	*Ne odgovara mi to.*	ne od·*go*·va·ra mi to
small	*sitna*	*sit*·na
medium	*srednja*	*sred*·nya
large	*krupna*	*krup*·na

books & music

I'd like (a) ...	Želio/Željela bih ... m/f	zhe·li·o/zhe·lye·la bih ...
newspaper	novine	no·vi·ne
(in English)	(na engleskom)	(na en·gles·kom)
pen	kemijsku	ke·miy·sku

Is there an English-language bookshop?

Postoji li knjižara za	po·stoy·i li knyi·zha·ra za
engleski jezik?	en·gle·ski ye·zik

I'm looking for something by (Oliver Dragojević).

Tražim nešto od	tra·zhim nesh·to od
(Olivera Dragojevića).	(o·li·ve·ra dra·goy·e·vi·cha)

Can I listen to this?

Mogu li ovo poslušati?	mo·gu li o·vo po·slu·sha·ti

photography

Can you ...?	Možete li ...?	mo·zhe·te li ...
develop this film	razviti ovaj film	raz·vi·ti o·vai film
load my film	staviti moj film	sta·vi·ti moy film
	u foto-aparat	u fo·to·a·pa·rat
transfer photos	prebaciti	pre·ba·tsi·ti
from my	fotografije sa	fo·to·gra·fi·ye sa
camera to CD	mog aparata na CD	mog a·pa·ra·ta na tse de
I need a/an ... film	Trebam ... film	tre·bam ... film
for this camera.	za ovaj foto-aparat.	za o·vai fo·to·a·pa·rat
APS	APS	a pe es
B&W	crno-bijeli	tsr·no·bi·ye·li
colour	kolor	ko·lor
I need a ... film	Trebam film ...	tre·bam film ...
for this camera.	za ovaj foto-aparat.	za o·vai fo·to·a·pa·rat
slide	za dijapozitive	za di·ya·po·zi·ti·ve
(200) speed	brzine (dvijesto)	br·zi·ne (dvi·ye·sto)
When will it	Kada će to biti	ka·da che to bi·ti
be ready?	gotovo?	go·to·vo

meeting people

greetings, goodbyes & introductions

Hello.	Bog/Zdravo. ©/⑤	bog/zdra·vo
Hi.	Ćao.	cha·o
Good night.	Laku noć.	la·ku noch
Goodbye.	Zbogom.	zbo·gom
Bye.	Ćao.	cha·o
See you later.	Doviđenja.	do·vi·je·nya
Mr	Gospodin	go·spo·din
Mrs	Gospođa	go·spo·ja
Miss	Gospođica	go·spo·ji·tsa
How are you?	Kako ste/si? pol/inf	ka·ko ste/si
Fine. And you?	Dobro. A vi/ti? pol/inf	do·bro a vi/ti
What's your name?	Kako se zovete/zoveš? pol/inf	ka·ko se zo·ve·te/zo·vesh
My name is ...	Zovem se ...	zo·vem se ...
I'm pleased to meet you.	Drago mi je da smo se upoznali.	dra·go mi ye da smo se u·poz·na·li
This is my ...	Ovo je moj/moja ... m/f	o·vo ye moy/moy·a ...
boyfriend	dečko	dech·ko
brother	brat	brat
daughter	ćerka	cher·ka
father	otac	o·tats
friend	prijatelj/prijateljica m/f	pri·ya·tel'/pri·ya·te·lyi·tsa
girlfriend	cura/devojka ©/⑤	tsu·ra/de·voy·ka
husband	muž	muzh
mother	majka	mai·ka
partner (intimate)	suprug/supruga m/f	su·prug/su·pru·ga
sister	sestra	ses·tra
son	sin	sin
wife	žena	zhe·na
Here's my ...	Ovo je moj/moja ... m/f	o·vo ye moy/moy·a ...
What's your ...?	Koji je tvoj ...? m	koy·i ye tvoy ...
	Koja je tvoja ...? f	koy·a ye tvoy·a ...
(email) address	(email) adresa f	(i·meyl) a·dre·sa
fax number	broj faksa m	broy fak·sa
phone number	broj telefona m	broy te·le·fo·na

occupations

What's your occupation?	*Čime se bavite?*	chi·me se ba·vi·te
I'm a/an ...	*Ja sam ...*	ya sam ...
artist	*umjetnik* m	um·yet·nik
	umjetnica f	um·yet·ni·tsa
businessperson	*poslovna osoba*	po·slo·vna o·so·ba
farmer	*poljodjelac* ©	po·lyo·dye·lats
	zemljoradnik ⑤	zem·lyo·rad·nik
office worker	*službenik* m	sluzh·be·nik
	službenica f	sluzh·be·ni·tsa
scientist	*znanstvenik* ©	znans·tve·nik
	naučnik ⑤	na·uch·nik
tradesperson	*zanatlija*	za·nat·li·ya

background

Where are you from?	*Odakle ste?*	o·da·kle ste
I'm from ...	*Ja sam iz ...*	ya sam iz ...
Australia	*Australije*	a·u·stra·li·ye
Canada	*Kanade*	ka·na·de
England	*Engleske*	en·gles·ke
New Zealand	*Novog Zelanda*	no·vog ze·lan·da
the USA	*Amerike*	a·me·ri·ke
Are you married?	*Jeste li vi vjenčani?*	ye·ste li vi vyen·cha·ni
I'm married.	*Ja sam u braku.*	ya sam u bra·ku
I'm single.	*Ja sam neoženjen.* m	ya sam ne·o·zhe·nyen
	Ja sam neudata. f	ya sam ne·u·da·ta

age

How old ...?	*Koliko ... godina?*	ko·li·ko ... go·di·na
are you	*imate/imaš* pol/inf	i·ma·te/i·mash
is your daughter	*vaša kći ima*	va·sha k·chi i·ma
is your son	*vaš sin ima*	vash sin i·ma
I'm ... years old.	*Imam ... godina.*	i·mam ... go·di·na
He/She is ... years old.	*On/Ona ima ... godina.*	on/o·na i·ma ... go·di·na

74

feelings

I'm (not) ...	Ja (ni)sam ...	ya (ni·)sam ...
Are you ...?	Jeste li ...?	ye·ste li ...
happy	sretni	sret·ni
hungry	gladni	glad·ni
OK	dobro	dob·ro
sad	tužni	tuzh·ni
thirsty	žedni	zhed·ni
tired	umorni	u·mor·ni

Are you hot/cold?
Je li vam toplo/hladno?   ye li vam to·plo/hlad·no

I'm (not) hot/cold.
Meni (ni)je toplo/hladno.   me·ni (ni·)ye to·plo/hlad·no

entertainment

going out

Where can	Gdje mogu	gdye mo·gu
I find ...?	pronaći ...?	pro·na·chi ...
clubs	noćne klubove	noch·ne klu·bo·ve
gay venues	gay lokale	gey lo·ka·le
pubs	gostionice	go·sti·o·ni·tse

I feel like going to a/the ...	Želim otići ...	zhe·lim o·ti·chi ...
concert	na koncert	na kon·tsert
movies	u kino/bioskop ©/ⓢ	u ki·no/bi·os·kop
party	na zabavu	na za·ba·vu
restaurant	u restoran	u re·sto·ran
theatre	u kazalište	u ka·za·lish·te

interests

Do you like ...?	*Volite li ...?*	*vo*·li·te li ...
I (don't) like ...	*Ja (ne) volim ...*	ya (ne) *vo*·lim ...
art	*umjetnost*	*um*·yet·nost
cooking	*kuhanje*	*ku*·ha·nye
movies	*filmove*	*fil*·mo·ve
reading	*čitanje*	*chi*·ta·nye
shopping	*kupovanje*	ku·*po*·va·nye
sport	*sport*	sport
travelling	*putovanja*	pu·to·*va*·nya
Do you like to ...?	*Da li volite da ...?*	da li *vo*·li·te da ...
dance	*plešete*	*ple*·she·te
listen to music	*slušate glazbu/ muziku* ©/Ⓢ	*slu*·sha·te *glaz*·bu/ *mu*·zi·ku

food & drink

finding a place to eat

Can you recommend a ...?	*Možete li preporučiti neki ...?*	*mo*·zhe·te li pre·po·*ru*·chi·ti *ne*·ki ...
bar	*bar*	bar
café	*kafić*	*ka*·fich
restaurant	*restoran*	re·*sto*·ran
I'd like ...	*Želim ...*	*zhe*·lim ...
a table for (five)	*stol za (petoro)*	stol za (*pe*·to·ro)
the (non)smoking section	*(ne)pušačko mjesto*	(*ne*·)*pu*·shach·ko *mye*·sto

ordering food

breakfast	*doručak* m	*do*·ru·chak
lunch	*ručak* m	*ru*·chak
dinner	*večera* f	*ve*·che·ra
snack	*užina* f	*u*·zhi·na
today's special	*specijalitet dana* m	spe·tsi·ya·*li*·tet *da*·na

What would you recommend?	Što biste nam preporučili?	shto *bi*·ste nam pre·po·*ru*·chi·li
I'd like (the) ..., please.	Mogu li dobiti ..., molim?	*mo*·gu li *do*·bi·ti ... *mo*·lim
bill	račun	ra·chun
drink list	cjenik pića	*tsye*·nik *pi*·cha
menu	jelovnik	ye·*lov*·nik
that dish	ono jelo	o·no ye·lo

drinks

coffee/tea ...	kava/čaj ...	*ka*·va/chai ...
with milk	sa mlijekom	sa mli·*ye*·kom
without sugar	bez šećera	bez *she*·che·ra
(orange) juice	sok (od naranče) m	sok (od *na*·ran·che)
mineral water	mineralna voda f	*mi*·ne·ral·na *vo*·da
soft drink	bezalkoholno piće m	be·zal·ko·hol·no *pi*·che
(hot) water	(topla) voda f	(to·pla) *vo*·da

in the bar

I'll have ...	Želim naručiti ...	*zhe*·lim na·*ru*·chi·ti ...
I'll buy you a drink.	Častim vas/te pićem. pol/inf	*cha*·stim vas/te *pi*·chem
What would you like?	Što želite/želiš? pol/inf	shto *zhe*·li·te/*zhe*·lish
Cheers!	Živjeli!	*zhi*·vye·li
brandy	rakija f	*ra*·ki·ya
champagne	šampanjac m	sham·*pa*·nyats
cocktail	koktel m	kok·*tel*
plum brandy	šljivovica f	*shlyi*·vo·vi·tsa
a bottle/glass of beer	boca/čaša piva	*bo*·tsa/*cha*·sha *pi*·va
a shot of (whiskey)	jedna čašica (viskija)	*yed*·na *cha*·shi·tsa (*vi*·ski·ya)
a bottle/glass of ... wine	boca/čaša ... vina	*bo*·tsa/*cha*·sha ... *vi*·na
red	crnog	*tsr*·nog
sparkling	pjenušavog	pye·*nu*·sha·vog
white	bijelog	bi·*ye*·log

What's the local speciality?

Što je ovdje područni/lokalni
specijalitet? ©/®

shto ye *ov*·dye po·*druch*·ni/*lo*·kal·ni
spe·tsi·ya·*li*·tet

What's that?

Što je to?

shto ye to

How much is (a kilo of cheese)?

Koliko stoji/košta (kila sira)? ©/®

ko·*li*·ko *sto*·yi/*kosh*·ta (*ki*·la *si*·ra)

I'd like ...	*Želim ...*	zhe·lim ...
(200) grams	*(dvijesto) grama*	(dvi·*ye*·sto) *gra*·ma
(two) kilos	*(dvije) kile*	(dvi·ye) *ki*·le
(three) pieces	*(tri) komada*	(tri) ko·*ma*·da
(six) slices	*(šest) krišaka*	(shest) *kri*·sha·ka

Less.	*Manje.*	*ma*·nye
Enough.	*Dosta.*	*do*·sta
More.	*Više.*	*vi*·she

special diets & allergies

Is there a vegetarian restaurant near here?

Da li znate za vegetarijanski
restoran ovdje blizu?

da li *zna*·te za ve·ge·ta·*ri*·yan·ski
re·*sto*·ran *ov*·dye *bli*·zu

Do you have vegetarian food?

Da li imate vegetarijanski obrok?

da li *i*·ma·te ve·ge·ta·*ri*·yan·ski *o*·brok

Could you prepare a	*Možete li prirediti*	*mo*·zhe·te li pri·*re*·di·ti
meal without ...?	*obrok koji ne sadrži ...?*	*o*·brok *koy*·i ne *sa*·dr·zhi ...
butter	*maslac*	*ma*·slats
eggs	*jaja*	*yai*·a
meat stock	*mesni bujon*	*mes*·ni *bu*·yon

I'm allergic	*Ja sam alergičan/*	ya sam a·*ler*·gi·chan/
to ...	*alergična na ...* m/f	a·*ler*·gich·na na ...
dairy produce	*mliječne proizvode*	mli·*yech*·ne pro·*iz*·vo·de
gluten	*gluten*	*glu*·ten
MSG	*glutaminat*	glu·ta·mi·*nat*
nuts	*razne orahe*	*raz*·ne *o*·ra·he
seafood	*morske plodove*	*mor*·ske *plo*·do·ve

menu reader

baklava f	ba-*kla*-va	*pastry with layers of nuts, sugar & cinnamon, soaked in syrup*
bečki odrezak m	*bech*-ki o-dre-zak	*Wiener schnitzel*
burek m	*bu*-rek	*flaky pastry stuffed with cheese or meat*
čevapčići m pl	che-*vap*-chi-chi	*skinless minced beef & lamb sausages*
džuveč m	ju-vech	*tomatoey casserole made from mixed vegetables, pork cutlets & rice*
gulaš od divljači m	*gu*-lash od *div*-lya-chi	*game goulash*
hladetina f	*hla*-de-ti-na	*pork brawn with vegetables, boiled eggs, garlic, parsley & paprika*
hladni pladanj m	*hlad*-ni *pla*-dan'	*cold cuts*
janjeća čorba f	*ya*-nye-cha *chor*-ba	*lamb stew*
janjetina na ražnju f	*ya*-nye-ti-na na *razh*-nyu	*lamb cooked on a spit*
japraci m pl	ya-*pra*-tsi	*mincemeat parcels rolled in vine or silver beet leaves (also called* **arambašići** a-ram-*ba*-shi-chi*)*
juha od graha f	*yu*-ha od *gra*-ha	*soup made from dried kidney or borlotti beans, smoked bacon bones (or smoked pork hock), onion, carrot, bay leaf & garlic*
kiseli kupus m	*ki*-se-li *ku*-pus	*sauerkraut – prepared from whole cored cabbage heads layered with horseradish, bay leaves, garlic, dried red pepper & salt*
kobasica f	ko-*ba*-si-tsa	*sausage*
kotlovina f	*kot*-lo-vi-na	*fried pork chops simmered in a piquant sauce*

ledene kocke f pl	*le·de·ne kots·ke*	coffee- or chocolate-flavoured sponge cake layered with chocolate cream
lička kisela čorba f	*lich·ka ki·se·la chor·ba*	stew prepared with cubed meat, mixed vegetables & cabbage
mađarica f	*ma·ja·ri·tsa*	layers of a rich sweet baked dough interspersed with a chocolate cream filling & topped with melted chocolate
miješano meso n	*mi·ye·sha·no me·so*	mixed grill
musaka f	*mu·sa·ka*	layered lasagne-style dish containing meat & vegetables
odojak na ražnju m	*o·doy·ak na razh·nyu*	suckling pig roasted on a spit
paprikaš m	*pa·pri·kash*	beef or fish stew flavoured with paprika
pastičada f	*pa·sti·cha·da*	beef rounds larded with smoked bacon & stewed with fried vegetables – served with a white wine sauce
pastirska juha f	*pa·stir·ska yu·ha*	soup made from cubed lamb, veal chops & pork neck
pita sa špinatom f	*pi·ta sa shpi·na·tom*	spinach pie & cottage cheese pie
pršut m	*pr·shut*	smoke-dried ham
punjene paprike f pl	*pu·nye·ne pa·pri·ke*	capsicums stuffed with rice, tomato paste, parsley, onion & mincemeat then oven baked
ražnjiči m pl	*razh·nyi·chi*	shish kebabs
riblja juha f	*rib·lya yu·ha*	fish chowder made of freshwater fish
sarma f	*sar·ma*	sour cabbage leaves stuffed with a mixture of ground meat, rice & garlic
štrudla f	*shtru·dla*	strudel with a sweet or savoury filling
tartuf m	*tar·tuf*	truffle – sometimes served shaved over scrambled eggs or risotto

emergencies

basics

Help!	*Upomoć!*	u-po-moch
Stop!	*Stanite!*	sta-ni-te
Go away!	*Maknite se!*	mak-ni-te se
Thief!	*Lopov!*	lo-pov
Fire!	*Požar!*	po-zhar
Watch out!	*Pazite!*	pa-zi-te
Call ...!	*Zovite ...!*	zo-vi-te ...
a doctor	*liječnika/lekara* ©/⑤	li-yech-ni-ka/le-ka-ra
an ambulance	*hitnu pomoć*	hit-nu po-moch
the police	*policiju*	po-li-tsi-yu

It's an emergency!
Imamo hitan slučaj.   i-ma-mo hi-tan slu-chai

Could you help me, please?
Molim vas, možete li mi pomoći?   mo-lim vas mo-zhe-te li mi po-mo-chi

Can I use your phone?
Mogu li koristiti vaš telefon?   mo-gu li ko-ri-sti-ti vash te-le-fon

I'm lost.
Izgubio/Izgubila sam se. m/f   iz-gu-bi-o/iz-gu-bi-la sam se

Where are the toilets?
Gdje se nalaze zahodi/toaleti? ©/⑤   gdye se na-la-ze za-ho-di/to-a-le-ti

police

Where's the police station?
Gdje se nalazi policijska stanica?   gdye se na-la-zi po-li-tsiy-ska sta-ni-tsa

I want to report an offence.
Želim prijaviti prekršaj.   zhe-lim pri-ya-vi-ti pre-kr-shai

I have insurance.
Imam osiguranje.   i-mam o-si-gu-ra-nye

I've been ...	*Ja sam bio/bila ...* m/f	ya sam bi-o/bi-la ...
assaulted	*napadnut/napadnuta* m/f	na-pad-nut/na-pad-nu-ta
raped	*silovan/silovana* m/f	si-lo-van/si-lo-va-na
robbed	*opljačkan* m	op-lyach-kan
	opljačkana f	op-lyach-ka-na

My ... was/were stolen.	Ukrali su mi ...	u·kra·li su mi ...
I've lost my ...	Izgubio/Izgubila sam ... m/f	iz·gu·bi·o/iz·gu·bi·la sam ...
backpack	svoj ranac	svoy ra·nats
bags	svoje torbe	svoy·e tor·be
credit card	svoju kreditnu karticu	svoy·oo kre·dit·nu kar·ti·tsu
jewellery	svoj nakit	svoy na·kit
money	svoj novac	svoy no·vats
passport	svoju putovnicu ©	svoy·oo pu·tov·ni·tsu
	svoj pasoš ⑤	svoy pa·sosh
travellers cheques	svoje putničke čekove	svoy·e put·nich·ke che·ko·ve

I want to contact my ...	Želim stupiti u kontakt sa ...	zhe·lim stu·pi·ti u kon·takt sa ...
consulate	svojom ambasadom	svoy·om am·ba·sa·dom
embassy	svojim konzulatom	svoy·im kon·zu·la·tom

health

medical needs

Where's the nearest ...?	Gdje je najbliži/ najbliža ...? m/f	gdye ye nai·bli·zhi/ nai·bli·zha ...
dentist	zubar m	zu·bar
doctor	liječnik/lekar m ©/⑤	li·yech·nik/le·kar
hospital	bolnica f	bol·ni·tsa
(night) pharmacist	(noćna) ljekarna/ apoteka f ©/⑤	(noch·na) lye·kar·na/ a·po·te·ka

I need a doctor (who speaks English).
Trebam liječnika/lekara (koji govori engleski). ©/⑤
tre·bam li·yech·ni·ka/le·ka·ra (koy·i go·vo·ri en·gle·ski)

Could I see a female doctor?
Mogu li dobiti ženskog liječnika/lekara? ©/⑤
mo·gu li do·bi·ti zhen·skog li·yech·ni·ka/le·ka·ra

I've run out of my medication.
Nestalo mi je lijekova.
ne·sta·lo mi ye li·ye·ko·va

symptoms, conditions & allergies

I'm sick.	Ja sam bolestan/ bolesna. m/f	ya sam *bo*·le·stan/ *bo*·le·sna
It hurts here.	Boli me ovdje.	*bo*·li me *ov*·dye
I have ...	Imam ...	*i*·mam ...

asthma	astma f	*ast*·ma
bronchitis	bronhitis m	bron·*hi*·tis
constipation	zatvorenje n	zat·vo·*re*·nye
cough	kašalj m	*ka*·shal'
diarrhoea	proljev m	*pro*·lyev
fever	groznica f	*gro*·zni·tsa
headache	glavobolja f	gla·*vo*·bo·lya
heart condition	poremećaj srca m	po·re·me·chai *sr*·tsa
nausea	mučnina f	much·*ni*·na
pain	bol m	bol
sore throat	grlobolja f	gr·*lo*·bo·lya
toothache	zubobolja f	zu·*bo*·bo·lya

I'm allergic to ...	Ja sam alergičan/ alergična na ... m/f	ya sam a·*ler*·gi·chan/ a·*ler*·gich·na na ...
antibiotics	antibiotike	an·ti·bi·*o*·ti·ke
anti-inflammatories	lijekove protiv upale	li·*ye*·ko·ve *pro*·tiv *u*·pa·le
aspirin	aspirin	a·*spi*·rin
bees	pčele	*pche*·le
codeine	kodein	ko·*de*·in
penicillin	penicilin	pe·ni·*tsi*·lin

antiseptic	antiseptik m	an·ti·*sep*·tik
bandage	zavoj m	*za*·voy
contraceptives	sredstva za sprječavanje trudnoće n pl	*sreds*·tva za spri·ye·*cha*·va·nye trud·*no*·che
diarrhoea medicine	lijekovi protiv proljeva m pl	li·*ye*·ko·vi *pro*·tiv *pro*·lye·va
insect repellent	sredstvo za odbijanje insekata n	*sreds*·tvo za od·*bi*·ya·nye in·se·ka·ta
laxatives	laksativi m pl	lak·*sa*·ti·vi
painkillers	tablete protiv bolova f pl	ta·*ble*·te *pro*·tiv *bo*·lo·va
rehydration salts	soli za rehidrataciju f	*so*·li za re·hi·dra·*ta*·tsi·yu
sleeping tablets	tablete za spavanje f pl	ta·*ble*·te za *spa*·va·nye

english–croatian dictionary

Croatian nouns in this dictionary have their gender indicated by ⓜ (masculine), ⓕ (feminine) or ⓝ (neuter). If it's a plural noun, you'll also see pl. Adjectives are given in the masculine form only. Words are also marked as a (adjective), v (verb), sg (singular), pl (plural), inf (informal), pol (polite), ⓒ (Croatian) or ⓢ (Serbian) where necessary.

A

accident *nezgoda* ⓕ *nez-go-da*
accommodation *smještaj* ⓜ *smye-shtai*
adaptor *konverter* ⓜ *kon-ver-ter*
address *adresa* ⓕ *a-dre-sa*
after *poslije* *po-sli-ye*
air-conditioned *klimatiziran* kli-ma-*ti-zi-ran*
airplane *zrakoplov/avion* ⓜ *zra-ko-plov/a-vi-on* ⓒ/ⓢ
airport *zračna luka* ⓕ/*aerodrom* ⓜ *zrach-na lu-ka/a-e-ro-drom* ⓒ/ⓢ
alcohol *alkohol* ⓜ *al-ko-hol*
all *sve* sve
allergy *alergija* ⓕ a-*ler-gi-ya*
ambulance *hitna pomoć* ⓕ *hit-na po-moch*
and *i* i
ankle *gležanj/članak* ⓜ *gle-zhan'/chla-nak* ⓒ/ⓢ
arm *ruka* ⓕ *ru-ka*
ashtray *pepeljara* ⓕ *pe-pe-lya-ra*
ATM *bankovni automat* ⓜ *ban-kov-ni a-u-to-mat*

B

baby *beba* ⓕ *be-ba*
back (body) *leđa* ⓕ pl *le-ja*
backpack *ranac* ⓜ *ra-nats*
bad *loš* losh
bag *torba* ⓕ *tor-ba*
baggage claim *šalter za podizanje prtljage* *shal-ter za po-di-za-nye prt-lya-ge*
bank *banka* ⓕ *ban-ka*
bar *bar* ⓜ bar
bathroom *kupaonica* ⓕ ku-pa-o-*ni-tsa*
battery (car) *akumulator* ⓜ a-ku-mu-*la-tor*
battery (general) *baterija* ⓕ ba-*te-ri-ya*
beautiful *lijep* li-yep
bed *krevet* ⓜ *kre-vet*
beer *pivo* ⓝ *pi-vo*
before *prije* *pri-ye*
behind *iza* i-*za*
bicycle *bicikl* ⓜ bi-*tsi*-kl
big *velik* *ve-lik*
bill *račun* ⓜ *ra-chun*

black *crn* tsrn
blanket *deka* ⓕ *de-ka*
blood group *krvna grupa* ⓕ *krv-na gru-pa*
blue *plav* plav
boat (ship) *brod* ⓜ brod
boat (smaller/private) *čamac* ⓜ *cha-mats*
book (make a reservation) v *rezervirati* re-zer-*vi-ra-ti*
Bosnia-Hercegovina *Bosna i Hercegovina* ⓕ *bos-na i her-tse-go-vi-na*
Bosnian (language) *bosanski jezik* ⓜ *bo-san-ski ye-zik*
bottle *boca* ⓕ *bo-tsa*
bottle opener *otvarač za boce* ⓜ ot-va-rach za *bo-tse*
boy *dječak* ⓜ *dye-chak*
brakes (car) *kočnice* ⓕ pl *koch-ni-tse*
breakfast *doručak* ⓜ *do-ru-chak*
broken (faulty) *pokvaren* po-*kva-ren*
bus *autobus* ⓜ a-u-to-bus
business *biznis* ⓝ *biz-nis*
buy *kupiti* *ku-pi-ti*

C

café *kafić/kavana* ⓜ/ⓕ *ka-fich/ka-va-na*
camera *foto-aparat* ⓜ *fo-to-a-pa-rat*
camp site *mjesto za kampiranje* ⓜ *mye-sto za kam-pi-ra-nye*
cancel *poništiti* po-*nish-ti-ti*
can opener *otvarač za limenke/konzerve* ⓜ ot-*va-rach za li-men-ke/kon-zer-ve* ⓒ/ⓢ
car *automobil* ⓜ a-u-to-mo-bil
cash *gotovina* ⓕ go-to-*vi-na*
cash (a cheque) v *unovčiti* u-nov-*chi-ti*
cell phone *mobilni telefon* ⓜ *mo-bil-ni te-le-fon*
centre *centar* ⓜ *tsen-tar*
change (money) v *zamijeniti* za-mi-ye-*ni-ti*
cheap *jeftin* *yef-tin*
check (bill) *račun* ⓜ *ra-chun*
check-in *prijemni šalter* *pri-yem-ni shal-ter*
chest *prsa/grudi* ⓕ pl *pr-sa/gru-di* ⓒ/ⓢ
child *dijete* ⓝ *di-ye-te*
cigarette *cigareta* ⓕ *tsi-ga-re-ta*
city *grad* ⓜ grad
clean a *čist* chist
closed *zatvoren* *zat-vo-ren*
coffee *kava* ⓕ *ka-va*

coins *novčići* ⓜ pl nov-chi-chi
cold a *hladan* hla-dan
collect call *poziv na račun nazvane osobe* ⓜ
  po-ziv na ra-chun naz-va-ne o-so-be
come *doći* do-chi
computer *računalo* ⓝ/*kompjuter* ⓜ
  ra-chu-na-lo/komp-yu-ter ⓒ/ⓢ
condom *prezervativ* ⓜ pre-zer-va-tiv
contact lenses *kontakt leče* ⓕ pl/*kontaktna sočiva*
  ⓝ pl kon-takt le-che/kon-takt-na so-chi-va ⓒ/ⓢ
cook v *kuhati* ku-ha-ti
cost *cijena* ⓕ tsi-ye-na
credit card *kreditna kartica* ⓕ kre-dit-na kar-ti-tsa
Croatia *Hrvatska* ⓕ hr-vat-ska
Croatian (language) *hrvatski* ⓜ hr-vat-ski
Croatian a *hrvatski* hr-vat-ski
cup *šalica/šoljica* ⓕ sha-li-tsa/sho-l'i-tsa ⓒ/ⓢ
currency exchange *tečaj/kurs stranih valuta* ⓜ
  te-chai/kurs stra-nih va-lu-ta ⓒ/ⓢ
customs (immigration) *carinarnica* ⓕ tsa-ri-nar-ni-tsa

D

dangerous *opasan* o-pa-san
date (time) *datum* ⓜ da-tum
day *dan* ⓜ dan
delay *zakašnjenje* ⓝ za-kash-nye-nye
dentist *zubar* ⓜ zu-bar
depart *otići* o-ti-chi
diaper *pelene* ⓕ pl pe-le-ne
dictionary *rječnik* ⓜ ryech-nik
dinner *večera* ⓕ ve-che-ra
direct *direktan* di-rek-tan
dirty *prljav* pr-lyav
disabled *onesposobljen* o-ne-spo-sob-lyen
discount *popust* ⓜ po-pust
doctor *liječnik/lekar* ⓜ li-yech-nik/le-kar ⓒ/ⓢ
double bed *dupli krevet* ⓜ du-pli kre-vet
double room *dvokrevetna soba* ⓕ dvo-kre-vet-na so-ba
drink *piće* ⓝ pi-che
drive v *voziti* vo-zi-ti
drivers licence *vozačka dozvola* ⓕ vo-zach-ka doz-vo-la
drug (illicit) *droga* ⓕ dro-ga
dummy (pacifier) *duda/cucla* ⓕ du-da/tsu-tsla ⓒ/ⓢ

E

ear *uho* ⓝ u-ho
east *istok* ⓜ i-stok
eat *jesti* ye-sti
economy class *drugi razred* ⓜ dru-gi raz-red
electricity *struja* ⓕ stru-ya
elevator *dizalo* ⓝ/*lift* ⓜ di-za-lo/lift ⓒ/ⓢ

email *e-mail* ⓜ i-me-il
embassy *ambasada* ⓕ am-ba-sa-da
emergency *hitan slučaj* ⓜ hi-tan slu-chai
English (language) *engleski* ⓜ en-gle-ski
entrance *ulaz* ⓜ u-laz
evening *večer* ⓕ ve-cher
exchange rate *tečaj/kurs razmjene* ⓜ
  te-chai/kurs raz-mye-ne ⓒ/ⓢ
exit *izlaz* ⓜ iz-laz
expensive *skup* skup
express mail *ekspres pošta* ⓕ eks-pres posh-ta
eye *oko* ⓝ o-ko

F

far *daleko* da-le-ko
fast *brz* brz
father *otac* ⓜ o-tats
film (camera) *film* ⓜ film
finger *prst* ⓜ prst
first-aid kit *pribor za prvu pomoć* ⓜ
  pri-bor za pr-vu po-moch
first class *prvi razred* ⓜ pr-vi raz-red
fish *riba* ⓕ ri-ba
food *hrana* ⓕ hra-na
foot *stopalo* ⓝ sto-pa-lo
fork *viljuška* ⓕ vi-lyush-ka
free (of charge) *besplatan* be-spla-tan
friend *prijatelj/prijateljica* ⓜ/ⓕ
  pri-ya-tel'/pri-ya-te-lyi-tsa
fruit *voće* ⓝ vo-che
full *pun* pun
funny *smiješan* smye-shan

G

gift *dar/poklon* ⓜ dar/pok-lon ⓒ/ⓢ
girl *djevojčica* ⓕ dye-voy-chi-tsa
glass (drinking) *čaša* ⓕ cha-sha
glasses *naočale* ⓕ pl na-o-cha-le
go *ići* i-chi
good *dobar* do-bar
green *zelen* ze-len
guide *vodič* ⓜ vo-dich

H

half *polovina* ⓕ po-lo-vi-na
hand *ruka* ⓕ ru-ka
handbag *ručna torbica* ⓕ ruch-na tor-bi-tsa
happy *sretan* sre-tan
have *imati* i-ma-ti
he *on* on

head *glava* ① *gla*-va
heart *srce* ⑩ *sr*-tse
heat *vrućina* ① *vru-chi*-na
heavy *težak* *te*-zhak
help v *pomoći* po-mo-chi
here *ovdje* ov-dye
high *visok* vi-sok
highway *autoput* ⑩ *a-u-to*-put
hike v *pješačiti* pye-sha-chi-ti
holidays *praznici* ⑩ pl *praz*-ni-tsi
homosexual *homoseksualac/homoseksualka* ⑩/①
   ho-mo-sek-su-*a*-lats/ho-mo-sek-su-*a*-ka
hospital *bolnica* ① *bol*-ni-tsa
hot *vruć* vruch
hotel *hotel* ⑩ ho-*tel*
hungry *gladan/gladna* ⑩/① *gla*-dan/*gla*-dna
husband *muž* ⑩ muzh

I

I *ja* ya
identification (card) *osobna iskaznica/lična karta* ①
   o-sob-na i-skaz-ni-tsa/lich-na kar-ta ⓒ/ⓢ
ill *bolestan* bo-le-stan
important *važan* va-zhan
included *uključen* uk-lyu-chen
injury *povreda* ① po-vre-da
insurance *osiguranje* ⑩ o-si-gu-ra-nye
Internet *internet* ⑩ in-ter-net
interpreter *tumač* ⑩ tu-mach

J

jewellery *nakit* ⑩ *na*-kit
job *posao* ⑩ *po*-sa-o

K

key *ključ* ⑩ klyuch
kilogram *kilogram* ⑩ *ki*-lo-gram
kitchen *kuhinja* ① *ku*-hi-nya
knife *nož* ⑩ nozh

L

laundry (place) *praonica* ① pra-o-ni-tsa
lawyer *pravnik* ⑩ *prav*-nik
left (direction) *lijevi* li-ye-vi
left-luggage office *ured za odlaganje prtljage* ⑩
   u-red za od-la-ga-nye prt-*lya*-ge
leg *noga* ① *no*-ga
lesbian *lezbijka* ① lez-*biy*-ka
less *manje* *ma*-nye

letter (mail) *pismo* ① *pi*-smo
lift (elevator) *dizalo/lift* di-za-lo/lift ⓒ/ⓢ
light *svjetlost* ① svyet-lost
like v *dopadati se* do-pa-da-ti se
lock *brava* ① *bra*-va
long *dugačak* du-ga-chak
lost *izgubljen* iz-gub-lyen
lost-property office *ured za izgubljene stvari* ⑩
   u-red za iz-gub-lye-ne stva-ri
love v *voljeti* vo-lye-ti
luggage *prtljaga* ① prt-*lya*-ga
lunch *ručak* ⑩ *ru*-chak

M

mail *pošta* ① posh-ta
man *čovjek* ⑩ cho-vyek
map (of country) *karta* ① *kar*-ta
map (of town) *plan grada* ⑩ plan *gra*-da
market *tržnica/pijaca* ① trzh-ni-tsa ⓒ/ⓢ
matches *šibice* ① pl *shi*-bi-tse
meat *meso* ⑩ *me*-so
medicine *lijekovi* ⑩ pl li-ye-ko-vi
menu *jelovnik* ⑩ ye-*lov*-nik
message *poruka* ① po-ru-ka
milk *mlijeko* ⑩ mli-ye-ko
minute *minuta* ① mi-nu-ta
mobile phone *mobilni telefon* ⑩ mo-bil-ni te-*le*-fon
money *novac* ⑩ no-vats
Montenegro *Crna Gora* ① tsr-na go-ra
month *mjesec* ⑩ mye-sets
morning *jutro* ⑩ yu-tro
mother *majka* ① mai-ka
motorcycle *motocikl* ⑩ mo-to-tsi-kl
motorway *autoput* ⑩ a-u-to-put
mouth *usta* ① pl u-sta
music *glazba* ① glaz-ba

N

name *ime* ⑩ *i*-me
napkin *salveta* ① sal-ve-ta
nappy *pelene* ① pl pe-le-ne
near *blizu* bli-zu
neck *vrat* ⑩ vrat
new *nov* nov
news *vijesti* ① pl vi-ye-sti
newspaper *novine* ① pl *no*-vi-ne
night *noć* ① noch
no *ne* ne
noisy *bučan* bu-chan
nonsmoking *nepušački* ⑩ ne-pu-shach-ki
north *sjever* ⑩ sye-ver

nose *nos* ⓜ nos
now *sada* sa-da
number *broj* ⓜ broy

O

oil (engine) *ulje* ⓝ u-lye
old *star* star
one-way ticket *jednosmjerna karta* ⓕ
yed-no-smyer-na kar-ta
open a *otvoren* ot-vo-ren
outside *vani/napolju* va-ni/na-po-l'u ⓒ/Ⓢ

P

package *paket* ⓜ pa-ket
paper *papir* ⓜ pa-pir
park (car) v *parkirati* par-ki-ra-ti
passport *putovnica* ⓕ/*pasoš* ⓜ
pu-tov-ni-tsa/pa-sosh ⓒ/Ⓢ
pay *platiti* pla-ti-ti
pen *kemijska* ⓕ ke-miy-ska
petrol *benzin* ⓜ ben-zin
pharmacy *ljekarna/apoteka* ⓕ
lye-kar-na/a-po-te-ka ⓒ/Ⓢ
phonecard *telefonska kartica* ⓕ
te-le-fon-ska kar-ti-tsa
photo *fotografija* ⓕ fo-to-gra-fi-ya
plate *tanjur* ⓜ ta-nyur
police *policija* ⓕ po-li-tsi-ya
postcard *dopisnica* ⓕ do-pi-sni-tsa
post office *poštanski ured* ⓜ posh-tan-ski u-red
pregnant *trudna* trud-na
price *cijena* ⓕ tsi-ye-na

Q

quiet *tih* tih

R

rain *kiša* ⓕ ki-sha
razor *brijač* ⓜ bri-yach
receipt *račun* ⓜ ra-chun
red *crven* tsr-ven
refund *povrat novca* ⓜ pov-rat nov-tsa
registered mail *preporučena pošta* ⓕ
pre-po-ru-che-na posh-ta
rent v *iznajmiti* iz-nai-mi-ti
repair v *popraviti* po-pra-vi-ti
reservation *rezervacija* ⓕ re-zer-va-tsi-ya
restaurant *restoran* ⓜ re-sto-ran
return v *vratiti se* vra-ti-ti se

return ticket *povratna karta* ⓕ po-vra-tna kar-ta
right (direction) *desno* de-sno
road *cesta* ⓕ/*put* ⓜ tse-sta/put ⓒ/Ⓢ
room *soba* ⓕ so-ba

S

safe a *siguran* si-gu-ran
sanitary napkin *higijenski uložak* ⓜ
hi-gi-yen-ski u-lo-zhak
seat *sjedište* ⓝ sye-dish-te
send *poslati* po-sla-ti
Serbia *Srbija* ⓕ sr-bi-ya
Serbian (language) *srpski jezik* ⓜ srp-ski ye-zik
service station *benzinska stanica* ⓕ
ben-zin-ska sta-ni-tsa
sex *seks* ⓜ seks
shampoo *šampon* ⓜ sham-pon
share (a dorm) *dijeliti* di-ye-li-ti
shaving cream *pjena za brijanje* ⓕ
pye-na za bri-ya-nye
she *ona* o-na
sheet (bed) *plahta* ⓕ/*čaršav* ⓜ
pla-hta/char-shav ⓒ/Ⓢ
shirt *košulja* ⓕ ko-shu-lya
shoes *cipele* ⓕ pl tsi-pe-le
shop *prodavaonica* ⓕ pro-da-va-o-ni-tsa
short *kratak* kra-tak
shower *tuš* ⓜ tush
single room *jednokrevetna soba* ⓕ
yed-no-kre-vet-na so-ba
skin *koža* ⓕ ko-zha
skirt *suknja* ⓕ suk-nya
sleep v *spavati* spa-va-ti
slowly *sporo* spo-ro
small *mali* ma-li
smoke (cigarettes) v *pušiti* pu-shi-ti
soap *sapun* ⓜ sa-pun
some *malo* ma-lo
soon *uskoro* u-sko-ro
south *jug* ⓜ yug
souvenir shop *prodavaonica suvenira* ⓕ
pro-da-va-o-ni-tsa su-ve-ni-ra
speak *govoriti* go-vo-ri-ti
spoon *žlica/kašika* ⓕ zhli-tsa/ka-shi-ka ⓒ/Ⓢ
stamp *poštanska marka* ⓕ posh-tan-ska mar-ka
stand-by ticket *uvjetna/uslovna karta* ⓕ
uv-yet-na/us-lov-na kar-ta ⓒ/Ⓢ
station (train) *stanica* ⓕ sta-ni-tsa
stomach *želudac* ⓜ zhe-lu-dats
stop v *zaustaviti* za-u-sta-vi-ti
stop (bus) *stanica* ⓕ sta-ni-tsa
street *ulica* ⓕ u-li-tsa

student *student* m & ① *stu*-dent
sun *sunce* ① *sun*-tse
sunscreen *losion za zaštitu od sunca* m
  lo-si-on za zash-ti-tu od *sun*-tsa
swim v *plivati* *pli*-va-ti

T

tampon *tampon* m *tam*-pon
taxi *taksi* m *tak*-si
teaspoon *žličica/kašičica* ①
  zhli-chi-tsa/*ka*-shi-chi-tsa ©/⑤
teeth *zubi* m pl *zu*-bi
telephone *telefon* m te-*le*-fon
television *televizija* ① te-le-*vi*-zi-ya
temperature (weather) *temperatura* ① tem-pe-ra-*tu*-ra
tent *šator* m *sha*-tor
that (one) *ono* o-no
they *oni/one/ona* m/①/① o-ni/o-ne/o-na
thirsty *žedan* zhe-dan
this (one) *ovo* o-vo
throat *grlo* ① *gr*-lo
ticket *karta* ① *kar*-ta
time *vrijeme* ① vri-ye-me
tired *umoran* u-mo-ran
tissues *papirnati rupčići* m pl pa-pir-na-ti *rup*-chi-chi ©
  papirne maramice ① pl pa-pir-ne ma-ra-mi-tse ⑤
today *danas* *da*-nas
toilet *zahod/toalet* m *za*-hod/to-a-*let* ©/⑤
tomorrow *sutra* su-tra
tonight *večeras* ve-che-ras
toothbrush *četkica za zube* ① *chet*-ki-tsa za *zu*-be
toothpaste *pasta za zube* ① *pa*-sta za *zu*-be
torch (flashlight) *ručna svjetiljka* ① *ruch*-na svye-til'-ka
tour *ekskurzija* ① ek-*skur*-zi-ya
tourist office *turistička agencija* ①
  tu-*ri*-stich-ka a-*gen*-tsi-ya
towel *ručnik/peškir* m *ruch*-nik/*pesh*-kir ©/⑤
train *vlak/voz* m vlak/voz ©/⑤
translate *prevesti* pre-*ve*-sti
travel agency *putna agencija* ① *put*-na a-*gen*-tsi-ya
travellers cheque *putnički ček* m *put*-nich-ki chek
trousers *hlače/pantalone* ① pl
  hla-che/pan-ta-lo-ne ©/⑤
twin beds *dva kreveta* m pl dva *kre*-ve-ta
tyre *guma* ① *gu*-ma

U

underwear *donje rublje* ① *do*-nye rub-lye
urgent *hitan* hi-tan

V

vacant *prazan* pra-zan
vacation *praznici* m pl *praz*-ni-tsi
vegetable *povrće* ① *po*-vr-che
vegetarian a *vegetarijanski* ve-ge-ta-*ri*-yan-ski
visa *viza* ① *vi*-za

W

waiter *konobar* m ko-no-bar
walk v *hodati* ho-da-ti
wallet *novčanik* m *nov*-cha-nik
warm a *topao* to-pa-o
wash (something) *oprati* o-*pra*-ti
watch *sat* m sat
water *voda* ① *vo*-da
we *mi* mi
weekend *vikend* m *vi*-kend
west *zapad* m *za*-pad
wheelchair *invalidska kolica* ① pl in-*va*-lid-ska ko-*li*-tsa
when *kada* ka-da
where *gdje* gdye
white *bijel* bi-yel
who *tko* tko
why *zašto* zash-to
wife *žena* ① zhe-na
window *prozor* m *pro*-zor
wine *vino* ① *vi*-no
with *sa* sa
without *bez* bez
woman *žena* ① zhe-na
write *napisati* na-*pi*-sa-ti

Y

yellow *žut* zhut
yes *da* da
yesterday *jučer* yu-cher
you sg inf *ti* ti
you sg pol & pl *vi* vi

French

french alphabet

A a a	*B b* be	*C c* se	*D d* de	*E e* eu
F f ef	*G g* zhe	*H h* ash	*I i* i	*J j* zhi
K k ka	*L l* el	*M m* em	*N n* en	*O o* o
P p pe	*Q q* kew	*R r* er	*S s* es	*T t* te
U u ew	*V v* ve	*W w* dubl ve	*X x* iks	*Y y* i grek
Z z zed				

■ french

FRANÇAIS

introduction

What do you think of when the word 'French' comes up? A *bon vivant*, drinking an *apéritif tête-à-tête* with a friend at a *café*, while studying the *à la carte* menu and making some witty *double entendres*? Are you getting *déjà vu* yet? Chances are you already know a few fragments of French (*français* fron-sey) – *bonjour*, *oui*, *au revoir*, *bon voyage* and so on. Even if you missed out on French lessons, though, that first sentence (forgive the stereotyping) is evidence that you probably know quite a few French words without realising it. And thanks to the Norman invasion of England in the 11th century, many common English words have a French origin – some estimate, in fact, that three-fifths of everyday English vocabulary arrived via French.

So, after centuries of contact with English, French offers English speakers a relatively smooth path to communicating in another language. The structure of a French sentence won't come as a surprise and the sounds of the language are generally common to English as well. The few sounds that do differ will be familiar to most through television and film examples of French speakers – the silent 'h' and the throaty 'r', for example. French is a distant cousin of English, but is most closely related to its Romance siblings, Italian and Spanish. These languages developed from the Latin spoken by the Romans during their conquests of the 1st century BC.

Almost 30 countries cite French as an official language (not always the only language, of course), in many cases due to France's colonisation of various countries in Africa, the Pacific and the Caribbean. It's the mother tongue of around 80 million people in places like Belgium, Switzerland, Luxembourg, Monaco, Canada and Senegal as well as France, and another 50 million speak it as a second language. French was the language of international diplomacy until the early 20th century, and is still an official language of a number of international organisations, including the Red Cross, the United Nations and the International Olympic Committee.

As well as the advantage of learning a language that's spoken all around the world, there are more subtle benefits to French. Being told of a wonderful vineyard off the tourist track, for example, or discovering that there's little truth in the cliché that the French are rude. And *regardez* the significant body of literature (the Nobel Prize for Literature has gone to French authors a dozen times), film and music ... You'll find the reasons to speak French just keep growing.

pronunciation

vowel sounds

Generally, French vowel sounds are short and don't glide into other vowels. Note that the ey in *café* is close to the English sound, but it's shorter and sharper.

symbol	english equivalent	french example	transliteration
a	run	*tasse*	tas
ai	aisle	*travail*	tra·vai
air	fair	*faire*	fair
e	bet	*fesses*	fes
ee	see	*lit*	lee
eu	nurse	*deux*	deu
ew	ee pronounced with rounded lips	*tu*	tew
ey	as in 'bet', but longer	*musée*	moo·zey
o	pot	*pomme*	pom
oo	moon	*chou*	shoo

There are also four nasal vowels in French. They're pronounced as if you're trying to force the sound out of your nose rather than your mouth. In French, nasal vowels cause the following nasal consonant sound to be omitted, but a 'hint' of what the implied consonant is can sometimes be heard. We've used nasal consonant sounds (m, n, ng) with the nasal vowel to help you produce the sound with more confidence. Since the four nasal sounds can be quite close, we've simplified it this way:

symbol	english equivalent	french example	transliteration
om/on/ong	like the 'o' in 'pot', plus nasal consonant sound	*mouton*	moo·ton
um/un/ung	similar to the 'a' in 'bat', plus nasal consonant sound	*magasin*	ma·ga·zun

consonant sounds

symbol	english equivalent	french example	transliteration
b	**bed**	*billet*	bee-yey
d	**dog**	*date*	dat
f	**fat**	*femme*	fam
g	**go**	*grand*	gron
k	**kit**	*carte*	kart
l	**lot**	*livre*	leev-re
m	**man**	*merci*	mair-see
n	**not**	*non*	non
ny	**canyon**	*signe*	see-nye
ng	**ring**	*cinquante*	sung-kont
p	**pet**	*parc*	park
r	**run (throaty)**	*rue*	rew
s	**sun**	*si*	see
sh	**shot**	*changer*	shon-zhey
t	**top**	*tout*	too
v	**very**	*verre*	vair
w	**win**	*oui*	wee
y	**yes**	*payer*	pe-yey
z	**zero**	*vous avez*	voo-za-vey
zh	**pleasure**	*je*	zhe

word stress

Syllables in French words are, for the most part, equally stressed. English speakers tend to stress the first syllable, so try adding a light stress on the final syllable to compensate. The rhythm of a French sentence is based on breaking the phrase into meaningful sections, then stressing the final syllable pronounced in each section. The stress at these points is characterised by a slight rise in intonation.

tools

language difficulties

Do you speak English?
Parlez-vous anglais? — par·ley·voo ong·gley

Do you understand?
Comprenez-vous? — kom·pre·ney·voo

I understand.
Je comprends. — zhe kom·pron

I don't understand.
Je ne comprends pas. — zhe ne kom·pron pa

What does (*beaucoup*) mean?
Que veut dire (beaucoup)? — ke veu deer (bo·koo)

How do you ...?	*Comment ...?*	ko·mon ...
pronounce this	*le prononcez-vous*	le pro·non·sey voo
write (*bonjour*)	*est-ce qu'on écrit (bonjour)*	es kon ey·kree (bon·zhoor)

Could you please ...?	*Pourriez-vous ..., s'il vous plaît?*	poo·ree·yey voo ... seel voo pley
repeat that	*répéter*	rey·pey·tey
speak more slowly	*parler plus lentement*	par·ley plew lon·te·mon
write it down	*l'écrire*	ley·kreer

essentials

Yes.	*Oui.*	wee
No.	*Non.*	non
Please.	*S'il vous plaît.*	seel voo pley
Thank you (very much).	*Merci (beaucoup).*	mair·see (bo·koo)
You're welcome.	*Je vous en prie.*	zhe voo zon·pree
Excuse me.	*Excusez-moi.*	ek·skew·zey·mwa
Sorry.	*Pardon.*	par·don

numbers

0	*zéro*	zey·ro	16	*seize*	sez
1	*un*	un	17	*dix-sept*	dee·set
2	*deux*	deu	18	*dix-huit*	dee·zweet
3	*trois*	trwa	19	*dix-neuf*	deez·neuf
4	*quatre*	ka·tre	20	*vingt*	vung
5	*cinq*	sungk	21	*vingt et un*	vung tey un
6	*six*	sees	22	*vingt-deux*	vung·deu
7	*sept*	set	30	*trente*	tront
8	*huit*	weet	40	*quarante*	ka·ront
9	*neuf*	neuf	50	*cinquante*	sung·kont
10	*dix*	dees	60	*soixante*	swa·sont
11	*onze*	onz	70	*soixante-dix*	swa·son·dees
12	*douze*	dooz	80	*quatre-vingts*	ka·tre·vung
13	*treize*	trez	90	*quatre-vingt-dix*	ka·tre·vung·dees
14	*quatorze*	ka·torz	100	*cent*	son
15	*quinze*	kunz	1000	*mille*	meel

time & dates

What time is it?	*Quelle heure est-il?*	kel eur ey·teel
It's one o'clock.	*Il est une heure.*	ee·ley ewn eu
It's (10) o'clock.	*Il est (dix) heures.*	ee·ley (deez) eu
Quarter past (one).	*Il est (une) heure et quart.*	ee·ley (ewn) eu ey kar
Half past (one).	*Il est (une) heure et demie.*	ee·ley (ewn) eu ey de·mee
Quarter to (one).	*Il est (une) heure moins le quart.*	ee·ley (ewn) eu mwun le kar
At what time ...?	*À quelle heure ...?*	a kel eu ...
At ...	*À ...*	a ...
in the morning	*du matin*	dew ma·tun
in the afternoon	*de l'après-midi*	de la·prey·mee·dee
in the evening	*du soir*	dew swar
Monday	*lundi*	lun·dee
Tuesday	*mardi*	mar·dee
Wednesday	*mercredi*	mair·kre·dee
Thursday	*jeudi*	zheu·dee
Friday	*vendredi*	von·dre·dee
Saturday	*samedi*	sam·dee
Sunday	*dimanche*	dee·monsh

January	*janvier*	zhon·vyey
February	*février*	feyv·ryey
March	*mars*	mars
April	*avril*	a·vreel
May	*mai*	mey
June	*juin*	zhwun
July	*juillet*	zhwee·yey
August	*août*	oot
September	*septembre*	sep·tom·bre
October	*octobre*	ok·to·bre
November	*novembre*	no·vom·bre
December	*décembre*	dey·som·bre

What date is it today?

    C'est quel jour aujourd'hui?   sey kel zhoor o·zhoor·dwee

It's (18 October).

    C'est le (dix-huit octobre).   sey le (dee·zwee tok·to·bre)

since (May)	*depuis (mai)*	de·pwee (mey)
until (June)	*jusqu'à (juin)*	zhoos·ka (zhwun)

today	*aujourd'hui*	o·zhoor·dwee
tonight	*ce soir*	se swar

last ...		
night	*hier soir*	ee·yair swar
week	*la semaine dernière*	la se·men dair·nyair
month	*le mois dernier*	le mwa dair·nyey
year	*l'année dernière*	la·ney dair·nyair

next ...		
week	*la semaine prochaine*	la se·men pro·shen
month	*le mois prochain*	le mwa pro·shen
year	*l'année prochaine*	la·ney pro·shen

yesterday/tomorrow ...	*hier/demain ...*	ee·yair/de·mun ...
morning	*matin*	ma·tun
afternoon	*après-midi*	a·pre·mee·dee
evening	*soir*	swar

weather

What's the weather like?	*Quel temps fait-il?*	kel tom fey·teel
It's ...		
cloudy	*Le temps est couvert.*	le tom ey koo·vair
cold	*Il fait froid.*	eel fey frwa
hot	*Il fait chaud.*	eel fey sho
raining	*Il pleut.*	eel pleu
snowing	*Il neige.*	eel nezh
sunny	*Il fait beau.*	eel fey bo
warm	*Il fait chaud.*	eel fey sho
windy	*Il fait du vent.*	eel fey dew von
spring	*printemps* m	prun·tom
summer	*été* m	ey·tey
autumn	*automne* m	o·ton
winter	*hiver* m	ee·vair

border crossing

I'm here ...	*Je suis ici ...*	zhe swee zee·see ...
in transit	*de passage*	de pa·sazh
on business	*pour le travail*	poor le tra·vai
on holiday	*pour les vacances*	poor ley va·kons
I'm here for ...	*Je suis ici pour ...*	zhe swee zee·see poor ...
(10) days	*(dix) jours*	(dees) zhoor
(three) weeks	*(trois) semaines*	(trwa) se·men
(two) months	*(deux) mois*	(deu) mwa

I'm going to (Paris).
Je vais à (Paris).   zhe vey a (pa·ree)

I'm staying at the (Hotel Grand).
Je loge à (l'hotel Grand).   zhe lozh a (lo·tel gron)

I have nothing to declare.
Je n'ai rien à déclarer.   zhe ney ryun a dey·kla·rey

I have something to declare.
J'ai quelque chose à déclarer.   zhey kel·ke·shoz a dey·kla·rey

That's not mine.
Ce n'est pas à moi.   se ney pa a mwa

transport

tickets & luggage

Where can I buy a ticket?
Où peut-on acheter un billet? oo pe·ton ash·tey um bee·yey

Do I need to book a seat?
Est-ce qu'il faut réserver une place? es·keel fo rey·zer·vey ewn plas

One ... ticket (to Bordeaux), please.	*Un billet ... (pour Bordeaux), s'il vous plaît.*	um bee·yey ... (poor bor·do) seel voo pley
one-way	*simple*	sum·ple
return	*aller et retour*	a·ley ey re·toor

I'd like to ... my ticket, please.	*Je voudrais ... mon billet, s'il vous plaît.*	zhe voo·drey ... mom bee·yey seel voo pley
cancel	*annuler*	a·new·ley
change	*changer*	shon·zhey
collect	*retirer*	re·tee·rey
confirm	*confirmer*	kon·feer·mey

I'd like a ... seat, please.	*Je voudrais une place ..., s'il vous plaît.*	zhe voo·drey ewn plas ... seel voo pley
(non)smoking	*non-fumeur*	non few·me
smoking	*fumeur*	few·me

How much is it?
C'est combien? sey kom·byun

Is there air conditioning?
Est-qu'il y a la climatisation? es·keel ya la klee·ma·tee·za·syon

Is there a toilet?
Est-qu'il y a des toilettes? es·keel ya dey twa·let

How long does the trip take?
Le trajet dure combien de temps? le tra·zhey dewr kom·byun de tom

Is it a direct route?
Est-ce que c'est direct? es·ke sey dee·rekt

I'd like a luggage locker.
Je voudrais une consigne automatique. zhe voo·drey ewn kon·see·nye o·to·ma·teek

My luggage	Mes bagages	mey ba-gazh
has been ...	ont été ...	on tey-tey ...
damaged	endommagés	on-do-ma-zhey
lost	perdus	per-dew
stolen	volés	vo-ley

getting around

Where does flight (008) arrive?
Où atteri le vol (008)? oo a-te-ree le vol (zey-ro zey-ro weet)

Where does flight (008) depart?
D'où décolle le vol (008)? doo dey-kol le vol (zey-ro zey-ro weet)

Where's (the) ...?	Où se trouve ...?	oo se troo-ve ...
arrivals hall	le hall d'arrivée	le hol da-ree-vey
departures hall	le hall des departs	le hol dey dey-par
duty-free shop	le magasin duty-free	le ma-ga-zun dyoo-tee free
gate (12)	porte (douze)	port (dooz)

Is this the ... to (Nice)?	Est ce ... pour (Nice)?	es se ... poor (nees)
boat	le bateau	le ba-to
bus	le bus	le bews
plane	l'avion	la-vyon
train	le train	le trun

What time's	Le ... bus passe	le ... bews pas
the ... bus?	à quelle heure?	a kel e
first	premier	pre-myey
last	dernier	dair-nyey
next	prochain	pro-shun

At what time does it arrive/leave?
A quelle heure est ce qu'il arrive/part? a kel eur es se keel a-ree-ve/par

How long will it be delayed?
De combien de temps est-il retardé? de kom-byun de tom es-teel re-tar-dey

What station is this?
C'est quelle gare? sey kel gar

What's the next station?
Quelle est la prochaine gare? kel ey la pro-shen gar

Does it stop at (Amboise)?
Est-ce qu'il s'arrête à (Amboise)? es-kil sa-ret a (om-bwaz)

Please tell me when we get to (Nantes).
Pouvez-vous me dire quand   poo·vey·voo me deer kon
nous arrivons à (Nantes)?   noo za·ree·von a (nont)

How long do we stop here?
Combien de temps on s'arrête ici?   kom·byun de tom on sa·ret ee·see

Is this seat available?
Est-ce que cette place est libre?   es·ke set plas ey lee·bre

That's my seat.
C'est ma place.   sey ma plas

I'd like a taxi ...	*Je voudrais un taxi ...*	zhe voo·drey un tak·see ...
at (9am)	*à (neuf heures*	a (neu veur
	du matin)	dew ma·tun)
now	*maintenant*	mun·te·non
tomorrow	*demain*	de·mun

Is this taxi available?
Vous êtes libre?   voo·zet lee·bre

How much is it to ...?
C'est combien pour aller à ...?   sey kom·byun poor a·ley a ...

Please put the meter on.
Mettez le compteur, s'il vous plaît.   me·tey le kon·teseel voo pley

Please take me to (this address).
Conduisez-moi à (cette adresse),   kon·dwee·zey mwa a (set a·dres)
s'il vous plaît.   seel voo pley

Please ...	*..., s'il vous plaît.*	... seel voo pley
slow down	*Roulez plus lentement*	roo·ley plew lont·mon
stop here	*Arrêtez-vous ici*	a·rey·tey voo ee·see
wait here	*Attendez ici*	a·ton·dey ee·see

car, motorbike & bicycle hire

I'd like to hire a ...	*Je voudrais louer ...*	zhe voo·drey loo·wey ...
bicycle	*un vélo*	un vey·lo
car	*une voiture*	ewn vwa·tewr
motorbike	*une moto*	ewn mo·to
with ...	*avec ...*	a·vek ...
a driver	*un chauffeur*	un sho·feur
air conditioning	*climatisation*	klee·ma·tee·za·syon

How much for … hire?	Quel est le tarif par …?	kel ey le ta·reef par …
hourly	heure	eur
daily	jour	zhoor
weekly	semaine	se·men

air	air m	air
oil	huile f	weel
petrol	essence f	es·sons
tyres	pneus f pl	pneu

I need a mechanic.
J'ai besoin d'un mécanicien.   zhey be·zwun dun mey·ka·nee·syun

I've run out of petrol.
Je suis en panne d'essence.   zhe swee zon pan de·sons

I have a flat tyre.
Mon pneu est à plat.   mom pneu ey ta pla

directions

Where's the …?	Où est-ce qu'il y a …?	oo es·keel ya …
bank	la banque	la bongk
city centre	le centre-ville	ler son·tre·veel
hotel	l'hôtel	lo·tel
market	le marché	le mar·shey
police station	le commissariat	le kom·mee·sar·ya
	de police	de po·lees
post office	le bureau de poste	le bew·ro de post
public toilet	des toilettes	dey twa·let
tourist office	l'office de tourisme	lo·fees de too·rees·me

Is this the road to (Toulouse)?
C'est la route pour (Toulouse)?   sey la root poor (too·looz)

Can you show me (on the map)?
Pouvez-vous m'indiquer (sur la carte)?   poo·vey·voo mun·dee·key (sewr la kart)

What's the address?
Quelle est l'adresse?   kel ey la·dres

How far is it?
C'est loin?   sey lwun

How do I get there?
Comment faire pour y aller?   ko·mon fair poor ee a·ley

Turn ...	Tournez ...	toor·ney ...
at the corner	au coin	o kwun
at the traffic lights	aux feux	o feu
left/right	à gauche/droite	a gosh/drwat

It's ...	C'est ...	sey ...
behind ...	derrière ...	dair·yair ...
far away	loin d'ici	lwun dee·see
here	ici	ee·see
in front of ...	devant ...	de·von ...
left	à gauche	a gosh
near (to ...)	près (de ...)	prey (de ...)
next to ...	à côté de ...	a ko·tey de ...
opposite ...	en face de ...	on fas de ...
right	à droite	a drwat
straight ahead	tout droit	too drwa
there	là	la

north	nord m	nor
south	sud m	sewd
east	est m	est
west	ouest m	west

by bus	en bus	om bews
by taxi	en taxi	on tak·see
by train	en train	on trun
on foot	à pied	a pyey

signs

Entrée/Sortie	on·trey/sor·tee	**Entrance/Exit**
Ouvert/Fermé	oo·vair/fair·mey	**Open/Closed**
Chambre Libre	shom·bre lee·bre	**Rooms Available**
Complet	kom·pley	**No Vacancies**
Renseignements	ron·sen·ye·mon	**Information**
Commissariat De Police	ko·mee·sar·ya de po·lees	**Police Station**
Interdit	in·teyr·dee	**Prohibited**
Toilettes	twa·let	**Toilets**
Hommes	om	**Men**
Femmes	fam	**Women**
Chaude/Froide	shod/frwad	**Hot/Cold**

102

accommodation

finding accommodation

Where's a . . .?	*Où est-ce qu'on peut trouver . . .?*	oo es·kon peu troo·vey . . .
camping ground	*un terrain de camping*	un tey·run de kom·peeng
guesthouse	*une pension*	ewn pon·see·on
hotel	*un hôtel*	un o·tel
youth hostel	*une auberge de jeunesse*	ewn o·bairzh de zhe·nes
Can you	*Est-ce que vous*	es·ke voo
recommend	*pouvez recommander*	poo·vey re·ko·mon·dey
somewhere . . .?	*un logement . . .?*	un lozh·mon . . .
cheap	*pas cher*	pa shair
good	*de bonne qualité*	de bon ka·lee·tey
nearby	*près d'ici*	prey dee·see

I'd like to book a room, please.
Je voudrais réserver — zhe voo·drey rey·zair·vey
une chambre, s'il vous plaît. — ewn shom·bre seel voo pley

I have a reservation.
J'ai une réservation. — zhey ewn rey·zair·va·syon

My name is . . .
Mon nom est . . . — mon nom ey . . .

Do you have	*Avez-vous*	a·vey·voo
a . . . room?	*une chambre . . .?*	ewn shom·bre . . .
single	*à un lit*	a un lee
double	*avec un grand lit*	a·vek ung gron lee
twin	*avec des lits jumeaux*	a·vek dey lee zhew·mo
Can I pay by . . .?	*Est-ce qu'on peut payer avec . . .?*	es·kom peu pey·yey a·vek . . .
credit card	*une carte de crédit*	ewn kart de krey·dee
travellers cheque	*des chèques de voyage*	dey shek de vwa·yazh
How much is it per . . .?	*Quel est le prix par . . .?*	kel ey le pree par . . .
night	*nuit*	nwee
person	*personne*	pair·son

I'd like to stay for (two) nights.
Je voudrais rester pour (deux) nuits. zhe voo·drey res·tey poor (der) nwee

From (July 2) to (July 6).
Du (deux juillet) au (six juillet). dew (de zhwee·yey) o (see zhwee·yey)

Can I see it?
Est-ce que je peux la voir? es·ke zhe peu la vwar

Am I allowed to camp here?
Est-ce que je peux camper ici? es·ke zhe peu kom·pey ee·see

Where's the nearest camp site?
Où est le terrain de camping oo ey ler tey·run de kom·peeng
le plus proche? le plew prosh

requests & queries

When/Where is breakfast served?
Quand/Où le petit kon/oo le pe·tee
déjeuner est-il servi? dey·zhe·ney ey·teel sair·vee

Please wake me at (seven).
Réveillez-moi à (sept) rey·vey·yey·mwa a (set)
heures, s'il vous plaît. eur seel voo pley

Could I have my key, please?
Est-ce que je pourrais avoir es·ke zhe poo·rey a·vwar
la clé, s'il vous plaît? la kley seel voo pley

Can I get another (blanket)?
Est-ce que je peux avoir es·ke zhe pe a·vwar
une autre (couverture)? ewn o·tre (koo·vair·tewr)

Is there a/an ...? *Avez-vous un ...?* a·vey·voo un ...
   elevator *ascenseur* a·son·seur
   safe *coffre-fort* ko·fre·for

The room is too ... *C'est trop ...* sey tro ...
   expensive *cher* shair
   noisy *bruyant* brew·yon
   small *petit* pe·tee

The ... doesn't work.	... ne fonctionne pas.	... ne fong·syon pa
air conditioning	La climatisation	klee·ma·tee·za·syon
fan	Le ventilateur	le von·tee·la·teur
toilet	Les toilettes	le twa·let

This ... isn't clean.	... n'est pas propre.	... ney pa pro·pre
pillow	Cet oreiller	set o·rey·yey
sheet	Ce drap	se drap
towel	Cette serviette	set sair·vee·et

checking out

What time is checkout?
Quand faut-il régler? — kon fo·teel rey·gley

Can I leave my luggage here?
Puis-je laisser mes bagages? — pweezh ley·sey mey ba·gazh

Could I have my ..., please?	Est-ce que je pourrais avoir ..., s'il vous plaît?	es·ke zhe poo·rey a·vwar ... seel voo pley
deposit	ma caution	ma ko·syon
passport	mon passeport	mon pas·por
valuables	mes biens précieux	mey byun prey·syeu

communications & banking

the internet

Where's the local Internet café?
Où est le cybercafé du coin? — oo ey le see·bair·ka·fey dew kwun

How much is it per hour?
C'est combien l'heure? — sey kom·byun leur

I'd like to ...	Je voudrais ...	zhe voo·drey ...
check my email	consulter mon courrier électronique	kon·sewl·tey mong koor·yey ey·lek·tro·neek
get Internet access	me connecter à l'internet	me ko·nek·tey a lun·tair·net
use a printer	utiliser une imprimante	ew·tee·lee·zey ewn um·pree·mont
use a scanner	utiliser un scanner	ew·tee·lee·zey un ska·nair

mobile/cell phone

I'd like a ...	Je voudrais ...	zhe voo-drey ...
mobile/cell phone for hire	louer un portable	loo-ey um por-ta-ble
SIM card for your network	une carte SIM pour le réseau	ewn kart seem poor le rey-zo

What are the rates?	Quels sont les tarifs?	kel son ley ta-reef

telephone

What's your phone number?
Quel est votre numéro de téléphone?   kel ey vo-tre new-mey-ro de tey-ley-fon

The number is ...
Le numéro est ...   le new-mey-ro ey ...

Where's the nearest public phone?
Où est le téléphone   oo ey le tey-ley-fon
public le plus proche?   pewb-leek le plew prosh

I'd like to buy a phone card.
Je voudrais acheter   zhe voo-drey ash-tey
une carte téléphonique.   ewn kart tey-ley-fo-neek

I want to ...	Je veux ...	zhe ve ...
call (Singapore)	téléphoner avec préavis (à Singapour)	tey-ley-fo-ney a-vek prey-a-vee (a sung-ga-poor)
make a local call	faire un appel local	fair un a-pel lo-kal
reverse the charges	téléphoner en PCV	tey-ley-fo-ney om pey-sey-vey

How much does ... cost?	Quel est le prix ...?	kel ey le pree ...
a (three)-minute call	d'une communication de (trois) minutes	dewn ko-mew-nee-ka-syon de (trwa) mee-newt
each extra minute	de chaque minute supplémentaire	de shak mee-newt sew-pley-mon-tair

It's (one euro) per (minute).
(Un euro) pour (une minute).   (un eu-ro) poor (ewn mee-newt)

post office

I want to send a ...	Je voudrais envoyer ...	zhe voo·drey on·vwa·yey ...
fax	un fax	un faks
letter	une lettre	ewn le·tre
parcel	un colis	ung ko·lee
postcard	une carte postale	ewn kart pos·tal

I want to buy a/an ...	Je voudrais acheter ...	zhe voo·drey ash·tey ...
envelope	une enveloppe	ewn on·vlop
stamp	un timbre	un tum·bre

Please send it (to Australia) by ...	Envoyez-le (en Australie), s'il vous plaît.	on·vwa·yey·le (on os·tra·lee) ... seel voo pley
airmail	par avion	par a·vyon
express mail	en exprès	on neks·pres
registered mail	en recommandé	on re·ko·mon·dey
surface mail	par voie de terre	par vwa de tair

Is there any mail for me?
Y a-t-il du courrier pour moi? ya·teel dew koor·yey poor mwa

bank

Where's a/an ...?	Où est ...?	oo ey ...
ATM	le guichet automatique	le gee·shey o·to·ma·teek
foreign exchange office	le bureau de change	le bew·ro de shonzh

I'd like to ...	Je voudrais ...	zhe voo·drey ...
arrange a transfer	faire un virement	fair un veer·mon
cash a cheque	encaisser un chèque	ong·key·sey un shek
change a travellers cheque	changer des chèques de voyage	shon·zhey dey shek de vwa·yazh
change money	changer de l'argent	shon·zhey de lar·zhon
get a cash advance	une avance de crédit	ewn a·vons de krey·dee
withdraw money	retirer de l'argent	re·tee·rey de lar·zhon

What's the ...?	Quel est ...?	kel ey ...
charge for that	le tarif	le ta·reef
exchange rate	le taux de change	le to de shonzh

It's ...	C'est ...	sey ...
(12) euros	(douze) euros	(dooz) eu·ro
free	gratuit	gra·twee

What time does the bank open?
À quelle heure ouvre la banque?   a kel eur oo·vre la bongk

Has my money arrived yet?
Mon argent est-il arrivé?   mon ar·zhon ey·teel a·ree·vey

sightseeing

getting in

What time does it ...?	Quelle est l'heure ...?	kel ey leur ...
close	de fermeture	de fer·me·tewr
open	d'ouverture	doo·vair·tewr

What's the admission charge?
Quel est le prix d'admission?   kel ey le pree dad·mee·syon

Is there a discount for children/students?
Il y a une réduction pour les   eel ya ewn rey·dewk·syon poor ley
enfants/étudiants?   zon·fon/zey·tew·dyon

I'd like a ...	Je voudrais ...	zhe voo·drey ...
catalogue	un catalogue	ung ka·ta·log
guide	un guide	ung geed
local map	une carte de la région	ewn kart de la rey·zhyon

I'd like to see ...	J'aimerais voir ...	zhem·rey vwar ...
What's that?	Qu'est-ce que c'est?	kes·ke sey
Can I take photos?	Je peux prendre	zhe peu pron·dre
	des photos?	dey fo·to

tours

When's the next ...?	C'est quand la prochaine ...?	sey kon la pro·shen ...
day trip	excursion d'une journée	eks·kewr·syon dewn zhoor·ney
tour	excursion	eks·kewr·syon

Is ... included?	Est-ce que ... est	es·ke ... ey
	inclus/incluse? m/f	tung·klew/tung·klewz
accommodation	le logement m	le lozh·mon
the admission charge	l'admission f	lad·mee·syon
food	la nourriture f	la noo·ree·tewr
transport	le transport m	le trons·por

How long is the tour?
L'excursion dure combien de temps?   leks·kewr·syon dewr kom·byun de tom

What time should we be back?
On doit rentrer pour quelle heure?   on dwa ron·trey poor kel eur

sightseeing

castle	château m	sha·to
cathedral	cathédrale f	ka·tey·dral
church	église f	ey·gleez
main square	place centrale f	plas son·tral
monastery	monastère m	mo·na·stair
monument	monument m	mo·new·mon
museum	musée m	mew·zey
old city	vieille ville f	vyey veel
palace	palais m	pa·ley
ruins	ruines f pl	rween
stadium	stade m	stad
statues	statues f pl	sta·tew

shopping

enquiries

Where's a ...?	Où est ...?	oo es ...
bank	la banque	la bongk
bookshop	la librairie	la lee·brey·ree
camera shop	le magasin photo	le ma·ga·zun fo·to
department store	le grand magasin	le gron ma·ga·zun
grocery store	l'épicerie	ley·pee·sree
market	le marché	le mar·shey
newsagency	le marchand de journaux	le mar·shon de zhoor·no
supermarket	le supermarché	le sew·pair·mar·shey

Where can I buy (a padlock)?
Où puis-je acheter (un cadenas)? oo pweezh ash·tey (un kad·na)

I'm looking for ...
Je cherche ... zhe shairsh ...

Can I look at it?
Est-ce que je peux le voir? es·ke zhe peu le vwar

Do you have any others?
Vous en avez d'autres? voo zon a·vey do·tre

Does it have a guarantee?
Est-ce qu'il y a une garantie? es keel ya ewn ga·ron·tee

Can I have it sent overseas?
Pouvez-vous me l'envoyer poo·vey·voo me lon·vwa·yey
à l'étranger? a ley·tron·zhey

Can I have my ... repaired?
Puis-je faire réparer ...? pwee·zhe fair rey·pa·rey ...

It's faulty.
C'est défectueux. sey dey·fek·tweu

I'd like ..., please.	*Je voudrais ...,*	zhe voo·drey ...
	s'il vous plaît.	seel voo pley
a bag	*un sac*	un sak
a refund	*un remboursement*	un rom·boors·mon
to return this	*rapporter ceci*	ra·por·tey se·see

paying

How much is it?
C'est combien? sey kom·byun

Can you write down the price?
Pouvez-vous écrire le prix? poo·vey·voo ey·kreer le pree

That's too expensive.
C'est trop cher. sey tro shair

Can you lower the price?
Vous pouvez baisser le prix? voo poo·vey bey·sey le pree

I'll give you (five) euros.
Je vous donnerai (cinq) euros. zhe voo don·rey (sungk) eu·ro

There's a mistake in the bill.
Il y a une erreur dans la note. eel ya ewn ey·reur don la not

Do you accept ...?	Est-ce que je peux payer avec ....?	es·ke zhe pe pey·yey a·vek ...
credit cards	une carte de crédit	ewn kart de krey·dee
debit cards	une carte de débit	ewn kart de dey·bee
travellers cheques	des chèques de voyages	dey shek de vwa·yazh

I'd like ..., please.	Je voudrais ..., s'il vous plaît.	zhe voo·drey ... seel voo pley
a receipt	un reçu	un re·sew
my change	ma monnaie	ma mo·ney

clothes & shoes

Can I try it on?	Puis-je l'essayer?	pwee·zhe ley·sey·yey
My size is (42).	Je fais du (quarante-deux).	zhe fey dew (ka·ront·deu)
It doesn't fit.	Ce n'est pas la bonne taille.	se ney pa la bon tai

small	petit	pe·tee
medium	moyen	mwa·yen
large	grand	gron

books & music

I'd like a ...	Je voudrais ...	zhe voo·drey ...
newspaper	un journal	un zhoor·nal
(in English)	(en anglais)	(on ong·gley)
pen	un stylo	un stee·lo

Is there an English-language bookshop?
Y a-t-il une librairie anglaise? — ya·teel ewn lee·brey·ree ong·gleyz

I'm looking for something by (Camus).
Je cherche quelque chose de (Camus). — zhe shairsh kel·ke shoz de (ka·mew)

Can I listen to this?
Je peux l'écouter ici? — zhe peu ley·koo·tey ee·see

photography

Can you ...?	Pouvez-vous ...?	poo·vey·voo ...
burn a CD from my memory card	copier un CD de ma carte memoire	ko·pyey un se·de de ma kart mey·mwar
develop this film	développer cette pellicule	dey·vlo·pey set pey·lee·kewl
load my film	charger ma pellicule	shar·zhey ma pey·lee·kewl

I need a/an ... film for this camera.	J'ai besoin d'une pellicule ... pour cet appareil.	zhey be·zwun dewn pey·lee·kewl ... poor sey·ta·pa·rey
APS	APS	a·pey·es
B&W	en noir et blanc	on nwar ey·blong
colour	couleur	koo·leur
slide	diapositive	dya·po·zee·teev
(200) speed	rapidité (deux cent)	ra·pee·dee·tey (deu son)

When will it be ready?
Quand est-ce que cela sera prêt?   kon tes·ke se·la se·ra prey

meeting people

greetings, goodbyes & introductions

Hello.	Bonjour.	bon·zhoor
Hi.	Salut.	sa·lew
Good night.	Bonsoir.	bon·swar
Goodbye.	Au revoir.	o re·vwar
See you later.	À bientôt.	a byun·to

Mr	Monsieur	me·syeu
Mrs	Madame	ma·dam
Miss	Mademoiselle	mad·mwa·zel

How are you?	Comment allez-vous?	ko·mon ta·ley·voo
Fine, thanks. And you?	Bien, merci. Et vous?	byun mair·see ey voo
What's your name?	Comment vous appelez-vous?	ko·mon voo za·pley·voo
My name is ...	Je m'appelle ...	zhe ma·pel ...
I'm pleased to meet you.	Enchanté/Enchantée. m/f	on·shon·tey

This is my ...	*Voici mon/ma ...* m/f	vwa·see mon/ma ...
boyfriend	*petit ami*	pe·tee ta·mee
brother	*frère*	frair
daughter	*fille*	fee·ye
father	*père*	pair
friend	*ami/amie* m/f	a·mee
girlfriend	*petite amie*	pe·teet a·mee
husband	*mari*	ma·ree
mother	*mère*	mair
partner (intimate)	*partenaire*	par·te·nair
sister	*sœur*	seur
son	*fils*	fees
wife	*femme*	fam
Here's my ...	*Voici mon ...*	vwa·see mon ...
What's your ...?	*Quel est votre ...?* pol	kel ey vo·tre ...
	Quel est ton ...? inf	kel ey ton ...
address	*adresse*	a·dress
email address	*e-mail*	ey·mel
fax number	*numéro de fax*	new·mey·ro de faks
phone number	*numéro de téléphone*	new·mey·ro de tey·ley·fon

occupations

What's your occupation?

Vous faites quoi comme métier? pol	voo fet kwa kom mey·tyey
Tu fais quoi comme métier? inf	tew fey kwa kom mey·tyey

I'm a/an ...	*Je suis un/une ...* m/f	zhe swee zun/zewn ...
artist	*artiste* m&f	ar·teest
businessperson	*homme/femme d'affaires* m/f	om/fem da·fair
farmer	*agriculteur* m	a·gree·kewl·teur
	agricultrice f	a·gree·kewl·trees
manual worker	*ouvrier/ouvrière* m/f	oo·vree·yey/oo·vree·yair
office worker	*employé/employée de bureau* m/f	om·plwa·yey de bew·ro
scientist	*scientifique* m&f	syon·tee·feek
student	*étudiant/étudiante* m/f	ey·tew·dyon/ey·tew·dyont
tradesperson	*ouvrier qualifié* m&f	oo·vree·yey ka·lee·fyey

background

Where are you from?	*Vous venez d'où?* pol	voo ve·ney doo
	Tu viens d'où? inf	tew vyun doo
I'm from ...	*Je viens ...*	zhe vyun ...
Australia	*d'Australie*	dos·tra·lee
Canada	*du Canada*	dew ka·na·da
England	*d'Angleterre*	dong·gle·tair
New Zealand	*de la Nouvelle-Zélande*	de la noo·vel·zey·lond
the USA	*des USA*	dey zew·es·a

Are you married?
Est-ce que vous êtes marié(e)? m/f pol   es·ke voo zet mar·yey
Est-ce que tu es marié(e)? m/f inf   es·ke tew ey mar·yey

I'm married.
Je suis marié/mariée. m/f   zhe swee mar·yey

I'm single.
Je suis célibataire. m&f   zhe swee sey·lee·ba·tair

age

How old ...?	*Quel âge ...?*	kel azh ...
are you	*avez-vous* pol	a·vey·voo
	as-tu inf	a·tew
is your daughter	*a votre fille* pol	a vo·tre fee·ye
is your son	*a votre fils* pol	a vo·tre fees

I'm ... years old.   *J'ai ... ans.*   zhey ... on
He/She is ... years old.   *Il/Elle a ... ans.*   eel/el a ... on

feelings

I'm (not) ...	*Je (ne) suis (pas)...*	zhe (ne) swee (pa) ...
Are you ...?	*Êtes-vous ...?* pol	et voo ...
	Es-tu ...? inf	ey·tew ...
happy	*heureux/heureuse* m/f	er·reu/er·reuz
sad	*triste* m&f	treest

I'm ...	J'ai ...	zhey ...
I'm not ...	Je n'ai pas ...	zhe ney pa ...
Are you ...?	Avez-vous ...? pol	a·vey voo ...
	As-tu ...? inf	a·tew ...
cold	froid/froide m/f	frwa/frwad
hot	chaud/chaude m/f	sho/shod
hungry	faim m&f	fum
thirsty	soif m&f	swaf

entertainment

going out

Where can I find ...?	Où sont les ...?	oo son ley ...
clubs	clubs	kleub
gay venues	boîtes gaies	bwat gey
pubs	pubs	peub
I feel like going to a/the ...	Je voudrais aller ...	zhe voo·drey a·ley ...
concert	à un concert	a ung kon·sair
movies	au cinéma	o see·ney·ma
party	à la fête	a la feyt
restaurant	au restaurant	o res·to·ron
theatre	au théâtre	o tey·a·tre

interests

Do you like ...?	Aimes-tu ...? inf	em·tew ...
I like ...	J'aime ...	zhem ...
I don't like ...	Je n'aime pas ...	zhe nem pa ...
art	l'art	lar
cooking	cuisiner	kwee·zee·ney
movies	le cinéma	le see·ney·ma
nightclubs	les boîtes	ley bwat
reading	lire	leer
shopping	faire des courses	fair dey koors
sport	le sport	le spor
travelling	voyager	vwa·ya·zhey

Do you like to ...?	Aimes-tu ...? inf	em·tew ...
dance	danser	don·sey
go to concerts	aller aux concerts	a·ley o kon·sair
listen to music	écouter de	ey·koo·tey de la
	la musique	mew·zeek

food & drink

finding a place to eat

Can you	Est-ce que vous pouvez	es·ke voo poo·vey
recommend a ...?	me conseiller ...?	me kon·sey·yey ...
bar	un bar	um bar
café	un café	ung ka·fey
restaurant	un restaurant	un res·to·ron

I'd like ..., please.	Je voudrais ...,	zhe voo·drey ...
	s'il vous plaît.	seel voo pley
a table for (five)	une table pour	ewn ta·ble poor
	(cinq) personnes	(sungk) pair·son
the (non)smoking	un endroit pour	un on·drwa poor
section	(non-)fumeurs	non·few·me

ordering food

breakfast	petit déjeuner m	pe·tee dey·zhe·ney
lunch	déjeuner m	dey·zhe·ney
dinner	dîner m	dee·ney
snack	casse-croûte m	kas·kroot

What would you recommend?
Qu'est-ce que vous conseillez?   kes·ke voo kon·sey·yey

I'd like (the) ...,	Je voudrais ...,	zhe voo·drey ...
please.	s'il vous plaît.	seel voo pley
bill	l'addition	la·dee·syon
drink list	la carte des boissons	la kart dey bwa·son
menu	la carte	la kart
that dish	ce plat	ser pla
wine list	la carte des vins	la kart dey vun

drinks

(cup of) coffee ...	*(un) café ...*	(ung) ka·fey ...
(cup of) tea ...	*(un) thé ...*	(un) tey ...
with milk	*au lait*	o ley
without sugar	*sans sucre*	son sew·kre
(orange) juice	*jus (d'orange)* m	zhew (do·ronzh)
soft drink	*boisson non-alcoolisée* f	bwa·son non·al·ko·lee·zey
... water	*eau ...*	o ...
hot	*chaude*	shod
sparkling mineral	*minérale gazeuse*	mee·ney·ral ga·zeuz
still mineral	*minérale non-gazeuse*	mee·ney·ral nong·ga·zeuz

in the bar

I'll have ...	*Je prends ...*	zhe pron ...
I'll buy you a drink.	*Je vous offre un verre.*	zhe voo zo·fre un vair
What would you like?	*Qu'est-ce que vous voulez?*	kes·ke voo voo·ley
Cheers!	*Santé!*	son·tey
brandy	*cognac* m	ko·nyak
champagne	*champagne* m	shom·pan·ye
cocktail	*cocktail* m	kok·tel
a shot of (whisky)	*un petit verre de (whisky)*	um pe·tee vair de (wees·kee)
a bottle of ... wine	*une bouteille de vin ...*	ewn boo·tey de vun ...
a glass of ... wine	*un verre de vin ...*	un vair de vun ...
red	*rouge*	roozh
sparkling	*mousseux*	moo·seu
white	*blanc*	blong
a ... of beer	*... de bière*	... de byair
glass	*un verre*	un vair
bottle	*une bouteille*	ewn boo·tey

self-catering

What's the local speciality?
Quelle est la spécialité locale? — kel ey la spey·sya·lee·tey lo·kal

What's that?
Qu'est-ce que c'est, ça? — kes·ke sey sa

How much is (a kilo of cheese)?
C'est combien (le kilo de fromage)? — sey kom·byun (le kee·lo de fro·mazh)

I'd like …	Je voudrais …	zhe voo·drey …
(200) grams	(deux cents) grammes	(deu son) gram
(two) kilos	(deux) kilos	(deu) kee·lo
(three) pieces	(trois) morceaux	(trwa) mor·so
(six) slices	(six) tranches	(sees) tronsh

Less.	Moins.	mwun
Enough.	Assez.	a·sey
More.	Plus.	plew

special diets & allergies

Is there a vegetarian restaurant near here?
Y a-t-il un restaurant — ya·teel un res·to·ron
végétarien par ici? — vey·zhey·ta·ryun par ee·see

Do you have vegetarian food?
Vous faites les repas végétarien? — voo fet ley re·pa vey·zhey·ta·ryun

Could you prepare	Pouvez-vous préparer	poo·vey·voo prey·pa·rey
a meal without …?	un repas sans …?	un re·pa son …
butter	beurre	beur
eggs	œufs	zeu
meat stock	bouillon gras	boo·yon gra

I'm allergic to …	Je suis allergique …	zhe swee za·lair·zheek …
dairy produce	aux produits laitiers	o pro·dwee ley·tyey
gluten	au gluten	o glew·ten
MSG	au glutamate	o glew·ta·mat
	de sodium	de so·dyom
nuts	au noix	no nwa
seafood	aux fruits de mer	o frwee de mair

baba au rhum m	ba-ba o rom	small sponge cake, often with raisins, soaked in a rum-flavoured syrup
béarnaise f	bey-ar-neyz	white sauce of wine or vinegar beaten with egg yolks & flavoured with herbs
blanquette de veau f	blong-ket de vo	veal stew in white sauce with cream
bombe glacée f	bom-be gla-sey	ice cream with candied fruits, glazed chestnuts & cream
bouillabaisse f	bwee-ya-bes	fish soup stewed in a broth with garlic, orange peel, fennel, tomatoes & saffron
brioche f	bree-yosh	small roll or cake sometimes flavoured with nuts, currants or candied fruits
brochette f	bro-shet	grilled skewer of meat or vegetables
consommé m	kon-so-mey	clarified meat or fish-based broth
contre-filet m	kon-tre-fee-ley	beef sirloin roast
coulis m	koo-lee	fruit or vegetable purée, used as a sauce
croque-madame m	krok-ma-dam	grilled or fried ham & cheese sandwich, topped with a fried egg
croquembouche m	kro-kom-boosh	cream puffs dipped in caramel
croque-monsieur m	krok-mes-yeu	grilled or fried ham & cheese sandwich
croustade f	kroo-stad	puff pastry filled with fish, seafood, meat, mushrooms or vegetables
dijonnaise	dee-zho-nez	dishes with a mustard-based sauce
estouffade f	es-too-fad	meat stewed in wine with carrots & herbs
friand m	free-yon	pastry stuffed with minced sausage meat, ham & cheese, or almond cream
fricandeau m	free-kon-do	veal fillet simmered in white wine, vegetables herbs & spices • a pork pâté

fricassée f	free-ka-sey	*lamb, veal or poultry in a thick creamy sauce with mushrooms & onions*
grenadin m	gre-na-dun	*veal (or sometimes poultry) fillet, wrapped in a thin slice of bacon*
michette f	mee-shet	*savoury bread stuffed with cheese, olives, onions & anchovies*
pan-bagnat m	pun ban-ya	*small round bread loaves, filled with onions, vegetables, anchovies & olives*
plateau de fromage m	pla-to de fro-mazh	*cheese board or platter*
pomme duchesse f	pom dew-shes	*fritter of mashed potato, butter & egg yolk*
pot-au-feu m	po-to-fe	*beef, root vegetable & herb stockpot*
potée f	po-tey	*meat & vegetables cooked in a pot*
profiterole m	pro-fee-trol	*small pastry with savoury or sweet fillings*
puits d'amour m	pwee da-moor	*puff pastry filled with custard or jam*
quenelle f	ke-nel	*fish or meat dumpling, often poached*
quiche f	keesh	*tart with meat, fish or vegetable filling*
raclette f	ra-klet	*hot melted cheese, served with potatoes & gherkins*
ragoût m	ra-goo	*stew of meat, fish and/or vegetables*
ratatouille f	ra-ta-too-ye	*vegetable stew*
roulade f	roo-lad	*slice of meat or fish rolled around stuffing*
savarin m	sa-va-run	*sponge cake soaked with a rum syrup & filled with custard, cream & fruits*
savoie f	sav-wa	*light cake made with beaten egg whites*
tartiflette f	tar-tee-flet	*dish of potatoes, cheese & bacon*
velouté m	ver-loo-tey	*rich, creamy soup, usually prepared with vegetables, shellfish or fish purée*
vol-au-vent m	vo-lo-von	*puff pastry filled with a mixture of sauce & meat, seafood or vegetables*

emergencies

basics

Help!	*Au secours!*	o skoor
Stop!	*Arrêtez!*	a·rey·tey
Go away!	*Allez-vous-en!*	a·ley·voo·zon
Thief!	*Au voleur!*	o vo·leur
Fire!	*Au feu!*	o feu
Watch out!	*Faites attention!*	fet a·ton·syon
Call ...!	*Appelez ...!*	a·pley ...
a doctor	*un médecin*	un meyd·sun
an ambulance	*une ambulance*	ewn om·bew·lons
the police	*la police*	la po·lees

It's an emergency!
C'est urgent! — sey tewr·zhon

Could you help me, please?
Est-ce que vous pourriez — es·ke voo poo·ryey
m'aider, s'il vous plaît? — mey·dey seel voo pley

Could I use the telephone?
Est-ce que je pourrais utiliser — es·ke zhe poo·rey ew·tee·lee·zey
le téléphone? — le tey·ley·fon

I'm lost.
Je suis perdu/perdue. m/f — zhe swee pair·dew

Where are the toilets?
Où sont les toilettes? — oo son ley twa·let

police

Where's the police station?
Où est le commissariat de police? — oo ey le ko·mee·sar·ya de po·lees

I want to report an offence.
Je veux signaler un délit. — zhe veu see·nya·ley un dey·lee

I have insurance.
J'ai une assurance. — zhey ewn a·sew·rons

I've been assaulted.
J'ai été attaqué/attaquée. m/f — zhey ey·tey a·ta·key

I've been raped.
J'ai été violé/violée. m/f   zhey ey·tey vyo·ley

I've been robbed.
On m'a volé.   on ma vo·ley

I've lost my ...	*J'ai perdu ...*	zhey pair·dew ...
My ... was/were stolen.	*On m'a volé ...*	on ma vo·ley ...
backpack	*mon sac à dos*	mon sak a do
bags	*mes valises*	mey va·leez
credit card	*ma carte de crédit*	ma kart de krey·dee
handbag	*mon sac à main*	mon sak a mun
jewellery	*mes bijoux*	mey bee·zhoo
money	*mon argent*	mon ar·zhon
passport	*mon passeport*	mom pas·por
travellers cheques	*mes chèques de voyage*	mey shek de vwa·yazh
wallet	*mon portefeuille*	mom por·te·feu·ye

I want to contact my ...	*Je veux contacter mon ...*	zher veu kon·tak·tey mon ...
consulate	*consulat*	kon·sew·la
embassy	*ambassade*	om·ba·sad

health

medical needs

Where's the nearest ...?	*Où y a t-il ... par ici?*	oo ee a teel ... par ee·see
dentist	*un dentiste*	un don·teest
doctor	*un médecin*	un meyd·sun
hospital	*un hôpital*	u·no·pee·tal
(night) pharmacist	*une pharmacie (de nuit)*	ewn far·ma·see (de nwee)

I need a doctor (who speaks English).
J'ai besoin d'un médecin (qui parle anglais).   zhey be·zwun dun meyd·sun (kee parl ong·gley)

Could I see a female doctor?
Est-ce que je peux voir une femme médecin?   es·ke zhe peu vwar ewn fam meyd·sun

I've run out of my medication.
Je n'ai plus de médicaments.   zhe ney plew de mey·dee·ka·mon

symptoms, conditions & allergies

I'm sick.	Je suis malade.	zhe swee ma·lad
It hurts here.	J'ai une douleur ici.	zhey ewn doo·leur ee·see

I have (a) ...	J'ai ...	zhey ...
asthma	de l'asthme	de las·me
bronchitis	la bronchite	la bron·sheet
constipation	la constiptation	la kon·stee·pa·syon
cough	la toux	la too
diarrhoea	la diarrhée	la dya·rey
fever	la fièvre	la fyev·re
headache	mal à la tête	mal a la tet
heart condition	maladie de cœur	ma·la·dee de keur
nausea	la nausée	la no·zey
pain	une douleur	ewn doo·leur
sore throat	mal à la gorge	mal a la gorzh
toothache	mal aux dents	mal o don

I'm allergic to ...	Je suis allergique ...	zhe swee za·lair·zheek ...
antibiotics	aux antibiotiques	o zon·tee·byo·teek
anti-inflammatories	aux antiinflammatoires	o zun·tee·un·fla·ma·twar
aspirin	à l'aspirine	a las·pee·reen
bees	aux abeilles	o za·bey·ye
codeine	à la codéine	a la ko·dey·een
penicillin	à la pénicilline	a la pey·nee·see·leen

antiseptic	antiseptique m	on·tee·sep·teek
bandage	pansement m	pons·mon
condoms	préservatifs m pl	prey·zair·va·teef
contraceptives	contraceptifs m pl	kon·tre·sep·teef
diarrhoea medicine	médecine pour la diarrhée f	med·seen poor la dya·ey
insect repellent	repulsif anti-insectes m	rey·pewl·seef on·tee·un·sekt
laxatives	laxatifs m pl	lak·sa·teef
painkillers	analgésiques m pl	a·nal·zhey·zeek
rehydration salts	sels de réhydratation m pl	seyl de rey·ee·dra·ta·syon
sleeping tablets	somnifères m pl	som·nee·fair

english–french dictionary

French nouns and adjectives in this dictionary have their gender indicated by ⓜ (masculine) or ⓕ (feminine). If it's a plural noun, you'll also see pl. Words are also marked as n (noun), a (adjective), v (verb), sg (singular), pl (plural), inf (informal) and pol (polite) where necessary.

A

accident *accident* ⓜ ak-see-don
accommodation *logement* ⓜ lozh-mon
adaptor *adaptateur* ⓜ a-dap-ta-teur
address *adresse* ⓕ a-dres
after *après* a-prey
air-conditioned *climatisé* kee-ma-tee-zey
airplane *avion* ⓜ a-vyon
airport *aéroport* ⓜ a-ey-ro-por
alcohol *alcool* ⓜ al-kol
all a *tout/toute* ⓜ/ⓕ too/toot
allergy *allergie* ⓕ a-lair-zhee
ambulance *ambulance* ⓕ om-bew-lons
and *et* ey
ankle *cheville* ⓕ she-vee-ye
arm *bras* ⓜ bra
ashtray *cendrier* ⓜ son-dree-yey
ATM *guichet automatique de banque* ⓜ
　gee-shey o-to-ma-teek de bonk

B

baby *bébé* ⓜ bey-bey
back (body) *dos* ⓜ do
backpack *sac à dos* ⓜ sak a do
bad *mauvais/mauvaise* ⓜ/ⓕ mo-vey/mo-veyz
bag *sac* ⓜ sak
baggage claim *retrait des bagages* ⓜ
　re-trey dey ba-gazh
bank *banque* ⓕ bonk
bar *bar* ⓜ bar
bathroom *salle de bain* ⓕ sal de bun
battery (car) *batterie* ⓕ bat-ree
battery (general) *pile* ⓕ peel
beautiful *beau/belle* ⓜ/ⓕ bo/bel
bed *lit* ⓜ lee
beer *bière* ⓕ byair
before *avant* a-von
behind *derrière* dair-yair
Belgium *Belgique* ⓕ bel-zheek
bicycle *vélo* ⓜ vey-lo

big *grand/grande* ⓜ/ⓕ gron/grond
bill *addition* ⓕ a-dee-syon
black *noir/noire* ⓜ/ⓕ nwar
blanket *couverture* ⓕ koo-vair-tewr
blood group *groupe sanguin* ⓜ groop song-gun
blue *bleu/bleue* ⓜ/ⓕ bler
book (make a reservation) v *réserver* rey-zair-vey
bottle *bouteille* ⓕ boo-tey
bottle opener *ouvre-bouteille* ⓜ oo-vre-boo-tey
boy *garçon* ⓜ gar-son
brakes (car) *freins* ⓜ frun
breakfast *petit déjeuner* ⓜ pe-tee dey-zheu-ney
broken (faulty) *défectueux/défectueuse* ⓜ/ⓕ
　dey-fek-tweu/dey-fek-tweuz
bus *(auto)bus* ⓜ (o-to)bews
business *affaires* ⓕ a-fair
buy *acheter* ash-tey

C

café *café* ⓜ ka-fey
camera *appareil photo* ⓜ a-pa-rey fo-to
camp site *terrain de camping* ⓜ tey-run de kom-peeng
cancel *annuler* a-new-ley
can opener *ouvre-boîte* ⓜ oo-vre-bwat
car *voiture* ⓕ vwa-tewr
cash *argent* ⓜ ar-zhon
cash (a cheque) v *encaisser* ong-key-sey
cell phone *téléphone portable* ⓜ tey-ley-fon por-ta-ble
centre *centre* ⓜ son-tre
change (money) v *échanger* ey-shon-zhey
cheap *bon marché* ⓜ&ⓕ bon mar-shey
check (bill) *addition* ⓕ la-dee-syon
check-in n *enregistrement* ⓜ on-re-zhee-stre-mon
chest *poitrine* ⓕ pwa-treen
child *enfant* ⓜ&ⓕ on-fon
cigarette *cigarette* ⓕ see-ga-ret
city *ville* ⓕ veel
clean a *propre* ⓜ&ⓕ pro-pre
closed *fermé/fermée* ⓜ/ⓕ fair-mey
coffee *café* ⓜ ka-fey
coins *pièces* ⓕ pyes
cold a *froid/froide* ⓜ/ⓕ frwa/frwad

collect call *appel en PCV* ⓜ a-pel on pey-sey-vey
come *venir* ve-neer
computer *ordinateur* ⓜ or-dee-na-teur
condom *préservatif* ⓜ prey-zair-va-teef
contact lenses *verres de contact* ⓜ vair de kon-takt
cook v *cuire* kweer
cost *coût* ⓜ koo
credit card *carte de crédit* ⓕ kart de krey-dee
cup *tasse* ⓕ tas
currency exchange *taux de change* ⓜ to de shonzh
customs (immigration) *douane* ⓕ dwan

D

dangerous *dangereux/dangereuse* ⓜ/ⓕ
    don-zhreu/don-zhreuz
date (time) *date* ⓕ dat
day *date de naissance* ⓕ dat de ney-sons
delay *retard* ⓜ re-tard
dentist *dentiste* ⓜ don-teest
depart *partir* par-teer
diaper *couche* ⓕ koosh
dictionary *dictionnaire* ⓜ deek-syo-nair
dinner *dîner* ⓜ dee-ney
direct *direct/directe* ⓜ/ⓕ dee-rekt
dirty *sale* ⓜ&ⓕ sal
disabled *handicapé/handicapée* ⓜ/ⓕ on-dee-ka-pey
discount *remise* ⓕ re-meez
doctor *médecin* ⓜ meyd-sun
double bed *grand lit* ⓜ gron lee
double room *chambre pour deux personnes* ⓕ
    shom-bre poor de pair-son
drink *boisson* ⓕ bwa-son
drive v *conduire* kon-dweer
drivers licence *permis de conduire* ⓜ
    pair-mee de kon-dweer
drugs (illicit) *drogue* ⓕ drog
dummy (pacifier) *tétine* ⓕ tey-teen

E

ear *oreille* ⓕ o-rey
east *est* ⓜ est
eat *manger* mon-zhey
economy class *classe touriste* ⓕ klas too-reest
electricity *électricité* ⓕ ey-lek-tree-see-tey
elevator *ascenseur* ⓜ a-son-seur
email *e-mail* ⓜ ey-mel
embassy *ambassade* ⓕ om-ba-sad
emergency *cas urgent* ⓜ ka ewr-zhon

English (language) *anglais/anglaise* ⓜ/ⓕ
    ong-gley/ong-gleyz
entrance *entrée* ⓕ on-trey
evening *soir* ⓜ swar
exchange rate *taux de change* ⓜ to de shonzh
exit *sortie* ⓕ sor-tee
expensive *cher/chère* ⓜ/ⓕ shair
express mail *exprès* eks-pres
eye *œil* ⓜ eu-yee

F

far *lointain/lointaine* ⓜ/ⓕ lwun-tun/lwun-ten
fast *rapide* ⓜ&ⓕ ra-peed
father *père* ⓜ pair
film (camera) *pellicule* ⓕ pey-lee-kewl
finger *doigt* ⓜ dwa
first-aid kit *trousse à pharmacie* ⓕ troos a far-ma-see
first class *première classe* ⓕ pre-myair klas
fish *poisson* ⓜ pwa-son
food *nourriture* ⓕ noo-ree-tewr
foot *pied* ⓜ pyey
fork *fourchette* ⓕ foor-shet
France *France* frons
free (of charge) *gratuit/gratuite* ⓜ/ⓕ
    gra-twee/gra-tweet
French (language) *Français* fron-sey
friend *ami/amie* ⓜ/ⓕ a-mee
fruit *fruit* ⓜ frwee
full *plein/pleine* ⓜ/ⓕ plun/plen
funny *drôle* ⓜ&ⓕ drol

G

gift *cadeau* ⓜ ka-do
girl *fille* ⓕ fee-ye
glass (drinking) *verre* ⓜ vair
glasses *lunettes* ⓕ pl lew-net
go *aller* a-ley
good *bon/bonne* ⓜ/ⓕ bon
green *vert/verte* ⓜ/ⓕ vairt
guide n *guide* ⓜ geed

H

half *moitié* ⓕ mwa-tyey
hand *main* ⓕ mun
handbag *sac à main* ⓜ sak a mun
happy *heureux/heureuse* ⓜ/ⓕ eu-reu/eu-reuz
have *avoir* a-vwar

he *il* eel
head *tête* ① tet
heart *cœur* ⓜ keur
heat *chaleur* ① sha-leur
heavy *lourd/lourde* ⓜ/① loor/loord
help ∨ *aider* ey-dey
here *ici* ee-see
high *haut/haute* ⓜ/① o/ot
highway *autoroute* ① o-to-root
hike ∨ *faire la randonnée* fair la ron-do-ney
holiday *vacances* ① pl va-kons
homosexual n *homosexuel/homosexuelle* ⓜ/①
    o-mo-sek-swel
hospital *hôpital* ⓜ o-pee-tal
hot *chaud/chaude* ⓜ/① sho/shod
hotel *hôtel* ⓜ o-tel
(be) hungry *avoir faim* a-vwar fum
husband *mari* ⓜ ma-ree

I

I *je* zhe
identification (card) *carte d'identité* ①
    kart dee-don-tee-tey
ill *malade* ⓜ&① ma-lad
important *important/importante* ⓜ/①
    um-por-ton/um-por-tont
included *compris/comprise* ⓜ/①
    kom-pree/kom-preez
injury *blessure* ① bley-sewr
insurance *assurance* ① a-sew-rons
Internet *Internet* ⓜ un-tair-net
interpreter *interprète* ⓜ&① un-tair-pret

J

jewellery *bijoux* ⓜ pl bee-zhoo
job *travail* ⓜ tra-vai

K

key *clé* ① kley
kilogram *kilogramme* ⓜ kee-lo-gram
kitchen *cuisine* ① kwee-zeen
knife *couteau* ⓜ koo-to

L

laundry (place) *blanchisserie* ① blon-shees-ree
lawyer *avocat/avocate* ⓜ/① a-vo-ka/a-vo-kat

left (direction) *à gauche* a gosh
left-luggage office *consigne* ① kon-see-nye
leg *jambe* ① zhomb
lesbian n *lesbienne* ① les-byen
less *moins* mwun
letter (mail) *lettre* ① ley-trer
lift (elevator) *ascenseur* ⓜ a-son-seur
light *lumière* ① lew-myair
like ∨ *aimer* ey-mey
lock *serrure* ① sey-rewr
long *long/longue* ⓜ/① long(k)
lost *perdu/perdue* ⓜ/① pair-dew
lost-property office *bureau des objets trouvés* ⓜ
    bew-ro dey zob-zhey troo-vey
love ∨ *aimer* ey-mey
luggage *bagages* ⓜ pl ba-gazh
lunch *déjeuner* ⓜ dey-zheu-ney

M

mail *courrier* ⓜ koo-ryey
man *homme* ⓜ om
map *carte* ① kart
market *marché* ⓜ mar-shey
matches *allumettes* ① pl a-lew-met
meat *viande* ① vyond
medicine *médecine* ① med-seen
menu *carte* kart
message *message* ⓜ mey-sazh
milk *lait* ⓜ ley
minute *minute* ① mee-newt
mobile phone *téléphone portable* ⓜ
    tey-ley-fon por-ta-ble
money *argent* ⓜ ar-zhon
month *mois* ⓜ mwa
morning *matin* ⓜ ma-tun
mother *mère* ① mair
motorcycle *moto* ① mo-to
motorway *autoroute* ① o-to-root
mouth *bouche* ① boosh
music *musique* ① mew-zeek

N

name *nom* ⓜ nom
napkin *serviette* ① sair-vyet
nappy *couche* ① koosh
near *près de* prey de
neck *cou* ⓜ koo
new *nouveau/nouvelle* ⓜ/① noo-vo/noo-vel

news *les nouvelles* ley noo-vel
newspaper *journal* ⓜ zhoor-nal
night *nuit* ⓕ nwee
no *non* non
noisy *bruyant/bruyante* ⓜ/ⓕ brew-yon/brew-yont
nonsmoking *non-fumeur* non-few-meur
north *nord* ⓜ nor
nose *nez* ⓜ ney
now *maintenant* mun-te-non
number *numéro* ⓜ new-mey-ro

O

oil (engine) *huile* ⓕ weel
old *vieux/vieille* ⓜ/ⓕ vyeu/vyey
one-way ticket *billet simple* ⓜ bee-yey sum-ple
open a *ouvert/ouverte* ⓜ/ⓕ oo-vair/oo-vairt
outside *dehors* de-or

P

package *paquet* ⓜ pa-key
paper *papier* ⓜ pa-pyey
park (car) v *garer (une voiture)* ga-rey (ewn vwa-tewr)
passport *passeport* ⓜ pas-por
pay *payer* pey-yey
pen *stylo* ⓜ stee-lo
petrol *essence* ⓕ ey-sons
pharmacy *pharmacie* ⓕ far-ma-see
phonecard *télécarte* ⓕ tey-ley-kart
photo *photo* ⓕ fo-to
plate *assiette* ⓕ a-syet
police *police* ⓕ po-lees
postcard *carte postale* ⓕ kart pos-tal
post office *bureau de poste* ⓜ bew-ro de post
pregnant *enceinte* on-sunt
price *prix* ⓜ pree

Q

quiet *tranquille* ⓜ&ⓕ trong-keel

R

rain n *pluie* ⓕ plwee
razor *rasoir* ⓜ ra-zwar
receipt *reçu* ⓜ re-sew
red *rouge* roozh
refund *remboursement* ⓜ rom-boor-se-mon
registered mail *en recommandé* on re-ko-mon-dey

rent v *louer* loo-ey
repair v *réparer* rey-pa-rey
reservation *réservation* ⓕ rey-zair-va-syon
restaurant *restaurant* ⓜ res-to-ron
return v *revenir* rev-neer
return ticket *aller retour* ⓜ a-ley re-toor
right (direction) *à droite* a drwat
road *route* ⓕ root
room *chambre* ⓕ shom-bre

S

safe a *sans danger* ⓜ&ⓕ son don-zhey
sanitary napkin *serviette hygiénique* ⓕ
  sair-vyet ee-zhyey-neek
seat *place* ⓕ plas
send *envoyer* on-vwa-yey
service station *station-service* ⓕ sta-syon-sair-vees
sex *sexe* ⓜ seks
shampoo *shampooing* ⓜ shom-pwung
share (a dorm) *partager* par-ta-zhey
shaving cream *mousse à raser* ⓕ moos a ra-zey
she *elle* el
sheet (bed) *drap* ⓜ dra
shirt *chemise* ⓕ she-meez
shoes *chaussures* ⓕ pl sho-sewr
shop *magasin* ⓜ ma-ga-zun
short *court/courte* ⓜ/ⓕ koor/koort
shower *douche* ⓕ doosh
single room *chambre pour une personne* ⓕ
  shom-bre poor ewn pair-son
skin *peau* ⓕ po
skirt *jupe* ⓕ zhewp
sleep v *dormir* dor-meer
slowly *lentement* lon-te-mon
small *petit/petite* ⓜ/ⓕ pe-tee/pe-teet
smoke (cigarettes) v *fumer* few-mey
soap *savon* ⓜ sa-von
some *quelques* kel-ke
soon *bientôt* byun-to
south *sud* ⓜ sewd
souvenir shop *magasin de souvenirs* ⓜ
  ma-ga-zun de soov-neer
speak *parler* par-ley
spoon *cuillère* ⓕ kwee-yair
stamp *timbre* ⓜ tum-bre
stand-by ticket *billet stand-by* ⓜ bee-yey stond-bai
station (train) *gare* ⓕ gar
stomach *estomac* ⓜ es-to-ma
stop v *arrêter* a-rey-tey

stop (bus) *arrêt* ⓜ a-rey
street *rue* ⓕ rew
student *étudiant/étudiante* ⓜ/ⓕ
  ey-tew-dyon/ey-tew-dyont
sun *soleil* ⓜ so-ley
sunscreen *écran solaire* ⓜ ey-kron so-lair
swim v *nager* na-zhey
Switzerland *Suisse* swees

T

tampons *tampons* ⓜ pl tom-pon
taxi *taxi* ⓜ tak-see
teaspoon *petite cuillère* ⓕ pe-teet kwee-yair
teeth *dents* ⓕ don
telephone n *téléphone* ⓜ tey-ley-fon
television *télé(vision)* ⓕ tey-ley(vee-zyon)
temperature (weather) *température* ⓕ
  tom-pey-ra-tewr
tent *tente* ⓕ tont
that (one) *cela* se-la
they *ils/elles* ⓜ/ⓕ eel/el
(be) thirsty *avoir soif* a-vwar swaf
this (one) *ceci* se-see
throat *gorge* ⓕ gorzh
ticket *billet* ⓜ bee-yey
time *temps* ⓜ tom
tired *fatigué/fatiguée* ⓜ/ⓕ fa-tee-gey
tissues *mouchoirs en papier* ⓜ pl
  moo-shwar om pa-pyey
today *aujourd'hui* o-zhoor-dwee
toilet *toilettes* ⓕ pl twa-let
tomorrow *demain* de-mun
tonight *ce soir* se swar
toothbrush *brosse à dents* ⓕ bros a don
toothpaste *dentifrice* ⓜ don-tee-frees
torch (flashlight) *lampe de poche* ⓕ lomp de posh
tour *voyage* ⓜ vwa-yazh
tourist office *office de tourisme* ⓜ
  o-fees-de too-rees-me
towel *serviette* ⓕ sair-vyet
train *train* ⓜ trun
translate *traduire* tra-dweer
travel agency *agence de voyage* ⓕ
  a-zhons de vwa-yazh
travellers cheque *chèque de voyage* ⓜ
  shek de vwa-yazh
trousers *pantalon* ⓜ pon-ta-lon

twin beds *lits jumeaux* ⓜ pl dey lee zhew-mo
tyre *pneu* ⓜ pneu

U

underwear *sous-vêtements* ⓜ soo-vet-mon
urgent *urgent/urgente* ⓜ/ⓕ ewr-zhon/ewr-zhont

V

vacant *libre* ⓜ&ⓕ lee-bre
vacation *vacances* ⓕ pl va-kons
vegetable n *légume* ⓜ ley-gewm
vegetarian a *végétarien/végétarienne* ⓜ/ⓕ
  vey-zhey-ta-ryun/vey-zhey-ta-ryen
visa *visa* ⓜ vee-za

W

waiter *serveur/serveuse* ⓜ/ⓕ sair-veur/sair-veurz
walk v *marcher* mar-shey
wallet *portefeuille* ⓜ por-te-feu-ye
warm a *chaud/chaude* ⓜ/ⓕ sho/shod
wash (something) *laver* la-vey
watch *montre* ⓕ mon-tre
water *eau* ⓕ o
we *nous* noo
weekend *week-end* ⓜ week-end
west *ouest* ⓜ west
wheelchair *fauteuil roulant* ⓜ fo-teu-ye roo-lon
when *quand* kon
where *où* oo
white *blanc/blanche* ⓜ/ⓕ blong/blonsh
who *qui* kee
why *pourquoi* poor-kwa
wife *femme* ⓕ fam
window *fenêtre* ⓕ fe-ney-tre
wine *vin* ⓜ vun
with *avec* a-vek
without *sans* son
woman *femme* ⓕ fam
write *écrire* ey-kreer

Y

yellow *jaune* zhon
yes *oui* wee
yesterday *hier* ee-yair
you sg inf *tu* tew
you sg pol *vous* voo
you pl *vous* voo

Greek

greek alphabet

A α *al*·pha	**B β** *vi*·ta	**Γ γ** *gha*·ma	**Δ δ** *dhel*·ta	**E ε** *ep*·si·lon
Z ζ *zi*·ta	**H η** *i*·ta	**Θ θ** *thi*·ta	**I ι** *yio*·ta	**K κ** *ka*·pa
Λ λ *lam*·dha	**M μ** mi	**N ν** ni	**Ξ ξ** ksi	**O o** *o*·mi·kron
Π π pi	**P ρ** ro	**Σ σ/ς*** *sigh*·ma	**T τ** taf	**Y υ** *ip*·si·lon
Φ φ fi	**X χ** hi	**Ψ ψ** psi	**Ω ω** *o*·me·gha	

* The letter Σ has two forms for the lower case – σ and ς. The second one is used at the end of words.

greek

introduction

Aristotle, Plato, Homer, Sappho and Herodotus can't all be wrong in their choice of language – if you've ever come across arcane concepts such as 'democracy', exotic disciplines like 'trigonometry' or a little-known neurosis termed 'the Oedipus complex', then you'll have some inkling of the widespread influence of Greek (Ελληνικά e·li·ni·ka). With just a little Modern Greek under your belt, you'll have a richer understanding of this language's impact on contemporary Western culture.

Modern Greek is a separate branch of the Indo-European language family, with Ancient Greek its only (extinct) relative. The first records of written Ancient Greek date from the 14th to the 12th centuries BC. By the 9th century BC, the Greeks had adapted the Phoenician alphabet to include vowels – the first alphabet to do so – and the script in use today came to its final form some time in the 5th century BC. The Greek script was the foundation for both the Cyrillic and the Latin alphabet.

Although written Greek has been remarkably stable over the millennia, the spoken language has evolved considerably. In the 5th century, the dialect spoken around Athens (known as 'Attic') became the dominant speech as a result of the city-state's cultural and political prestige. Attic gained even greater influence as the medium of administration for the vast empire of Alexander the Great, and remained the official language of the Eastern Roman Empire and the Orthodox Church after the demise of the Hellenistic world. Once the Ottoman Turks took Constantinople in 1453, the Attic dialect lost its official function. In the meantime, the common language, known as Koine (Κοινή ki·ni), continued to evolve, absorbing vocabulary from Turkish, Italian, Albanian and other Balkan languages.

When an independent Greece returned to the world stage in 1832, it needed to choose a national language. Purists advocated a slightly modernised version of Attic known as Καθαρεύουσα ka·tha·re·vu·sa (from the Greek word for 'clean'), which no longer resembled the spoken language. However, Koine had strong support as it was spoken and understood by the majority of Greeks, and in the end it gained official recognition, although it was banned during the military dictatorship (1967–74). Today, Greek is the official language of Greece and a co-official language of Cyprus, and has over 13 million speakers worldwide. Start your Greek adventure with this chapter – and if you're having one of those days when you're dying to say 'It's all Greek to me!', remember that in your shoes, a Greek speaker would say: Αυτά για μένα είναι Κινέζικα af·ta yia me·na i·ne ki·ne·zi·ka (This is Chinese to me)!

pronunciation

vowel sounds

Greek vowels are pronounced separately even when they're written in sequence, eg ζώο *zo·o* (animal). You'll see though, in the table below, that some letter combinations correspond to a single sound – ουρά (queue) is pronounced *u·ra*. When a word ending in a vowel is followed by another word that starts with the same or a similar vowel sound, one vowel is usually omitted and the two words are pronounced as if they were one – Σε ευχαριστώ se ef·kha·ris·*to* becomes Σ' ευχαριστώ sef·kha·ris·*to* (Thank you). Note that the apostrophe (') is used in written Greek to show that two words are joined together.

symbol	english equivalent	greek example	transliteration
a	father	αλλά	a·*la*
e	bet	πλένομαι	*ple*·no·me
i	hit	πίσω, πόλη, υποφέρω, είδος, οικογένεια, υιός	*pi*·so, *po*·li, i·po·*fe*·ro, *i*·dhos, i·ko·ye·ni·a, *i*·os
ia	nostalgia	ζητιάνος	zi·*tia*·nos
io	ratio	πιο	pio
o	pot	πόνος, πίσω	*po*·nos, *pi*·so
u	put	ουρά	u·*ra*

word stress

Stress can fall on any of the last three syllables. In our pronunciation guides, the stressed syllable is always in italics, but in written Greek, the stressed syllable is always indicated by an accent over the vowel, eg καλά ka·*la* (good). If a vowel is represented by two letters, it's written on the second letter, eg ζητιάνος zi·*tia*·nos (beggar). If the accent is marked on the first of these two letters, they should be read separately, eg Μάιος *ma*·i·os (May). Where two vowels occur together but are not stressed, a diaeresis (¨) is used to indicate that they should be pronounced separately, eg λαϊκός la·i·*kos* (popular).

consonant sounds

Most Greek consonant sounds are also found in English – only the guttural gh and kh might need a bit of practice. Double consonants are only pronounced once – άλλος a·los (other). However, you'll notice that sometimes two Greek letters in combination form one single consonant sound – the combination of the letters μ and π makes the sound b, and the combination of the letters ν and τ makes the sound d.

symbol	english equivalent	greek example	transliteration
b	bed	μπαρ	bar
d	dog	ντομάτα	do-*ma*-ta
dh	that	δεν	dhen
dz	adds	τζάμι	dza-*mi*
f	fat	φως, αυτή	fos, af-*ti*
g	go	γκαρσόν	gar-*son*
gh	guttural sound, between 'goat' and 'loch'	γάτα	*gha*-ta
h	hat	χέρι	*he*-ri
k	kit	καλά	ka-*la*
kh	loch (guttural sound)	χαλί	kha-*li*
l	let	λάδι	*la*-dhi
m	man	μαζί	ma-*zi*
n	not	ναός	na-*os*
ng	ring	ελέγχω	e-*leng*-kho
p	pet	πάνω	*pa*-no
r	red (trilled)	ράβω	*ra*-vo
s	sun	στυλό	sti-*lo*
t	top	τι	ti
th	thin	θέα	*the*-a
ts	hats	τσέπη	*tse*-pi
v	very	βίζα, αύριο	*vi*-za, *av*-ri-o
y	yes	γέρος	*ye*-ros
z	zero	ζέστη	*ze*-sti

tools

language difficulties

Do you speak English?
Μιλάς Αγγλικά;
mi-*las* ang-gli-*ka*

Do you understand?
Καταλαβαίνεις;
ka-ta-la-*ve*-nis

I understand.
Καταλαβαίνω.
ka-ta-la-*ve*-no

I don't understand.
Δεν καταλαβαίνω.
dhen ka-ta-la-*ve*-no

What does (μώλος) mean?
Τι σημαίνει (μώλος);
ti si-*me*-ni (*mo*-los)

How do you ...? Πως ...; pos ...
  pronounce this προφέρεις αυτό pro-*fe*-ris af-*to*
  write (Madhuri) γράφουν (Μαδουρή) *ghra*-foun (ma-dhu-*ri*)

Could you Θα μπορούσες tha bo-*ru*-ses
please ...? παρακαλώ να ...; pa-ra-ka-*lo* na ...
  repeat that το επαναλάβεις to e-pa-na-*la*-vis
  speak more slowly μιλάς πιο σιγά mi-*las* pio si-*gha*
  write it down το γράψεις to *ghrap*-sis

essentials

Yes.	Ναι.	ne
No.	Οχι.	*o*-hi
Please.	Παρακαλώ.	pa-ra-ka-*lo*
Thank you (very much).	Ευχαριστώ (πολύ).	ef-kha-ri-*sto* (po-*li*)
You're welcome.	Παρακαλώ.	pa-ra-ka-*lo*
Excuse me.	Με συγχωρείτε.	me sing-kho-*ri*-te
Sorry.	Συγνώμη.	si-*ghno*-mi

0	μηδέν	mi-*dhen*		15	δεκαπέντε	dhe-ka-*pe*-de
1	ένας/μία/ένα m/f/n	*e*-nas/*mi*-a/*e*-na		16	δεκαέξι	dhe-ka-*ek*-si
2	δύο	*dhi*-o		17	δεκαεφτά	dhe-ka-ef-*ta*
3	τρεις m&f	tris		18	δεκαοχτώ	dhe-ka-okh-*to*
	τρία n	*tri*-a		19	δεκαεννέα	dhe-ka-e-*ne*-a
4	τέσσερις m&f	*te*-se-ris		20	είκοσι	*i*-ko-si
	τέσσερα n	*te*-se-ra		21	είκοσι	*i*-ko-si
5	πέντε	*pe*-de			ένας/μία/	*e*-nas/*mi*-a/
6	έξι	*ek*-si			ένα m/f/n	*e*-na
7	εφτά	ef-*ta*		22	είκοσι δύο	*i*-ko-si *dhi*-o
8	οχτώ	okh-*to*		30	τριάντα	tri-*a*-da
9	εννέα	e-*ne*-a		40	σαράντα	sa-*ra*-da
10	δέκα	*dhe*-ka		50	πενήντα	pe-*ni*-da
11	έντεκα	*e*-de-ka		60	εξήντα	ek-*si*-da
12	δώδεκα	*dho*-dhe-ka		70	εβδομήντα	ev-dho-*mi*-da
13	δεκατρείς m&f	dhe-ka-*tris*		80	ογδόντα	ogh-*dho*-da
	δεκατρία n	dhe-ka-*tri*-a		90	ενενήντα	e-ne-*ni*-da
14	δεκατέσσερις m&f	dhe-ka-*te*-se-ris		100	εκατό	e-ka-*to*
	δεκατέσσερα n	dhe-ka-*te*-se-ra		1000	χίλια	*hi*-lia

time & dates

What time is it?	Τι ώρα είναι;	ti *o*-ra *i*-ne
It's one o'clock.	Είναι (μία) η ώρα.	*i*-ne (*mi*-a) i *o*-ra
It's (10) o'clock.	Είναι (δέκα) η ώρα.	*i*-ne (*dhe*-ka) i *o*-ra
Quarter past (10).	(Δέκα) και τέταρτο.	(*dhe*-ka) ke *te*-tar-to
Half past (10).	(Δέκα) και μισή.	(*dhe*-ka) ke mi-*si*
Quarter to (10).	(Δέκα) παρά τέταρτο.	(*dhe*-ka) pa-*ra* te-*tar*-to
At what time ...?	Τι ώρα ...;	ti *o*-ra ...
At ...	Στις ...	stis ...
Monday	Δευτέρα	dhef-*te*-ra
Tuesday	Τρίτη	*tri*-ti
Wednesday	Τετάρτη	te-*tar*-ti
Thursday	Πέμπτη	*pem*-ti
Friday	Παρασκευή	pa-ra-ske-*vi*
Saturday	Σάββατο	*sa*-va-to
Sunday	Κυριακή	ki-ria-*ki*

January	Ιανουάριος	i·a·nu·*a*·ri·os
February	Φεβρουάριος	fev·ru·*a*·ri·os
March	Μάρτιος	*mar*·ti·os
April	Απρίλιος	a·*pri*·li·os
May	Μάιος	*ma*·i·os
June	Ιούνιος	i·*u*·ni·os
July	Ιούλιος	i·*u*·li·os
August	Αύγουστος	*av*·ghu·stos
September	Σεπτέμβριος	sep·*tem*·vri·os
October	Οκτώβριος	ok·*tov*·ri·os
November	Νοέμβριος	no·*em*·vri·os
December	Δεκέμβριος	dhe·*kem*·vri·os

What date is it today?

Τι ημερομηνία είναι σήμερα;   ti i·me·ro·mi·*ni*·a *i*·ne *si*·me·ra

It's (18 October).

Είναι (δεκαοχτώ Οκτωβρίου).   *i*·ne (dhe·ka·okh·*to* ok·tov·*ri*·u)

| since (May) | από (το Μάιο) | a·*po* (to *ma*·i·o) |
| until (June) | μέχρι (τον Ιούνιο) | *meh*·ri (ton i·*u*·ni·o) |

yesterday	χτες	khtes
today	σήμερα	*si*·me·ra
tonight	απόψε	a·*pop*·se
tomorrow	αύριο	*av*·ri·o

last ...

night	την περασμένη νύχτα	tin pe·raz·*me*·ni *nikh*·ta
week	την περασμένη εβδομάδα	tin pe·raz·*me*·ni ev·dho·*ma*·dha
month	τον περασμένο μήνα	ton pe·raz·*me*·no *mi*·na
year	τον περασμένο χρόνο	ton pe·raz·*me*·no *khro*·no

next ...

week	την επόμενη εβδομάδα	tin e·*po*·me·ni ev·dho·*ma*·dha
month	τον επόμενο μήνα	ton e·*po*·me·no *mi*·na
year	τον επόμενο χρόνο	ton e·*po*·me·no *khro*·no

yesterday/	χτες/	khtes/
tomorrow ...	αύριο το ...	*av*·ri·o to ...
morning	πρωί	pro·*i*
afternoon	απόγευμα	a·*po*·yev·ma
evening	βράδι	*vra*·dhi

weather

What's the weather like?	Πως είναι ο καιρός;	pos *i*-ne o ke-*ros*

It's ...

cloudy	Είναι συννεφιά.	*i*-ne si-ne-*fia*
cold	Κάνει κρύο.	*ka*-ni *kri*-o
hot	Κάνει πολλή ζέστη.	*ka*-ni po-*li* ze-sti
raining	Βρέχει.	*vre*-hi
snowing	Χιονίζει.	hio-*ni*-zi
sunny	Είναι λιακάδα.	*i*-ne lia-*ka*-dha
warm	Κάνει ζέστη.	*ka*-ni ze-sti
windy	Φυσάει.	fi-*sa*-i

spring	άνοιξη f	*a*-nik-si
summer	καλοκαίρι n	ka-lo-*ke*-ri
autumn	φθινόπωρο n	fthi-*no*-po-ro
winter	χειμώνας m	hi-*mo*-nas

border crossing

I'm here ...	Είμαι εδώ...	*i*-me e-*dho*...
in transit	τράνζιτ	*tran*-zit
on business	για δουλειά	yia dhu-*lia*
on holiday	σε διακοπές	se dhia-ko-*pes*

I'm here for (three) ...	Είμαι εδώ για (τρεις) ...	*i*-me e-*dho* yia (tris) ...
days	μέρες	*me*-res
weeks	εβδομάδες	ev-dho-*ma*-dhes
months	μήνες	*mi*-nes

I'm going to (Limassol).
Πηγαίνω στη (Λεμεσό).   pi-*ye*-no sti (le-me-*so*)

I'm staying at the (Xenia).
Μένω στο (Ξενία).   *me*-no sto (kse-*ni*-a)

I have nothing to declare.
Δεν έχω τίποτε να δηλώσω.   dhen *e*-kho *ti*-po-te na dhi-*lo*-so

I have something to declare.
Εχω κάτι να δηλώσω.   *e*-kho *ka*-ti na dhi-*lo*-so

That's (not) mine.
Αυτό (δεν) είναι δικό μου.   af-*to* (dhen) *i*-ne dhi-*ko* mu

transport

tickets & luggage

| Where can I buy a ticket? | Που αγοράζω εισιτήριο; | pu a·gho·ra·zo i·si·ti·ri·o |
| Do I need to book a seat? | Χρειάζεται να κλείσω θέση; | khri·a·ze·te na kli·so the·si |

One ... ticket	Ένα εισιτήριο ...	e·na i·si·ti·ri·o ...
to (Patras), please.	για την (Πάτρα), παρακαλώ.	yia tin (pa·tra) pa·ra·ka·lo
one-way	απλό	a·plo
return	με επιστροφή	me e·pi·stro·fi

I'd like to ... my	Θα ήθελα να ... το	tha i·the·la na ... to
ticket, please.	εισιτήριό μου, παρακαλώ.	i·si·ti·ri·o mu pa·ra·ka·lo
cancel	ακυρώσω	a·ki·ro·so
change	αλλάξω	a·lak·so
confirm	επικυρώσω	e·pi·ki·ro·so

I'd like a ... seat.	Θα ήθελα μια θέση ...	tha i·the·la mia the·si ...
nonsmoking	στους μη καπνίζοντες	stus mi kap·ni·zo·des
smoking	στους καπνίζοντες	stus kap·ni·zo·des

| How much is it? | | |
| Πόσο κάνει; | | po·so ka·ni |

| Is there air conditioning? | | |
| Υπάρχει έρκοντίσιον; | | i·par·hi e·kon·di·si·on |

| Is there a toilet? | | |
| Υπάρχει τουαλέτα; | | i·par·hi tu·a·le·ta |

| How long does the trip take? | | |
| Πόσο διαρκεί το ταξίδι; | | po·so dhi·ar·ki to tak·si·dhi |

| Is it a direct route? | | |
| Πηγαίνει κατ'ευθείαν; | | pi·ye·ni ka·tef·thi·an |

Where can I find a luggage locker?		
Που μπορώ να βρω τη φύλαξη		pu bo·ro na vro ti fi·lak·si
αντικειμένων;		a·di·ki·me·non

My luggage has	Οι αποσκευές	i a·pos·ke·ves
been ...	μου έχουν ...	mu e·khun ...
damaged	πάθει ζημιά	pa·thi zi·mia
lost	χαθεί	kha·thi
stolen	κλαπεί	kla·pi

Where does flight (10) arrive/depart?

	Πού προσγειώνεται/	pu pros-yi-*o*-ne-te/
	απογειώνεται η πτήση (δέκα);	a-po-yi-*o*-ne-te i *pti*-si (*dhe*-ka)

Where's (the) ...? Πού είναι ...; pu *i*-ne ...
arrivals hall	η αίθουσα των αφίξεων	i *e*-thu-sa tona-*fik*-se-on
departures hall	η αίθουσα των	i *e*-thu-sa ton
	ανα χωρήσεων	a-na kho-*ri*-se-on
duty-free shop	τα αφορολόγητα	ta a-fo-ro-*lo*-yi-ta
gate (nine)	η θύρα (εννέα)	i *thi*-ra (e-*ne*-a)

Is this the ... Είναι αυτό το ... *i*-ne af-*to* to ...
to (Athens)? για την (Αθήνα); yia tin (a-*thi*-na)
boat	πλοίο	*pli*-o
bus	λεωφορείο	le-o-fo-*ri*-o
ferry	φέρυ	*fe*-ri
plane	αεροπλάνο	a-e-ro-*pla*-no
train	τρένο	*tre*-no

What time's the Πότε είναι το ... *po*-te *i*-ne to ...
... (bus)? (λεωφορείο); (le-o-fo-*ri*-o)
first	πρώτο	*pro*-to
last	τελευταίο	te-lef-*te*-o
next	επόμενο	e-*po*-me-no

At what time does it arrive/depart?
Τι ώρα φτάνει/φεύγει; ti *o*-ra *fta*-ni/*fev*-yi

What time does it get to (Thessaloniki)?
Τι ώρα φτάνει στη (Θεσσαλονίκη); ti *o*-ra *fta*-ni sti (the-sa-lo-*ni*-ki)

How long will it be delayed?
Πόση ώρα θα καθυστερήσει; *po*-si *o*-ra tha ka-thi-ste-*ri*-si

What station is this?
Ποιος σταθμός είναι αυτός; pios stath-*mos i*-ne af-*tos*

What stop is this?
Ποια στάση είναι αυτή; pia *sta*-si *i*-ne af-*ti*

What's the next station?
Ποιος είναι ο επόμενος σταθμός; pios *i*-ne o e-*po*-me-nos stath-*mos*

What's the next stop?
Ποια είναι η επόμενη στάση; pia *i*-ne i e-*po*-me-ni *sta*-si

Does it stop at (Iraklio)?

Σταματάει στο (Ηράκλειο);   sta·ma·*ta*·i sto (i·*ra*·kli·o)

Please tell me when we get to (Thessaloniki).

Παρακαλώ πέστε μου όταν   pa·ra·ka·*lo* pe·ste mu *o*·tan
φτάσουμε στη (Θεσσαλονίκη).   *fta*·su·me sti (the·sa·lo·*ni*·ki)

How long do we stop here?

Πόση ώρα θα σταματήσουμε εδώ;   *po*·si o·ra tha sta·ma·*ti*·su·me e·*dho*

Is this seat available?

Είναι αυτή η θέση ελεύθερη;   *i*·ne af·*ti* i *the*·si e·*lef*·the·ri

That's my seat.

Αυτή η θέση είναι δική μου.   af·*ti* i *the*·si *i*·ne dhi·*ki* mu

I'd like a taxi ...	θα ήθελα ένα ταξί ...	tha *i*·the·la *e*·na tak·*si* ...
at (9am)	στις (εννέα	stis (e·*ne*·a
	πριν το μεσημέρι)	prin to me·si·*me*·ri)
now	τώρα	*to*·ra
tomorrow	αύριο	*av*·ri·o

Is this taxi available?

Είναι αυτό το ταξί ελεύθερο;   *i*·ne af·*to* to tak·*si* e·*lef*·the·ro

How much is it to ...?

Πόσο κάνει για ...;   *po*·so ka·ni yia ...

Please put the meter on.

Παρακαλώ βάλε το ταξίμετρο.   pa·ra·ka·*lo* va·le to tak·*si*·me·tro

Please take me to (this address).

Παρακαλώ πάρε με σε   pa·ra·ka·*lo* pa·re me se
(αυτή τη διεύθυνση).   (af·*ti* ti dhi·*ef*·thin·si)

Please ...	Παρακαλώ ...	pa·ra·ka·*lo* ...
slow down	πήγαινε πιο σιγά	*pi*·ye·ne pio si·*gha*
stop here	σταμάτα εδώ	sta·*ma*·ta e·*dho*
wait here	περίμενε εδώ	pe·*ri*·me·ne e·*dho*

car, motorbike & bicycle hire

I'd like to	θα ήθελα να	tha *i*·the·la na
hire a ...	ενοικιάσω ένα ...	e·ni·ki·*a*·so *e*·na ...
bicycle	ποδήλατο	po·*dhi*·la·to
car	αυτοκίνητο	af·to·*ki*·ni·to
motorbike	μοτοσικλέτα	mo·to·si·*kle*·ta

with ...	με ...	me ...
a driver	οδηγό	o-dhi-*gho*
air conditioning	έρκοντίσιον	e-kon-*di*-si-on

How much for ... hire?	Πόσο νοικάζεται την ...;	*po*-so ni-*kia*-ze-te tin ...
hourly	ώρα	*o*-ra
daily	ημέρα	i-*me*-ra
weekly	εβδομάδα	ev-dho-*ma*-dha

air	αέρας m	a-*e*-ras
oil	λάδι αυτοκινήτου n	*la*-dhi af-to-ki-*ni*-tu
petrol	βενζίνα f	ven-*zi*-na
tyres	λάστιχα n	*la*-sti-kha

I need a mechanic.	Χρειάζομαι μηχανικό.	khri-*a*-zo-me mi-kha-ni-*ko*
I've run out of petrol.	Μου τελείωσε η βενζίνα.	mu te-*li*-o-se i ven-*zi*-na
I have a flat tyre.	Μ'έπιασε λάστιχο.	*me*-pia-se *la*-sti-kho

directions

Where's the ...?	Που είναι ...;	pu *i*-ne ...
bank	η τράπεζα	i *tra*-pe-za
city centre	το κέντρο της πόλης	to *ke*-dro tis *po*-lis
hotel	το ξενοδοχείο	to kse-no-dho-*hi*-o
market	η αγορά	i a-gho-*ra*
police station	ο αστυνομικός σταθμός	o a-sti-no-mi-*kos* stath-*mos*
post office	το ταχυδρομείο	to ta-hi-dhro-*mi*-o
public toilet	τα δημόσια αποχωρητήρια	ta dhi-*mo*-si-a a-po-kho-ri-*ti*-ria
tourist office	το τουριστικό γραφείο	to tu-ri-sti-*ko* ghra-*fi*-o

Is this the road to (Lamia)?
Είναι αυτός ο δρόμος για (τη Λαμία);   *i*-ne af-*tos* o *dhro*-mos yia (ti la-*mi*-a)

Can you show me (on the map)?
Μπορείς να μου δείξεις (στο χάρτη);   bo-*ris* na mu *dhik*-sis (sto *khar*-ti)

What's the address?
Ποια είναι η διεύθυνση;   pia *i*-ne i dhi-*ef*-thin-si

How far is it?
Πόσο μακριά είναι;   *po*-so ma-kri-*a i*-ne

How do I get there?
Πως πηγαίνω εκεί;   pos pi-*ye*-no e-*ki*

Turn ...	Στρίψε ...	*strip·se ...*
at the corner	στη γωνία	sti gho·*ni*·a
at the traffic lights	στα φανάρια	sta fa·*na*·ria
left/right	αριστερά/δεξιά	a·ris·te·*ra*/dhek·si·*a*

It's ...	Είναι ...	*i·ne ...*
behind ...	πίσω ...	*pi*·so ...
far away	μακριά	ma·kri·*a*
here	εδώ	e·*dho*
in front of ...	μπροστά από ...	bros·*ta* a·*po* ...
near ...	κοντά ...	ko·*da* ...
next to ...	δίπλα από ...	*dhip*·la a·*po* ...
on the corner	στη γωνία	sti gho·*ni*·a
opposite ...	απέναντι ...	a·*pe*·na·di ...
straight ahead	κατ'ευθείαν	ka·tef·*thi*·an
there	εκεί	e·*ki*

by bus	με λεωφορείο	me le·o·fo·*ri*·o
by boat	με πλοίο	me *pli*·o
by taxi	με ταξί	me tak·*si*
by train	με τρένο	me *tre*·no
on foot	με πόδια	me *po*·dhia

north	βόρια	*vo*·ri·a
south	νότια	*no*·ti·a
east	ανατολικά	a·na·to·li·*ka*
west	δυτικά	dhi·ti·*ka*

signs

Είσοδος/Έξοδος	*i*·so·dhos/*ek*·so·dhos	Entrance/Exit
Ανοικτός/Κλειστός	a·nik·*tos*/kli·*stos*	Open/Closed
Ελεύθερα Δωμάτια	e·*lef*·the·ra dho·*ma*·ti·a	Rooms Available
Πλήρες	*pli*·res	No Vacancies
Πληροφορίες	pli·ro·fo·*ri*·es	Information
Αστυνομικός Σταθμός	a·sti·no·mi·*kos* stath·*mos*	Police Station
Απαγορεύεται	a·pa·gho·*re*·ve·te	Prohibited
Τουαλέτες	tu·a·*le*·tes	Toilets
Ανδρών	an·*dhron*	Men
Γυναικών	yi·ne·*kon*	Women
Ζεστό/Κρύο	zes·*to*/khri·o	Hot/Cold

142

accommodation

finding accommodation

Where's a ...?	Που είναι ...;	pu *i*-ne ...
camping ground	χώρος για κάμπινγκ	*kho*-ros yia *kam*-ping
guesthouse	ξενώνας	kse-*no*-nas
hotel	ξενοδοχείο	kse-no-dho-*hi*-o
youth hostel	γιουθ χόστελ	yiuth *kho*-stel
Can you recommend somewhere ...?	Μπορείτε να συστήσετε κάπου ...;	bo-*ri*-te na si-*sti*-se-te *ka*-pu ...
cheap	φτηνό	fti-*no*
good	καλό	ka-*lo*
nearby	κοντινό	ko-di-*no*

I'd like to book a room, please.
Θα ήθελα να κλείσω ένα
δωμάτιο, παρακαλώ.
tha *i*-the-la na *kli*-so e-na
dho-*ma*-ti-o pa-ra-ka-*lo*

I have a reservation.
Εχω κάνει κάποια κράτηση.
e-kho *ka*-ni *ka*-pia *kra*-ti-si

My name's ...
Με λένε ...
me *le*-ne ...

Do you have a ... room?	Εχετε ένα ... δωμάτιο;	*e*-he-te e-na ... dho-*ma*-ti-o
single	μονό	mo-*no*
double	διπλό	dhi-*plo*
twin	δίκλινο	*dhi*-kli-no
How much is it per ...?	Πόσο είναι για κάθε ...;	*po*-so *i*-ne yia *ka*-the ...
night	νύχτα	*nikh*-ta
person	άτομο	*a*-to-mo
Can I pay ...?	Μπορώ να πληρώσω με ...;	bo-*ro* na pli-*ro*-so me ...
by credit card	πιστωτική κάρτα	pi-sto-ti-*ki kar*-ta
with a travellers cheque	ταξιδιωτική επιταγή	tak-si-dhio-ti-*ki* e-pi-ta-*yi*

For (three) nights/weeks.
Για (τρεις) νύχτες/εβδομάδες.   yia *(tris)* nikh·tes/ev·dho·*ma*·dhes

From (2 July) to (6 July).
Από (τις δύο Ιουλίου)   a·*po* (tis *dhi*·o i·u·*li*·u)
μέχρι (τις έξι Ιουλίου).   me·khri (tis ek·si i·u·*li*·u)

Can I see it?
Μπορώ να το δω;   bo·*ro* na to dho

Am I allowed to camp here?
Μπορώ να κατασκηνώσω εδώ;   bo·*ro* na ka·ta·ski·*no*·so e·*dho*

Where can I find a camp site?
Που μπορώ να βρω το   pu bo·*ro* na vro to
χώρο του κάμπινγκ;   *kho*·ro tu *kam*·ping

requests & queries

When/Where is breakfast served?
Πότε/Που σερβίρεται το πρόγευμα;   *po*·te/pu ser·*vi*·re·te to *pro*·yev·ma

Please wake me at (seven).
Παρακαλώ ξύπνησέ με στις (εφτά).   pa·ra·ka·*lo* ksip·ni·*se* me stis (ef·*ta*)

Could I have my key, please?
Μπορώ να έχω το κλειδί μου   bo·*ro* na *e*·kho to kli·*dhi* mu
παρακαλώ;   pa·ra·ka·*lo*

Can I get another (blanket)?
Μπορώ να έχω και άλλη (κουβέρτα);   bo·*ro* na *e*·kho ke *a*·li (ku·*ver*·ta)

This (towel) isn't clean.
Αυτή (η πετσέτα) δεν είναι καθαρό.   af·*ti* (i pet·*se*·ta) dhen *i*·ne ka·tha·*ri*

Is there a/an ...?	Έχετε ...;	*e*·he·te ...
elevator	ασανσέρ	a·san·*ser*
safe	χρηματοκιβώτιο	khri·ma·to·ki·*vo*·ti·o

The room is too ...	Είναι πάρα πολύ ...	*i*·ne *pa*·ra po·*li* ...
expensive	ακριβό	a·kri·*vo*
noisy	θορυβώδες	tho·ri·*vo*·dhes
small	μικρό	mi·*kro*

The ... doesn't work.	... δεν λειτουργεί.	... dhen li·tur·*ghi*
air conditioning	Το έρκοντίσιον	to er·kon·*di*·si·on
fan	Ο ανεμιστήρας	o a·ne·mi·*sti*·ras
toilet	Η τουαλέτα	i tu·a·*le*·ta

144

checking out

What time is checkout?
Τι ώρα είναι η αναχώρηση;   ti o·ra i·ne i a·na·kho·ri·si

Can I leave my luggage here?
Μπορώ να αφήσω τις βαλίτσες μου εδώ;   bo·ro na a·fi·so tis va·lit·ses mu e·dho

Could I have my ..., please?	Μπορώ να έχω ... μου παρακαλώ;	bo·ro na e·kho ... mu pa·ra·ka·lo
deposit	την προκαταβολή	tin pro·ka·ta·vo·li
passport	το διαβατήριο	to dhia·va·ti·ri·o
valuables	τα κοσμήματά	ta koz·mi·ma·ta

communications & banking

the internet

Where's the local Internet cafe?
Που είναι το τοπικό   pu i·ne to to·pi·ko
καφενείο με διαδίκτυο;   ka·fe·ni·o me dhia·dhik·ti·o

How much is it per hour?
Πόσο κοστίζει κάθε ώρα;   po·so ko·sti·zi ka·the o·ra

I'd like to ...	θα ήθελα να ...	tha i·the·la na ...
check my email	ελέγξω την ηλεκτρονική αλληλογραφία μου	e·leng·so tin i·lek·tro·ni·ki a·li·lo·ghra·fi·a mu
get Internet access	έχω πρόσβαση στο διαδίκτυο	e·kho pros·va·si sto dhi·a·dhik·ti·o
use a printer	χρησιμοποιήσω έναν εκτυπωτή	khri·si·mo·pi·i·so e·nan ek·ti·po·ti
use a scanner	χρησιμοποιήσω ένα σκάνερ	khri·si·mo·pi·i·so e·na ska·ner

mobile/cell phone

I'd like a ...	Θα ήθελα ...	tha *i*-the-la ...
mobile/cell phone for hire	να νοικιάσω ένα κινητό τηλέφωνο	na ni-*kia*-so e-na ki-ni-*to* ti-*le*-fo-no
SIM card for your network	μια κάρτα SIM για το δίκτυό σας	mia *kar*-ta sim yia to *dhik*-tio sas
What are the rates?	Ποιες είναι οι τιμές;	pies *i*-ne i ti-*mes*

telephone

What's your phone number?

Τι αριθμό τηλεφώνου έχεις;
ti a-rith-*mo* ti-le-*fo*-nu *e*-his

The number is ...

Ο αριθμός είναι ...
o a-rith-*mos i*-ne ...

Where's the nearest public phone?

Που είναι το πιο κοντινό
δημόσιο τηλέφωνο;
pu *i*-ne to pio ko-di-*no*
dhi-*mo*-si-o ti-*le*-fo-no

I'd like to buy a phonecard.

Θέλω να αγοράσω μια
τηλεφωνική κάρτα.
the-lo na a-gho-*ra*-so mia
ti-le-fo-ni-*ki kar*-ta

I want to ...	Θέλω να ...	*the*-lo na ...
call (Singapore)	τηλεφωνήσω (στη Σιγγαπούρη)	ti-le-fo-*ni*-so (sti sing-ga-*pu*-ri)
make a local call	κάνω ένα τοπικό τηλέφωνο	*ka*-no e-na to-pi-*ko* ti-*le*-fo-no
reverse the charges	αντιστρέψω τα έξοδα	a-di-*strep*-so ta *ek*-so-dha

How much does ... cost?	Πόσο κοστίζει ...;	*po*-so ko-*sti*-zi ...
a (three)- minute call	ένα τηλεφώνημα (τριών) λεπτών	*e*-na ti-le-*fo*-ni-ma (tri-*on*) lep-*ton*
each extra minute	κάθε έξτρα λεπτό	*ka*-the *eks*-tra lep-*to*

It's (40c) per (30) seconds.

(Σαράντα λεπτά) για (τριάντα)
δευτερόλεπτα.
(sa-*ra*-da lep-*ta*) yia (tri-*a*-da)
dhef-te-*ro*-lep-ta

post office

I want to send a ...	Θέλω να στείλω ...	the-lo na sti-lo ...
fax	ένα φαξ	e-na faks
letter	ένα γράμμα	e-na ghra-ma
parcel	ένα δέμα	e-na dhe-ma
postcard	μια κάρτα	mia kar-ta

I want to buy a/an ...	Θέλω να αγοράσω ένα ...	the-lo na a-gho-ra-so e-na ...
envelope	φάκελο	fa-ke-lo
stamp	γραμματόσημο	ghra-ma-to-si-mo

Please send it (to Australia) by ...	Παρακαλώ στείλτε το ... (στην Αυστραλία).	pa-ra-ka-lo stil-te to ... (stin af-stra-li-a)
airmail	αεροπορικώς	a-e-ro-po-ri-kos
express mail	εξπρές	eks-pres
registered mail	συστημένο	si-sti-me-no
surface mail	δια ξηράς	dhia ksi-ras

Is there any mail for me?
Υπάρχουν γράμματα για μένα; i-par-khun ghra-ma-ta yia me-na

bank

Where's a/an ...?	Που είναι ...;	pu i-ne ...
ATM	μια αυτόματη μηχανή χρημάτων	mia af-to-ma-ti mi-kha-ni khri-ma-ton
foreign exchange office	ένα γραφείο αλλαγής χρημάτων	e-na ghra-fi-o a-la-yis khri-ma-ton

I'd like to ...	Θα ήθελα να ...	tha i-the-la na ...
Where can I ...?	Που μπορώ να ...;	pu bo-ro na ...
arrange a transfer	τακτοποιήσω μια μεταβίβαση	tak-to-pi-i-so mia me-ta-vi-va-si
cash a cheque	εξαργυρώσω μια επιταγή	ek-sar-yi-ro-so mia e-pi-ta-yi
change a travellers cheque	αλλάξω μια ταξιδιωτική επιταγή	a-lak-so mia tak-si-dhio-ti-ki e-pi-ta-yi
change money	αλλάξω χρήματα	a-lak-so khri-ma-ta
get a cash advance	κάνω μια ανάληψη σε μετρητά	ka-no mia a-na-lip-si se me-tri-ta
withdraw money	αποσύρω χρήματα	a-po-si-ro khri-ma-ta

What's the ...?	Ποια είναι ... ;	pia *i*·ne ...
charge for that	η χρέωση για αυτό	i *khre*·o·si yia af·*to*
exchange rate	η τιμή συναλλάγματος	i ti·*mi* si·na·*lagh*·ma·tos

It's (12) ...	Κάνει (δώδεκα) ...	*ka*·ni (*dho*·dhe·ka) ...
Cyprus pounds	λίρες Κύπρου	*li*·res *ki*·pru
euros	ευρώ	ev·*ro*

It's free.
Είναι δωρεάν.   *i*·ne dho·re·*an*

What time does the bank open?
Τι ώρα ανοίγει η τράπεζα;   ti *o*·ra a·*ni*·yi i *tra*·pe·za

Has my money arrived yet?
Έχουν φτάσει τα χρήματά μου;   *e*·khun *fta*·si ta *khri*·ma·*ta* mu

sightseeing

getting in

What time does it open/close?
Τι ώρα ανοίγει/κλείνει;   ti *o*·ra a·*ni*·yi/*kli*·ni

What's the admission charge?
Πόσο κοστίζει η είσοδος;   *po*·so ko·*sti*·zi i *i*·so·dhos

Is there a discount for students/children?
Υπάρχει έκπτωση για   i·*par*·hi *ek*·pto·si yia
σπουδαστές/παιδιά;   spu·dha·*stes*/pe·*dhia*

I'd like a ...	Θα ήθελα ...	tha *i*·the·la ...
catalogue	ένα κατάλογο	*e*·na ka·*ta*·lo·gho
guide	έναν οδηγό	*e*·nan o·dhi·*gho*
local map	ένα τοπικό χάρτη	*e*·na to·pi·*ko* *khar*·ti

I'd like to see ...	Θα ήθελα να δω ...	tha *i*·the·la na dho ...
What's that?	Τι είναι εκείνο;	ti *i*·ne e·*ki*·no
Can I take a photo?	Μπορώ να πάρω μια	bo·*ro* na *pa*·ro mia
	φωτογραφία;	fo·to·ghra·*fi*·a

When's the next tour?

Πότε είναι η επόμενη περιήγηση;   *po*·te *i*·ne i e·*po*·me·ni pe·ri·*i*·yi·si

When's the next ...?   Πότε είναι το επόμενο ...;   *po*·te *i*·ne to e·*po*·me·no ...

     boat trip   ταξίδι με τη βάρκα   tak·*si*·dhi me ti *var*·ka

     day trip   ημερήσιο ταξίδι   i·me·*ri*·si·o tak·*si*·dhi

Is ... included?   Συμπεριλαμβάνεται ...;   si·be·ri·lam·*va*·ne·te ...

     accommodation   κατάλυμα   ka·*ta*·li·ma

     the admission charge   τιμή εισόδου   ti·*mi* i·so·dhu

     food   φαγητό   fa·yi·*to*

     transport   μεταφορά   me·ta·fo·*ra*

How long is the tour?

Πόση ώρα διαρκεί η περιήγηση;   *po*·si o·ra dhi·ar·*ki* i pe·ri·*i*·yi·si

What time should we be back?

Τι ώρα πρέπει να επιστρέψουμε;   ti o·ra *pre*·pi na e·pi·*strep*·su·me

sightseeing

amphitheatre	αμφιθέατρο n	am·fi·*the*·a·tro
castle	κάστρο n	*ka*·stro
cathedral	μητρόπολη f	mi·*tro*·po·li
church	εκκλησία f	e·kli·*si*·a
fresco	φρέσκο n	*fres*·ko
labyrinth	λαβύρινθος m	la·*vi*·rin·thos
main square	κεντρική πλατεία f	ken·dhri·*ki* pla·*ti*·a
monastery	μοναστήρι n	mo·na·*sti*·ri
monument	μνημείο n	mni·*mi*·o
mosaic	μωσαϊκό n	mo·sa·i·*ko*
museum	μουσείο n	mu·*si*·o
old city	αρχαία πόλι	ar·*khe*·a *po*·li
palace	παλάτι n	pa·*la*·ti
ruins	ερρίπια n pl	e·*ri*·pi·a
sculpture	γλυπτική f	ghlip·ti·*ki*
stadium	στάδιο n	*sta*·dhi·o
statue	άγαλμα n	*a*·ghal·ma
temple	ναός m	na·*os*

shopping

enquiries

Where's a ...?	Που είναι ...;	pu *i*·ne ...
bank	μια τράπεζα	mia *tra*·pe·za
bookshop	ένα βιβλιοπωλείο	e·na viv·li·o·po·*li*·o
camera shop	ένα κατάστημα φωτογραφικών ειδών	e·na ka·*ta*·sti·ma fo·to·ghra·fi·*kon* i·*dhon*
department store	ένα κατάστημα	e·na ka·*ta*·sti·ma
grocery store	ένα οπωροπωλείο	e·na o·po·ro·po·*li*·o
kiosk	ένα περίπτερο	e·na pe·*rip*·te·ro
market	μια αγορά	mia a·gho·*ra*
newsagency	το εφημεριδοπωλείο	to e·fi·me·ri·dho·po·*li*·o
supermarket	ένα σούπερμάρκετ	e·na *su*·per·*mar*·ket

Where can I buy (a padlock)?
Που μπορώ να αγοράσω
(μια κλειδαριά);
pu bo·*ro* na a·gho·*ra*·so
(mia kli·dha·*ria*)

I'd like to buy ...
Θα ήθελα να αγοράσω ...
tha *i*·the·la na a·gho·*ra*·so ...

Can I look at it?
Μπορώ να το κοιτάξω;
bo·*ro* na to ki·*tak*·so

Do you have any others?
Έχετε άλλα;
e·he·te *a*·la

Does it have a guarantee?
Έχει εγγύηση;
e·hi e·*gi*·i·si

Can I have it sent overseas?
Μπορείς να το στείλεις
στο εξωτερικό;
bo·*ris* na to *sti*·lis
sto ek·so·te·ri·*ko*

Can I have ... repaired?
Μπορώ να επισκευάσω εδώ ...;
bo·*ro* na e·pi·ske·*va*·so e·*dho* ...

Can I have a bag, please?
Μπορώ να έχω μια τσάντα, παρακαλώ;
bo·*ro* na *e*·kho mia *tsa*·da pa·ra·ka·*lo*

It's faulty.
Είναι ελαττωματικό.
i·ne e·la·to·ma·ti·*ko*

I'd like ..., please.
Θα ήθελα ..., παρακαλώ.
tha *i*·the·la ... pa·ra·ka·*lo*

| a refund | επιστροφή χρημάτων | e·pi·stro·*fi* khri·*ma*·ton |
| to return this | να επιστρέψω αυτό | na e·pi·*strep*·so af·*to* |

paying

How much is it?
Πόσο κάνει;   po·so ka·ni

Can you write down the price?
Μπορείς να γράψεις την τιμή;   bo·ris na ghrap·sis tin ti·mi

That's too expensive.
Είναι πάρα πολύ ακριβό.   i·ne pa·ra po·li a·kri·vo

Can you lower the price?
Μπορείς να κατεβάσεις την τιμή;   bo·ris na ka·te·va·sis tin ti·mi

I'll give you (five) euros.
Θα σου δώσω (πέντε) ευρώ.   tha su dho·so (pe·de) ev·ro

I'll give you (five) Cyprus pounds.
Θα σου δώσω (πέντε) λίρες Κύπρου.   tha su dho·so (pe·de) li·res ki·pru

There's a mistake in the bill.
Υπάρχει κάποιο λάθος   i·par·hi ka·pio la·thos
στο λογαριασμό.   sto lo·gha·riaz·mo

Do you accept ...?	Δέχεστε ...;	dhe·he·ste ...
credit cards	πιστωτικές κάρτες	pi·sto·ti·kes kar·tes
debit cards	χρεωτικές κάρτες	khre·o·ti·kes kar·tes
travellers cheques	ταξιδιωτικές	tak·si·dhio·ti·kes
	επιταγές	e·pi·ta·yes

I'd like my change, please.
Θα ήθελα τα ρέστα μου, παρακαλώ.   tha i·the·la ta re·sta mu pa·ra·ka·lo

Can I have a receipt, please?
Μπορώ να έχω μια   bo·ro na e·kho mia
απόδειξη, παρακαλώ;   a·po·dhik·si pa·ra·ka·lo

clothes & shoes

Can I try it on?	Μπορώ να το προβάρω;	bo·ro na to pro·va·ro
My size is (40).	Το νούμερό μου είναι	to nu·me·ro mu i·ne
	(σαράντα).	(sa·ra·da)
It doesn't fit.	Δε μου κάνει.	dhe mu ka·ni
small	μικρό	mi·kro
medium	μεσαίο	me·se·o
large	μεγάλο	me·gha·lo

books & music

I'd like a ...	Θα ήθελα ...	tha *i*·the·la ...
newspaper	μια εφημερίδα	mia e·fi·me·*ri*·dha
(in English)	(στα Αγγλικά)	(sta ang·gli·*ka*)
pen	ένα στυλό	*e*·na sti·*lo*

Is there an English-language bookshop?
Υπάρχει ένα βιβλιοπωλείο
Αγγλικής γλώσσας;
i·*par*·hi e·na viv·li·o·po·*li*·o
ang·gli·*kis ghlo*·sas

I'm looking for something by (Anna Vissi).
Ψάχνω για κάτι (της Άννας Βίση). *psakh*·no yia *ka*·ti (tis *a*·nas *vi*·si)

Can I listen to this?
Μπορώ να το ακούσω; bo·*ro* na to a·*ku*·so

photography

Can you ...?	Μπορείς να ...;	bo·*ris* na ...
develop this	εμφανίσεις αυτό	em·fa·*ni*·sis af·*to*
film	το φιλμ	to film
load my film	βάλεις το φιλμ	*va*·lis to film
	στη μηχανή μου	sti mi·kha·*ni* mu
transfer photos	μεταφέρεις	me·ta·*fe*·ris
from my	φωτογραφίες από	fo·to·ghra·*fi*·es a·*po*
camera to CD	την φωτογραφική	ti fo·to·ghra·fi·*ki*
	μου μηχανή στο CD	mu mi·kha·*ni* sto si·*di*

I need a/an ... film	Χρειάζομαι φιλμ ...	khri·*a*·zo·me film ...
for this camera.	για αυτή τη μηχανή.	yia af·*ti* ti mi·kha·*ni*
APS	APS	*e*·i·pi·es
B&W	μαυρόασπρο	mav·*ro*·a·spro
colour	έγχρωμο	*eng*·khro·mo
slide	σλάιντ	*sla*·id
(200) speed	ταχύτητα (διακοσίων)	ta·*hi*·ti·ta (dhia·ko·*si*·on)

| When will it be ready? | Πότε θα είναι έτοιμο; | *po*·te tha *i*·ne *e*·ti·mo |

meeting people

greetings, goodbyes & introductions

Hello/Hi.	Γεια σου.	yia su
Good night.	Καληνύχτα.	ka·li·*nikh*·ta
Goodbye/Bye.	Αντίο.	a·*di*·o
Mr	Κύριε	*ki*·ri·e
Mrs	Κυρία	ki·*ri*·a
Miss	Δις	dhes·pi·*nis*
How are you?	Τι κάνεις;	ti *ka*·nis
Fine. And you?	Καλά. Εσύ;	ka·*la* e·si
What's your name?	Πως σε λένε;	pos se *le*·ne
My name is ...	Με λένε ...	me *le*·ne ...
I'm pleased to meet you.	Χαίρω πολύ.	*he*·ro po·*li*

This is my ...	Από εδώ ... μου.	a·po e·*dho* ... mu
boyfriend	ο φίλος	o *fi*·los
brother	ο αδερφός	o a·dher·*fos*
daughter	η κόρη	i *ko*·ri
father	ο πατέρας	o pa·*te*·ras
friend	ο φίλος/η φίλη m/f	o *fi*·los/i *fi*·li
girlfriend	η φιλενάδα	i fi·le·*na*·dha
husband	ο σύζυγός	o *si*·zi·ghos
mother	η μητέρα	i mi·*te*·ra
partner (intimate)	ο/η σύντροφός m/f	o/i si·dro·*fos*
sister	η αδερφή	i a·dher·*fi*
son	ο γιος	o yios
wife	η σύζυγός	i *si*·zi·ghos

Here's my ...	Εδώ είναι ... μου.	e·*dho* *i*·ne ... mu
What's your ...?	Ποιο είναι ... σου;	pio *i*·ne ... su
email address	το ημέιλ	to i·*me*·il
fax number	το φαξ	to faks
phone number	το τηλέφωνό	to ti·*le*·fo·*no*

Here's my address.
Εδώ είναι η διεύθυνσή μου.   e·*dho* *i*·ne i dhi·*ef*·thin·*si* mu

What's your address?
Ποια είναι η δική σου διεύθυνση;   pia *i*·ne i dhi·*ki* su dhi·*ef*·thin·si

occupations

What's your occupation?	Τι δουλειά κάνεις;	ti dhu·*lia* ka·nis
I'm a/an ...	Είμαι/Δουλεύω ...	*i*·me/dhou·*lev*·o ...
businessperson	επιχειρηματίας m&f	e·pi·hi·ri·ma·*ti*·as
farmer	γεωργός m&f	ye·or·*ghos*
manual worker	εργάτης/εργάτρια m/f	er·*gha*·tis/er·*gha*·tri·a
office worker	σε γραφείο	se ghra·*phi*·o
scientist	επιστήμονας m&f	e·pi·*sti*·mo·nas
tradesperson	έμπορος m&f	*e*·bo·ros

background

Where are you from?	Από που είσαι;	a·*po* pu *i*·se
I'm from ...	Είμαι από ...	*i*·me a·*po* ...
Australia	την Αυστραλία	tin af·stra·*li*·a
Canada	τον Καναδά	ton ka·na·*dha*
England	την Αγγλία	tin ang·*gli*·a
New Zealand	την Νέα Ζηλανδία	tin *ne*·a zi·lan·*dhi*·a
the USA	την Αμερική	tin A·me·ri·*ki*
Are you married?	Είσαι παντρεμένος/ παντρεμένη; m/f	*i*·se pa·dre·*me*·nos/ pa·dre·*me*·ni
I'm married.	Είμαι παντρεμένος/ παντρεμένη. m/f	*i*·me pa·dre·*me*·nos/ pa·dre·*me*·ni
I'm single.	Είμαι ανύπαντρος/ ανύπαντρη. m/f	*i*·me a·*ni*·pa·dros/ a·*ni*·pa·dri

age

How old ...?	Πόσο χρονών ...;	*po*·so khro·*non* ...
are you	είσαι	*i*·se
is your daughter	είναι η κόρη σου	*i*·ne i *ko*·ri su
is your son	είναι ο γιος σου	*i*·ne o yios su
I'm ... years old.	Είμαι ... χρονών.	*i*·me ... khro·*non*
He/She is ... years old.	Αυτός/αυτή είναι ... χρονών.	af·*tos*/af·*ti* i·ne ... khro·*non*

feelings

I'm (not) ...	(Δεν) Είμαι ...	(dhen) *i*-me ...
Are you ...?	Είσαι ...;	*i*-se ...
happy	ευτυχισμένος m	ef-ti-hiz-*me*-nos
	ευτυχισμένη f	ef-ti-hiz-*me*-ni
hot	ζεστός/ζεστή m/f	ze-*stos*/ze-*sti*
hungry	πεινασμένος m	pi-naz-*me*-nos
	πεινασμένη f	pi-naz-*me*-ni
sad	στενοχωρημένος m	ste-no-kho-ri-*me*-nos
	στενοχωρημένη f	ste-no-kho-ri-*me*-ni
thirsty	διψασμένος m	dhip-saz-*me*-nos
	διψασμένη f	dhip-saz-*me*-ni

entertainment

going out

Where can I find ...?	Που μπορώ να βρω ...;	pu bo-*ro* na vro ...
clubs	κλαμπ	klab
gay venues	Χώρους συνάντησης	*kho*-rus si-*na*-di-sis
	για γκέη	yia *ge*-i
pubs	μπυραρίες	bi-ra-*ri*-es
I feel like going to a/the ...	Εχω όρεξι να πάω σε ...	*e*-kho o-rek-si na *pa*-o se ...
concert	κονσέρτο	kon-*ser*-to
the movies	φιλμ	film
party	πάρτυ	*par*-ti
restaurant	εστιατόριο	e-sti-a-*to*-ri-o
theatre	θέατρο	*the*-a-tro

interests

Do you like ...?	Σου αρέσει ...;	su a-*re*-si ...
I (don't) like ...	(Δεν) μου αρέσει ...	(dhen) mu a-*re*-si ...
cooking	η μαγειρική	i ma-yi-ri-*ki*
reading	το διάβασμα	to *dhia*-vaz-ma

Do you like ...?	Σου αρέσουν ...;	su a·*re*·sun ...
I (don't) like ...	(Δεν) μου αρέσουν τα ...	(dhen) mu a·*re*·sun ta ...
art	καλλιτεχνικά	ka·li·tekh·ni·*ka*
movies	φιλμ	film
nightclubs	νάιτ κλαμπ	*na*·it klab
sport	σπορ	spor

Do you like to ...?	Σου αρέσει να ...;	sou a·*re*·si na ...
dance	χορεύεις	kho·*re*·vis
go to concerts	πηγαίνεις σε κονσέρτα	pi·*ye*·nis se kon·*ser*·ta
listen to music	ακούς μουσική	a·*kus* mu·si·*ki*

food & drink

finding a place to eat

Can you recommend a ...?	Μπορείς να συστήσεις ...;	bo·*ris* na si·*sti*·sis ...
bar	ένα μπαρ	*e*·na bar
café	μία καφετέρια	*mi*·a ka·fe·*te*·ria
restaurant	ένα εστιατόριο	*e*·sti·a·*to*·ri·o

I'd like ..., please.	Θα ήθελα ..., παρακαλώ.	tha *i*·thela ... pa·ra·ka·*lo*
a table for (five)	ένα τραπέζι για (πέντε)	*e*·na tra·*pe*·zi yia (*pe*·de)
the (non)smoking section	στους (μη) καπνίζοντες	stus (mi) kap·*ni*·zo·des

ordering food

breakfast	πρόγευμα n	*pro*·yev·ma
lunch	γεύμα n	*yev*·ma
dinner	δείπνο n	*dhip*·no
snack	μεζεδάκι n	me·ze·*dha*·ki

What would you recommend?
Τι θα συνιστούσες;   ti tha si·ni·*stu*·ses

I'd like (a/the) ...,	Θα ήθελα ...,	tha *i*-the-la ...
please.	παρακαλώ.	pa·ra·ka·*lo*
bill	το λογαριασμό	to lo·gha·riaz·*mo*
drink list	τον κατάλογο	ton ka·*ta*·lo·gho
	με τα ποτά	me ta po·*ta*
menu	το μενού	to me·*nu*
that dish	εκείνο το φαγητό	e·*ki*·no to fa·yi·*to*

drinks

(cup of) coffee ...	(ένα φλυτζάνι) καφέ ...	(e·na fli-*dza*-ni) ka·*fe* ...
(cup of) tea ...	(ένα φλυτζάνι) τσάι ...	(e·na fli-*dza*-ni) *tsa*·i ...
with milk	με γάλα	me *gha*·la
without sugar	χωρίς ζάχαρη	kho·*ris* za·kha·ri
(orange) juice	χυμός (πορτοκάλι) m	hi·*mos* (por·to·*ka*·li)
soft drink	αναψυκτικό n	a·nap·sik·ti·*ko*
... water	... νερό	... ne·*ro*
hot	ζεστό	ze·*sto*
(sparkling) mineral	(γαζόζα) μεταλλικό	(gha·*zo*·za) me·ta·li·*ko*

in the bar

I'll have ...	θα πάρω ...	tha *pa*·ro ...
I'll buy you a drink.	θα σε κεράσω εγώ.	tha se ke·*ra*·so e·*gho*
What would you like?	Τι θα ήθελες;	ti tha *i*·the·les
Cheers!	Εις υγείαν!	is i·*yi*·an
brandy	μπράντι n	*bran*·di
champagne	σαμπάνια f	sam·*pa*·nia
a glass/bottle of	ένα ποτήρι/μπουκάλι	e·na po·*ti*·ri/bu·*ka*·li
beer	μπύρα	*bi*·ra
ouzo	ούζο n	*u*·zo
a shot of (whisky)	ένα (ουίσκι)	*e*·na (u·*i*·ski)
a glass/bottle	ένα ποτήρι/μπουκάλι	e·na po·*ti*·ri/bu·*ka*·li
of ... wine	... κρασί	... kra·*si*
red	κόκκινο	*ko*·ki·no
sparkling	σαμπάνια	sam·*pa*·nia
white	άσπρο	*a*·spro

self-catering

What's the local speciality?
Ποιες είναι οι τοπικές λιχουδιές;   pies i·ne i to·pi·*kes* li·khu·*dhies*

What's that?
Τι είναι εκείνο;   ti *i*·ne e·*ki*·no

How much is (a kilo of cheese)?
Πόσο κάνει (ένα κιλό τυρί);   *po*·so ka·ni (e·na ki·*lo* ti·*ri*)

I'd like ...	Θα ήθελα ...	tha *i*·the·la ...
(100) grams	(εκατό) γραμμάρια	(e·ka·to) ghra·ma·ria
(two) kilos	(δύο) κιλά	(dhi·o) ki·la
(three) pieces	(τρία) κομμάτια	(tri·a) ko·ma·tia
(six) slices	(έξι) φέτες	(ek·si) fe·tes

Less.	Πιο λίγο.	pio *li*·gho
Enough.	Αρκετά.	ar·ke·*ta*
More.	Πιο πολύ.	pio po·*li*

special diets & allergies

Is there a vegetarian restaurant near here?
Υπάρχει ένα εστιατόριο χορτοφάγων   i·*par*·hi e·na e·sti·a·*to*·ri·o hor·to·*fa*·ghon
εδώ κοντά;   e·dho ko·da

Do you have vegetarian food?
Έχετε φαγητό για χορτοφάγους;   e·he·te fa·yi·*to* yia khor·to·*fa*·ghus

I don't eat ...	Δεν τρώω ...	dhen *tro*·gho ...
butter	βούτυρο	*vu*·ti·ro
eggs	αβγά	av·*gha*
meat stock	ζουμί από κρέας	zu·*mi* a·*po* kre·as

I'm allergic to ...	Είμαι αλλεργικός/	*i*·me a·ler·yi·*kos*
	αλλεργική ... m/f	a·ler·yi·*ki* ...
dairy produce	στα γαλακτικά	sta gha·lak·ti·*ka*
gluten	στη γλουτένη	sti ghlu·*te*·ni
MSG	στο MSG	sto em es dzi
nuts	στους ξηρούς καρπούς	stus ksi·*rus* kar·*pus*
seafood	στα θαλασσινά	sta tha·la·si·*na*

αρνί κοκκινιστό n	ar-*ni* ko-ki-ni-*sto*	lamb braised in white wine
αστακός m	a-sta-*kos*	lobster, boiled or chargrilled
γιαουρτογλού f	yia-ur-to-*ghlu*	grilled meat & yogurt pie
γιουβέτσι n	yiu-*vet*-si	casserole of meat & seafood with tomatoes & pasta
δάχτυλα n pl	*dhakh*-ti-la	deep-fried, nut-filled pastries
ελιές τσακιστές f pl	e-*lies* tsa-ki-*stes*	marinated green olives
ελιές τουρσί f pl	e-*lies* tur-*si*	pickled olives
ιμάμ-μπαϊλντί n	i-*mam*-ba-il-*di*	stuffed eggplant
καβούρι βραστό n	ka-*vu*-ri vra-*sto*	boiled crab with dressing
κακαβιά f	ka-ka-*via*	saltwater fish soup
καλαμάρι Λεβριανά n	ka-la-*ma*-ri lev-ria-*na*	squid stewed in wine
καλαμάρι τηγανητό n	ka-la-*ma*-ri ti-gha-ni-*to*	battered & fried squid rings
καρυδόπιτα f	ka-ri-*dho*-pi-ta	rich moist walnut cake
καταΐφι n	ka-ta-*i*-fi	syrupy nut-filled rolls
κεφτέδες m pl	kef-*te*-dhes	lamb, pork or veal rissoles
κοντοσούβλι n	kon-do-*suv*-li	spit-roast pieces of lamb or pork
κοφίσι n	ko-*fi*-si	fish pie
κρεατόπιτα f	kre-a-*to*-pi-ta	lamb or veal pie
λάχανα με λαρδί n pl	*la*-kha-na me lar-*dhi*	greens & bacon casserole
μηλοπιτάκια n pl	mi-lo-pi-*ta*-kia	apple & walnut pies
μπακλαβάς m pl	ba-kla-*vas*	nut-filled pastry in honey syrup
μπάμιες γιαχνί f pl	*ba*-mies yia-*khni*	braised okra
μπιζελόσουπα f	bi-ze-*lo*-su-pa	fragrant pea soup with dill
μπουρδέτο n	bur-*dhe*-to	salt cod stew

μπριάμι n	bri-*a*-mi	mixed vegetables casserole
μπριζόλες f pl	bri-*zo*-les	chops • steak
μύδια κρασάτα n pl	*mi*-dhia kra-*sa*-ta	poached mussels in wine sauce
ντολμάδες m pl	dol-*ma*-dhes	stuffed vine or cabbage leaves
ντοματόσουπα f	do-ma-*to*-su-pa	tomato soup with pasta
παλικάρια n pl	pa-li-*ka*-ri-a	boiled legumes & grains
ρέγγα f	*reng*-ga	smoked herrings, plain or grilled
ριζάδα f	ri-*za*-dha	thick soup with rice & shellfish
σαλιγκάρια n pl	sa-ling-*ga*-ri-a	snails cooked in the shell
σουβλάκι n	suv-*la*-ki	seasoned or marinated meat or fish, skewered & chargrilled
σπανακόπιτα f	spa-na-*ko*-pi-ta	spinach pie
συκόψωμο n	si-*kop*-so-mo	heavy aromatic fig cake
ταβάς m	ta-*vas*	seasoned beef or lamb casserole
τζατζίκι n	dza-*dzi*-ki	cucumber, yogurt & garlic salad
τυρόπιτα f	ti-*ro*-pi-ta	cheese pie
φακές σούπα f pl	fa-*kes* su-pa	lentil soup
φασολάδα f	fa-so-*la*-dha	thick fragrant bean soup
χαλβάς m	khal-*vas*	sweet of sesame seeds & honey, with pistachio or almonds
χαμψοπίλαφο n	kham-pso-*pi*-la-fo	onion & anchovy pilau
χόρτα τσιγάρι n pl	*khor*-ta tsi-*gha*-ri	lightly fried wild greens
χορτόπιτα f	khor-*to*-pi-ta	pie with seasonal greens
χορτοσαλάτα f	khor-to-sa-*la*-ta	warm salad of greens & dressing
χταπόδι βραστό n	khta-*po*-dhi vra-*sto*	boiled octopus
χωριάτικη σαλάτα f	kho-ri-*a*-ti-ki sa-*la*-ta	salad of tomatoes, cucumber, olives & feta

emergencies

basics

Help!	Βοήθεια!	vo-*i*-thia
Stop!	Σταμάτα!	sta-*ma*-ta
Go away!	Φύγε!	*fi*-ye
Thief!	Κλέφτης!	*klef*-tis
Fire!	Φωτιά!	fo-*tia*
Watch out!	Πρόσεχε!	*pro*-se-he

Call ...!	Κάλεσε ...!	ka-*le*-se ...
an ambulance	το ασθενοφόρο	to as-the-no-*fo*-ro
the doctor	ένα γιατρό	*e*-na yia-*tro*
the police	την αστυνομία	tin a-sti-no-*mi*-a

It's an emergency.
Είναι μια έκτακτη ανάγκη.
i-ne mia *ek*-tak-ti a-*na*-gi

Could you help me, please?
Μπορείς να βοηθήσεις, παρακαλώ;
bo-*ris* na vo-i-*thi*-sis pa-ra-ka-*lo*

Can I make a phone call?
Μπορώ να κάνω ένα τηλεφώνημα;
bo-*ro* na *ka*-no *e*-na ti-le-*fo*-ni-ma

I'm lost.
Εχω χαθεί.
e-kho kha-*thi*

Where are the toilets?
Που είναι η τουαλέτα;
pu *i*-ne i tu-a-*le*-ta

police

Where's the police station?
Που είναι ο αστυνομικός σταθμός;
pu *i*-ne o a-sti-no-mi-*kos* stath-*mos*

I want to report an offence.
Θέλω να αναφέρω μια παρανομία.
the-lo na a-na-*fe*-ro mia pa-ra-no-*mi*-a

I have insurance.
Εχω ασφάλεια.
e-kho as-*fa*-li-a

I've been ...	Με έχουν ...	me *e*-khun ...
assaulted	κακοποιήσει	ka-ko-pi-*i*-si
raped	βιάσει	vi-*a*-si
robbed	ληστέψει	li-*step*-si

I've lost my …	Έχασα … μου.	e-kha-sa … mu
My … was/were stolen.	Έκλεψαν … μου.	e-klep-san … mu
backpack	το σακίδιο	to sa-ki-dhio
bags	τις βαλίτσες	tis va-lits-es
credit card	την πιστωτική κάρτα	tin pi-sto-ti-ki kar-ta
handbag	την τσάντα	tin tsa-da
jewellery	τα κοσμήματά	ta koz-mi-ma-ta
money	τα χρήματά	ta khri-ma-ta
passport	το διαβατήριό	to dhia-va-ti-rio
travellers cheques	τις ταξιδιωτικές επιταγές	tis tak-si-dhio-ti-kes e-pi-ta-yes
wallet	το πορτοφόλι	to por-to-fo-li
I want to contact my …	Θέλω να έρθω σε επαφή με … μου.	the-lo na er-tho se e-pa-fi me … mu
consulate	τηνπρεσβεία	tin prez-vi-a
embassy	το προξενείο	to pro-ksee-ni-o

health

medical needs

Where's the nearest …?	Που είναι ο πιο κοντινός …;	pu i-ne o pio ko-di-nos …
dentist	οδοντίατρος	o-dho-di-a-tros
doctor	γιατρός	yia-tros
Where's the nearest …?	Που είναι το πιο κοντινό…;	pu i-ne to pio ko-di-no …
hospital	νοσοκομείο	no-so-ko-mi-o
(night) pharmacy	(νυχτερινό) φαρμακείο	(nikh-te-ri-no) far-ma-ki-o

I need a doctor (who speaks English).
Χρειάζομαι ένα γιατρό (που να μιλάει αγγλικά).   khri-a-zo-me e-na yia-tro (pu na mi-la-i ang-gli-ka)

Could I see a female doctor?
Μπορώ να δω μια γυναίκα γιατρό;   bo-ro na dho mia yi-ne-ka yia-tro

I've run out of my medication.
Μου έχουν τελειώσει τα φάρμακά μου.   mu e-khun te-li-o-si ta far-ma-ka mu

I'm sick.	Είμαι άρρωστος/άρρωστη m/f	i-me a-ro-stos/a-ro-sti
It hurts here.	Πονάει εδώ.	po-na-i e-dho
I have (a/an) ...	Εχω ...	e-kho ...

asthma	άσθμα n	as-thma
bronchitis	βροχίτιδα f	vro-hi-ti-dha
constipation	δυσκοιλιότητα f	dhis-ki-li-o-ti-ta
cough	βήχα m	vi-kha
diarrhoea	διάρροια f	dhi-a-ri-a
fever	πυρετό m	pi-re-to
headache	πονοκέφαλο m	po-no-ke-fa-lo
heart condition	καρδιακή	kar-dhi-a-ki
	κατάσταση f	ka-ta-sta-si
nausea	ναυτία f	naf-ti-a
pain	πόνο m	po-no
sore throat	πονόλαιμο m	po-no-le-mo
toothache	πονόδοντο m	po-no-dho-do

I'm allergic to ...	Είμαι αλλεργικός/	i-me a-ler-yi-kos
	αλλεργική ... m/f	a-ler-yi-ki ...
antibiotics	στα αντιβιωτικά	sta a-di-vi-o-ti-ka
anti-inflammatories	στα αντιφλεγμονώδη	sta a-di-flegh-mo-no-dhi
aspirin	στην ασπιρίνη	stin as-pi-ri-ni
bees	στις μέλισσες	stis me-li-ses
codeine	στην κωδεΐνη	stin ko-dhe-i-ni
penicillin	στην πενικιλλίνη	stin pe-ni-ki-li-ni

antiseptic	αντισηπτικό n	a-di-sip-ti-ko
bandage	επίδεσμος m	e-pi-dhez-mos
condoms	προφυλακτικά n	pro-fi-lak-ti-ka
contraceptives	αντισυλληπτικά n pl	a-di-si-lip-ti-ka
diarrhoea medicine	φάρμακο διάροιας	far-ma-ko dhiar-ghias
insect repellent	εντομοαπωθητικό n	e-do-mo-a-po-thi-ti-ko
laxatives	καθαρτικό n	ka-thar-ti-ko
painkillers	παυσίπονα	paf-si-po-na
rehydration salts	ενυδρωτικά άλατα n pl	en-i-dhro-ti-ka a-la-ta
sleeping tablets	υπνωτικά χάπια n pl	ip-no-ti-ka kha-pia

english–greek dictionary

Greek nouns in this dictionary have their gender indicated by ⓜ (masculine), ⓕ (feminine) or ⓝ (neuter). If it's a plural noun you'll also see pl. Adjectives are given in the masculine form only. Words are also marked as n (noun), a (adjective), v (verb), sg (singular), pl (plural), inf (informal) and pol (polite) where necessary.

A

accident ατύχημα ⓝ a-*ti*-hi-ma
accommodation κατάλυμα ⓝ ka-*ta*-li-ma
adaptor μετασχηματιστής ⓜ me-ta-shi-ma-ti-*stis*
address διεύθυνση ⓕ dhi-*ef*-thin-si
aeroplane αεροπλάνο ⓝ a-e-ro-*pla*-no
after μετά me-*ta*
air-conditioned με έρκοντίσιον me-er-kon-*di*-si-on
airport αεροδρόμιο ⓝ a-e-ro-*dhro*-mi-o
alcohol αλκοόλ ⓝ al-ko-*ol*
all όλοι ⓝ *o*-li
allergy αλλεργία ⓕ a-ler-*yi*-a
ambulance νοσοκομειακό ⓝ no-so-ko-mi-a-*ko*
and και ke
ankle αστράγαλος ⓜ a-*stra*-gha-los
arm χέρι ⓝ *he*-ri
ashtray σταχτοθήκη ⓕ stakh-to-*thi*-ki
ATM αυτόματη μηχανή χρημάτων ⓕ
    af-to-ma-ti mi-kha-*ni* khri-*ma*-ton

B

baby μωρό ⓝ mo-*ro*
back (body) πλάτη ⓕ *pla*-ti
backpack σακίδιο ⓝ sa-ki-dhi-o
bad κακός ka-*kos*
bag σάκος ⓜ *sa*-kos
baggage claim παραλαβή αποσκευών ⓕ
    pa-ra-la-*vi* a-po-ske-*von*
bank τράπεζα ⓕ *tra*-pe-za
bar μπαρ ⓝ bar
bathroom μπάνιο ⓝ *ba*-nio
battery μπαταρία ⓕ ba-ta-*ri*-a
beautiful όμορφος *o*-mor-fos
bed κρεβάτι ⓝ kre-*va*-ti
beer μπύρα ⓕ *bi*-ra
before πριν prin
behind πίσω *pi*-so
bicycle ποδήλατο ⓝ po-*dhi*-la-to
big μεγάλος me-*gha*-los

bill λογαριασμός ⓜ lo-gha-riaz-*mos*
black a μαύρος *mav*-ros
blanket κουβέρτα ⓕ ku-*ver*-ta
blood group ομάδα αίματος ⓕ o-*ma*-dha e-ma-tos
blue a μπλε ble
boat βάρκα ⓕ *var*-ka
book (make a reservation) v κλείσω θέση *kli*-so the-si
bottle μπουκάλι ⓝ bu-*ka*-li
bottle opener ανοιχτήρι ⓝ a-nikh-*ti*-ri
boy αγόρι ⓝ a-*gho*-ri
brakes (car) φρένα ⓝ pl *fre*-na
breakfast πρωινό ⓝ pro-i-no
broken (faulty) ελαττωματικός e-la-to-ma-ti-*kos*
bus λεωφορείο ⓝ le-o-fo-*ri*-o
business επιχείρηση ⓕ e-pi-*hi*-ri-si
buy αγοράζω a-gho-*ra*-zo

C

café καφετέρια ⓕ ka-fe-*te*-ria
camera φωτογραφική μηχανή ⓕ
    fo-to-ghra-fi-*ki* mi-kha-*ni*
camp site χώρος για κάμπινγκ ⓝ *kho*-ros yia *kam*-ping
cancel ακυρώνω a-ki-*ro*-no
can opener ανοιχτήρι ⓝ a-nikh-*ti*-ri
car αυτοκίνητο ⓝ af-to-*ki*-ni-to
cash μετρητά ⓝ pl me-tri-*ta*
cash (a cheque) v εξαργυρώνω ek-sar-yi-*ro*-no
cell phone κινητό ⓝ ki-ni-*to*
centre κέντρο ⓝ *ke*-dro
change (money) v αλλάζω a-*la*-zo
cheap φτηνός fti-*nos*
check (bill) λογαριασμός ⓜ lo-gha-riaz-*mos*
check-in ρεσεψιόν ⓕ re-sep-sion
chest στήθος ⓝ *sti*-thos
child παιδί ⓝ pe-*dhi*
cigarette τσιγάρο ⓝ tsi-*gha*-ro
city πόλη ⓕ *po*-li
clean a καθαρός ka-tha-*ros*
closed κλεισμένος kliz-*me*-nos
coffee καφές ⓜ ka-*fes*
coins κέρματα ⓝ pl *ker*-ma-ta
cold a κρυωμένος kri-o-*me*-nos

collect call κλήση με αντιστροφή της επιβάρυνσης ⓕ
   kli-si me a-dis-tro-fi tis e-pi-va-rin-sis
come έρχομαι *er-kho-me*
computer κομπιούτερ ⓝ *kom-piu-ter*
condom προφυλακτικό *pro-fi-lak-ti-ko*
contact lenses φακοί επαφής ⓝ pl *fa-ki e-pa-fis*
cook v μαγειρεύω *ma-yi-re-vo*
cost τιμή ⓕ *ti-mi*
credit card πιστωτική κάρτα ⓕ *pi-sto-ti-ki kar-ta*
cup φλιτζάνι *fli-dza-ni*
currency exchange τιμή συναλλάγματος ⓕ
   ti-mi si-na-lagh-ma-tos
customs (immigration) τελωνείο ⓝ *te-lo-ni-o*
Cypriot (nationality) Κύπριος/Κύπρια ⓜ/ⓕ
   ki-pri-os/ki-pri-a
Cypriot a κυπριακός/κυπριακή ⓜ/ⓕ
   ki-pri-a-kos/ki-pri-a-ki
Cyprus Κύπρος ⓕ *ki-pros*

D

dangerous επικίνδυνος *e-pi-kin-dhi-nos*
date (time) ημερομηνία ⓕ *i-me-ro-mi-ni-a*
day ημέρα ⓕ *i-me-ra*
delay καθυστέρηση ⓕ *ka-thi-ste-ri-si*
dentist οδοντίατρος ⓜ & ⓕ *o-dho-di-a-tros*
depart αναχωρώ *a-na-kho-ro*
diaper πάνα ⓕ *pa-na*
dictionary λεξικό ⓝ *lek-si-ko*
dinner δείπνο ⓝ *dhip-no*
direct άμεσος *a-me-sos*
dirty βρώμικος *vro-mi-kos*
disabled ανάπηρος *a-na-pi-ros*
discount έκπτωση ⓕ *ek-pto-si*
doctor γιατρός ⓜ & ⓕ *yia-tros*
double bed διπλό κρεβάτι ⓝ *dhi-plo kre-va-ti*
double room διπλό δωμάτιο ⓝ *dhi-plo dho-ma-ti-o*
drink ποτό ⓝ *po-to*
drive v οδηγώ *o-dhi-gho*
drivers licence άδεια οδήγησης ⓕ *a-dhi-a o-dhi-yi-sis*
drugs (illicit) ναρκωτικό ⓝ *nar-ko-ti-ko*
dummy (pacifier) πιπίλα ⓕ *pi-pi-la*

E

ear αφτί ⓝ *af-ti*
east ανατολή ⓕ *a-na-to-li*
eat τρώγω *tro-gho*
economy class τουριστική θέση ⓕ *tu-ri-sti-ki the-si*
electricity ηλεκτρισμός ⓜ *i-lek-triz-mos*

elevator ασανσέρ ⓝ *a-san-ser*
email ημέιλ ⓝ *i-me-il*
embassy πρεσβεία ⓕ *pre-zvi-a*
emergency έκτακτη ανάγκη ⓕ *ek-tak-ti a-na-gi*
English (language) Αγγλικά ⓝ *ang-gli-ka*
entrance είσοδος ⓕ *i-so-dhos*
evening βράδι ⓝ *vra-dhi*
exchange rate τιμή συναλλάγματος ⓕ
   ti-mi si-na-lagh-ma-tos
exit έξοδος ⓕ *ek-so-dhos*
expensive ακριβός *a-kri-vos*
express mail επείγον ταχυδρομείο ⓝ
   e-pi-ghon ta-hi-dhro-mi-o
eye μάτι ⓝ *ma-ti*

F

far μακριά *ma-kri-a*
fast γρήγορος *ghri-gho-ros*
father πατέρας ⓜ *pa-te-ras*
film (camera) φιλμ ⓝ *film*
finger δάκτυλο ⓝ *dhak-ti-lo*
first-aid kit κυτίο πρώτων βοηθειών ⓝ
   ki-ti-o pro-ton vo-i-thi-on
first class πρώτη τάξη ⓕ *pro-ti tak-si*
fish ψάρι ⓝ *psa-ri*
food φαγητό ⓝ *fa-yi-to*
foot πόδι ⓝ *po-dhi*
fork πιρούνι ⓝ *pi-ru-ni*
free (of charge) δωρεάν *dho-re-an*
friend φίλος/φίλη ⓜ/ⓕ *fi-los/fi-li*
fruit φρούτα ⓝ pl *fru-ta*
full γεμάτο *ye-ma-to*
funny αστείος *a-sti-os*

G

gift δώρο ⓝ *dho-ro*
girl κορίτσι ⓝ *ko-rit-si*
glass (drinking) ποτήρι ⓝ *po-ti-ri*
glasses γιαλιά ⓝ *yia-lia*
go πηγαίνω *pi-ye-no*
good καλός *ka-los*
Greece Ελλάδα ⓕ *e-la-dha*
Greek (language) Ελληνικά ⓝ *e-li-ni-ka*
Greek (nationality) Έλληνες ⓜ pl *e-li-nes*
green πράσινος *pra-si-nos*
guide οδηγός ⓜ & ⓕ *o-dhi-ghos*

H

half μισό ⊚ mi-so
hand χέρι ⊚ he-ri
handbag τσάντα ⊕ tsa-da
happy ευτυχισμένος ef-ti-hiz-me-nos
have έχω e-kho
he αυτός ⊚ af-tos
head κεφάλι ⊚ ke-fa-li
heart καρδιά ⊕ kar-dhia
heat ζέστη ⊕ ze-sti
heavy βαρύς va-ris
help v βοηθώ vo-i-tho
here εδώ e-dho
high ψηλός psi-los
highway δημόσιος δρόμος ⊚ dhi-mo-si-os dhro-mos
hike v πεζοπορώ pe-zo-po-ro
holiday διακοπές ⊕ dhia-ko-pes
homosexual ομοφυλόφιλος ⊚ o-mo-fi-lo-fi-los
hospital νοσοκομείο ⊚ no-so-ko-mi-o
hot ζεστός ze-stos
hotel ξενοδοχείο ⊚ kse-no-dho-hi-o
hungry πεινασμένος pi-naz-me-nos
husband σύζυγος ⊚ si-zi-ghos

I

I εγώ e-gho
identification (card) ταυτότητα ⊕ taf-to-ti-ta
ill άρρωστος a-ro-stos
important σπουδαίος spu-dhe-os
included συμπεριλαμβανομένου si-be-ri-lam-va-no-me-nu
injury πληγή ⊕ pli-yi
insurance ασφάλεια ⊕ as-fa-li-a
Internet διαδίκτυο ⊚ dhi-a-dhik-ti-o
interpreter διερμηνέας ⊚ & ⊕ dhi-er-mi-ne-as

J

jewellery κοσμήματα ⊚ pl koz-mi-ma-ta
job δουλειά ⊕ dhu-lia

K

key κλειδί ⊚ kli-dhi
kilogram χιλιόγραμμο ⊚ hi-lio-gra-mo
kitchen κουζίνα ⊕ ku-zi-na
knife μαχαίρι ⊚ ma-he-ri

L

laundry (place) πλυντήριο ⊚ pli-di-ri-o
lawyer δικηγόρος ⊚ & ⊕ dhi-ki-gho-ros
left (direction) αριστερός ⊚ a-ri-ste-ros
left-luggage office γραφείο φύλαξη αποσκευών ⊚ gra-fi-o fi-lak-si a-po-ske-von
leg πόδι ⊚ po-dhi
lesbian λεσβία ⊕ les-vi-a
less λιγότερο li-gho-te-ro
letter (mail) γράμμα ⊚ ghra-ma
lift (elevator) ασανσέρ ⊚ a-san-ser
light φως ⊚ fos
like v μου αρέσει mu a-re-si
lock κλειδαριά ⊕ kli-dha-ria
long μακρύς ma-kris
lost χαμένος kha-me-nos
lost-property office γραφείο απωλεσθέντων αντικειμένων ⊚ gra-fi-o a-po-les-the-don a-di-ki-me-non
love v αγαπώ a-gha-po
luggage αποσκευές ⊕ a-po-ske-ves
lunch μεσημεριανό φαγητό ⊚ me-si-me-ria-no fa-yi-to

M

mail (letters) αλληλογραφία ⊕ a-li-lo-ghra-fi-a
mail (postal system) ταχυδρομείο ⊚ ta-hi-dhro-mi-o
man άντρας ⊚ a-dras
map χάρτης ⊚ khar-tis
market αγορά ⊕ a-gho-ra
matches σπίρτα ⊚ pl spir-ta
meat κρέας ⊚ kre-as
medicine φάρμακο ⊚ far-ma-ko
menu μενού ⊚ me-nu
message μήνυμα ⊚ mi-ni-ma
milk γάλα ⊚ gha-la
minute λεπτό ⊚ lep-to
mobile phone κινητό ⊚ ki-ni-to
money χρήματα ⊚ khri-ma-ta
month μήνας ⊚ mi-nas
morning πρωί ⊚ pro-i
mother μητέρα ⊕ mi-te-ra
motorcycle μοτοσυκλέτα ⊕ mo-to-si-kle-ta
motorway αυτοκινητόδρομος ⊚ af-to-ki-ni-to-dhro-mos
mouth στόμα ⊚ sto-ma
music μουσική ⊕ mu-si-ki

N

name όνομα ⊚ o-no-ma
napkin πετσετάκι ⊚ pet-se-ta-ki
nappy πάνα ⊕ pa-na

near κοντά ko-*da*

neck λαιμός ⓜ le-*mos*

new νέος ne-*os*

news νέα ⓝ ne-*a*

newspaper εφημερίδα ⓕ e-fi-me-*ri*-dha

night νύχτα ⓕ *nikh*-ta

no όχι o-*hi*

noisy a θορυβώδης thro-*vo*-dhis

nonsmoking μη καπνίζοντες mi kap-*ni*-zo-des

north βοράς ⓜ *vo*-ras

nose μύτη ⓕ *mi*-ti

now τώρα *to*-ra

number αριθμός ⓜ a-rith-*mos*

O

oil (engine) λάδι αυτοκινήτου ⓝ *la*-dhi af-to-ki-*ni*-tu

old παλιός pa-*lios*

one-way ticket απλό εισιτήριο ⓝ a-*plo* i-si-*ti*-ri-o

open a ανοιχτός a-nikh-*tos*

outside έξω *ek*-so

P

package πακέτο ⓝ pa-*ke*-to

paper χαρτί ⓝ khar-*ti*

park (car) v παρκάρω par-*ka*-ro

passport διαβατήριο ⓝ dhia-va-*ti*-ri-o

pay v πληρώνω pli-*ro*-no

pen στυλό ⓝ sti-*lo*

petrol πετρέλαιο ⓝ pe-*tre*-le-o

pharmacy φαρμακείο ⓝ far-ma-*ki*-o

phonecard τηλεκάρτα ⓕ ti-le-*kar*-ta

photo φωτογραφία ⓕ fo-to-gra-*fi*-a

plate πιάτο ⓝ *pia*-to

police αστυνομία ⓕ a-sti-no-*mi*-a

postcard κάρτα ⓕ *kar*-ta

post office ταχυδρομείο ⓝ ta-hi-dhro-*mi*-o

pregnant έγκυος e-gi-os

price τιμή ⓕ ti-*mi*

Q

quiet ήσυχος *i*-si-khos

R

rain βροχή vro-*hi*

razor ξυριστική μηχανή ⓕ ksi-ri-sti-*ki* mi-kha-*ni*

receipt απόδειξη ⓕ a-*po*-dhik-si

red κόκκινο *ko*-ki-no

refund ⓝ επιστροφή χρημάτων ⓕ e-pi-stro-*fi* khri-*ma*-ton

registered mail συστημένο sis-ti-*me*-no

rent v ενοικιάζω e-ni-ki-*a*-zo

repair v επισκευάζω e-pi-ske-*va*-zo

reservation κράτηση ⓕ *kra*-ti-si

restaurant εστιατόριο ⓝ e-sti-a-*to*-ri-o

return v επιστρέφω e-pi-*stre*-fo

return ticket εισιτήριο μετ' επιστροφής ⓝ i-si-*ti*-ri-o me-te-pis-tro-*fis*

right (direction) δεξιός dhek-si-*os*

road δρόμος ⓜ *dhro*-mos

room δωμάτιο ⓝ dho-*ma*-ti-o

S

safe a ασφαλής as-fa-*lis*

sanitary napkin πετσετάκι υγείας ⓝ pet-se-*ta*-ki i-*yi*-as

seat θέση ⓕ *the*-si

send στέλνω *stel*-no

service station βενζινάδικο ⓝ ven-zi-*na*-dhi-ko

sex σεξ ⓝ seks

shampoo σαμπουάν ⓝ sam-pu-*an*

share (a dorm) μοιράζομαι mi-*ra*-zo-me

shaving cream κρέμα ξυρίσματος ⓕ *kre*-ma ksi-*riz*-ma-tos

she αυτή af-*ti*

sheet (bed) σεντόνι ⓝ se-*do*-ni

shirt πουκάμισο ⓝ pu-*ka*-mi-so

shoes παπούτσια ⓝ pl pa-*put*-si-a

shop μαγαζί ⓝ ma-gha-*zi*

short κοντός ko-*dos*

shower ντους ⓜ duz

single room μονό δωμάτιο ⓝ mo-*no* dho-*ma*-tio

skin δέρμα ⓝ *dher*-ma

skirt φούστα ⓕ *fu*-sta

sleep v κοιμάμαι ki-*ma*-me

slowly αργά ar-*gha*

small μικρός mi-*kros*

smoke (cigarettes) v καπνίζω kap-*ni*-zo

soap σαπούνι ⓝ sa-*pu*-ni

some μερικοί me-ri-*ki*

soon σύντομα *si*-do-ma

south νότος ⓜ *no*-tos

souvenir shop κατάστημα για σουβενίρ ⓝ ka-*ta*-sti-ma yia su-ve-*nir*

speak μιλάω mi-*la*-o

spoon κουτάλι ⓝ ku-*ta*-li

stamp γραμματόσημο ⓝ ghra-ma-*to*-si-mo

stand-by ticket εισιτήριο σταντ μπάι ⓝ
i-si-ti-ri-o stand *ba*-i
station (train) σταθμός ⓜ stath-*mos*
stomach στομάχι ⓝ sto-*ma*-hi
stop v σταματάω sta-ma-*ta*-o
stop (bus) στάση ① *sta*-si
street οδός ① o-*dhos*
student σπουδαστής/σπουδάστρια ⓜ/①
spu-dha-*stis*/spu-dha-stri-a
sun ήλιος ⓜ *i*-li-os
sunscreen αντιηλιακό ⓝ a-di-i-li-a-*ko*
swim v κολυμπώ ko-li-*bo*

T

tampon ταμπόν ⓝ ta-*bon*
taxi ταξί ⓝ tak-*si*
teaspoon κουτάλι τσαγιού ① ku-*ta*-li tsa-*yiu*
teeth δόντια ⓝ *dho*-dia
telephone τηλέφωνο ⓝ ti-*le*-fo-no
television τηλεόραση ① ti-le-o-ra-si
temperature (weather) θερμοκρασία ①
ther-mo-kra-*si*-a
tent τέντα ① *te*-da
that (one) εκείνο e-ki-no
they αυτοί af-*ti*
thirsty διψασμένος dhip-saz-*me*-nos
this (one) αυτός af-*tos*
throat λαιμός ⓜ le-*mos*
ticket εισιτήριο ⓝ i-si-*ti*-ri-o
time ώρα ① *o*-ra
tired κουρασμένος ku-raz-*me*-nos
tissues χαρτομάντηλα ⓝ pl khar-to-*ma*-di-la
today σήμερα *si*-me-ra
toilet τουαλέτα ① tu-a-*le*-ta
tomorrow αύριο *av*-ri-o
tonight απόψε a-*pop*-se
toothbrush οδοντόβουρτσα ① o-dho-*do*-vur-tsa
toothpaste οδοντόπαστα ① o-dho-*do*-pa-sta
torch (flashlight) φακός ⓜ fa-*kos*
tour περιήγηση ① pe-ri-*i-yi*-si
tourist office τουριστικό γραφείο ⓝ
tu-ri-sti-*ko* ghra-*fi*-o
towel πετσέτα ① pet-*se*-ta
train τρένο ⓝ *tre*-no
translate v μεταφράζω me-ta-*fra*-zo
travel agency ταξιδιωτικό γραφείο ⓝ
tak-si-dhi-o-ti-*ko* ghra-*fi*-o
travellers cheque ταξιδιωτική επιταγή ①
tak-si-dhi-o-ti-*ki* e-pi-ta-*yi*

trousers παντελόνι ⓝ pa-de-*lo*-ni
twin beds δίκλινο δωμάτιο ⓝ *dhi*-kli-no dho-*ma*-ti-o
tyre λάστιχο ⓝ *la*-sti-kho

U

underwear εσώρουχα ⓝ pl e-*so*-ru-kha
urgent επείγον e-*pi*-ghon

V

vacant ελεύθερος e-*lef*-the-ros
vacation διακοπές ① dhia-ko-*pes*
vegetable λαχανικά ⓝ pl la-kha-ni-*ka*
vegetarian n χορτοφάγος ⓜ&① khor-to-*fa*-ghos
visa βίζα ① *vi*-za

W

waiter γκαρσόν ⓝ gar-*son*
walk v περπατάω per-pa-*ta*-o
wallet πορτοφόλι ⓝ por-to-*fo*-li
warm a ζεστός ze-*stos*
wash (something) v πλένω *ple*-no
watch ρολόι ⓝ ro-*lo*-i
water νερό ⓝ ne-*ro*
we εμείς e-*mis*
weekend Σαββατοκύριακο ⓝ sa-va-to-*ki*-ria-ko
west δύση ① *dhi*-si
wheelchair αναπηρική καρέκλα ①
a-na-pi-ri-*ki* ka-*re*-kla
when όταν o-tan
where πού pu
white άσπρος *as*-pros
who ποιος pios
why γιατί yia-*ti*
wife σύζυγος ① *si*-zi-ghos
window παράθυρο ⓝ pa-*ra*-thi-ro
wine κρασί ⓝ kra-*si*
with με me
without χωρίς kho-*ris*
woman γυναίκα ① yi-*ne*-ka
write v γράφω *ghra*-fo

Y

yellow a κίτρινος *ki*-tri-nos
yes ναι ne
yesterday χτες khtes
you sg inf εσύ e-*si*
you sg pol & pl εσείς e-*sis*

Italian

italian alphabet

A a	B b	C c	D d	E e
a	bee	chee	dee	e
F f	G g	H h	I i	L l
e·fe	jee	a·ka	ee	e·le
M m	N n	O o	P p	Q q
e·me	e·ne	o	pee	koo
R r	S s	T t	U u	V v
e·re	e·se	tee	oo	voo
Z z				
tse·ta				

■ italian

ITALIANO

introduction

All you need for *la dolce vita* is to be able to tell your *Moschino* from your *macchiato* and your *Fellini* from your *fettuccine*. Happily, you'll find Italian (*italiano* ee·ta·*lya*·no) an easy language to start speaking as well as a beautiful one to listen to. When even a simple sentence sounds like an aria it can be difficult to resist striking up a conversation – and thanks to widespread migration and the huge popularity of Italian culture and cuisine, you're probably familiar with words like *ciao, pasta* and *bella* already.

There are also many similarities between Italian and English which smooth the way for language learners. Italian is a Romance language – a descendent of Latin, the language of the Romans (as are French, Spanish, Portuguese and Romanian), and English has been heavily influenced by Latin, particularly via contact with French.

Up until the 19th century, Italy was a collection of autonomous states, rather than a nation-state. As a result, Italian has many regional dialects, including Sardinian and Sicilian. Some dialects are so different from standard Italian as to be considered distinct languages in their own right. It wasn't until the 19th century that the Tuscan dialect – the language of Dante, Boccaccio and Petrarch – became the standard language of the nation, and the official language of schools, media and administration. 'Standard Italian' is the variety that will take you from the top of the boot to the very toe – all the language in this phrasebook is in standard Italian.

The majority of the approximately 65 million people who speak Italian live, of course, in Italy. However, the language also has official status in San Marino, Vatican City, parts of Switzerland, Slovenia and the Istrian peninsula of Croatia. Italian was the official language of Malta during the period of the Knights of St John (1530–1798) and afterwards shared that status with English during the British rule. Only in 1934 was Italian withdrawn and substituted with the native Maltese language. Today, Maltese people are generally fluent in Italian. It might surprise you to learn that Italian is also spoken in the African nation of Eritrea, which was a colony of Italy from 1880 until 1941. Most Eritreans nowadays speak Italian only as a second language. Italian is widely used in Albania, Monaco and France, and spoken by large communities of immigrants worldwide. This chapter is designed to help you on your adventures in the Italian-speaking world – so, as the Italians would say, *In bocca al lupo!* een bo·ka·*loo*·po (lit: in the mouth of the wolf) – good luck!

pronunciation

vowel sounds

Italian vowel sounds are generally shorter than those in English. They also tend not to run together to form vowel sound combinations (diphthongs), though it can often sound as if they do to English speakers.

symbol	english equivalent	italian example	transliteration
a	father	*pane*	*pa*·ne
ai	aisle	*mai*	mai
ay	say	*vorrei*	vo·*ray*
e	bet	*letto*	*le*·to
ee	see	*vino*	*vee*·no
o	pot	*molo*	*mo*·lo
oo	zoo	*frutta*	*froo*·ta
oy	toy	*poi*	poy
ow	how	*ciao, autobus*	chow, *ow*·to·boos

word stress

In Italian, you generally emphasise the second-last syllable of a word. When a written word has an accent marked on a vowel, though, the stress is on that syllable. The stressed syllable is always italicised in our pronunciation guides. The characteristic sing-song quality of an Italian sentence is created by pronouncing the syllables evenly and rhythmically, then swinging down on the last word.

consonant sounds

In addition to the sounds described on the next page, Italian consonants can also have a stronger, more emphatic pronunciation. The actual sounds are basically the same, though meaning can be altered between a normal consonant sound and this double consonant sound. The phonetic guides in this book don't distinguish between the two forms. Refer to the written Italian beside each phonetic guide as the cue –

if the word is written with a double consonant, use the stronger form. Even if you never distinguish them, you'll always be understood in context. Here are some examples where this 'double consonant' effect can make a difference:

sonno	*son·no*	**sleep**	*sono*	*so·no*	**I am**
pappa	*pap·pa*	**baby food**	*papa*	*pa·pa*	**pope**

symbol	english equivalent	italian example	transliteration
b	bed	*bello*	*be·lo*
ch	cheat	*centro*	*chen·tro*
d	dog	*denaro*	*de·na·ro*
dz	adds	*mezzo, zaino*	*me·dzo, dzai·no*
f	fat	*fare*	*fa·re*
g	go	*gomma*	*go·ma*
j	joke	*cugino*	*ku·jee·no*
k	kit	*cambio, quanto*	*kam·byo, kwan·to*
l	lot	*linea*	*lee·ne·a*
ly	million	*figlia*	*fee·lya*
m	man	*madre*	*ma·dre*
n	not	*numero*	*noo·me·ro*
ny	canyon	*bagno*	*ba·nyo*
p	pet	*pronto*	*pron·to*
r	red (stronger and rolled)	*ristorante*	*ree·sto·ran·te*
s	sun	*sera*	*se·ra*
sh	shot	*sciare*	*shya·re*
t	top	*teatro*	*te·a·tro*
ts	hits	*grazie, sicurezza*	*gra·tsye, see·koo·re·tsa*
v	very	*viaggio*	*vya·jo*
w	win	*uomo*	*wo·mo*
y	yes	*italiano*	*ee·ta·lya·no*
z	zero	*casa*	*ka·za*

tools

language difficulties

Do you speak English?
Parla inglese?   *par*·la een·*gle*·ze

Do you understand?
Capisce?   ka·*pee*·she

I (don't) understand.
(Non) capisco.   (non) ka·*pee*·sko

What does (giorno) mean?
Che cosa vuol dire (giorno)?   ke *ko*·za vwol *dee*·re (*jor*·no)

How do you ...?   *Come si ...?*   *ko*·me see ...
   pronounce this   *pronuncia questo*   pro·*noon*·cha *kwe*·sto
   write (arrivederci)   *scrive (arrivederci)*   *skree*·ve (a·ree·ve·*der*·chee)

Could you please ...?   *Può ... per favore?*   pwo ... per fa·*vo*·re
   repeat that   *ripeterlo*   ree·*pe*·ter·lo
   speak more   *parlare più*   par·*la*·re pyoo
   slowly   *lentamente*   len·ta·*men*·te
   write it down   *scriverlo*   *skree*·ver·lo

essentials

Yes.	*Sì.*	see
No.	*No.*	no
Please.	*Per favore.*	per fa·*vo*·re
Thank you (very much).	*Grazie (mille).*	*gra*·tsye (*mee*·le)
You're welcome.	*Prego.*	*pre*·go
Excuse me.	*Mi scusi.* pol	mee *skoo*·zee
	Scusami. inf	*skoo*·za·mee
Sorry.	*Mi dispiace.*	mee dees·*pya*·che

numbers

0	zero	dze·ro	16	sedici	se·dee·chee
1	uno	oo·no	17	diciassette	dee·cha·se·te
2	due	doo·e	18	diciotto	dee·cho·to
3	tre	tre	19	diciannove	dee·cha·no·ve
4	quattro	kwa·tro	20	venti	ven·tee
5	cinque	cheen·kwe	21	ventuno	ven·too·no
6	sei	say	22	ventidue	ven·tee·doo·e
7	sette	se·te	30	trenta	tren·ta
8	otto	o·to	40	quaranta	kwa·ran·ta
9	nove	no·ve	50	cinquanta	cheen·kwan·ta
10	dieci	dye·chee	60	sessanta	se·san·ta
11	undici	oon·dee·chee	70	settanta	se·tan·ta
12	dodici	do·dee·chee	80	ottanta	o·tan·ta
13	tredici	tre·dee·chee	90	novanta	no·van·ta
14	quattordici	kwa·tor·dee·chee	100	cento	chen·to
15	quindici	kween·dee·chee	1000	mille	mee·le

time & dates

What time is it?	Che ora è?	ke o·ra e
It's one o'clock.	È l'una.	e loo·na
It's (two) o'clock.	Sono le (due).	so·no le (doo·e)
Quarter past (one).	(L'una) e un quarto.	(loo·na) e oon kwar·to
Half past (one).	(L'una) e mezza.	(loo·na) e me·dza
Quarter to (eight).	(Le otto) meno un quarto.	(le o·to) me·no oon kwar·to
At what time ...?	A che ora ...?	a ke o·ra ...
At ...	Alle ...	a·le ...
am	di mattina	dee ma·tee·na
pm	di pomeriggio	dee po·me·ree·jo
Monday	lunedì	loo·ne·dee
Tuesday	martedì	mar·te·dee
Wednesday	mercoledì	mer·ko·le·dee
Thursday	giovedì	jo·ve·dee
Friday	venerdì	ve·ner·dee
Saturday	sabato	sa·ba·to
Sunday	domenica	do·me·nee·ka

tools – ITALIAN

January	gennaio	je·na·yo
February	febbraio	fe·bra·yo
March	marzo	mar·tso
April	aprile	a·pree·le
May	maggio	ma·jo
June	giugno	joo·nyo
July	luglio	loo·lyo
August	agosto	a·gos·to
September	settembre	se·tem·bre
October	ottobre	o·to·bre
November	novembre	no·vem·bre
December	dicembre	dee·chem·bre

What date is it today?
Che giorno è oggi?   ke *jor*·no e *o*·jee

It's (15 December).
È (il quindici) dicembre.   e (eel *kween*·dee·chee) dee·*chem*·bre

| since (May) | da (maggio) | da (ma·jo) |
| until (June) | fino a (giugno) | fee·no a (joo·nyo) |

yesterday	ieri	ye·ree
today	oggi	o·jee
tonight	stasera	sta·se·ra
tomorrow	domani	do·ma·nee

last ...

night	ieri notte	ye·ree no·te
week	la settimana scorsa	la se·tee·ma·na skor·sa
month	il mese scorso	eel me·ze skor·so
year	l'anno scorso	la·no skor·so

next ...

week	la settimana prossima	la se·tee·ma·na pro·see·ma
month	il mese prossimo	eel me·ze pro·see·mo
year	l'anno prossimo	la·no pro·see·mo

yesterday/tomorrow ...   *ieri/domani ...*   ye·ree/do·ma·nee ...

morning	mattina	ma·tee·na
afternoon	pomeriggio	po·me·ree·jo
evening	sera	se·ra

weather

What's the weather like?	*Che tempo fa?*	ke *tem*·po fa
It's ...		
cloudy	*È nuvoloso.*	e noo·vo·*lo*·zo
cold	*Fa freddo.*	fa *fre*·do
hot	*Fa caldo.*	fa *kal*·do
raining	*Piove.*	*pyo*·ve
snowing	*Nevica.*	ne·*vee*·ka
sunny	*È soleggiato.*	e so·le·*ja*·to
warm	*Fa bel tempo.*	fa bel *tem*·po
windy	*Tira vento.*	*tee*·ra *ven*·to
spring	*primavera* f	pree·ma·*ve*·ra
summer	*estate* f	es·*ta*·te
autumn	*autunno* m	ow·*too*·no
winter	*inverno* m	een·*ver*·no

border crossing

I'm here ...	*Sono qui ...*	*so*·no kwee ...
in transit	*in transito*	een *tran*·see·to
on business	*per affari*	per a·*fa*·ree
on holiday	*in vacanza*	een va·*kan*·tsa
I'm here for ...	*Sono qui per ...*	*so*·no kwee per ...
(10) days	*(dieci) giorni*	*(dye*·chee) *jor*·nee
(three) weeks	*(tre) settimane*	(tre) se·tee·*ma*·ne
(two) months	*(due) mesi*	*(doo*·e) *me*·zee

I'm going to (Perugia).
Vado a (Perugia). va·do a (pe·*roo*·ja)

I'm staying at the (Minerva Hotel).
Alloggio al (Minerva). a·*lo*·jo al (mee·*ner*·va)

I have nothing to declare.
Non ho niente da dichiarare. non o *nyen*·te da dee·kya·*ra*·re

I have something to declare.
Ho delle cose da dichiarare. o *de*·le *ko*·ze da dee·kya·*ra*·re

That's (not) mine.
(Non) è mio/mia. m/f (non) e *mee*·o/*mee*·a

transport

tickets & luggage

Where can I buy a ticket?
Dove posso comprare un biglietto?   do·ve po·so kom·pra·re oon bee·lye·to

Do I need to book a seat?
Bisogna prenotare un posto?   bee·zo·nya pre·no·ta·re oon pos·to

One ... ticket	*Un biglietto ... (per*	oon bee·*lye*·to ... (per
(to Rome), please.	*Roma), per favore.*	*ro*·ma) per fa·*vo*·re
one-way	*di sola andata*	dee *so*·la an·*da*·ta
return	*di andata e ritorno*	dee an·*da*·ta e ree·*tor*·no
I'd like to ... my	*Vorrei ... il mio*	vo·*ray* ... eel *mee*·o
ticket, please.	*biglietto, per favore.*	bee·*lye*·to per fa·*vo*·re
cancel	*cancellare*	kan·che·*la*·re
change	*cambiare*	kam·*bya*·re
collect	*ritirare*	ree·tee·*ra*·re
confirm	*confermare*	kon·fer·*ma*·re
I'd like a ... seat,	*Vorrei un posto ...,*	vo·*ray* oon *pos*·to ...
please.	*per favore.*	per fa·*vo*·re
nonsmoking	*per non fumatori*	per non foo·ma·*to*·ree
smoking	*per fumatori*	per foo·ma·*to*·ree

How much is it?
Quant'è?   kwan·te

Is there air conditioning?
C'è l'aria condizionata?   che *la*·rya kon·dee·tsyo·*na*·ta

Is there a toilet?
C'è un gabinetto?   che oon ga·bee·*ne*·to

How long does the trip take?
Quanto ci vuole?   kwan·to chee *vwo*·le

Is it a direct route?
È un itinerario diretto?   e oo·nee·tee·ne·*ra*·ryo dee·*re*·to

I'd like a luggage locker.
Vorrei un armadietto per il bagaglio.   vo·*ray* oon ar·ma·*dye*·to per eel ba·*ga*·lyo

My luggage	Il mio bagaglio	eel *mee*·o ba·*ga*·lyo
has been ...	è stato ...	e *sta*·to ...
damaged	danneggiato	da·ne·*ja*·to
lost	perso	*per*·so
stolen	rubato	roo·*ba*·to

getting around

Where does flight (004) arrive?
Dove arriva il volo (004)?   do·ve a·*ree*·va eel *vo*·lo (*dze*·ro *dze*·ro *kwa*·tro)

Where does flight (004) depart?
Da dove parte il volo (004)?   da *do*·ve *par*·te eel *vo*·lo (*dze*·ro *dze*·ro *kwa*·tro)

Where's the ...?	Dove sono ...?	*do*·ve *so*·no ...
arrivalls hall	gli arrivi	lyee a·*ree*·vee
departures hall	le partenze	le par·*ten*·dze

Is this the ...	È questo/questa ...	e *kwes*·to/*kwes*·ta ...
to (Venice)? m/f	per (Venezia)? m/f	per (ve·*ne*·tsya)
boat	la nave f	la *na*·ve
bus	l'autobus m	*low*·to·boos
plane	l'aereo m	la·*e*·re·o
train	il treno m	eel *tre*·no

What time's	A che ora passa	a ke *o*·ra *pa*·sa
the ... bus?	... autobus?	... *ow*·to·boos
first	il primo	eel *pree*·mo
last	l'ultimo	*lool*·tee·mo
next	il prossimo	eel *pro*·see·mo

At what time does it arrive/leave?
A che ora arriva/parte?   a ke *o*·ra a·*ree*·va/*par*·te

How long will it be delayed?
Di quanto ritarderà?   dee *kwan*·to ree·tar·de·*ra*

What station/stop is this?
Che stazione/fermata è questa?   ke sta·*tsyo*·ne/fer·*ma*·ta e *kwe*·sta

What's the next station/stop?
Qual'è la prossima stazione/   kwa·*le* la *pro*·see·ma sta·*tsyo*·ne/
fermata?   fer·*ma*·ta

Does it stop at (Milan)?
Si ferma a (Milano)?   see *fer*·ma a (mee·*la*·no)

Please tell me when we get to (Taranto).
Mi dica per favore quando   mee *dee*·ka per fa·*vo*·re *kwan*·do
arriviamo a (Taranto).   a·ree·*vya*·mo a (ta·*ran*·to)

How long do we stop here?
Per quanto tempo ci fermiamo qui?   per *kwan*·to *tem*·po chee fer·*mya*·mo kwee

Is this seat available?
È libero questo posto?   e *lee*·be·ro *kwe*·sto *pos*·to

That's my seat.
Quel posto è mio.   kwel *pos*·to e *mee*·o

I'd like a taxi ...	*Vorrei un tassì ...*	vo·*ray* oon ta·*see* ...
at (9am)	*alle (nove*	*a*·le (*no*·ve
	di mattina)	dee ma·*tee*·na)
now	*adesso*	a·*de*·so
tomorrow	*domani*	do·*ma*·nee

Is this taxi available?
È libero questo tassi?   e *lee*·be·ro *kwe*·sto ta·*see*

How much is it to ...?
Quant'è per ...?   kwan·*te* per ...

Please put the meter on.
Usi il tassametro, per favore.   *oo*·zee eel ta·sa·*me*·tro per fa·*vo*·re

Please take me to (this address).
Mi porti a (questo indirizzo),   mee *por*·tee a (*kwe*·sto een·dee·*ree*·tso)
per piacere.   per pya·*che*·re

Please ...	*..., per favore.*	... per fa·*vo*·re
slow down	*Rallenti*	ra·*len*·tee
stop here	*Si fermi qui*	see *fer*·mee kwee
wait here	*Mi aspetti qui*	mee as·*pe*·tee kwee

car, motorbike & bicycle hire

I'd like to hire a/an ...	*Vorrei noleggiare ...*	vo·*ray* no·le·*ja*·re ...
bicycle	*una bicicletta*	*oo*·na bee·chee·*kle*·ta
car	*una macchina*	*oo*·na *ma*·kee·na
motorbike	*una moto*	*oo*·na *mo*·to
with ...	*con ...*	kon ...
a driver	*un'autista*	oo·now·*tee*·sta
air conditioning	*aria condizionata*	*a*·rya kon·dee·tsyo·*na*·ta

How much for … hire?	Quanto costa …?	kwan·to kos·ta …
hourly	all'ora	a·lo·ra
daily	al giorno	al jor·no
weekly	alla settimana	a·la se·tee·ma·na

air	aria f	a·rya
oil	olio m	o·lyo
petrol	benzina f	ben·dzee·na
tyres	gomme f pl	go·me

I need a mechanic.
  Ho bisogno di un meccanico.   o bee·zo·nyo dee oon me·ka·nee·ko

I've run out of petrol.
  Ho esaurito la benzina.   o e·zow·ree·to la ben·dzee·na

I have a flat tyre.
  Ho una gomma bucata.   o oo·na go·ma boo·ka·ta

directions

Where's the …?	Dov'è …?	do·ve …
bank	la banca	la ban·ka
city centre	il centro città	eel chen·tro chee·ta
hotel	l'albergo	lal·ber·go
market	il mercato	eel mer·ka·to
police station	il posto di polizia	eel pos·to dee po·lee·tsee·a
post office	l'ufficio postale	loo·fee·cho pos·ta·le
public toilet	il gabinetto pubblico	eel ga·bee·ne·to poo·blee·ko
tourist office	l'ufficio del turismo	loo·fee·cho del too·reez·mo

Is this the road to (Milan)?
  Questa strada porta a (Milano)?   kwe·sta stra·da por·ta a (mee·la·no)

Can you show me (on the map)?
  Può mostrarmi (sulla pianta)?   pwo mos·trar·mee (soo·la pyan·ta)

What's the address?
  Qual'è l'indirizzo?   kwa·le leen·dee·ree·tso

How far is it?
  Quant'è distante?   kwan·te dees·tan·te

How do I get there?
  Come ci si arriva?   ko·me chee see a·ree·va

Turn ...	Giri ...	jee·ree ...
at the corner	all'angolo	a·lan·go·lo
at the traffic lights	al semaforo	al se·ma·fo·ro
left/right	a sinistra/destra	a see·nee·stra/de·stra

It's ...	È...	e ...
behind ...	dietro ...	dye·tro ...
far away	lontano	lon·ta·no
here	qui	kwee
in front of ...	davanti a ...	da·van·tee a ...
left	a sinistra	a see·nee·stra
near (to ...)	vicino (a ...)	vee·chee·no (a ...)
next to ...	accanto a ...	a·kan·to a ...
on the corner	all'angolo	a·lan·go·lo
opposite ...	di fronte a ...	dee fron·te a ...
right	a destra	a de·stra
straight ahead	sempre diritto	sem·pre dee·ree·to
there	là	la

by bus	con l'autobus	kon low·to·boos
by taxi	con il tassì	ko·neel ta·see
by train	con il treno	ko·neel tre·no
on foot	a piedi	a pye·dee

north	nord m	nord
south	sud m	sood
east	est m	est
west	ovest m	o·vest

signs

Entrata/Uscita	en·tra·ta/oo·shee·ta	Entrance/Exit
Aperto/Chiuso	a·per·to/kyoo·zo	Open/Closed
Camere Libere	ka·me·re lee·be·re	Rooms Available
Completo	kom·ple·to	No Vacancies
Informazioni	een·for·ma·tsyo·nee	Information
Posto di Polizia	pos·to de po·lee·tsee·a	Police Station
Proibito	pro·ee·bee·to	Prohibited
Gabinetti	ga·bee·ne·tee	Toilets
Uomini	wo·mee·nee	Men
Donne	do·ne	Women
Caldo/Freddo	kal·do/fre·do	Hot/Cold

accommodation

finding accommodation

Where's a/an ...?	*Dov'è ...?*	do·ve ...
camping ground	*un campeggio*	oon kam·pe·jo
guesthouse	*una pensione*	oo·na pen·syo·ne
inn	*una locanda*	oo·na lo·kan·da
hotel	*un albergo*	oo·nal·ber·go
youth hostel	*un ostello della*	oo·nos·te·lo de·la
	gioventù	jo·ven·too
Can you recommend	*Può consigliare*	pwo kon·see·lya·re
somewhere ...?	*qualche posto ...?*	kwal·ke pos·to ...
cheap	*economico*	e·ko·no·mee·ko
good	*buono*	bwo·no
nearby	*vicino*	vee·chee·no

I'd like to book a room, please.
Vorrei prenotare una camera,   vo·ray pre·no·ta·re oo·na ka·me·ra
per favore.   per fa·vo·re

I have a reservation.
Ho una prenotazione.   o oo·na pre·no·ta·tsyo·ne

My name's ...
Mi chiamo ...   mee kya·mo ...

Do you have	*Avete una*	a·ve·te oo·na
a ... room?	*camera ...?*	ka·me·ra ...
single	*singola*	seen·go·la
double	*doppia con letto*	do·pya kon le·to
	matrimoniale	ma·tree·mo·nya·le
twin	*doppia a due letti*	do·pya a doo·e le·tee
How much is it per ...?	*Quanto costa per ...?*	kwan·to kos·ta per ...
night	*una notte*	oo·na no·te
person	*persona*	per·so·na
Can I pay by ...?	*Posso pagare con ...?*	po·so pa·ga·re kon ...
credit card	*la carta di credito*	la kar·ta dee kre·dee·to
travellers	*un assegno*	oo·na·se·nyo
cheque	*di viaggio*	dee vee·a·jo

I'd like to stay for (two) nights.
Vorrei rimanere (due) notti.   vo·ray ree·ma·ne·re (doo·e) no·tee

From (July 2) to (July 6).
Dal (due luglio) al (sei luglio).   dal (doo·e loo·lyo) al (say loo·lyo)

Can I see it?
Posso vederla?   po·so ve·der·la

Am I allowed to camp here?
Si può campeggiare qui?   see pwo kam·pe·ja·re kwee

Is there a camp site nearby?
C'è un campeggio qui vicino?   che oon kam·pe·jo kwee vee·chee·no

requests & queries

When's breakfast served?
A che ora è la prima colazione?   a ke o·ra e la pree·ma ko·la·tsyo·ne

Where's breakfast served?
Dove si prende la prima colazione?   do·ve see pren·de la pree·ma ko·la·tsyo·ne

Please wake me at (seven).
Mi svegli alle (sette), per favore.   mee sve·lyee a·le (se·te) per fa·vo·re

Could I have my key, please?
Posso avere la chiave, per favore?   po·so a·ve·re la kya·ve per fa·vo·re

Can I get another (blanket)?
Può darmi un altra (coperta)?   pwo dar·mee oo·nal·tra (ko·per·ta)

This (sheet) isn't clean.
Questo (lenzuolo) non è pulito.   kwe·sto (len·tzwo·lo) non e poo·lee·to

Is there a/an ...?	*C'è ...?*	che ...
elevator	*un ascensore*	oo·na·shen·so·re
safe	*una cassaforte*	oo·na ka·sa·for·te
The room is too ...	*La camera è troppo ...*	la ka·me·ra e tro·po ...
expensive	*cara*	ka·ra
noisy	*rumorosa*	roo·mo·ro·za
small	*piccola*	pee·ko·la
The ... doesn't work.	*... non funziona.*	... non foon·tsyo·na
air conditioning	*L'aria condizionata*	la·rya kon·dee·tsyo·na·ta
fan	*Il ventilatore*	eel ven·tee·la·to·re
toilet	*Il gabinetto*	eel ga·bee·ne·to

4

checking out

What time is checkout?
A che ora si deve lasciar   a ke o·*ra* see *de*·ve la·*shar*
libera la camera?   *lee*·be·ra la *ka*·me·ra

Can I leave my luggage here?
Posso lasciare ili mio bagaglio qui?   po·so la·*sha*·re eel *mee*·o ba·*ga*·lyo kwee

Could I have my ..., please?	*Posso avere ..., per favore?*	po·so a·*ve*·re ... per fa·*vo*·re
deposit	*la caparra*	la ka·*pa*·ra
passport	*il mio passaporto*	eel *mee*·o pa·sa·*por*·to
valuables	*i miei oggetti di valore*	ee myay o·*je*·tee dee va·*lo*·re

communications & banking

the internet

Where's the local Internet café?
Dove si trova l'Internet point?   *do*·ve see *tro*·va *leen*·ter·net poynt

How much is it per hour?
Quanto costa all'ora?   *kwan*·to *kos*·ta a·*lo*·ra

I'd like to ...	*Vorrei ...*	vo·*ray* ...
check my email	*controllare le mie email*	kon·tro·*la*·re le *mee*·e e·*mayl*
get Internet access	*usare Internet*	oo·*za*·re *een*·ter·net
use a printer	*usare una stampante*	oo·*za*·re *oo*·na stam·*pan*·te
use a scanner	*scandire*	skan·*dee*·re

mobile/cell phone

I'd like a ...	*Vorrei ...*	vo·*ray* ...
mobile/cell phone for hire	*un cellulare da noleggiare*	oon che·loo·*la*·re da no·le·*ja*·re
SIM card for your network	*un SIM card per la rete telefonica*	oon seem kard per la *re*·te te·le·*fo*·nee·ka

What are the rates?
Quali sono le tariffe?   *kwa*·lee *so*·no le ta·*ree*·fe

telephone

What's your phone number?
Qual'è il Suo/tuo numero
di telefono? pol/inf

kwa-*le* eel soo-o/*too*-o *noo*-me-ro
dee te-*le*-fo-no

The number is ...
Il numero è ...

eel *noo*-me-ro e ...

Where's the nearest public phone?
Dov'è il telefono pubblico
più vicino?

do-*ve* eel te-*le*-fo-no *poo*-blee-ko
pyoo vee-*chee*-no

I'd like to buy a phonecard.
Vorrei comprare una
scheda telefonica.

vo-*ray* kom-*pra*-re *oo*-na
ske-da te-le-*fo*-nee-ka

I want to ...	Vorrei ...	vo-*ray* ...
call (Singapore)	fare una chiamata	*fa*-re *oo*-na kya-*ma*-ta
	a (Singapore)	a (seen-ga-*po*-re)
make a local call	fare una chiamata	*fa*-re *oo*-na kya-*ma*-ta
	locale	lo-*ka*-le
reverse the charges	fare una chiamata a	*fa*-re *oo*-na kya-*ma*-ta a
	carico del destinatario	ka-*ree*-ko del des-tee-na-*ta*-ryo

How much does ... cost?	Quanto costa ...?	*kwan*-to *kos*-ta ...
a (three)-minute	una telefonata	*oo*-na te-le-fo-*na*-ta
call	di (tre) minuti	dee (tre) mee-*noo*-tee
each extra minute	ogni minuto in più	*o*-nyee mee-*noo*-to een pyoo

It's (one euro) per (minute).
(Un euro) per (un minuto).

(oon e-*oo*-ro) per (oon mee-*noo*-to)

post office

I want to send a ...	Vorrei mandare ...	vo-*ray* man-*da*-re ...
fax	un fax	oon faks
letter	una lettera	*oo*-na *le*-te-ra
parcel	un pacchetto	oon pa-*ke*-to
postcard	una cartolina	*oo*-na kar-to-*lee*-na

I want to buy ...	Vorrei comprare ...	vo-*ray* kom-*pra*-re ...
an envelope	una busta	*oo*-na *boo*-sta
stamps	dei francobolli	day fran-ko-*bo*-lee

Please send it (to Australia) by ...	Lo mandi ... (in Australia), per favore.	lo man·dee ... (een ow·stra·lya) per fa·vo·re
airmail	via aerea	vee·a a·e·re·a
express mail	posta prioritaria	pos·ta pryo·ree·ta·rya
registered mail	posta raccomandata	pos·ta ra·ko·man·da·ta
surface mail	posta ordinaria	pos·ta or·dee·na·rya
Is there any mail for me?	C'è posta per me?	che pos·ta per me

bank

Where's a/an ...?	Dov'è ... più vicino?	do·ve ... pyoo vee·chee·no
ATM	il Bancomat	eel ban·ko·mat
foreign exchange office	il cambio	eel kam·byo
I'd like to ...	Vorrei ...	vo·ray ...
Where can I ...?	Dove posso ...?	do·ve po·so ...
arrange a transfer	trasferire soldi	tras·fe·ree·re sol·dee
cash a cheque	riscuotere un assegno	ree·skwo·te·re oo·na·se·nyo
change a travellers cheque	cambiare un assegno di viaggio	kam·bya·re oo·na·se·nyo dee vee·a·jo
change money	cambiare denaro	kam·bya·re de·na·ro
get a cash advance	prelevare con carta di credito	pre·le·va·re kon kar·ta dee kre·dee·to
withdraw money	fare un prelievo	fa·re oon pre·lye·vo
What's the ...?	Quant'è ...?	kwan·te ...
commission	la commissione	la ko·mee·syo·ne
exchange rate	il cambio	eel kam·byo
It's ...	È ...	e ...
(12) euros	(dodici) euro	(do·dee·chee) e·oo·ro
free	gratuito	gra·too·ee·to

What's the charge for that?
Quanto costa?   kwan·to kos·ta

What time does the bank open?
A che ora apre la banca?   a ke o·ra a·pre la ban·ka

Has my money arrived yet?
È arrivato il mio denaro?   e a·ree·va·to eel mee·o de·na·ro

sightseeing

getting in

What time does it open/close?
A che ora apre/chiude? — a ke *o*·ra *a*·pre/*kyoo*·de

What's the admission charge?
Quant'è il prezzo d'ingresso? — kwan·*te* eel *pre*·tso deen·*gre*·so

Is there a discount for children/students?
C'è uno sconto per — che *oo*·no *skon*·to per
bambini/studenti? — bam·*bee*·nee/stoo·*den*·tee

I'd like a ...	*Vorrei* ...	vo·*ray* ...
catalogue	*un catalogo*	oon ka·*ta*·lo·go
guide	*una guida*	*oo*·na *gwee*·da
local map	*una cartina*	*oo*·na kar·*tee*·na
	della zona	de·la *dzo*·na

I'd like to see ...	*Vorrei vedere* ...	vo·*ray* ve·*de*·re ...
What's that?	*Cos'è?*	ko·*ze*
Can I take a photo?	*Posso fare una foto?*	*po*·so *fa*·re *oo*·na *fo*·to

tours

When's the next ...?	*A che ora parte la prossima ...?*	a ke *o*·ra *par*·te la *pro*·see·ma ...
day trip	*escursione in giornata*	es·koor·*syo*·ne een jor·*na*·ta
tour	*gita turistica*	*jee*·ta too·*ree*·stee·ka

Is ... included?	*È incluso ...?*	e een·*kloo*·zo ...
accommodation	*l'alloggio*	la·*lo*·jo
the admission charge	*il prezzo d'ingresso*	eel *pre*·tso deen·*gre*·so
food	*il vitto*	eel *vee*·to
transport	*il trasporto*	eel tras·*por*·to

How long is the tour?
Quanto dura la gita? — *kwan*·to *doo*·ra la *jee*·ta

What time should we be back?
A che ora dovremmo ritornare? — a ke *o*·ra dov·*re*·mo ree·tor·*na*·re

sightseeing

castle	*castello* m	kas-*te*-lo
cathedral	*duomo* m	*dwo*-mo
church	*chiesa* f	*kye*-za
main square	*piazza principale* f	*pya*-tsa preen-chee-*pa*-le
monastery	*monastero* m	mo-nas-*te*-ro
monument	*monumento* m	mo-noo-*men*-to
museum	*museo* m	moo-*ze*-o
old city	*centro storico* m	*chen*-tro *sto*-ree-ko
palace	*palazzo* m	pa-*la*-tso
ruins	*rovine* f pl	ro-*vee*-ne
stadium	*stadio* m	*sta*-dyo
statues	*statue* f pl	*sta*-too-e

shopping

enquiries

Where's a ... ?	*Dov'è ... ?*	do-*ve* ...
bank	*la banca*	la *ban*-ka
bookshop	*la libreria*	la lee-bre-*ree*-a
camera shop	*il fotografo*	eel fo-*to*-gra-fo
department store	*il grande magazzino*	eel *gran*-de ma-ga-*dzee*-no
grocery store	*la drogheria*	la dro-ge-*ree*-a
market	*il mercato*	eel mer-*ka*-to
newsagency	*l'edicola*	le-*dee*-ko-la
supermarket	*il supermercato*	eel soo-per-mer-*ka*-to

Where can I buy (a padlock)?
Dove posso comprare (un lucchetto)?   do-ve *po*-so kom-*pra*-re (oon loo-*ke*-to)

I'm looking for ...
Sto cercando ...   sto cher-*kan*-do ...

Can I look at it?
Posso dare un'occhiata?   po·so da·re oo·no·kya·ta

Do you have any others?
Ne avete altri?   ne a·ve·te al·tree

Does it have a guarantee?
Ha la garanzia?   a la ga·ran·tsee·a

Can I have it sent overseas?
Può spedirlo all'estero?   pwo spe·deer·lo a·les·te·ro

Can I have my ... repaired?
Posso far aggiustare ... qui?   po·so far a·joo·sta·re ... kwee

It's faulty.
È difettoso.   e dee·fe·to·zo

I'd like (a) ..., please.	*Vorrei ..., per favore.*	vo·ray ... per fa·vo·re
bag	*un sacchetto*	oon sa·ke·to
refund	*un rimborso*	oon reem·bor·so
to return this	*restituire questo*	res·tee·twee·re kwe·sto

paying

How much is it?
Quant'è?   kwan·te

Can you write down the price?
Può scrivere il prezzo?   pwo skree·ve·re eel pre·tso

That's too expensive.
È troppo caro.   e tro·po ka·ro

Can you lower the price?
Può farmi lo sconto?   pwo far·mee lo skon·to

I'll give you (five) euros.
Le offro (cinque) euro.   le o·fro (cheen·kwe) e·oo·ro

There's a mistake in the bill.
C'è un errore nel conto.   che oon e·ro·re nel kon·to

Do you accept ...?	*Accettate ...?*	a·che·ta·te ...
credit cards	*la carta di credito*	la kar·ta dee kre·dee·to
debit cards	*la carta di debito*	la kar·ta dee de·bee·to
travellers cheques	*gli assegni di viaggio*	lyee a·se·nyee dee vee·a·jo

I'd like …, please.	Vorrei …, per favore.	vo·ray … per fa·vo·re
a receipt	una ricevuta	oo·na ree·che·voo·ta
my change	il mio resto	eel mee·o res·to

clothes & shoes

Can I try it on?	Potrei provarmelo?	po·tray pro·var·me·lo
My size is (40).	Sono una taglia (quaranta).	so·no oo·na ta·lya (kwa·ran·ta)
It doesn't fit.	Non va bene.	non va be·ne
small	piccola	pee·ko·la
medium	media	me·dya
large	forte	for·te

books & music

I'd like a …	Vorrei …	vo·ray …
newspaper	un giornale	oon jor·na·le
(in English)	(in inglese)	(een een·gle·ze)
pen	una penna	oo·na pe·na

Is there an English-language bookshop?

| C'è una libreria specializzata | che oo·na lee·bre·ree·a spe·cha·lee·dza·ta |
| in lingua inglese? | een leen·gwa een·gle·ze |

I'm looking for something by (Alberto Moravia).

| Sto cercando qualcosa di | sto cher·kan·do kwal·ko·za dee |
| (Alberto Moravia). | (al·ber·to mo·ra·vee·a) |

Can I listen to this?

| Potrei ascoltarlo? | po·tray as·kol·tar·lo |

photography

Can you …?	Potrebbe …?	po·tre·be …
burn a CD from	masterizzare un	mas·te·ree·tsa·re oon
my memory card	CD dalla mia	chee dee da·la mee·a
	memory card	me·mo·ree kard
develop this	sviluppare	svee·loo·pa·re
film	questo rullino	kwe·sto roo·lee·no
load my film	inserire il	een·se·ree·re eel
	mio rullino	mee·o roo·lee·no

I need a/an ... film for this camera.	Vorrei un rullino ... per questa macchina fotografica.	vo-ray oon roo-lee-no ... per kwe-sta ma-kee-na fo-to-gra-fee-ka
APS	da APS	da a-pee-e-se
B&W	in bianco e nero	een byan-ko e ne-ro
colour	a colori	a ko-lo-ree
slide	per diapositive	per dee-a-po-zee-tee-ve
(200) speed	da (duecento) ASA	da (doo-e chen-to) a-za
When will it be ready?	Quando sarà pronto?	kwan-do sa-ra pron-to

meeting people

greetings, goodbyes & introductions

Hello.	Buongiorno.	bwon-jor-no
Hi.	Ciao.	chow
Good night.	Buonanotte.	bwo-na-no-te
Goodbye.	Arrivederci.	a-ree-ve-der-chee
Bye.	Ciao.	chow
See you later.	A più tardi.	a pyoo tar-dee
Mr	Signore	see-nyo-re
Mrs	Signora	see-nyo-ra
Miss	Signorina	see-nyo-ree-na
How are you?	Come sta? pol	ko-me sta
	Come stai? inf	ko-me stai
Fine. And you?	Bene. E Lei? pol	be-ne e lay
	Bene. E tu? inf	be-ne e too
What's your name?	Come si chiama? pol	ko-me see kya-ma
	Come ti chiami? inf	ko-me tee kya-mee
My name is ...	Mi chiamo ...	mee kya-mo ...
I'm pleased to meet you.	Piacere.	pya-che-re

This is my ...	Le/Ti presento ... pol/inf	le/tee pre·zen·to ...
boyfriend	mio ragazzo	mee·o ra·ga·tso
brother	mio fratello	mee·o fra·te·lo
daughter	mia figlia	mee·a fee·lya
father	mio padre	mee·o pa·dre
friend	il mio amico m	eel mee·o a·mee·ko
	la mia amica f	la mee·a a·mee·ka
girlfriend	mia ragazza	mee·a ra·ga·tsa
husband	mio marito	mee·o ma·ree·to
mother	mia madre	mee·a ma·dre
partner (intimate)	il mio compagno m	eel mee·o kom·pa·nyo
	la mia compagna f	la mee·a kom·pa·nya
sister	mia sorella	mee·a so·re·la
son	mio figlio	mee·o fee·lyo
wife	mia moglie	mee·a mo·lye

Here's my ...	Ecco il mio ...	e·ko eel mee·o ...
What's your ...?	Qual'è il	kwa·le eel
	Suo/tuo ...? pol/inf	soo·o/too·o ...
address	indirizzo	een·dee·ree·tso
email address	indirizzo di email	een·dee·ree·tso dee e·mayl
fax number	numero di fax	noo·me·ro dee faks
phone number	numero di telefono	noo·me·ro dee te·le·fo·no

occupations

What's your occupation?	Che lavoro fa/fai? pol/inf	ke la·vo·ro fa/fai
I'm a/an ...	Sono ...	so·no ...
artist	artista m&f	ar·tees·ta
business person	uomo/donna	wo·mo/do·na
	d'affari m/f	da·fa·ree
farmer	agricoltore m	a·gree·kol·to·re
	agricoltrice f	a·gree·kol·tree·che
manual worker	manovale m&f	ma·no·va·le
office worker	impiegato/a m/f	eem·pye·ga·to/a
scientist	scienziato/a m/f	shen·tsee·a·to/a
student	studente m	stoo·den·te
	studentessa f	stoo·den·te·sa
tradesperson	operaio/a m/f	o·pe·ra·yo/a

background

Where are you from?	Da dove viene/vieni? pol/inf	da do·ve vye·ne/vye·nee
I'm from ...	Vengo ...	ven·go ...
Australia	dall'Australia	dal·ow·stra·lya
Canada	dal Canada	dal ka·na·da
England	dall'Inghilterra	da·leen·geel·te·ra
New Zealand	dalla Nuova Zelanda	da·la nwo·va ze·lan·da
the USA	dagli Stati Uniti	da·lyee sta·tee oo·nee·tee
Are you married?	È sposato/a? m/f pol	e spo·za·to/a
	Sei sposato/a? m/f inf	say spo·za·to/a
I'm married.	Sono sposato/a. m/f	so·no spo·za·to/a
I'm single.	Sono celibe/nubile. m/f	che·lee·be/noo·bee·le

age

How old ...?	Quanti anni ...?	kwan·tee a·nee ...
are you	ha/hai pol/inf	a/ai
is your daughter	ha Sua/tua	a soo·a/too·a
	figlia pol/inf	fee·lya
is your son	ha Suo/tuo	a soo·o/too·o
	figlio pol/inf	fee·lyo
I'm ... years old.	Ho ... anni.	o ... a·nee
He/She is ... years old.	Ha ... anni.	a ... a·nee

feelings

I'm (not) ...	(Non) Ho ...	(non) o ...
Are you ...?	Ha/Hai ...? pol/inf	a/ai ...
cold	freddo	fre·do
hot	caldo	kal·do
hungry	fame	fa·me
thirsty	sete	se·te
I'm (not) ...	(Non) Sono ...	(non) so·no ...
Are you ...?	È/Sei ...? pol/inf	e/say ...
happy	felice	fe·lee·che
sad	triste	tree·ste

entertainment

going out

Where can I find ...?	Dove sono ...?	do·ve so·no ...
clubs	dei clubs	day kloob
gay venues	dei locali gay	day lo·ka·lee ge
pubs	dei pub	day pab
I feel like going to a/the ...	Ho voglia d'andare ...	o vo·lya dan·da·re ...
concert	a un concerto	a oon kon·cher·to
movies	al cinema	al chee·nee·ma
party	a una festa	a oo·na fes·ta
restaurant	in un ristorante	een oon rees·to·ran·te
theatre	a teatro	a te·a·tro

interests

Do you like ...?	Ti piace/ piacciono ...? sg/pl	tee pya·che/ pya·cho·no ...
I (don't) like ...	(Non) Mi piace/ piacciono ... sg/pl	(non) mee pya·che/ pya·cho·no ...
art	l'arte sg	lar·te
cooking	cucinare sg	koo·chee·na·re
movies	i film pl	ee feelm
nightclubs	le discoteche pl	le dees·ko·te·ke
reading	leggere sg	le·je·re
shopping	lo shopping sg	lo sho·ping
sport	lo sport sg	lo sport
travelling	viaggiare sg	vee·a·ja·re
Do you like to ...?	Ti piace ...?	tee pya·che ...
dance	ballare	ba·la·re
go to concerts	andare ai concerti	an·da·re ai kon·cher·tee
listen to music	ascoltare la musica	as·kol·ta·re la moo·zee·ka

food & drink

finding a place to eat

Can you recommend a ...?	Potrebbe consigliare un ...?	po·*tre*·be kon·see·*lya*·re oon ...
bar	locale	lo·*ka*·le
café	bar	bar
restaurant	ristorante	rees·to·*ran*·te
I'd like ..., please.	Vorrei ..., per favore.	vo·*ray* ... per fa·*vo*·re
a table for (four)	un tavolo per (quattro)	oon *ta*·vo·lo per (*kwa*·tro)
the (non)smoking section	(non) fumatori	(non) foo·ma·*to*·ree

ordering food

breakfast	prima colazione f	*pree*·ma ko·la·*tsyo*·ne
lunch	pranzo m	*pran*·dzo
dinner	cena f	*che*·na
snack	spuntino m	spoon·*tee*·no

What would you recommend?
Cosa mi consiglia?   *ko*·za mee kon·*see*·lya

I'd like (the) ..., please.	Vorrei ..., per favore.	vo·*ray* ... per fa·*vo*·re
bill	il conto	eel *kon*·to
drink list	la lista delle bevande	la *lee*·sta *de*·le be·*van*·de
menu	il menù	eel me·*noo*
that dish	questo piatto	*kwe*·sto *pya*·to

drinks

(cup of) coffee ...	(un) caffè ...	(oon) ka·fe ...
(cup of) tea ...	(un) tè ...	(oon) te ...
with milk	con latte	kon la·te
without sugar	senza zucchero	sen·tsa tsoo·ke·ro
orange juice (bottled)	succo d'arancia m	soo·ko da·ran·cha
orange juice (fresh)	spremuta d'arancia f	spre·moo·ta da·ran·cha
soft drink	bibita f	bee·bee·ta
... water	acqua ...	a·kwa ...
boiled	bollita	bo·lee·ta
mineral	minerale	mee·ne·ra·le
sparkling mineral	frizzante	free·tsan·te
still mineral	naturale	na·too·ra·le

in the bar

I'll have ...	Prendo ...	pren·do ...
I'll buy you a drink.	Ti offro da bere. inf	tee of·ro da be·re
What would you like?	Cosa prendi?	ko·za pren·dee
Cheers!	Salute!	sa·loo·te
brandy	cognac m	ko·nyak
champagne	champagne m	sham·pa·nye
cocktail	cocktail m	kok·tayl
a shot of (whisky)	un sorso di (whisky)	oon sor·so dee (wee·skee)
a ... of beer	... di birra	... dee bee·ra
bottle	una bottiglia	oo·na bo·tee·lya
glass	un bicchiere	oon bee·kye·re
a bottle of ...	una bottiglia di	oo·na bo·tee·lya dee
wine	vino ...	vee·no ...
a glass of ...	un bicchiere di	oon bee·kye·re dee
wine	vino ...	vee·no ...
red	rosso	ro·so
sparkling	spumante	spoo·man·te
white	bianco	byan·ko

food & drink – ITALIAN

197

self-catering

What's the local speciality?
   Qual'è la specialità   kwa·*le* la spe·cha·lee·*ta*
   di questa regione?   dee *kwe*·sta re·*jo*·ne

What's that?
   Cos'è?   ko·*ze*

How much is (a kilo of cheese)?
   Quanto costa (un chilo   *kwan*·to *kos*·ta (oon *kee*·lo
   di formaggio)?   dee for·*ma*·jo)

I'd like ...	*Vorrei ...*	vo·*ray* ...
100 grams	*un etto*	oo·*ne*·to
(two) kilos	*(due) chili*	(*doo*·e) *kee*·lee
(three) pieces	*(tre) pezzi*	(tre) *pe*·tsee
(six) slices	*(sei) fette*	(say) *fe*·te
Less.	*Meno.*	*me*·no
Enough.	*Basta.*	*bas*·ta
More.	*Più.*	pyoo

special diets & allergies

Is there a vegetarian restaurant near here?
   C'è un ristorante vegetariano   che oon rees·to·*ran*·te ve·je·ta·*rya*·no
   qui vicino?   kwee vee·*chee*·no

Do you have vegetarian food?
   Avete piatti vegetariani?   a·*ve*·te *pya*·tee ve·je·ta·*rya*·nee

Could you prepare	*Potreste preparare*	po·*tres*·te pre·pa·*ra*·re
a meal without ...?	*un pasto senza ...?*	oon *pas*·to *sen*·tsa ...
butter	*burro*	*boo*·ro
eggs	*uova*	*wo*·va
meat stock	*brodo di carne*	*bro*·do de *kar*·ne
I'm allergic to ...	*Sono allergico/a ...* m/f	*so*·no a·*ler*·jee·ko/a ...
dairy produce	*ai latticini*	ai la·tee·*chee*·nee
gluten	*al glutine*	al *gloo*·tee·ne
MSG	*al glutammato*	al glu·ta·*ma*·to
	monosodico	mo·no·*so*·dee·ko
nuts	*alle noci*	*a*·le *no*·chee
seafood	*ai frutti di mare*	ai *froo*·tee dee *ma*·re

acciughe f pl	a-*choo*-ge	anchovies
arancini m pl	a-ran-*chee*-nee	rice balls stuffed with a meat mixture
babà m	ba-*ba*	dessert containing sultanas
baccalà m	ba-ka-*la*	dried salted cod
bagna cauda f	*ban*-ya *cow*-da	anchovy, olive oil & garlic dip
brioche m	bree-*osh*	breakfast pastry
bruschetta f	broos-*ke*-ta	toasted bread with olive oil & toppings
budino m	boo-*dee*-no	milk-based pudding
cacciucco m	ka-*choo*-ko	seafood stew with wine, garlic & herbs
cannelloni m pl	ka-ne-*lo*-nee	pasta stuffed with spinach, minced roast veal, ham, eggs, parmesan & spices
caponata f	ka-po-*na*-ta	eggplant with a tomato sauce
ciabatta f	cha-*ba*-ta	crisp, flat & long bread
conchiglie f pl	kon-*kee*-lye	pasta shells
costine f pl	kos-*tee*-ne	ribs
cozze f pl	*ko*-tse	mussels
crostata f	kro-*sta*-ta	fruit tart
crostini m pl	kro-*stee*-nee	bread toasted with savoury toppings
farinata f	fa-ree-*na*-ta	thin, flat bread made from chickpea flour
fettuccine f pl	fe-too-*chee*-ne	long ribbon-shaped pasta
focaccia f	fo-*ka*-cha	flat bread filled or topped with cheese, ham, vegetables & other ingredients
frittata f	free-*ta*-ta	thick omelette slice, served hot or cold
funghi m pl	*foon*-gee	mushrooms
gamberoni m pl	gam-be-*ro*-nee	prawns
gelato m	je-*la*-to	ice cream

gnocchi m pl	*nyo·kee*	*small (usually potato) dumplings*
grappa f	*gra·pa*	*distilled grape must*
involtini m pl	*een·vol·tee·nee*	*stuffed rolls of meat or fish*
linguine f pl	*leen·gwee·ne*	*long thin ribbons of pasta*
lumache f pl	*loo·ma·ke*	*snails*
maccheroni m pl	*ma·ke·ro·nee*	*refers to any tube pasta*
mascarpone m	*mas·kar·po·ne*	*very soft & creamy cheese*
minestrone m	*mee·ne·stro·ne*	*traditional vegetable soup*
ostriche f pl	*os·tree·ke*	*oysters*
pancetta f	*pan·che·ta*	*salt-cured bacon*
panzanella f	*pan·tsa·ne·la*	*tomato, onion, garlic, olive oil, bread & basil salad*
penne f pl	*pe·ne*	*short & tubular pasta*
pesto m	*pes·to*	*paste of garlic, basil, pine nuts & parmesan*
polpette m	*pol·pe·te*	*meatballs*
prosciutto m	*pro·shoo·to*	*any type of thinly sliced ham*
quattro formaggi	*kwa·tro for·ma·jee*	*pasta sauce with four different cheeses*
quattro stagioni	*kwa·tro sta·jo·nee*	*pizza with different toppings on each quarter*
ragù m	*ra·goo*	*meat sauce (sometimes vegetarian)*
ravioli m pl	*ra·vee·o·lee*	*pasta squares usually stuffed with meat, parmesan cheese & breadcrumbs*
rigatoni m pl	*ree·ga·to·nee*	*short, fat tubes of pasta*
risotto m	*ree·zo·to*	*rice dish cooked in broth*
spaghetti m pl	*spa·ge·tee*	*ubiquitous long thin strands of pasta*
tagliatelle f	*ta·lya·te·le*	*long, ribbon-shaped pasta*
tiramisù m	*tee·ra·mee·soo*	*layered sponge cake soaked in coffee*
tortellini m pl	*tor·te·lee·nee*	*pasta filled with meat, parmesan & egg*
vongole f pl	*von·go·le*	*clams*

emergencies

basics

Help!	*Aiuto!*	ai·*yoo*·to
Stop!	*Fermi!*	*fer*·mee
Go away!	*Vai via!*	vai *vee*·a
Thief!	*Ladro!*	*la*·dro
Fire!	*Al fuoco!*	al *fwo*·ko
Watch out!	*Attenzione!*	a·ten·*tsyo*·ne
Call ...!	*Chiami ...!*	*kya*·mee ...
a doctor	*un medico*	oon *me*·dee·ko
an ambulance	*un'ambulanza*	o·nam·boo·*lan*·tsa
the police	*la polizia*	la po·lee·*tsee*·a

It's an emergency!
È un'emergenza!
e oo·ne·mer·*jen*·tsa

Could you help me, please?
Mi può aiutare, per favore?
mee pwo ai·yoo·*ta*·re per fa·*vo*·re

I have to use the telephone.
Devo fare una telefonata.
de·vo *fa*·re *oo*·na te·le·fo·*na*·ta

I'm lost.
Mi sono perso/a. m/f
mee *so*·no *per*·so/a

Where are the toilets?
Dove sono i gabinetti?
do·ve *so*·no ee ga·bee·ne·tee

police

Where's the police station?
Dov'è il posto di polizia?
do·*ve* eel *pos*·to dee po·lee·*tsee*·a

I want to report an offence.
Voglio fare una denuncia.
vo·lyo *fa*·re *oo*·na de·*noon*·cha

I have insurance.
Ho l'assicurazione.
o la·see·koo·ra·*tsyo*·ne

I've been ...	*Sono stato/a ...* m/f	*so*·no *sta*·to/a ...
assaulted	*aggredito/a* m/f	a·gre·*dee*·to/a
raped	*violentato/a* m/f	vyo·len·*ta*·to/a
robbed	*derubato/a* m/f	roo·*ba*·to/a

I've lost my ...	Ho perso ...	o *per*·so ...
My ... was/were stolen.	Mi hanno rubato ...	mee *a*·no roo·*ba*·to ...
backpack	il mio zaino	eel *mee*·o *dzai*·no
bags	i miei bagagli	ee mee·*ay* ba·*ga*·lyee
credit card	la mia carta di credito	la *mee*·a *kar*·ta dee *kre*·dee·to
handbag	la mia borsa	la *mee*·a *bor*·sa
jewellery	i miei gioielli	ee mee·*ay* jo·*ye*·lee
money	i miei soldi	ee mee·*ay* *sol*·dee
passport	il mio passaporte	eel *mee*·o pa·sa·*por*·te
travellers cheques	i miei assegni di viaggio	ee mee·*ay* a·*se*·nyee dee vee·*a*·jo
wallet	portafoglio	por·ta·*fo*·lyo
I want to contact my ...	Vorrei contattare ...	vo·*ray* kon·ta·*ta*·re ...
consulate	il mio consolato	eel *mee*·o kon·so·*la*·to
embassy	la mia ambasciata	la *mee*·a am·ba·*sha*·ta

health

medical needs

Where's the nearest ...?	Dov'è ... più vicino/a? m/f	do·*ve* ... pyoo vee·*chee*·no/a
dentist	il dentista m	eel den·*tee*·sta
doctor	il medico m	eel *me*·dee·ko
hospital	l'ospedale m	los·pe·*da*·le
(night) pharmacist	la farmacia (di turno) f	la far·ma·*chee*·a (dee *toor*·no)

I need a doctor (who speaks English).
Ho bisogno di un medico (che parli inglese).
o bee·*zo*·nyo dee oon *me*·dee·ko (ke *par*·lee een·*gle*·ze)

Could I see a female doctor?
Posso vedere una dottoressa?
po·so ve·*de*·re *oo*·na do·to·*re*·sa

I've run out of my medication.
Ho finito la mia medicina.
o fee·*nee*·to la *mee*·a me·dee·*chee*·na

2

symptoms, conditions & allergies

| I'm sick. | Mi sento male. | mee *sen*·to *ma*·le |
| It hurts here. | Mi fa male qui. | mee fa *ma*·le kwee |

I have (a) ...	Ho ...	o ...
asthma	asma	*as*·ma
bronchitis	la bronchite	la bron·*kee*·te
constipation	la stitichezza	la stee·tee·*ke*·tsa
cough	la tosse	la *to*·se
diarrhoea	la diarrea	la dee·a·*re*·a
fever	la febbre	la *fe*·bre
headache	mal di testa	mal dee *tes*·ta
heart condition	un problema cardiaco	oon pro·*ble*·ma kar·*dee*·a·ko
nausea	la nausea	la *now*·ze·a
pain	un dolore	oon do·*lo*·re
sore throat	mal di gola	mal dee *go*·la
toothache	mal di denti	mal dee *den*·tee

I'm allergic to ...	Sono allergico/a ... m/f	*so*·no a·*ler*·jee·ko/a ...
antibiotics	agli	*a*·lyee
	antibiotici	an·tee·bee·*o*·tee·chee
anti-	agli	*a*·lyee
inflammatories	antinfiammatori	an·teen·fya·ma·*to*·ree
aspirin	all'aspirina	a·las·pee·*ree*·na
bees	alle api	*a*·le *a*·pee
codeine	alla codeina	*a*·la ko·de·*ee*·na
penicillin	alla penicillina	*a*·la pe·nee·chee·*lee*·na

antiseptic	antisettico m	an·tee·*se*·tee·ko
bandage	fascia f	*fa*·sha
condoms	preservativi m pl	pre·zer·va·*tee*·vee
contraceptives	contraccettivi m pl	kon·tra·che·*tee*·vee
diarrhoea medicine	antidissenterico m	an·tee·dee·sen·te·*ree*·ko
insect repellent	repellente per	re·pe·*len*·te per
	gli insetti m	lyee een·*se*·tee
laxatives	lassativi m pl	la·sa·*tee*·vee
painkillers	analgesico m	a·nal·*je*·zee·ko
rehydration salts	sali minerali m pl	*sa*·lee mee·ne·*ra*·lee
sleeping tablets	sonniferi m pl	so·*nee*·fe·ree

english–italian dictionary

Italian nouns in this dictionary, and adjectives affected by gender, have their gender indicated by ⓜ (masculine) or ⓕ (feminine). If it's a plural noun, you'll also see pl. Words are also marked as n (noun), a (adjective), v (verb), sg (singular), pl (plural), inf (informal) and pol (polite) where necessary.

A

accident *incidente* ⓜ een-chee-*den*-te
accommodation *alloggio* ⓜ a-*lo*-jo
adaptor *presa multipla* ⓕ *pre*-sa mool-*tee*-pla
address *indirizzo* ⓜ een-dee-*ree*-tso
after *dopo* do-po
air-conditioned *ad aria condizionata*
   ad a-rya kon-dee-*tsyo*-na-ta
airplane *aereo* ⓜ a-e-re-o
airport *aeroporto* ⓜ a-e-ro-*por*-to
alcohol *alcol* ⓜ al-kol
all a *tutto/a* too-to/a
allergy *allergia* ⓕ a-ler-*jee*-a
ambulance *ambulanza* ⓕ am-boo-*lan*-tsa
and e e
ankle *caviglia* ⓕ ka-*vee*-lya
arm *braccio* ⓜ bra-cho
ashtray *portacenere* ⓜ por-ta-*che*-ne-re
ATM *Bancomat* ⓜ ban-ko-mat

B

baby *bimbo/a* ⓜ/ⓕ beem-bo/a
back (body) *schiena* ⓕ skye-na
backpack *zaino* ⓜ dzai-no
bad *cattivo/a* ⓜ/ⓕ ka-*tee*-vo/a
bag *borsa* ⓕ bor-sa
baggage claim *ritiro bagagli* ree-*tee*-ro ba-*ga*-lyee
bank *banca* ⓕ ban-ka
bar *locale* ⓜ lo-*ka*-le
bathroom *bagno* ⓜ ba-nyo
battery *pila* ⓕ pee-la
beautiful *bello/a* ⓜ/ⓕ be-lo/a
bed *letto* ⓜ le-to
beer *birra* ⓕ bee-ra
before *prima* pree-ma
behind *dietro* dye-tro
bicycle *bicicletta* ⓕ bee-chee-*kle*-ta
big *grande* gran-de
bill *conto* ⓜ kon-to

black *nero/a* ⓜ/ⓕ ne-ro/a
blanket *coperta* ⓕ ko-*per*-ta
blood group *gruppo sanguigno* ⓜ groo-po san-*gwee*-nyo
blue *azzurro/a* ⓜ/ⓕ a-dzoo-ro/a
boat *barca* ⓕ bar-ka
book (make a reservation) v *prenotare* pre-no-*ta*-re
bottle *bottiglia* ⓕ bo-*tee*-lya
bottle opener *apribottiglie* ⓜ a-pree-bo-*tee*-lye
boy *ragazzo* ⓜ ra-ga-tso
brakes (car) *freno* ⓜ fre-no
breakfast (prima) colazione ⓕ (*pree*-ma) ko-la-*tsyo*-ne
broken (faulty) *rotto/a* ⓜ/ⓕ ro-to/a
bus *autobus* ⓜ ow-to-boos
business *affari* ⓜ pl a-*fa*-ree
buy *comprare* kom-*pra*-re

C

café *bar* ⓜ bar
camera *macchina fotografica* ⓕ
   ma-kee-na fo-to-*gra*-fee-ka
camp site *campeggio* ⓜ kam-*pe*-jo
cancel *cancellare* kan-che-*la*-re
can opener *apriscatole* ⓜ a-pree-*ska*-to-le
car *macchina* ⓕ ma-kee-na
cash *soldi* ⓜ pl sol-dee
cash (a cheque) v *riscuotere un assegno*
   ree-skwo-te-re oon a-se-nyo
cell phone *telefono cellulare* ⓜ te-*le*-fo-no che-loo-*la*-re
centre *centro* ⓜ chen-tro
change (money) v *cambiare* kam-*bya*-re
cheap *economico/a* ⓜ/ⓕ e-ko-no-mee-ko/a
check (bill) *conto* ⓜ kon-to
check-in *registrazione* ⓕ re-jee-stra-*tsyo*-ne
chest *petto* ⓜ pe-to
child *bambino/a* ⓜ/ⓕ bam-*bee*-no/a
cigarette *sigaretta* ⓕ see-ga-*re*-ta
city *città* ⓕ chee-ta
clean a *pulito/a* ⓜ/ⓕ poo-lee-to/a
closed *chiuso/a* ⓜ/ⓕ kyoo-zo/a
coffee *caffè* ⓜ ka-fe
coins *monete* ⓕ pl mo-ne-te

cold a *freddo/a* ⓜ/ⓕ *fre*-do/a
collect call *chiamata a carico del destinatario* ⓕ
  kya-*ma*-ta a *ka*-ree-ko del des-tee-na-*ta*-ryo
come *venire* ve-*nee*-re
computer *computer* ⓜ kom-*pyoo*-ter
condom *preservativo* ⓜ pre-zer-va-*tee*-vo
contact lenses *lenti a contatto* ⓕ pl *len*-tee a kon-*ta*-to
cook v *cucinare* koo-chee-na-re
cost *prezzo* ⓜ *pre*-tso
credit card *carta di credito* ⓕ *kar*-ta dee *kre*-dee-to
cup *tazza* ⓕ *ta*-tsa
currency exchange *cambio valuta* ⓜ *kam*-byo va-*loo*-ta
customs (immigration) *dogana* ⓕ do-*ga*-na

D

dangerous *pericoloso/a* ⓜ/ⓕ pe-ree-ko-*lo*-zo/a
date (time) *data* ⓕ *da*-ta
day *giorno* ⓜ *jor*-no
delay *ritardo* ⓜ ree-*tar*-do
dentist *dentista* ⓜ den-*tee*-sta
depart *partire* par-*tee*-re
diaper *pannolino* ⓜ pa-no-*lee*-no
dictionary *vocabolario* ⓜ vo-ka-bo-*la*-ryo
dinner *cena* ⓕ *che*-na
direct *diretto/a* ⓜ/ⓕ dee-*re*-to/a
dirty *sporco/a* ⓜ/ⓕ *spor*-ko/a
disabled *disabile* dee-*za*-bee-le
discount *sconto* ⓜ *skon*-to
doctor *medico* ⓜ *me*-dee-ko
double bed *letto matrimoniale* ⓜ *le*-to ma-tree-mo-*nya*-le
double room *camera doppia* ⓕ *ka*-mer-a do-pya
drink *bevanda* ⓕ be-*van*-da
drive v *guidare* gwee-*da*-re
drivers licence *patente di guida* ⓕ pa-*ten*-te dee *gwee*-da
drugs (illicit) *droga* ⓕ *dro*-ga
dummy (pacifier) *ciucciotto* ⓜ choo-*cho*-to

E

ear *orecchio* ⓜ o-*re*-kyo
east *est* ⓜ est
eat *mangiare* man-*ja*-re
economy class *classe turistica* ⓕ *kla*-se too-*ree*-stee-ka
electricity *elettricità* ⓕ e-le-tree-chee-*ta*
elevator *ascensore* ⓜ a-shen-*so*-re
email *email* ⓜ e-*mayl*
embassy *ambasciata* ⓕ am-ba-*sha*-ta
emergency *emergenza* ⓕ e-mer-*jen*-tsa
English (language) *inglese* een-*gle*-ze

entrance *entrata* ⓕ en-*tra*-ta
evening *sera* ⓕ *se*-ra
exchange rate *tasso di cambio* ⓜ *ta*-so dee *kam*-byo
exit *uscita* ⓕ *ta*-so dee *kam*-byo
expensive *caro/a* ⓜ/ⓕ *ka*-ro/a
express mail *posta prioritaria* ⓕ *pos*-ta pree-o-ree-*ta*-rya
eye *occhio* ⓜ *o*-kyo

F

far *lontano/a* ⓜ/ⓕ lon-*ta*-no/a
fast *veloce* ve-*lo*-che
father *padre* ⓜ *pa*-dre
film (camera) *rullino* ⓜ roo-*lee*-no
finger *dito* ⓜ *dee*-to
first-aid kit *valigetta del pronto soccorso* ⓕ
  va-lee-*je*-ta del *pron*-to so-*kor*-so
first class *prima classe* ⓕ *pree*-ma *kla*-se
fish n *pesce* ⓜ *pe*-she
food *cibo* ⓜ *chee*-bo
foot *piede* ⓜ *pye*-de
fork *forchetta* ⓕ for-*ke*-ta
free (of charge) *gratuito/a* ⓜ/ⓕ gra-*too*-ee-to/a
friend *amico/a* ⓜ/ⓕ a-*mee*-ko/a
fruit *frutta* ⓕ *froo*-ta
full *pieno/a* ⓜ/ⓕ *pye*-no/a
funny *divertente* dee-ver-*ten*-te

G

gift *regalo* ⓜ re-*ga*-lo
girl *ragazza* ⓕ ra-*ga*-tsa
glass (drinking) *bicchiere* ⓜ bee-*kye*-re
glasses *occhiali* ⓜ pl o-*kya*-lee
go *andare* an-*da*-re
good *buono/a* ⓜ/ⓕ *bwo*-no/a
green *verde* *ver*-de
guide n *guida* ⓕ *gwee*-da

H

half *mezzo* ⓜ *me*-dzo
hand *mano* ⓕ *ma*-no
handbag *borsetta* ⓕ bor-*se*-ta
happy *felice* ⓜ/ⓕ fe-*lee*-che
have *avere* a-*ve*-re
he *lui* loo-ee
head *testa* ⓕ *te*-sta
heart *cuore* ⓜ *kwo*-re
heat n *caldo* ⓜ *kal*-do

heavy *pesante* pe-*zan*-te
help v *aiutare* a-yoo-*ta*-re
here *qui* kwee
high *alto/a* ⓜ/ⓕ *al*-to/a
highway *autostrada* ⓕ ow-to-*stra*-da
hike v *fare un'escursione a piedi*
  fa-re oon es-koor-*syo*-ne a *pye*-de
holiday *vacanze* ⓕ pl va-*kan*-tse
homosexual n *omosessuale* ⓜ&ⓕ o-mo-se-*swa*-le
hospital *ospedale* ⓜ os-pe-*da*-le
hot *caldo/a* ⓜ/ⓕ *kal*-do/a
hotel *albergo* ⓜ al-*ber*-go
hungry *affamato/a* ⓜ/ⓕ a-fa-*ma*-to
husband *marito* ⓜ ma-*ree*-to

I

I *io* ee-o
identification (card) *carta d'identità* ⓕ
  kar-ta dee-den-tee-*ta*
ill *malato/a* ⓜ/ⓕ ma-*la*-to/a
important *importante* eem-por-*tan*-te
included *compreso/a* ⓜ/ⓕ kom-*pre*-zo/a
injury *ferita* ⓕ fe-*ree*-ta
insurance *assicurazione* ⓕ a-see-koo-ra-*tsyo*-ne
Internet *Internet* ⓜ een-ter-net
interpreter *interprete* ⓜ/ⓕ een-*ter*-pre-te
Italy *Italia* ⓕ ee-*ta*-lya
Italian (language) *italiano* ⓜ ee-ta-*lya*-no

J

jewellery *gioielli* ⓜ pl jo-*ye*-lee
job *lavoro* ⓜ la-*vo*-ro

K

key *chiave* ⓕ *kya*-ve
kilogram *chilo* ⓜ *kee*-lo
kitchen *cucina* ⓕ koo-*chee*-na
knife *coltello* ⓜ kol-*te*-lo

L

laundry (place) *lavanderia* ⓕ la-van-de-*ree*-a
lawyer *avvocato/a* ⓜ/ⓕ a-vo-*ka*-to/a
left (direction) *sinistra* see-*nee*-stra
left-luggage office *deposito bagagli* ⓜ
  de-*po*-zee-to ba-*ga*-lyee
leg *gamba* ⓕ *gam*-ba

lesbian n *lesbica* ⓕ *lez*-bee-ka
less (di) *meno* (dee) *me*-no
letter (mail) *lettera* ⓕ *le*-te-ra
lift (elevator) *ascensore* ⓜ a-shen-*so*-re
light *luce* ⓕ *loo*-che
like v *piacere* pya-*che*-re
lock *serratura* ⓕ se-ra-*too*-ra
long *lungo/a* ⓜ/ⓕ *loon*-go/a
lost *perso/a* ⓜ/ⓕ *per*-so/a
lost-property office *ufficio oggetti smarriti* ⓜ
  oo-*fee*-cho o-*je*-tee sma-*ree*-tee
love v *amare* a-*ma*-re
luggage *bagaglio* ⓜ ba-*ga*-lyo
lunch *pranzo* ⓜ *pran*-dzo

M

mail *posta* ⓕ *pos*-ta
man *uomo* ⓜ *wo*-mo
map *pianta* ⓕ *pyan*-ta
market *mercato* ⓜ mer-*ka*-to
matches *fiammiferi* ⓜ pl fya-*mee*-fe-ree
meat *carne* ⓕ *kar*-ne
medicine *medicina* ⓕ me-dee-*chee*-na
menu *menu* ⓜ me-noo
message *messaggio* ⓜ me-*sa*-jo
milk *latte* ⓜ *la*-te
minute *minuto* ⓜ mee-*noo*-to
mobile phone *telefono cellulare* ⓜ te-*le*-fo-no che-loo-*la*-re
money *denaro* ⓜ de-*na*-ro
month *mese* ⓜ *me*-ze
morning *mattina* ⓕ ma-*tee*-na
mother *madre* ⓕ *ma*-dre
motorcycle *moto* ⓕ *mo*-to
motorway *autostrada* ⓕ ow-to-*stra*-da
mouth *bocca* ⓕ *bo*-ka
music *musica* ⓕ *moo*-zee-ka

N

name *nome* ⓜ *no*-me
napkin *tovagliolo* ⓜ to-va-*lyo*-lo
nappy *pannolino* ⓜ pa-no-*lee*-no
near *vicino (a)* vee-*chee*-no (a)
neck *collo* ⓜ *ko*-lo
new *nuovo/a* ⓜ/ⓕ *nwo*-vo/a
news *notizie* ⓕ pl no-*tee*-tsye
newspaper *giornale* ⓜ jor-*na*-le
night *notte* ⓕ *no*-te
no *no* no

noisy *rumoroso/a* m/f roo-mo-*ro*-zo/a
nonsmoking *non fumatore* non foo-ma-*to*-re
north *nord* m nord
nose *naso* m *na*-zo
now *adesso* a-*de*-so
number *numero* m *noo*-me-ro

O

oil (engine) *olio* m *o*-lyo
old *vecchio/a* m/f *ve*-kyo/a
one-way ticket *biglietto di solo andata*
  bee-*lye*-to dee *so*-lo an-*da*-ta
open a *aperto/a* m/f a-*per*-to/a
outside *fuori* fwo-ree

P

package *pacchetto* m pa-*ke*-to
paper *carta* f *kar*-ta
park (car) v *parcheggiare* par-ke-*ja*-re
passport *passaporto* m pa-sa-*por*-to
pay *pagare* pa-*ga*-re
pen *penna (a sfera)* f *pe*-na (a *sfe*-ra)
petrol *benzina* f ben-*dzee*-na
pharmacy *farmacia* f far-ma-*chee*-a
phonecard *scheda telefonica* f *ske*-da te-le-*fo*-nee-ka
photo *foto* f *fo*-to
plate *piatto* m *pya*-to
police *polizia* f po-lee-*tsee*-a
postcard *cartolina* f kar-to-*lee*-na
post office *ufficio postale* m oo-*fee*-cho pos-*ta*-le
pregnant *incinta* een-*cheen*-ta
price *prezzo* m *pre*-tso

Q

quiet *tranquillo/a* m/f tran-*kwee*-lo/a

R

rain n *pioggia* f *pyo*-ja
razor *rasoio* m ra-*zo*-yo
receipt *ricevuta* f re-che-*voo*-ta
red *rosso/a* m/f *ro*-so/a
refund *rimborso* m reem-*bor*-so
registered mail *posta raccomandata* f
  pos-ta ra-ko-man-*da*-ta
rent v *prendere in affitto* pren-*de*-re een a-*fee*-to
repair v *riparare* ree-pa-*ra*-re

reservation *prenotazione* f pre-no-ta-*tsyo*-ne
restaurant *ristorante* m rees-to-*ran*-te
return v *ritornare* ree-tor-*na*-re
return ticket *biglietto di andata e ritorno*
  bee-*lye*-to dee an-*da*-ta e ree-*tor*-no
right (direction) *destra* de-stra
road *strada* f *stra*-da
room *camera* f *ka*-me-ra

S

safe a *sicuro/a* m/f see-*koo*-ro/a
sanitary napkins *assorbenti igienici* m pl
  as-or-*ben*-tee ee-*je*-nee-chee
seat *posto* m *pos*-to
send *mandare* man-*da*-re
service station *stazione di servizio* f
  sta-*tsyo*-ne dee ser-*vee*-tsyo
sex *sesso* m *se*-so
shampoo *shampoo* m *sham*-poo
share (a dorm) *condividere* kon-dee-*vee*-de-re
shaving cream *crema da barba* f *kre*-ma da *bar*-ba
she *lei* lay
sheet (bed) *lenzuolo* f len-*tswo*-lo
shirt *camicia* f ka-*mee*-cha
shoes *scarpe* f pl *skar*-pe
shop *negozio* m ne-*go*-tsyo
short *corto/a* m/f *kor*-to/a
shower *doccia* f *do*-cha
single room *camera singola* f *ka*-me-ra *seen*-go-la
skin *pelle* f *pe*-le
skirt *gonna* f *go*-na
sleep v *dormire* dor-*mee*-re
slowly *lentamente* len-ta-*men*-te
small *piccolo/a* m/f *pee*-ko-lo/a
smoke (cigarettes) v *fumare* foo-*ma*-re
soap *sapone* f sa-*po*-ne
some *alcuni/e* m/f pl al-*koo*-nee/al-*koo*-ne
soon *fra poco* fra *po*-ko
south *sud* m sood
souvenir shop *negozio di souvenir* m
  ne-*go*-tsyo dee soo-ve-neer
speak *parlare* par-*la*-re
spoon *cucchiaio* m koo-*kya*-yo
stamp *francobollo* m fran-ko-*bo*-lo
stand-by ticket *in lista d'attesa* een *lee*-sta da-*te*-za
station (train) *stazione* f sta-*tsyo*-ne
stomach *stomaco* m *sto*-ma-ko
stop v *fermare* fer-*ma*-re
stop (bus) *fermata* f fer-*ma*-ta

street *strada* ① *stra*-da

student *studente/studentessa* ⓜ/① stoo-*den*-te/stoo-den-*te*-sa

sun *sole* ① *so*-le

sunscreen *crema solare* ① *kre*-ma so-*la*-re

swim v *nuotare* nwo-*ta*-re

Switzerland *Svizzera* ① svee-*tse*-ra

T

tampons *assorbenti interni* ⓜ pl a-sor-*ben*-tee een-*ter*-nee

taxi *tassi* ⓜ ta-*see*

teaspoon *cucchiaino* ⓜ koo-kya-ee-no

teeth *denti* ⓜ pl *den*-tee

telephone *telefono* ⓜ te-*le*-fo-no

television *televisione* ① te-le-vee-*zyo*-ne

temperature (weather) *temperatura* ① tem-pe-ra-*too*-ra

tent *tenda* ① *ten*-da

that (one) *quello/a* ⓜ/① *kwe*-lo/a

they *loro* lo-ro

thirsty *assetato/a* ⓜ/① a-se-*ta*-to

this (one) *questo/a* ⓜ/① *kwe*-sto/a

throat *gola* ① *go*-la

ticket *biglietto* ⓜ bee-*lye*-to

time *tempo* ⓜ *tem*-po

tired *stanco/a* ⓜ/① *stan*-ko/a

tissues *fazzolettini di carta* ⓜ pl fa-tso-le-*tee*-nee dee *kar*-ta

today *oggi* o-jee

toilet *gabinetto* ⓜ ga-bee-*ne*-to

tomorrow *domani* do-*ma*-nee

tonight *stasera* sta-*se*-ra

toothbrush *spazzolino da denti* ⓜ spa-tso-*lee*-no da *den*-tee

toothpaste *dentifricio* ⓜ den-tee-*free*-cho

torch (flashlight) *torcia elettrica* ① *tor*-cha e-*le*-tree-ka

tour *gita* ① *jee*-ta

tourist office *ufficio del turismo* ⓜ oo-*fee*-cho del too-*reez*-mo

towel *asciugamano* ⓜ a-shoo-ga-*ma*-no

train *treno* ⓜ *tre*-no

translate *tradurre* tra-*doo*-re

travel agency *agenzia di viaggio* ① a-jen-*tsee*-a dee vee-*a*-jo

travellers cheque *assegno di viaggio* ⓜ a-*se*-nyo dee vee-*a*-jo

trousers *pantaloni* ⓜ pl pan-ta-*lo*-nee

twin beds *due letti* doo-e *le*-tee

tyre *gomma* ① *go*-ma

U

underwear *biancheria intima* ⓜ byan-ke-*ree*-a *een*-tee-ma

urgent *urgente* ⓜ/① oor-*jen*-te

V

vacant *libero/a* ⓜ/① *lee*-be-ro/a

vacation *vacanza* ① va-*kan*-tsa

vegetable *verdura* ① ver-*doo*-ra

vegetarian a *vegetariano/a* ⓜ/① ve-je-ta-*rya*-no/a

visa *visto* ⓜ *vee*-sto

W

waiter *cameriere/a* ⓜ/① ka-mer-*ye*-re/a

walk v *camminare* ka-mee-*na*-re

wallet *portafoglio* ⓜ por-ta-*fo*-lyo

warm a *tiepido/a* ① *tye*-pee-do/a

wash (something) *lavare* la-*va*-re

watch *orologio* ⓜ o-ro-*lo*-jo

water *acqua* ① *a*-kwa

we *noi* noy

weekend *fine settimana* ⓜ *fee*-ne se-tee-*ma*-na

west *ovest* ⓜ o-*vest*

wheelchair *sedia a rotelle* ① *se*-dya a ro-*te*-le

when *quando* kwan-do

where *dove* do-ve

white *bianco/a* ⓜ/① *byan*-ko/a

who *chi* kee

why *perché* per-*ke*

wife *moglie* ① *mo*-lye

window *finestra* ① fee-*nes*-tra

wine *vino* ⓜ *vee*-no

with *con* kon

without *senza* sen-tsa

woman *donna* ① *do*-na

write *scrivere* skree-ve-re

Y

yellow *giallo/a* ⓜ/① *ja*-lo/a

yes *sì* see

yesterday *ieri* ye-ree

you sg inf *tu* too

you sg pol *Lei* lay

you pl *voi* voy

Macedonian

macedonian alphabet

A a a	Б б buh	В в vuh	Г г guh	Д д duh	Ѓ ѓ gyuh
E e e	Ж ж zhuh	З з zuh	S s dzuh	И и i	J j yuh
К к kuh	Л л luh	Љ љ lyuh	М м muh	Н н nuh	Њ њ nyuh
O o o	П п puh	Р р ruh	С с suh	Т т tuh	Ќ ќ kyuh
У у u	Ф ф fuh	Х х huh	Ц ц tsuh	Ч ч chuh	Џ џ juh
Ш ш shuh					

■ macedonian

МАКЕДОНСКИ

MACEDONIAN

introduction

Macedonian (македонски ma·ke·don·ski), the language spoken in the Balkan peninsula to the north of Greece, shares only the name with the ancient language usually thought of in relation to the empire of Alexander the Great. The present-day Macedonian is a South Slavic language (with Bulgarian and Serbian its closest relatives) and the official language of Macedonia, the former Yugoslav republic which became an independent state in 1992. For the speakers of Macedonian – about 2 million people living in Macedonia and the neighbouring countries, as well as the diaspora – it has extreme significance as a confirmation of their national identity.

From the arrival of the Slavs to the Balkans in the 6th century AD until the Turkish conquest in the 15th century, the present-day Macedonia was passed back and forth between Byzantium and the medieval Bulgarian and Serbian kingdoms, and the heavy interaction between the three Slavic languages explains many of their common features. Most notably, Macedonian and Bulgarian differ from the other Slavic languages in the absence of noun cases. During the five centuries of Turkish rule in the Ottoman Empire, Turkish linguistic influence on Macedonian (mostly in the vocabulary) was rivalled only by Greek, as the liturgic language of the Greek Orthodox Church. Stronger exposure to Serbian within the Yugoslav state for most of the 20th century is reflected in the vocabulary (particularly slang) of Macedonian today.

The history of the Macedonian literary language is centred around Old Church Slavonic and the Cyrillic alphabet. The Byzantine Orthodox missionaries, St Cyril and Methodius, themselves from Salonica in Aegean Macedonia and speakers of a Slavic dialect of the region, invented the Glagolitic alphabet in the 9th century. They translated Greek religious literature into Old Church Slavonic, the language of the earliest written records from which the modern South Slavic literary languages all evolved. The Cyrillic alphabet was later developed by the disciples of the two missionaries, using the Greek and Glagolitic characters. The Macedonian Cyrillic alphabet in its present form is phonetic and very similar to the Serbian alphabet, with only a few different letters.

The creation of a modern literary standard started in the latter half of the 19th century and ended with the official codification in 1945 of a standard based on the west-central dialects. This form is the most distinct from Bulgarian and Serbian, whose boundaries with Macedonian can often be blurry.

pronunciation

vowel sounds

The Macedonian vowel system is very straightforward – it consists of the five basic vowels.

symbol	english equivalent	macedonian example	transliteration
a	father	здраво	*zdra*·vo
e	bet	вера	*ve*·ra
i	hit	син	sin
o	pot	добро	*dob*·ro
u	put	југ	yug

word stress

In the Macedonian literary standard the stress usually falls on the third syllable from the end in words with three syllables or more. If the word has only two syllables, the first is usually stressed. There are exceptions to this rule, such as with many new borrowings and other words of foreign origin – eg литература li·te·ra·*tu*·ra, not li·te·*ra*·tu·ra (literature). Just follow our coloured pronunciation guide, in which the stressed syllable is indicated in italics.

consonant sounds

The consonant sounds in Macedonian mostly have equivalents in English. You might need a little practice with the 'soft' ѓ gy and ќ ky sounds. Don't be intimidated by the consonant clusters as in црква *tsrk*·va (church) or брзо *br*·zo (fast) – try putting a slight 'uh' sound before the r, which serves as a semi-vowel.

symbol	english equivalent	macedonian example	transliteration
b	bed	билет	*bi*·let
ch	cheat	чист	chist
d	dog	мед	med
dz	adds	sид	dzid
f	fat	кафе	*ka*·fe
g	go	гуми	*gu*·mi
gy	legume	госпоѓа	*gos*·po·**gya**
h	hat	храм	hram
j	joke	џамија	*ja*·mi·ya
k	kit	компир	*kom*·pir
ky	cure	ноќ	noky
l	lot	леб	leb
ly	million	љубов	*lyu*·bov
m	man	месо	*me*·so
n	not	бензин	*ben*·zin
ny	canyon	бања	*ba*·nya
p	pet	писмо	*pis*·mo
r	run	стар	star
s	sun	сега	*se*·ga
sh	shot	туш	tush
t	top	исток	*is*·tok
ts	hats	деца	*de*·tsa
v	very	север	*se*·ver
y	yes	јас	yas
z	zero	пазар	*pa*·zar
zh	pleasure	плажа	*pla*·zha

tools

language difficulties

Do you speak English?
Зборувате ли англиски?   zbo·*ru*·va·te li *an*·glis·ki

Do you understand?
Разбирате ли?   raz·*bi*·ra·te li

I (don't) understand.
Jac (не) разбирам.   yas (ne) *raz*·bi·ram

What does (добро) mean?
Што значи (добро)?   shto *zna*·chi (*dob*·ro)

How do you ...?   Како се ...?   *ka*·ko se ...
   pronounce this   изговара ова   iz·*go*·va·ra *o*·va
   write (утре)   пишува (утре)   *pi*·shu·va (*ut*·re)

Could you please ...?   ..., ве молам.   ... ve *mo*·lam
   repeat that   Повторете го тоа   pov·to·*re*·te go *to*·a
   speak more slowly   Зборувајте полека   zbo·*ru*·vay·te *po*·le·ka
   write it down   Напишете го тоа   na·pi·*she*·te go *to*·a

essentials

Yes.	Да.	da
No.	Не.	ne
Please.	Молам.	*mo*·lam
Thank you (very much).	Благодарам. **pol**	bla·*go*·da·ram
Thanks a lot.	Фала многу. **inf**	*fa*·la *mno*·gu
You're welcome.	Нема зошто.	*ne*·ma *zosh*·to
Excuse me.	Извинете.	iz·*vi*·ne·te
Sorry.	Простете.	*pros*·te·te

numbers

0	нула	*nu*·la	15	петнаесет	*pet*·*na*·e·set
1	еден/една m/f	e·den/ed·na	16	шеснаесет	shes·*na*·e·set
	едно n	ed·no	17	седумнаесет	se·dum·*na*·e·set
2	два m	dva	18	осумнаесет	o·sum·*na*·e·set
	две f&n	dve	19	деветнаесет	de·vet·*na*·e·set
3	три	tri	20	дваесет	*dva*·e·set
4	четири	*che*·ti·ri	21	дваесет и еден	*dva*·e·set i e·den
5	пет	pet	22	дваесет и два	*dva*·e·set i dva
6	шест	shest	30	триесет	*tri*·e·set
7	седум	*se*·dum	40	четириесет	che·ti·*ri*·e·set
8	осум	*o*·sum	50	педесет	*pe*·de·set
9	девет	*de*·vet	60	шеесет	*she*·e·set
10	десет	*de*·set	70	седумдесет	se·*dum*·de·set
11	единаесет	e·di·*na*·e·set	80	осумдесет	o·*sum*·de·set
12	дванаесет	dva·*na*·e·set	90	деведесет	de·*ve*·de·set
13	тринаесет	tri·*na*·e·set	100	сто	sto
14	четиринаесет	che·ti·ri·*na*·e·set	1000	илјада	*il*·ya·da

time & dates

What time is it?	Колку е часот?	*kol*·ku e *cha*·sot
It's one o'clock.	Часот е еден.	*cha*·sot e e·den
It's (two) o'clock.	Часот е (два).	*cha*·sot e (dva)
Quarter past (one).	(Еден) и петнаесет.	(e·den) i pet·*na*·e·set
Half past (one).	(Еден) и пол.	(e·den) i pol
Quarter to (eight).	Петнаесет до (осум).	pet·*na*·e·set do (*o*·sum)
At what time ...?	Во колку часот ...?	vo *kol*·ku *cha*·sot ...
At ...	Во ...	vo ...
am	претпладне	*pret*·plad·ne
pm	попладне	*po*·plad·ne
Monday	понеделник	po·*ne*·del·nik
Tuesday	вторник	*vtor*·nik
Wednesday	среда	*sre*·da
Thursday	четврток	*chet*·vr·tok
Friday	петок	*pe*·tok
Saturday	сабота	*sa*·bo·ta
Sunday	недела	*ne*·de·la

January	јануари	ya·nu·*a*·ri
February	февруари	fev·ru·*a*·ri
March	март	mart
April	април	*ap*·ril
May	мај	may
June	јуни	*yu*·ni
July	јули	*yu*·li
August	август	*av*·gust
September	септември	sep·*tem*·vri
October	октомври	ok·*tom*·vri
November	ноември	no·*em*·vri
December	декември	de·*kem*·vri

What date is it today?
Кој датум е денес?   koy *da*·tum e *de*·nes

It's (15 December).
Денес е (петнаесетти декември).   *de*·nes e (pet·na·e·set·ti de·*kem*·vri)

| since (May) | од (мај) | od (may) |
| until (June) | до (јуни) | do (*yu*·ni) |

last ...		
night	синока	*si*·no·kya
week	минатата недела	mi·*na*·ta·ta *ne*·de·la
month	минатиот месец	mi·*na*·ti·ot *me*·sets
year	минатата година	mi·*na*·ta·ta *go*·di·na

next ...		
week	следната недела	*sled*·na·ta *ne*·de·la
month	следниот месец	*sled*·ni·ot *me*·sets
year	следната година	*sled*·na·ta *go*·di·na

yesterday/tomorrow ...	вчера/утре ...	*vche*·ra/*ut*·re ...
morning	наутро	*na*·ut·ro
afternoon	попладне	*pop*·lad·ne
evening	вечер	*ve*·cher

weather

What's the weather like?	Какво е времето?	kak·vo e vre·me·to
It' snowing.	Паѓа снег.	pa·gya sneg

It's...	Времето е ...	vre·me·to e ...
cloudy	облачно	ob·lach·no
cold	студено	stu·de·no
hot	жешко	zhesh·ko
raining	врнежливо	vr·nezh·li·vo
sunny	сончево	son·che·vo
warm	топло	top·lo
windy	ветровито	vet·ro·vi·to

spring	пролет f	pro·let
summer	лето n	le·to
autumn	есен m	e·sen
winter	зима f	zi·ma

border crossing

I'm here ...	Јас сум овде ...	yas sum ov·de ...
in transit	транзит	tran·zit
on business	службено	sluzh·be·no
on holiday	на одмор	na od·mor

I'm here for ...	Јас овде останувам ...	yas ov·de os·ta·nu·vam ...
(10) days	(десет) дена	(de·set) de·na
(two) months	(два) месеца	(dva) me·se·tsa
(three) weeks	(три) недели	(tri) ne·de·li

I'm going to (Ohrid).
Јас одам во (Охрид). yas o·dam vo (oh·rid)

I'm staying at the (Hotel Park).
Јас престојувам во (хотел 'Парк'). yas pres·to·yu·vam vo (ho·tel park)

I have nothing to declare.
Јас немам да пријавам ништо. yas ne·mam da pri·ya·vam nish·to

I have something to declare.
Јас имам нешто да пријавам. yas i·mam nesh·to da pri·ya·vam

That's (not) mine.
Тоа (не) е мое. to·a (ne) e mo·e

transport

tickets & luggage

Where can I buy a ticket?
Каде можам да купам билет?   *ka*·de *mo*·zham da *ku*·pam *bi*·let

Do I need to book a seat?
Ми треба ли резервација?   mi *tre*·ba li re·zer·*va*·tsi·ya

One ... ticket	Еден ... (за Охрид),	*e*·den ... (za *oh*·rid)
(to Ohrid), please.	ве молам.	ve *mo*·lam
one-way	билет во еден	*bi*·let vo *e*·den
	правец	*pra*·vets
return	повратен билет	*pov*·ra·ten *bi*·let

I'd like to ... my	Сакам да го ... мојот	*sa*·kam da go ... *mo*·yot
ticket, please.	билет, ве молам.	*bi*·let ve *mo*·lam
cancel	откажам	*ot*·ka·zham
change	променам	*pro*·me·nam
collect	земам	*ze*·mam
confirm	потврдам	*pot*·vr·dam

I'd like a ...	Сакам едно седиште	*sa*·kam *ed*·no *se*·dish·te
seat, please.	за ..., ве молам.	za ... ve *mo*·lam
nonsmoking	непушачи	ne·*pu*·sha·chi
smoking	пушачи	*pu*·sha·chi

How much is it?
Колку чини тоа?   *kol*·ku *chi*·ni *to*·a

Is there air conditioning?
Дали има клима уред?   *da*·li *i*·ma *kli*·ma *u*·red

Is there a toilet?
Дали има тоалет?   *da*·li *i*·ma to·a·*let*

How long does the trip take?
Колку време се патува?   *kol*·ku *vre*·me se *pa*·tu·va

Is it a direct route? (train/bus)
Дали е овој воз/автобус директен?   *da*·li e *o*·voy voz/*av*·to·bus *di*·rek·ten

I'd like a luggage locker.
Сакам шкаф за багаж.   *sa*·kam shkaf za *ba*·gazh

My luggage has been ...	Мојот багаж е ...	*mo*-yot *ba*-gazh e ...
damaged	оштетен	*osh*-te-ten
lost	загубен	*za*-gu-ben
stolen	украден	*uk*-ra-den

getting around

Where does flight (912) arrive/depart?
Каде слетува/полетува
авионот со лет (912)?
ka-de sle-*tu*-va/po-*le*-tu-va
a-vi-*o*-not so let (*de*-vet *e*-den dva)

Where's (the) ...?	Каде е ...?	*ka*-de e ...
arrivals hall	чекалната за	che-*kal*-na-ta za
	пристигнување	pris-*tig*-*nu*-va-nye
departures hall	чекалната за	che-*kal*-na-ta za
	заминување	za-mi-*nu*-va-nye
duty-free shop	дјутифри	*dyu*-ti-fri
	продавницата	pro-dav-*ni*-tsa-ta
gate (12)	излезот (дванаесет)	*iz*-le-zot (dva-*na*-e-set)

Is this the ... to (Bitola)?	Дали овој ... оди за (Битола)?	*da*-li o-voy ... *o*-di za (*bi*-to-la)
boat	брод	brod
bus	автобус	*av*-to-bus
plane	авион	a-vi-*on*
train	воз	voz

What time's the ... bus?	Кога поаѓа ... автобус?	*ko*-ga po-a-*gya* ... *av*-to-bus
first	првиот	*pr*-vi-ot
last	последниот	pos-*led*-ni-ot
next	следниот	*sled*-ni-ot

At what time does it arrive/leave?
Кога пристигнува/поаѓа?
ko-ga pris-*tig*-nu-va/*po*-a-gya

How long will it be delayed?
Колку време ќе доцни?
kol-ku *vre*-me kye *dots*-ni

What station/stop is this?
Која е оваа станица?
ko-ya e o-va-a *sta*-ni-tsa

What's the next station/stop?
Која е следната станица?
ko-ya e *sled*-na-ta *sta*-ni-tsa

Does it stop at (Prilep)?
Дали застанува во (Прилеп)?   *da*·li zas·*ta*·nu·va vo (*pri*·lep)

Please tell me when we get to (Skopje).
Ве молам кажете ми кога   ve *mo*·lam ka·*zhe*·te mi *ko*·ga
ќе стигнеме во (Скопје).   kye *stig*·ne·me vo (*skop*·ye)

How long do we stop here?
Колку долго ќе стоиме овде?   *kol*·ku *dol*·go kye *sto*·i·me *ov*·de

Is this seat available?
Дали е ова седиште слободно?   *da*·li e *o*·va se·*dish*·te *slo*·bod·no

That's my seat.
Тоа е мое седиште.   *to*·a e *mo*·e se·*dish*·te

I'd like a taxi ...	Сакам такси ...	*sa*·kam *tak*·si ...
at (9am)	во (девет	vo (*de*·vet
	претпладне)	*pret*·plad·ne)
now	сега	*se*·ga
tomorrow	утре	*ut*·re

Is this taxi available?
Дали е ова такси слободно?   *da*·li e *o*·va *tak*·si *slo*·bod·no

How much is it to ...?
Колку ќе чини до ...?   *kol*·ku kye *chi*·ni do ...

Please put the meter on.
Ве молам вклучете го   ve *mo*·lam vklu·*che*·te go
таксиметарот.   tak·si·*me*·ta·rot

Please take me to (this address).
Ве молам одвезете ме до   ve *mo*·lam od·ve·*ze*·te me do
(оваа адреса).   (*o*·va·a *a*·dre·sa)

Please ...	Ве молам ...	ve *mo*·lam ...
slow down	возете побавно	*vo*·ze·te *po*·bav·no
stop here	застанете овде	zas·*ta*·ne·te *ov*·de
wait here	причекајте овде	pri·*che*·kay·te *ov*·de

car, motorbike & bicycle hire

I'd like to hire a ...	Сакам да изнајмам ...	*sa*·kam da *iz*·nay·mam ...
bicycle	точак	*to*·chak
car	кола	*ko*·la
motorbike	моторцикл	mo·tor·*tsikl*

with ...	со ...	so ...
a driver	возач	*vo*·zach
air conditioning	клима уред	*kli*·ma *u*·red
antifreeze	антифриз	*an*·ti·friz
snow chains	синџири за снег	*sin*·ji·ri za sneg

How much for ... hire?	Колку чини ...?	*kol*·ku *chi*·ni ...
hourly	на час	na chas
daily	дневно	*dnev*·no
weekly	неделно	*ne*·del·no

air	воздух m	*voz*·duh
oil	масло n	*mas*·lo
petrol	бензин m	*ben*·zin
tyres	гуми f pl	*gu*·mi

I need a mechanic.
Ми треба механичар.
mi *tre*·ba me·*ha*·ni·char

I've run out of petrol.
Останав без бензин.
os·ta·nav bez *ben*·zin

I have a flat tyre.
Имам издишена гума.
i·mam iz·*di*·she·na *gu*·ma

directions

Where's the ...?	Каде е ...?	*ka*·de e ...
bank	банката	*ban*·ka·ta
city centre	центарот на градот	*tsen*·ta·rot na *gra*·dot
hotel	хотелот	*ho*·te·lot
market	пазарот	*pa*·za·rot
police station	полициската	po·li·*tsis*·ka·ta
	станица	*sta*·ni·tsa
post office	поштата	*posh*·ta·ta
public toilet	јавниот тоалет	*yav*·ni·ot to·a·*let*
tourist office	туристичкото биро	tu·ris·*tich*·ko·to *bi*·ro

Is this the road to (Bitola)?
Дали овој пат води до (Битола)?
da·li *o*·voy pat *vo*·di do (*bi*·to·la)

Can you show me (on the map)?
Можете ли да ми покажете
(на картава)?
mo·zhe·te li da mi po·*ka*·zhe·te
(na *kar*·ta·va)

What's the address?
Која е адресата? — *ko*·ya e ad·*re*·sa·ta

How far is it?
Колку е тоа далеку? — *kol*·ku e *to*·a *da*·le·ku

How do I get there?
Како да стигнам до таму? — *ka*·ko da *stig*·nam do *ta*·mu

Turn ...	Свртете ...	*svr*·te·te ...
at the corner	на аголот	na *a*·go·lot
at the traffic lights	на семафорите	na se·ma·*fo*·ri·te
left/right	лево/десно	*le*·vo/*des*·no

It's ...	Тоа е ...	*to*·a e ...
behind ...	зад ...	zad ...
far away	далеку	*da*·le·ku
here	овде	*ov*·de
in front of ...	пред ...	pred ...
left	лево	*le*·vo
near (to ...)	блиску (до ...)	*blis*·ku (do ...)
next to ...	веднаш до ...	*ved*·nash do ...
on the corner	на аголот	na *a*·go·lot
opposite ...	спроти ...	*spro*·ti ...
right	десно	*des*·no
straight ahead	право напред	*pra*·vo *nap*·red
there	таму	*ta*·mu

by bus	со автобус	so *av*·to·bus
by taxi	со такси	so *tak*·si
by train	со воз	so voz
on foot	пешки	*pesh*·ki
north	север	*se*·ver
south	југ	yug
east	исток	*is*·tok
west	запад	*za*·pad

Влез/Излез	vlez/iz·lez	**Entrance/Exit**
Отворено/Затворено	ot·vo·re·no/zat·vo·re·no	**Open/Closed**
Соби за издавање	so·bi za iz·da·va·nye	**Rooms Available**
Нема место	ne·ma mes·to	**No Vacancies**
Информации	in·for·ma·tsi·i	**Information**
Полициска станица	po·li·tsis·ka sta·ni·tsa	**Police Station**
Забрането	za·bra·ne·to	**Prohibited**
Тоалети	to·a·le·ti	**Toilets**
Машки	mash·ki	**Men**
Женски	zhen·ski	**Women**
Топло/Ладно	top·lo/lad·no	**Hot/Cold**

accommodation

finding accommodation

Where's a ...?	Каде има ...?	ka·de i·ma ...
camping ground	камп	kamp
guesthouse	приватно сместување	pri·vat·no smes·tu·va·nye
hotel	хотел	ho·tel
youth hostel	младинско	mla·din·sko
	пренокиште	pre·no·kyish·te
Can you	Можете ли да ми	mo·zhe·te li da mi
recommend	препорачате	pre·po·ra·cha·te
somewhere ...?	нешто ...?	nesh·to ...
cheap	поевтино	po·ev·ti·no
good	добро	dob·ro
nearby	близу	bli·zu

I'd like to book a room, please.
Сакам да резервирам соба,   sa·kam da re·zer·vi·ram so·ba
ве молам.   ve mo·lam

I have a reservation.
Јас имам резервација.   yas i·mam re·zer·va·tsi·ya

My name's ...
Јас се викам ...   yas se vi·kam ...

Do you have a ... room?	Дали имате...?	*da*-li *i*-ma-te ...
single	еднокреветна соба	ed-no-*kre*-vet-na *so*-ba
double	соба со брачен кревет	*so*-ba so *bra*-chen *kre*-vet
twin	двокреветна соба	dvo-*kre*-vet-na *so*-ba

How much is it per ...?	Која е цената за ...?	*ko*-ya e *tse*-na-ta za ...
night	ноќ	noky
person	еден	e-den

Can I pay ...?	Примате ли ...?	*pri*-ma-te li ...
by credit card	кредитни картички	*kre*-dit-ni *kar*-tich-ki
with a travellers cheque	патнички чекови	*pat*-nich-ki *che*-ko-vi

I'd like to stay for (two) nights.
Сакам да останам (две) ноќи.　　*sa*-kam da *os*-ta-nam (dve) *no*-kyi

From (2 July) to (6 July).
Од (втори јули) до (шести јули).　　od (*vto*-ri *yu*-li) do (*shes*-ti *yu*-li)

Can I see it?
Може ли да ја видам?　　*mo*-zhe li da ya *vi*-dam

Am I allowed to camp here?
Може ли да кампувам овде?　　*mo*-zhe li da *kam*-pu-vam *ov*-de

Is there a camp site nearby?
Дали во близината има камп?　　*da*-li vo bli-*zi*-na-ta *i*-ma kamp

requests & queries

When's breakfast served?
Кога е појадокот?　　*ko*-ga e po-*ya*-do-kot

Where's breakfast served?
Каде се појадува?　　*ka*-de se po-*ya*-du-va

Please wake me at (seven).
Ве молам разбудете ме во (седум).　　ve *mo*-lam raz-bu-*de*-te me vo (*se*-dum)

Could I have my key, please?
Може ли да го добијам клучот, ве молам?　　*mo*-zhe li da go do-*bi*-yam *klu*-chot ve *mo*-lam

Is there a/an ...?	Дали има ...?	*da·*li *i·*ma ...
elevator	лифт	lift
safe	сеф	sef

The room is too ...	Собата е премногу ...	*so·*ba·ta e *prem·*no·gu ...
expensive	скапа	*ska·*pa
noisy	бучна	*buch·*na
small	мала	*ma·*la

The ... doesn't work.	Не работи ...	ne *ra·*bo·ti ...
air conditioning	клима уредот	*kli·*ma *u·*re·dot
fan	фенот	*fe·*not
toilet	тоалетот	to·a·*le·*tot

This ... isn't clean.	Овој ... не е чист.	*o·*voy ... ne e chist
sheet	чаршаф	*char·*shaf
towel	пешкир	*pesh·*kir

This pillow isn't clean.
Оваа перница не е чиста.

*o·*va·a *per·*ni·tsa ne e *chis·*ta

Can I get another (blanket)?
Може ли да добијам уште
едно (ќебе)?

*mo·*zhe li da *do·*bi·yam *ush·*te
*ed·*no (*kye·*be)

checking out

What time is checkout?
Во колку часот треба да се
одјавам?

vo *kol·*ku *cha·*sot *tre·*ba da se
*od·*ya·vam

Can I leave my luggage here?
Може ли да го оставам мојот
багаж овде?

*mo·*zhe li da go *os·*ta·vam *mo·*yot
*ba·*gazh *ov·*de

Could I have my valuables, please?
Може ли да ги добијам моите
вредни предмети, ве молам?

*mo·*zhe li da gi *do·*bi·yam *mo·*i·te
*vred·*ni *pred·*me·ti ve *mo·*lam

Could I have	Може ли да го добијам	*mo·*zhe li da go *do·*bi·yam
my ..., please?	мојот..., ве молам?	*mo·*yot ... ve *mo·*lam
deposit	депозит	*de·*po·zit
passport	пасош	*pa·*sosh

communications & banking

the internet

Where's the local Internet café?
Каде има тука интернет кафе? — *ka*·de *i*·ma *tu*·ka *in*·ter·net ka·*fe*

How much is it per hour?
Колку чини на час? — *kol*·ku *chi*·ni na chas

I'd like to ...	Сакам да ...	*sa*·kam da ...
check my email	си ја проверам електронската пошта	si ya *pro*·ve·ram e·lek·*tron*·ska·ta *posh*·ta
get Internet access	добијам пристап на интернет	do·*bi*·yam *pris*·tap na *in*·ter·net
use a printer	користам печатар	*ko*·ris·tam *pe*·cha·tar
use a scanner	користам скенер	*ko*·ris·tam *ske*·ner

mobile/cell phone

I'd like to buy ...	Сакам да купам ...	*sa*·kam da *ku*·pam ...
a mobile/cell phone	мобилен телефон	mo·*bi*·len *te*·le·fon
SIM card for your network	СИМ картичка за вашата мрежа	sim *kar*·tich·ka za *va*·sha·ta *mre*·zha

What are the rates?
Кои се цените? — *ko*·i se *tse*·ni·te

telephone

What's your phone number?
Кој е вашиот телефонски број? — koy e *va*·shi·ot te·le·*fon*·ski broy

The number is ...
Бројот е ... — *bro*·yot e ...

Where's the nearest public phone?
Каде е најблиската јавна говорница? — *ka*·de e nay·*blis*·ka·ta *yav*·na go·*vor*·ni·tsa

I'd like to buy a phonecard.
Сакам да купам телефонска картичка. — *sa*·kam da *ku*·pam te·le·*fon*·ska *kar*·tich·ka

I want to ...	Сакам да ...	sa·kam da ...
call (Singapore)	се јавам во (Сингапур)	se ya·vam vo (sin·ga·pur)
make a local call	телефонирам локално	te·le·fo·ni·ram lo·kal·no
reverse the	телефонирам	te·le·fo·ni·ram
charges	на нивна сметка	na niv·na smet·ka

How much does ... cost?	Колку чини ...?	kol·ku chi·ni ...
a (three)-minute	разговор од	raz·go·vor od
call	(три) минути	(tri) mi·nu·ti
each extra	секоја наредна	se·ko·ya na·red·na
minute	минута	mi·nu·ta

(Ten) denars per minute.

(Десет) денари за минута.   (de·set) de·na·ri za mi·nu·ta

post office

I want to send a ...	Сакам да испратам ...	sa·kam da is·pra·tam ...
letter	писмо	pis·mo
parcel	пакет	pa·ket
postcard	разгледница	raz·gled·ni·tsa

I want to buy ...	Сакам да купам ...	sa·kam da ku·pam ...
an envelope	плик	plik
stamps	поштенски марки	posh·ten·ski mar·ki

Please send it	Ве молам испратете	ve mo·lam is·pra·te·te
(to Australia) by ...	го (во Австралија) ...	go (vo av·stra·li·ya) ...
airmail	авионски	a·vi·on·ski
express mail	експресно	eks·pres·no
registered mail	препорачано	pre·po·ra·cha·no
surface mail	обично	o·bich·no

Is there any mail for me?

Дали има пошта за мене?   da·li i·ma posh·ta za me·ne

bank

Where's a/an ...?	Каде има ...?	ka·de i·ma ...
ATM	банкомат	ban·ko·mat
foreign exchange office	менувачница	me·nu·vach·ni·tsa

I'd like to ...	Сакам да ...	sa·kam da ...
Where can I ...?	Каде можам да ...?	ka·de mo·zham da ...
arrange a transfer	направам трансфер	na·pra·vam trans·fer
cash a cheque	разменам чек	raz·me·nam chek
change a travellers cheque	разменам патнички чекови	raz·me·nam pat·nich·ki che·ko·vi
change money	разменам пари	raz·me·nam pa·ri
get a cash advance	добијам кредит	do·bi·yam kre·dit
withdraw money	извадам пари	iz·va·dam pa·ri

What's the ...?	Колку ...?	kol·ku ...
charge for that	се наплаќа за тоа	se na·pla·kya za to·a
commission	е провизијата	e pro·vi·zi·ya·ta
exchange rate	е курсот	e kur·sot

It's (12) denars.	(Дванаесет) денари.	(dva·na·e·set) de·na·ri
It's free.	Бесплатно е.	bes·plat·no e

What time does the bank open?
Кога се отвора банката?   ko·ga se ot·vo·ra ban·ka·ta

Has my money arrived yet?
Дали пристигнаа моите пари?   da·li pris·tig·na·a mo·i·te pa·ri

sightseeing

getting in

What time does it open/close?
Кога се отвора/затвора?   ko·ga se ot·vo·ra/zat·vo·ra

What's the admission charge?
Колку чини влезница?   kol·ku chi·ni vlez·ni·tsa

Is there a discount for students/children?
Има ли попуст за студенти/деца?   i·ma li po·pust za stu·den·ti/de·tsa

I'd like a ...	Сакам ...	sa·kam ...
catalogue	каталог	ka·ta·log
guide	водич	vo·dich
local map	локална карта	lo·kal·na kar·ta

I'd like to see …
Сакам да видам…   *sa*-kam da *vi*-dam …

What's that?
Што е ова?   shto e *o*-va

Can I take a photo?
Може ли да сликам?   *mo*-zhe li da *sli*-kam

tours

When's the next …?	Кога е следната …?	*ko*-ga e *sled*-na-ta …
day trip	целодневна тура	tse-*lo*-dnev-na *tu*-ra
tour	тура	*tu*-ra
Is … included?	Дали е …?	*da*-li e …
accommodation	вклучено	*vklu*-che-no
	сместувањето	smes-tu-*va*-nye-to
the admission	вклучена цената	*vklu*-che-na *tse*-na-ta
charge	на влезниците	na vlez-*ni*-tsi-te
food	вклучена храна	*vklu*-che-na *hra*-na
transport	вклучен превоз	*vklu*-chen *pre*-voz

How long is the tour?
Колку долго трае турата?   *kol*-ku *dol*-go *tra*-e *tu*-ra-ta

What time should we be back?
Во колку часот ќе се вратиме?   vo *kol*-ku *cha*-sot kye se *vra*-ti-me

sightseeing		
castle	тврдина f	*tvr*-di-na
church	црква f	*tsrk*-va
main square	главен плоштад m	*gla*-ven *plosh*-tad
monastery	манастир m	*ma*-nas-tir
monument	споменик m	*spo*-me-nik
mosque	џамија f	*ja*-mi-ya
museum	музеј m	*mu*-zey
old city	стар град m	star grad
palace	палата f	pa-*la*-ta
ruins	урнатини f pl	ur-*na*-ti-ni
stadium	стадион m	sta-di-*on*
statue	статуа f	*sta*-tu-a

shopping

enquiries

Where's a ...?	Каде има ...?	ka·de i·ma ...
bank	банка	ban·ka
bookshop	книжарница	kni·zhar·ni·tsa
camera shop	продавница за	pro·dav·ni·tsa za
	фотоапарати	fo·to·a·pa·ra·ti
department store	стоковна куќа	sto·kov·na ku·kya
grocery store	бакалница	ba·kal·ni·tsa
market	пазар	pa·zar
newsagency	киоск за весници	ki·osk za ves·ni·tsi
supermarket	супермаркет	su·per·mar·ket

Where can I buy (a padlock)?
Каде можам да купам (катинар)?   ka·de mo·zham da ku·pam (ka·ti·nar)

I'm looking for ...
Барам ...   ba·ram ...

Can I look at it?
Може ли да ја видам?   mo·zhe li da ya vi·dam

Do you have any others?
Имате ли други?   i·ma·te li dru·gi

Does it have a guarantee?
Дали има гаранција?   da·li i·ma ga·ran·tsi·ya

Can I have it sent abroad?
Може ли да ми го испратите   mo·zhe li da mi go is·pra·ti·te
во странство?   vo strans·tvo

Can I have my ... repaired?
Може ли да ми го поправите ...?   mo·ze li da mi go pop·ra·vi·te ...

It's faulty.
Расипан е.   ra·si·pan e

I'd like ..., please.	Јас би сакал ...,	yas bi sa·kal ...
	ве молам.	ve mo·lam
a bag	торба	tor·ba
a refund	да ми ги вратите	da mi gi vra·ti·te
	парите	pa·ri·te
to return this	да го вратам ова	da go vra·tam o·va

paying

How much is it?
Колку чини тоа? — *kol*·ku *chi*·ni *to*·a

Can you write down the price?
Можете ли да ми ја напишете цената? — *mo*·zhe·te li da mi ya na·*pi*·she·te *tse*·na·ta

That's too expensive.
Тоа е многу скапо. — *to*·a e *mno*·gu *ska*·po

What's your lowest price?
Која е вашата најниска цена? — *ko*·ya e *va*·sha·ta *nai*·nis·ka *tse*·na

I'll give you (five) denars.
Јас ќе ви дадам (пет) денари. — yas kye vi *da*·dam (pet) *de*·na·ri

There's a mistake in the bill.
Има грешка во сметката. — *i*·ma *gresh*·ka vo *smet*·ka·ta

Do you accept ...?	Примате ли ...?	*pri*·ma·te li ...
credit cards	кредитни картички	*kre*·dit·ni *kar*·tich·ki
debit cards	дебитни картички	*de*·bit·ni *kar*·tich·ki
travellers cheques	патнички чекови	*pat*·nich·ki *che*·ko·vi
I'd like ..., please.	Сакам ..., ве молам.	*sa*·kam ... ve *mo*·lam
a receipt	признаница	priz·*na*·ni·tsa
my change	кусур	*ku*·sur

clothes & shoes

Can I try it on?
Може ли да го пробам тоа? — *mo*·zhe li da go *pro*·bam *to*·a

My size is (42).
Јас носам (четириесет и два). — yas *no*·sam (che·ti·*ri*·e·set i dva)

It doesn't fit.
Не ми е точно. — ne mi e *toch*·no

small	мал	mal
medium	среден	sre·den
large	голем	go·lem

books & music

I'd like a ...	Сакам ...	sa·kam ...
newspaper	весник	ves·nik
(in English)	(на англиски)	(na an·glis·ki)
pen	пенкало	pen·ka·lo

Is there an English-language bookshop?
Дали има англиска книжарница?   da·li i·ma an·glis·ka kni·zhar·ni·tsa

I'm looking for something by (Simon Trpcheski/Blazhe Koneski).
Барам нешто од (Симон   ba·ram nesh·to od (si·mon
Трпчески/Блаже Конески).   trp·ches·ki/bla·zhe ko·nes·ki)

Can I listen to this?
Може ли да го слушнам ова?   mo·zhe li da go slush·nam o·va

photography

Can you ...?	Можете ли ...?	mo·zhe·te li ...
burn a CD from	да преснимите од ЦД	da pres·ni·mi·te od tse·de
my memory card	од мојата картичка	od mo·ya·ta kar·tich·ka
	со меморија	so me·mo·ri·ya
develop this	да го развиете овој	da go raz·vi·e·te o·voy
film	филм	film
load my film	да го ставите филмот	da go sta·vi·te fil·mot
	во апаратот	vo a·pa·ra·tot

I need a/an ... film	Сакам ... за овој	sa·kam ... za o·voy
for this camera.	фотоапарат.	fo·to·a·pa·rat
APS	АПС филм	a·pe·es film
B&W	црно-бел филм	tsr·no·bel film
colour	филм во боја	film vo bo·ya
slide	слајд филм	slayd film
(200) speed	филм со брзина	film so br·zi·na
	(двеста)	(dves·ta)

When will it be ready? Кога ќе биде готов?   ko·ga kye bi·de go·tov

meeting people

greetings, goodbyes & introductions

Hello/Hi.	Здраво/Чао.	*zdra*·vo/*cha*·o
Good night.	Добра ноќ.	*dob*·ra noky
Goodbye/Bye.	До гледање/Чао.	do *gle*·da·nye/*cha*·o
See you later.	Се гледаме.	se *gle*·da·me
Mr	Господин	*gos*·po·din
Mrs	Госпоѓа	*gos*·po·gya
Miss	Госпоѓица	gos·*po*·gyi·tsa
How are you?	Како сте/си? pol/inf	*ka*·ko ste/si
Fine. And you?	Добро. А вие/ти? pol/inf	*dob*·ro a *vi*·e/ti
What's your name?	Како се викате/	*ka*·ko se *vi*·ka·te/
	викаш? pol/inf	*vi*·kash
My name is ...	Јас се викам ...	yas se *vi*·kam ...
I'm pleased to	Драго ми е што	*dra*·go mi e shto
meet you.	се запознавме.	se za·*poz*·nav·me
This is my ...	Ова е ...	*o*·va e ...
boyfriend	моето момче	*mo*·e·to *mom*·che
brother	мојот брат	*mo*·yot brat
daughter	мојата ќерка	*mo*·ya·ta *kyer*·ka
father	мојот татко	*mo*·yot *tat*·ko
friend	мојот пријател m	*mo*·yot *pri*·ya·tel
	мојата пријателка f	*mo*·ya·ta pri·*ya*·tel·ka
girlfriend	мојата девојка	*mo*·ya·ta *de*·voy·ka
husband	мојот сопруг	*mo*·yot *sop*·rug
mother	мојата мајка	*mo*·ya·ta *may*·ka
partner (intimate)	мојот партнер m&f	*mo*·yot *part*·ner
sister	мојата сестра	*mo*·ya·ta *ses*·tra
son	мојот син	*mo*·yot sin
wife	мојата сопруга	*mo*·ya·ta *so*·pru·ga
Here's my ...	Ова е мојата ...	*o*·va e *mo*·ya·ta ...
What's your ...?	Која е вашата ...?	*ko*·ya e *va*·sha·ta ...
address	адреса	*ad*·re·sa
email address	имеил адреса	*i*·me·il *ad*·re·sa

Here's my ...	Ова е мојот ...	o·va e mo·yot ...
What's your ...?	Кој е вашиот ...?	koy e va·shi·ot ...
fax number	број на факс	broy na faks
phone number	телефонски број	te·le·fon·ski broy

occupations

| What's your occupation? | Што работите? | shto ra·bo·ti·te |

I'm a/an ...	Јас сум ...	yas sum ...
artist	уметник m&f	u·met·nik
farmer	фармер m&f	far·mer
office worker	службеник m	sluzh·be·nik
	службеничка f	sluzh·be·nich·ka
scientist	научник m&f	na·uch·nik
tradesperson	трговец m&f	tr·go·vets

background

| Where are you from? | Од каде сте? | od ka·de ste |

I'm from ...	Јас сум од ...	yas sum od ...
Australia	Австралија	av·stra·li·ya
Canada	Канада	ka·na·da
England	Англија	an·gli·ya
New Zealand	Нов Зеланд	nov ze·land
the USA	Америка	a·me·ri·ka

Are you married?	Дали сте женет/	da·li ste zhe·net/
	мажена? m/f	ma·zhe·na
I'm married.	Јас сум женет/	yas sum zhe·net/
	мажена. m/f	ma·zhe·na
I'm single.	Јас сум нежена/	yas sum ne·zhe·net/
	немажена. m/f	ne·ma·zhe·na

age

How old ...?	Колку години ...?	kol·ku go·di·ni ...
are you	имате/имаш pol/inf	i·ma·te/i·mash
is your daughter	има вашата ќерка	i·ma va·sha·ta kyer·ka
is your son	има вашиот син	i·ma va·shi·ot sin

| I'm ... years old. | Јас имам ... години. | yas *i*·mam ... *go*·di·ni |
| He/She is ... years old. | Тој/Таа има ... години. | toy/*ta*·a *i*·ma ... *go*·di·ni |

feelings

I'm (not) ...	Јас (не) сум ...	yas (ne) sum ...
Are you ...?	Дали си ...?	*da*·li si ...
happy	среќен/среќна m/f	*sre*·kyen/*sreky*·na
hungry	гладен/гладна m/f	*gla*·den/*glad*·na
sad	тажен/тажна m/f	*ta*·zhen/*tazh*·na
thirsty	жеден/жедна m/f	*zhe*·den/*zhed*·na

I'm ...	Мене ми е ...	*me*·ne mi e ...
I'm not ...	Не ми е ...	ne mi e ...
Are you ...?	Дали ти е ...?	*da*·li ti e ...
cold	студено	*stu*·de·no
hot	топло	*top*·lo

entertainment

going out

Where can I find ...?	Каде можам да најдам ...?	*ka*·de *mo*·zham da *nay*·dam ...
clubs	клубови	*klu*·bo·vi
gay venues	собиралишта на хомосексуалци	so·bi·*ra*·lish·ta na ho·mo·sek·su·*al*·tsi
pubs	пабови	*pa*·bo·vi

I feel like going to a/the ...	Ми се оди ...	mi se *o*·di ...
concert	на концерт	na *kon*·tsert
movies	на кино	na *ki*·no
party	на забава	na *za*·ba·va
restaurant	во ресторан	vo res·to·*ran*
theatre	на театар	na te·*a*·tar

interests

Do you like ...?	Дали сакате ...?	da·li sa·ka·te ...
I (don't) like ...	Jac (не) сакам ...	yas (ne) sa·kam ...
art	уметност	u·met·nost
cooking	готвење	got·ve·nye
movies	филмови	fil·mo·vi
reading	читање	chi·ta·nye
shopping	купување	ku·pu·va·nye
sport	спорт	sport
travelling	патување	pa·tu·va·nye
Do you like to ...?	Дали сакате да ...?	da·li sa·ka·te da ...
dance	танцувате	tan·tsu·va·te
go to concerts	одите на концерти	o·di·te na kon·tsert
listen to music	слушате музика	slu·sha·te mu·zi·ka

food & drink

finding a place to eat

Can you recommend a ...?	Можете ли да ми препорачате ...?	mo·zhe·te li da mi pre·po·ra·cha·te ...
bar	некој бар	ne·koy bar
café	некое кафе	ne·ko·e ka·fe
restaurant	некој ресторан	ne·koy res·to·ran
I'd like ..., please.	Сакам ..., ве молам.	sa·kam ... ve mo·lam
a table for (four)	маса за (четворица)	ma·sa za (chet·vo·ri·tsa)
the (non)smoking section	на место за (не)пушачи	na mes·to za (ne·)pu·sha·chi

ordering food

breakfast	појадок m	po·ya·dok
lunch	ручек m	ru·chek
dinner	вечера f	ve·che·ra
snack	закуска f	za·kus·ka
today's special	специјалитет на денот m	spe·tsi·ya·li·tet na de·not

What would you recommend?
Што препорачувате вие?   shto pre·po·ra·*chu*·va·te *vi*·e

I'd like (the) …, please.   Ве молам …   ve *mo*·lam …
  bill   сметката   *smet*·ka·ta
  drink list   листа со пијалаци   *lis*·ta so pi·*ya*·la·tsi
  menu   мени   me·*ni*
  that dish   ова јадење   *o*·va *ya*·de·nye

drinks

(cup of) coffee …	(шоља) кафе …	(*sho*·lya) *ka*·fe …
(cup of) tea …	(шоља) чај …	(*sho*·lya) chay …
with milk	со млеко	so *mle*·ko
without sugar	без шеќер	bez *she*·kyer
(orange) juice	сок (од поморанџа) m	sok (od *po*·mo·*ran*·ja)
soft drink	безалкохолен пијалак m	bez·al·*ko*·ho·len *pi*·ya·lak
… water	… вода	… *vo*·da
boiled	превриена	pre·*vri*·e·na
mineral	минерална	mi·ne·*ral*·na

in the bar

I'll have …	Јас ќе земам …	yas kye *ze*·mam …
I'll buy you a drink.	Јас ќе ви/ти купам	yas kye vi/ti *ku*·pam
	пијалак. pol/inf	*pi*·ya·lak
What would you like?	Што сакате вие/ти? pol/inf	shto *sa*·ka·te *vi*·e/ti
Cheers!	На здравје!	na *zdrav*·ye
brandy	ракија f	*ra*·ki·ya
cocktail	коктел m	kok·*tel*
cognac	коњак m	*ko*·nyak
a bottle/glass of beer	шише/чаша пиво	*shi*·she/*cha*·sha *pi*·vo
a shot of (whisky)	чашка (виски)	*chash*·ka (*vis*·ki)
a bottle/glass	шише/чаша	*shi*·she/*cha*·sha
of … wine	… вино	… *vi*·no
red	црвено	*tsr*·ve·no
sparkling	пенливо	*pen*·li·vo
white	бело	*be*·lo

self-catering

What's the local speciality?
Што е локален специјалитет?   *shto e lo·ka·len spe·tsi·ya·li·tet*

What's that?
Што е тоа?   *shto e to·a*

How much is (a kilo of cheese)?
Колку чини (кило сирење)?   *kol·ku chi·ni (ki·lo si·re·nye)*

I'd like ...	Сакам ...	*sa·kam ...*
(100) grams	(сто) грама	*(sto) gra·ma*
(two) kilos	(две) кила	*(dve) ki·la*
(three) pieces	(три) парчиња	*(tri) par·chi·nya*
(six) slices	(шест) парчиња	*(shest) par·chi·nya*

Less.	Помалку.	*po·mal·ku*
Enough.	Доволно.	*do·vol·no*
More.	Повеќе.	*po·ve·kye*

special diets & allergies

Is there a vegetarian restaurant near here?
Дали овде близу има   *da·li ov·de bli·zu i·ma*
вегетаријански ресторан?   *ve·ge·ta·ri·yan·ski res·to·ran*

Do you have vegetarian food?
Дали имате вегетаријанска храна?   *da·li i·ma·te ve·ge·ta·ri·yan·ska hra·na*

Could you prepare a meal without ...?	Може ли да подготвите јадење без ...?	*mo·zhe li da pod·got·vi·te ya·de·nye bez ...*
butter	путер	*pu·ter*
eggs	јајца	*yay·tsa*
meat stock	производи од месо	*pro·iz·vo·di od me·so*

I'm allergic to ...	Јас сум алергичен/ алергична на ... m/f	*yas sum a·ler·gi·chen/ a·ler·gich·na na ...*
dairy produce	млечни производи	*mlech·ni pro·iz·vo·di*
gluten	глутен	*glu·ten*
MSG	МСГ	*muh suh guh*
nuts	ореви, бадеми, лешници	*o·re·vi, ba·de·mi, lesh·ni·tsi*
seafood	морска храна	*mor·ska hra·na*

ајвар m	ay·var	spicy mixture of grilled, ground & fried red peppers (sometimes with eggplant and/or carrots added)
алва f	al·va	sesame seeds crushed in honey
баклава f	bak·la·va	flaky pastry with nuts, soaked in syrup
бурек m	bu·rek	flaky pastry with layers of cheese, spinach, potato or minced meat & onion
ѓувеч m	gyu·vech	stew made of meat (usually chicken), rice, peppers, carrots & onion, baked in the oven
зелник m	zel·nik	thin, flaky pastry filled with leek, spinach, cabbage or potatoes, with cheese & eggs added
качамак m	ka·cha·mak	a paste-like entrée, made of ground maize cooked in salt water & served with feta cheese & fried bacon
мусака f	mu·sa·ka	alternate layers of minced meat & potato or eggplant
пастрмајлија f	pas·tr·may·li·ya	similar to a pizza, with meat (usually pork) & eggs
пилав m	pi·lav	meat cut into small pieces & mixed with seasoned rice before being cooked in the oven
пилешка супа f	pi·lesh·ka su·pa	chicken soup
пинџур m	pin·jur	a mixture of baked, ground or crushed & stir-fried green peppers, tomatoes, eggplant & garlic
пита/баница f	pi·ta/ba·ni·tsa	flaky pastry filled with spinach & cheese, eggs, or pumpkin

плескавица f	*ples-ka-vi-tsa*	*burger of minced pork, beef or lamb*
подварок m	*pod-va-rok*	*finely shredded sour cabbage cooked in the oven with slices of meat*
полнети пиперки f pl	*pol-ne-ti pi-per-ki*	*peppers stuffed with minced beef or pork & rice*
рибја чорба f	*rib-ya chor-ba*	*fish soup*
сарма f	*sar-ma*	*minced meat rolled in sour cabbage leaves*
селско месо n	*sel-sko me-so*	*fried meat, meatballs, smoked meat, mushrooms, tomatoes & onions, cooked in a clay pot in the oven*
сирење n	*si-re-nye*	*white cheese*
скара f	*ska-ra*	*barbecue (chicken, lamb or pork)*
слатко n	*slat-ko*	*fruit (either cherries, grapes, plums etc) cooked in sugar to get a thick mixture, kept in small jars & served with water*
сутлијаш m	*sut-li-yash*	*rice pudding garnished with almonds & cinnamon*
тавче гравче n	*tav-che grav-che*	*boiled beans cooked in a clay pot in the oven*
таратор m	*ta-ra-tor*	*cold appetiser made of yogurt, cucumbers & garlic*
телешка чорба f	*te-lesh-ka chor-ba*	*veal soup*
турли тава f	*tur-li ta-va*	*stew of meat (pork, veal & mutton) & vegetables, cooked in the oven*
ќофтиња n pl	*kyof-ti-nya*	*meatballs*
шампити f pl	*sham-pi-ti*	*whisked egg whites with sugar placed in a thick layer on baked pastry*
шопска салата f	*shop-ska sa-la-ta*	*salad of peppers, cucumbers, tomatoes, onions & feta cheese*

emergencies

basics

Help!	Помош!	po·mosh
Stop!	Застани!	za·sta·ni
Go away!	Одете си!	o·de·te si
Thief!	Крадец!	kra·dets
Fire!	Пожар!	po·zhar
Watch out!	Внимавајте!	vni·ma·vay·te
It's an emergency!	Итно е!	it·no e
I'm lost.	Се загубив.	se za·gu·biv
Where are the toilets?	Каде се тоалетите?	ka·de se to·a·le·ti·te

Call ...!	Викнете ...!	vik·ne·te ...
a doctor	лекар	le·kar
an ambulance	брза помош	br·za po·mosh
the police	полиција	po·li·tsi·ya

Could you help me, please?

Може ли да ми помогнете,
ве молам?

mo·zhe li da mi po·mog·ne·te ve mo·lam

I have to use the telephone.

Треба да телефонирам.

tre·ba da te·le·fo·ni·ram

police

Where's the police station?

Каде е полициската станица?

ka·de e po·li·tsis·ka·ta sta·ni·tsa

I want to report an offence.

Сакам да пријавам престап.

sa·kam da pri·ya·vam pres·tap

I have insurance.

Имам осигурување.

i·mam o·si·gu·ru·va·nye

I've been ...	Бев ...	bev ...
assaulted	нападнат m	na·pad·nat
	нападната f	na·pad·na·ta
raped	силуван/силувана m/f	si·lu·van/si·lu·va·na
robbed	опљачкан m	op·lyach·kan
	опљачкана f	op·lyach·ka·na

I've lost my ...	Го загубив мојот ...	go *za*-gu-biv *mo*-yot ...
My ...was stolen.	Мојот ... беше украден.	*mo*-yot ... *be*-she *uk*-ra-den
jewellery	накит	*na*-kit
passport	пасош	*pa*-sosh
wallet	паричник	*pa*-rich-nik

I've lost my ...	Ја загубив мојата ...	ya *za*-gu-biv *mo*-ya-ta ...
My ...was stolen.	Мојата ... беше украдена.	*mo*-ya-ta ... *be*-she uk-*ra*-de-na
credit card	кредитна картичка	*kre*-dit-na *kar*-tich-ka
handbag	чанта	*chan*-ta

I've lost my ...	Ги загубив моите ...	gi *za*-gu-biv *mo*-i-te ...
My ...were stolen.	Моите ... беа украдени.	*mo*-i-te ... *be*-a uk-*ra*-de-ni
bags	торби	*tor*-bi
travellers cheques	патнички чекови	*pat*-nich-ki *che*-ko-vi

I want to contact my ...	Сакам да се јавам во ...	*sa*-kam da se *ya*-vam vo ...
consulate	мојот конзулат	*mo*-yot kon-zu-*lat*
embassy	мојата амбасада	*mo*-ya-ta am-ba-*sa*-da

health

medical needs

Where's the nearest ...?	Каде има најблиску ...?	*ka*-de *i*-ma *nay*-blis-ku ...
dentist	заболекар	za-bo-*le*-kar
doctor	лекар	*le*-kar
hospital	болница	*bol*-ni-tsa
(night) pharmacist	(дежурна) аптека	(*de*-zhur-na) *ap*-te-ka

I need a doctor (who speaks English).
Ми треба доктор (што зборува англиски).
mi *tre*-ba *dok*-tor (shto *zbo*-ru-va *an*-glis-ki)

Could I see a female doctor?
Може ли да одам кај докторка?
mo-zhe li da *o*-dam kay *dok*-tor-ka

I've run out of my medication.
Останав без лекови.
os-ta-nav bez *le*-ko-vi

symptoms, conditions & allergies

| I'm sick. | Jac сум болен/болна. m/f | yas sum *bo*·len/*bol*·na |
| It hurts here. | Овде ме боли. | *ov*·de me *bo*·li |

I have a (a) ...	Имам ...	*i*·mam ...
asthma	астма	*ast*·ma
bronchitis	бронхитис	bron·*hi*·tis
constipation	констипација	kon·sti·*pa*·tsi·ya
cough	кашлица	*kash*·li·tsa
diarrhoea	пролив	*pro*·liv
fever	треска	*tres*·ka
headache	главоболка	gla·*vo*·bol·ka
heart condition	тешкотии со срцето	tesh·*ko*·ti·i so *sr*·tse·to
nausea	лошење	*lo*·she·nye
pain	болка	*bol*·ka
sore throat	воспаление на грлото	vos·pa·*le*·ni·e na *gr*·lo·to
toothache	забоболка	za·*bo*·bol·ka

I'm allergic to ...	Jac сум алергичен/	yas sum a·*ler*·gi·chen/
	алергична на ... m/f	a·*ler*·gich·na na ...
antibiotics	антибиотици	an·ti·bi·o·*ti*·tsi
anti-inflammatories	анти-инфламатори	an·ti·in·fla·*ma*·to·ri
aspirin	аспирин	as·pi·*rin*
bees	пчели	*pche*·li
codeine	кодеин	ko·de·*in*
penicillin	пеницилин	pe·ni·tsi·*lin*

antiseptic	антисептик m	an·ti·*sep*·tik
bandage	завој m	*za*·voy
condoms	кондоми m pl	kon·*do*·mi
contraceptives	средства за	*sreds*·tva za
	контрацепција n pl	kon·tra·*tsep*·tsi·ya
diarrhoea medicine	лекови против	*le*·ko·vi *pro*·tiv
	пролив m pl	*pro*·liv
insect repellent	средство против	*sreds*·tvo *pro*·tiv
	инсекти n	*in*·sek·ti
laxatives	лаксативи m pl	lak·sa·*ti*·vi
painkillers	средства против болки n pl	*sreds*·tva *pro*·tiv *bol*·ki
rehydration salts	соли за рехидрирање f pl	*so*·li za re·hid·*ri*·ra·nye
sleeping tablets	таблети за спиење f pl	tab·*le*·ti za *spi*·e·nye

english–macedonian dictionary

Macedonian nouns in this dictionary have their gender indicated by ⓜ (masculine), ⓕ (feminine) or ⓝ (neuter). If it's a plural noun, you'll also see pl. Adjectives are given in the masculine form only. Words are also marked as a (adjective), v (verb), sg (singular), pl (plural), inf (informal) or pol (polite) where necessary.

A

accident несреќа ⓕ *nes-kya*
accommodation сместување ⓝ *smes-tu-va-nye*
adaptor адаптер ⓜ *a-dap-ter*
address адреса ⓕ *a-dre-sa*
after потоа *po-to-a*
air-conditioned климатизиран kli-ma-ti-zi-ran
airplane авион ⓜ *a-vi-on*
airport аеродром ⓜ a-e-ro-*drom*
alcohol алкохол ⓜ *al*-ko-hol
all сите *si-*te
allergy алергија ⓕ a-*ler-*gi-ya
ambulance брза помош ⓕ *br*-za *po*-mosh
and и i
ankle зглоб ⓜ zglob
arm рака ⓕ *ra-*ka
ashtray пепелник ⓜ *pe*-pel-nik
ATM банкомат ⓜ ban-ko-*mat*

B

baby бебе ⓝ *be*-be
back (body) грб ⓜ grb
backpack ранец ⓜ *ra-*nets
bad лош losh
bag торба ⓕ *tor*-ba
baggage claim подигање на багаж ⓝ
  po-di-ga-nye na ba-gazh
bank банка ⓕ *ban*-ka
bar бар ⓜ bar
bathroom бања ⓕ *ba*-nya
battery батерија ⓕ ba-*te*-ri-ya
beautiful убав u-bav
bed кревет ⓜ *kre*-vet
beer пиво ⓝ *pi*-vo
before пред pred
behind зад zad
bicycle точак ⓜ *to*-chak
big голем *go*-lem
bill сметка ⓕ *smet*-ka
black црн tsrn
blanket ќебе ⓝ *kye*-be

blood group крвна група ⓕ *krv*-na *gru*-pa
blue син sin
boat брод ⓜ brod
book (make a reservation) v резервира re-zer-*vi*-ra
bottle шише ⓝ *shi*-she
bottle opener отворач за шишиња ⓜ
  o-*tvo*-rach za *shi*-shi-nya
boy момче ⓝ *mom*-che
brakes (car) кочници ⓕ pl *koch*-ni-tsi
breakfast појадок ⓜ *po*-ya-dok
broken (faulty) расипан *ra*-si-pan
bus автобус ⓜ *av*-to-bus
business бизнис ⓜ *biz*-nis
buy купува *ku*-pu-va

C

café кафуле ⓝ *ka*-fu-le
camera фото апарат ⓜ *fo*-to a-pa-*rat*
camp site камп ⓜ kamp
cancel откажува ot-*ka*-zhu-va
can opener отворач за конзерви ⓜ
  ot-*vo*-rach za kon-*zer*-vi
car автомобил ⓜ *av*-to-mo-bil
(pay) cash (плаќа) во готово (*pla*-kya) vo *go*-to-vo
cash (a cheque) v менува (чек) *me*-nu-va (chek)
cell phone мобилен телефон ⓜ *mo*-bi-len te-le-*fon*
centre центар ⓜ *tsen*-tar
change (money) v разменува (пари)
  raz-*me*-nu-va (*pa*-ri)
cheap евтин *ev*-tin
check (bill) сметка ⓕ *smet*-ka
check-in пријавување ⓝ pri-ya-*vu*-va-nye
chest гради ⓕ pl *gra*-di
child дете ⓝ *de*-te
cigarette цигара ⓕ *tsi*-ga-ra
city град ⓜ grad
clean a чист chist
closed затворен zat-*vo*-ren
coffee кафе ⓝ *ka*-fe
coins метални пари ⓕ pl *me*-tal-ni *pa*-ri
cold a студен *stu*-den
collect call разговор платен од примачот ⓜ
  raz-go-vor *pla*-ten od *pri*-ma-chot

come доаѓа *do-a-gya*
computer компјутер ⓜ *komp-yu-ter*
condom кондом ⓜ *kon-dom*
contact lenses контактни леќи ⓕ pl
  kon-tak-tni le-kyi
cook v готви *got-vi*
cost цена ⓕ *tse-na*
credit card кредитна картичка ⓕ
  kre-dit-na kar-tich-ka
cup шолја ⓕ *sho-lya*
currency exchange курс на валути ⓜ *kurs na va-lu-ti*
customs (immigration) царинарница ⓕ
  tsa-ri-*nar*-ni-tsa

D

dangerous опасен *o-pa-sen*
date (time) датум ⓜ *da-tum*
day ден ⓜ *den*
delay n доцнење ⓕ *dots-ne-nye*
dentist забар ⓜ *za-bar*
depart заминува *za-mi-nu-va*
diaper пелена ⓕ *pe-le-na*
dictionary речник ⓜ *rech-nik*
dinner вечера ⓕ *ve-che-ra*
direct директен *di-rek-ten*
dirty нечист *ne-chist*
disabled (person) инвалид ⓜ *in-va-lid*
discount попуст ⓜ *po-pust*
doctor доктор ⓜ *dok-tor*
double bed брачен кревет ⓜ *bra-chen kre-vet*
double room двокреветна соба ⓕ
  dvo-*kre*-vet-na *so*-ba
drink пијалак ⓜ *pi-ya-lak*
drive v вози *vo-zi*
drivers licence возачка дозвола ⓕ
  vo-zach-ka doz-vo-la
drug (illicit) дрога ⓕ *dro-ga*
dummy (pacifier) цуцла ⓕ *tsuts-la*

E

ear уво ⓝ *u-vo*
east исток ⓜ *is-tok*
eat јаде *ya-de*
economy class економска класа ⓕ
  e-*kon*-om-ska *kla*-sa
electricity електрична струја ⓕ *e-lek-trich-na stru-ya*
elevator лифт ⓜ *lift*
email имеил ⓜ *i-me-il*
embassy амбасада ⓕ am-ba-sa-da
emergency итна ситуација ⓕ *it-na si-tu-a-tsi-ya*

English (language) англиски ⓜ *an-glis-ki*
entrance влез ⓜ *vlez*
evening вечер ⓕ *ve-cher*
exchange rate курс ⓜ *kurs*
exit излез ⓜ *iz-lez*
expensive скап *skap*
express mail брза пошта ⓕ *br-za posh-ta*
eye око ⓝ *o-ko*

F

far далеку *da-le-ku*
fast брз *brz*
father татко ⓜ *tat-ko*
film (camera) филм ⓜ *film*
finger прст ⓜ *prst*
first-aid kit кутија за прва помош ⓕ
  ku-ti-ya za *pr*-va po-mosh
first class прва класа ⓕ *pr*-va *kla*-sa
fish риба ⓕ *ri-ba*
food храна ⓕ *hra-na*
foot нога ⓕ *no-ga*
fork виљушка ⓕ *vi-lyush-ka*
free (of charge) бесплатен *bes*-pla-ten
friend пријател/пријателка ⓜ/ⓕ
  pri-ya-tel/*pri-ya*-tel-ka
fruit овошје ⓝ *o-vosh-ye*
full полн *poln*
funny смешен *sme-shen*

G

gift подарок ⓜ *po-da-rok*
girl девојка ⓕ *de-voy-ka*
glass (drinking) чаша ⓕ *cha-sha*
glasses очила ⓝ pl *o-chi-la*
go оди *o-di*
good добар *do-bar*
green зелен *ze-len*
guide водич ⓜ *vo-dich*

H

half половина ⓕ *po-lo-vi-na*
hand рака ⓕ *ra-ka*
handbag женска чанта ⓕ *zhen*-ska *chan*-ta
happy среќен *sre*-kyen
have има *i-ma*
he тој *toy*
head глава ⓕ *gla-va*
heart срце ⓝ *sr-tse*
heat топлина ⓕ *to-pli-na*

heavy тежок *te-zhok*
help v помага *po-ma-ga*
here овде *ov-de*
high висок *vi-sok*
highway автопат ⓜ *av-to-pat*
hike v планинари *pla-ni-na-ri*
holiday годишен одмор ⓜ *go-di-shen od-mor*
homosexual хомосексуалец ⓜ *ho-mo-sek-su-a-lets*
hospital болница ⓕ *bol-ni-tsa*
hot жежок *zhe-zhok*
hotel хотел ⓜ *ho-tel*
hungry гладен *gla-den*
husband сопруг ⓜ *sop-rug*

I

I јас *yas*
identification (card) лична карта ⓕ *lich-na kar-ta*
ill болен *bo-len*
important важен *va-zhen*
included вклучен *vklu-chen*
injury повреда ⓕ *po-vre-da*
insurance осигурување ⓝ *o-si-gu-ru-va-nye*
Internet интернет ⓜ *in-ter-net*
interpreter толкувач ⓜ *tol-ku-vach*

J

jewellery накит ⓜ *na-kit*
job работа ⓕ *ra-bo-ta*

K

key клуч ⓜ *kluch*
kilogram килограм ⓜ *ki-lo-gram*
kitchen кујна ⓕ *kuy-na*
knife нож ⓜ *nozh*

L

laundry (place) перална ⓕ *pe-ral-na*
lawyer адвокат ⓜ *ad-vo-kat*
left (direction) лево *le-vo*
left-luggage office место за чување багаж ⓝ *mes-to za chu-va-nye ba-gazh*
leg нога ⓕ *no-ga*
lesbian лезбејка ⓕ *lez-bey-ka*
less помалку *po-mal-ku*
letter (mail) писмо ⓝ *pis-mo*
lift (elevator) лифт ⓜ *lift*
light светлина ⓕ *svet-li-na*

like v сака *sa-ka*
lock катанец ⓜ *ka-ta-nets*
long долг *dolg*
lost загубен *za-gu-ben*
lost-property office биро за загубени работи ⓝ *bi-ro za za-gu-be-ni ra-bo-ti*
love v љуби *lyu-bi*
luggage багаж ⓜ *ba-gazh*
lunch ручек ⓜ *ru-chek*

M

Macedonia Македонија ⓕ *ma-ke-do-ni-ya*
Macedonian (language) македонски ⓜ *ma-ke-don-ski*
Macedonian a македонски *ma-ke-don-ski*
mail пошта ⓕ *posh-ta*
man маж ⓜ *mazh*
map мапа ⓕ *ma-pa* ,
market пазар ⓜ *pa-zar*
matches кибрит ⓜ *kib-rit*
meat месо ⓝ *me-so*
medicine лек ⓜ *lek*
menu мени ⓝ *me-ni*
message порака ⓕ *po-ra-ka*
milk млеко ⓝ *mle-ko*
minute минута ⓕ *mi-nu-ta*
mobile phone мобилен телефон ⓜ *mo-bi-len te-le-fon*
money пари ⓝ pl *pa-ri*
month месец ⓜ *me-sets*
morning утро ⓝ *ut-ro*
mother мајка ⓕ *may-ka*
motorcycle мотор ⓜ *mo-tor*
motorway автопат ⓜ *av-to-pat*
mouth уста ⓕ *us-ta*
music музика ⓕ *mu-zi-ka*

N

name име ⓝ *i-me*
napkin салфета ⓕ *sal-fe-ta*
nappy пелена ⓕ *pe-le-na*
near блиску *blis-ku*
neck врат ⓜ *vrat*
new нов *nov*
news вести ⓝ pl *ves-ti*
newspaper весник ⓜ *ves-nik*
night ноќ ⓕ *noky*
no не *ne*
noisy бучен *bu-chen*
nonsmoking за непушачи *za ne-pu-sha-chi*

north север ⓜ se-ver
nose нос ⓜ nos
now сега se-ga
number број ⓜ broy

O

oil (engine) масло ⓝ mas-lo
old стар ⓜ star
one-way ticket билет во еден правец ⓜ bi-let vo e-den pra-vets
open a отворен ot-vo-ren
outside надвор nad-vor

P

package пакет ⓜ pa-ket
paper хартија ⓕ har-ti-ya
park (car) v паркира par-ki-ra
passport пасош ⓜ pa-sosh
pay плаќа pla-kya
pen пенкало ⓝ pen-ka-lo
petrol бензин ⓜ ben-zin
pharmacy аптека ⓕ ap-te-ka
phonecard телефонска картичка ⓕ te-le-fon-ska kar-tich-ka
photo фотографија ⓕ fo-to-gra-fi-ya
plate чинија ⓕ chi-ni-ya
police полиција ⓕ po-li-tsi-ya
postcard поштенска картичка ⓕ posh-ten-ska kar-tich-ka
post office пошта ⓕ posh-ta
pregnant бремена ⓕ bre-me-na
price цена ⓕ tse-na

Q

quiet тивок ti-vok

R

rain дожд ⓜ dozhd
razor жилет ⓜ zhi-let
receipt белешка ⓕ be-lesh-ka
red црвен tsr-ven
refund враќање на пари ⓝ vra-kya-nye na pa-ri
registered mail препорачано писмо ⓝ pre-po-ra-cha-no pis-mo
rent v изнајмува iz-nay-mu-va
repair v поправа pop-ra-va
reservation резервација ⓕ re-zer-va-tsi-ya

restaurant ресторан ⓜ res-to-ran
return v враќа vra-kya
return ticket повратен билет ⓜ po-vra-ten bi-let
right (direction) десно des-no
road пат ⓜ pat
room соба ⓕ so-ba

S

safe a безбеден bez-be-den
sanitary napkin хигиенска влошка ⓕ hi-gi-en-ska vlosh-ka
seat седиште ⓝ se-dish-te
send испраќа is-pra-kya
service station бензинска пумпа ⓕ ben-zin-ska pum-pa
sex секс ⓜ seks
shampoo шампон ⓜ sham-pon
share (a dorm) дели de-li
shaving cream крем за бричење ⓜ krem za bri-che-nye
she таа ta-a
sheet (bed) чаршаф ⓜ char-shaf
shirt кошула ⓕ ko-shu-la
shoes чевли ⓜ pl chev-li
shop продавница ⓕ pro-dav-ni-tsa
short кус kus
shower туш ⓜ tush
single room еднокреветна соба ⓕ ed-no-kre-vet-na so-ba
skin кожа ⓕ ko-zha
skirt здолниште ⓝ zdol-nish-te
sleep v спие spi-e
slowly полека po-le-ka
small мал mal
smoke (cigarettes) v пуши pu-shi
soap сапун ⓜ sa-pun
some неколку ne-kol-ku
soon наскоро nas-ko-ro
south југ ⓜ yug
souvenir shop продавница за сувенири ⓕ pro-dav-ni-tsa za su-ve-ni-ri
speak зборува zbo-ru-va
spoon лажица ⓕ la-zhi-tsa
stamp марка ⓕ mar-ka
stand-by ticket стендбај билет ⓜ stend-bay bi-let
station (train) (железничка) станица ⓕ (zhe-lez-nich-ka) sta-ni-tsa
stomach стомак ⓜ sto-mak
stop v запира za-pi-ra
(bus) stop (автобуска) станица ⓕ (av-to-bus-ka) sta-ni-tsa
street улица ⓕ u-li-tsa

student студент/студентка ⓜ/ⓕ
stu-dent/stu-*dent*-ka

sun сонце ⓝ *son*-tse

sunscreen лосион за сончање ⓜ
lo-si-*on* za *son*-cha-nye

swim v плива *pli*-va

T

tampons тампони ⓜ pl *tam*-*po*-ni

taxi такси ⓝ *tak*-si

teaspoon лажиче ⓝ *la*-zhi-che

teeth заби ⓜ pl *za*-bi

telephone телефон ⓜ te-le-*fon*

television телевизија ⓕ te-le-*vi*-zi-ya

temperature (weather) температура ⓕ
tem-pe-ra-*tu*-ra

tent шатор ⓜ *sha*-tor

that (one) она o-*na*

they тие *ti*-e

thirsty жеден *zhe*-den

this (one) ова o-va

throat грло ⓝ *gr*-lo

ticket билет ⓜ *bi*-let

time време ⓝ *vre*-me

tired уморен u-mo-ren

tissues книжни марамчиња ⓜ pl
knizh-ni ma-*ram*-chi-nya

today денес *de*-nes

toilet тоалет ⓜ to-a-*let*

tomorrow утре *ut*-re

tonight вечерва *ve*-cher-va

toothbrush четка за заби ⓕ *chet*-ka za *za*-bi

toothpaste паста за заби ⓕ *pas*-ta za *za*-bi

torch (flashlight) џепна ламба ⓕ *jep*-na *lam*-ba

tour патување ⓝ pa-*tu*-va-nye

tourist office туристичко биро ⓝ tu-*ris*-tich-ko bi-*ro*

towel пешкир ⓜ *pesh*-kir

train воз ⓜ voz

translate преведува pre-*ve*-du-va

travel agency туристичка агенција ⓕ
tu-*ris*-tich-ka a-*gen*-tsi-ya

travellers cheque патнички чек ⓜ *pat*-nich-ki chek

trousers панталони ⓕ pl pan-*ta*-lo-ni

twin beds двоен кревет ⓜ *dvo*-en *kre*-vet

tyre гума ⓕ *gu*-ma

U

underwear долна облека ⓕ *dol*-na *ob*-le-ka

urgent итен *i*-ten

V

vacant слободен *slo*-bo-den

vacation годишен одмор ⓜ *go*-di-shen *od*-mor

vegetable зеленчук ⓜ *ze*-len-chuk

vegetarian a вегетаријански ve-ge-ta-ri-*yan*-ski

visa виза ⓕ *vi*-za

W

waiter келнер ⓜ *kel*-ner

walk v пешачи pe-sha-chi

wallet паричник ⓜ *pa*-rich-nik

warm a топол *to*-pol

wash (something) мие *mi*-e

watch часовник ⓜ *cha*-sov-nik

water вода ⓕ *vo*-da

we ние *ni*-e

weekend викенд ⓜ *vi*-kend

west запад ⓜ *za*-pad

wheelchair инвалидска количка ⓕ
in-va-*lid*-ska ko-*lich*-ka

when кога *ko*-ga

where каде *ka*-de

white бел bel

who кој koy

why зошто *zosh*-to

wife сопруга ⓕ *so*-pru-ga

window прозорец ⓜ *pro*-zo-rets

wine вино ⓝ *vi*-no

with со so

without без bez

woman жена ⓕ *zhe*-na

write пишува *pi*-shu-va

Y

yellow жолт zholt

yes да da

yesterday вчера *vche*-ra

you sg inf ти ti

you sg pol & pl вие *vi*-e

Portuguese

portuguese alphabet

A a aa	B b be	C c se	D d de	E e e
F f e·fe	G g je	H h a·gaah	I i ee	J j jo·ta
K k ka·pa	L l e·le	M m e·me	N n e·ne	O o o
P p pe	Q q ke	R r e·rre	S s e·se	T t te
U u oo	V v ve	W w da·blyoo	X x sheesh	Y y eeps·lon
Z z ze				

■ portuguese

introduction

Portuguese (*português* poor·too·*gesh*), the language which produced words such as *albino*, *brocade* and *molasses*, comes from the Romance language family and is closely related to Spanish, French and Italian. Descended from the colloquial Latin spoken by Roman soldiers, it's now used by over 200 million people worldwide.

Linguists believe that before the Roman invasion of the Iberian Peninsula in 218 BC, the locals of modern-day Portugal spoke a Celtic language. That local language was supplanted by the vernacular form of Latin (sometimes called 'Romance') spoken by the occupying forces under the Romans' 500-year rule of the province of Lusitania (present-day Portugal and Spanish Galicia). During this period, Portuguese also absorbed elements of the languages of invading Germanic tribes. The greatest influence on today's Portuguese, however, was a result of the Moorish invasion of the peninsula in AD 711. Arabic was imposed as the official language of the region until the expulsion of the Moors in 1249, and although Romance was still spoken by the masses, the Moorish language left its mark on the vocabulary. From the 16th century on, there were only minor changes to the language, mostly influences from France and Spain. The earliest written documents were composed in the 12th century, and the Portuguese used in 1572 by Luís de Camões (author of the first great Portuguese classic, *Os Lusíadas*) was already identifiable as the language of José Saramago's Nobel Prize-winning works in the 20th century.

The global distribution of the Portuguese language began during the period know as *Os Descobrimentos* (the Discoveries), the golden era of Portugal's colonial expansion into Africa, Asia and South America. In the 15th and 16th centuries, the peninsular nation was a world power and had enormous economic, cultural and political influence. The empire's reach can be seen today in the number of countries besides Portugal where Portuguese still has the status of an official language – Brazil, Madeira and the Azores in the Atlantic Ocean off Europe, Cape Verde, São Tomé and Príncipe, Guinea-Bissau, Angola and Mozambique (all in Africa), and Macau and East Timor in Asia.

While there are differences between European Portuguese and that spoken elsewhere, you shouldn't have many problems being understood throughout the Portuguese-speaking world. As the Portuguese say, *Quem não arrisca, não petisca* keng nowng a·*rreesh*·ka, nowng pe·*teesh*·ka (If you don't take a risk, you won't eat delicacies).

pronunciation

vowel sounds

The vowel sounds in Portuguese are quite similar to those found in English. Most vowel sounds in Portuguese also have a nasal version with an effect similar to the silent '-ng' ending in English, as in *amanhã* aa·ma·*nyang* (tomorrow), for example. The letter 'n' or 'm' at the end of a syllable or a tilde (~) in written Portuguese indicate that the vowel is nasal.

symbol	english equivalent	portuguese example	transliteration
a	run	*maçã*	ma·*sang*
aa	father	*tomate*	too·*maa*·te
ai	aisle	*pai*	pai
ay	say	*lei*	lay
e	bet	*cedo*	*se*·doo
ee	see	*fino*	*fee*·noo
o	pot	*sobre*	*so*·bre
oh	oh	*couve*	*koh*·ve
oo	book	*gato*	*ga*·too
ow	how	*Austrália*	ow·*shtraa*·lya
oy	toy	*noite*	*noy*·te

word stress

In Portuguese, stress generally falls on the second-to-last syllable of a word, though there are exceptions. If a written vowel has a circumflex (ˆ) or an acute (´) or grave (`) accent marked on it, this cancels the general rule and the stress falls on that syllable. When a word ends in a written *i*, *im*, *l*, *r*, *u*, *um* or *z*, or is pronounced with a nasalised vowel, the stress falls on the last syllable. Don't worry too much about it when using phrases from this book though – the stressed syllable is always italicised in our coloured pronunciation guides.

consonant sounds

Most of the consonant sounds in Portuguese are also found in English, and even *r* (rr) will be familiar to many people (it's similar to the French 'r'). Note that the letter ç ('c' with a cedilla) is pronounced as s rather than k.

symbol	english equivalent	portuguese example	transliteration
b	bed	*beber*	be·*ber*
d	dog	*dedo*	de·doo
f	fat	*faca*	faa·ka
g	go	*gasolina*	ga·zoo·lee·na
k	kit	*cama*	ka·ma
l	lot	*lixo*	lee·shoo
ly	million	*muralhas*	moo·raa·lyash
m	man	*macaco*	ma·kaa·koo
n	not	*nada*	naa·da
ng	ring (indicates the nasalisation of the preceding vowel)	*ambos, uns, amanhã*	ang·boosh, oongsh, aa·ma·nyang
ny	canyon	*linha*	lee·nya
p	pet	*padre*	paa·dre
r	like 'tt' in 'butter' said fast	*hora*	o·ra
rr	run (throaty)	*relva*	rrel·va
s	sun	*criança*	kree·ang·sa
sh	shot	*chave*	shaa·ve
t	top	*tacho*	taa·shoo
v	very	*vago*	vaa·goo
w	win	*água*	aa·gwa
y	yes	*edifício*	ee·dee·fee·syoo
z	zero	*camisa*	ka·mee·za
zh	pleasure	*cerveja*	serr·ve·zha

tools

language difficulties

Do you speak English?
Fala inglês?   faa·la eeng·*glesh*

Do you understand?
Entende?   eng·*teng*·de

I (don't) understand.
(Não) Entendo.   (nowng) eng·*teng*·doo

What does (*bem-vindo*) mean?
O que quer dizer (bem-vindo)?   oo ke ker dee·*zer* (beng·*veeng*·doo)

How do you ...?	*Como é que se ...?*	ko·moo e ke se ...
pronounce this	*pronuncia isto*	proo·noong·*see*·a *esh*·too
write (*ajuda*)	*escreve (ajuda)*	shkre·ve (a·*zhoo*·da)

Could you please ...?	*Podia ..., por favor?*	poo·dee·a ... poor fa·*vor*
repeat that	*repetir isto*	rre·pe·*teer* eesh·too
speak more slowly	*falar mais devagar*	fa·*laar* maish de·va·*gaar*
write it down	*escrever isso*	shkre·*ver* ee·soo

PORTUGUES – tools

numbers

0	zero	ze·roo	16	dezasseis	de·za·saysh
1	um	oong	17	dezassete	de·za·se·te
2	dois	doysh	18	dezoito	de·zoy·too
3	três	tresh	19	dezanove	de·za·no·ve
4	quatro	kwaa·troo	20	vinte	veeng·te
5	cinco	seeng·koo	21	vinte e um	veeng·te e oong
6	seis	saysh	22	vinte e dois	veeng·te e doysh
7	sete	se·te	30	trinta	treeng·ta
8	oito	oy·too	40	quarenta	kwa·reng·ta
9	nove	no·ve	50	cinquenta	seeng·kweng·ta
10	dez	desh	60	sessenta	se·seng·ta
11	onze	ong·ze	70	setenta	se·teng·ta
12	doze	do·ze	80	oitenta	oy·teng·ta
13	treze	tre·ze	90	noventa	no·veng·ta
14	catorze	ka·tor·ze	100	cem	seng
15	quinze	keeng·ze	1000	mil	meel

time & dates

What time is it?	Que horas são?	kee o·rash sowng
It's one o'clock.	É uma hora.	e oo·ma o·ra
It's (10) o'clock.	São (dez) horas.	sowng (desh) o·rash
Quarter past (10).	(Dez) e quinze.	(desh) e keeng·ze
Half past (10).	(Dez) e meia.	(desh) e may·a
Quarter to (10).	Quinze para as (dez).	keeng·ze pa·ra ash (desh)
At what time ...?	A que horas ...?	a ke o·rash ...
At ...	Às ...	ash ...
in the morning	da manhã	da ma·nyang
in the afternoon	da tarde	da taar·de
in the evening	da noite	da noy·te
Monday	segunda-feira	se·goong·da·fay·ra
Tuesday	terça-feira	ter·sa·fay·ra
Wednesday	quarta-feira	kwaar·ta·fay·ra
Thursday	quinta-feira	keeng·ta·fay·ra
Friday	sexta-feira	saysh·ta·fay·ra
Saturday	sábado	saa·ba·doo
Sunday	domingo	doo·meeng·goo

January	*Janeiro*	zha-*nay*-roo
February	*Fevereiro*	fe-*vray*-roo
March	*Março*	maar-soo
April	*Abril*	a-*breel*
May	*Maio*	maa-yoo
June	*Junho*	zhoo-nyoo
July	*Julho*	zhoo-lyoo
August	*Agosto*	a-*gosh*-too
September	*Setembro*	se-*teng*-broo
October	*Outubro*	oh-*too*-broo
November	*Novembro*	no-*veng*-broo
December	*Dezembro*	de-*zeng*-broo

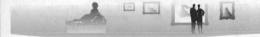

What date is it today?
Qual é a data de hoje? — kwaal e a *daa*-ta de o-zhe

It's (18 October).
Hoje é dia (dezoito de Outubro). — o-zhe e *dee*-a (de-*zoy*-too de oh-*too*-broo)

since (May)	*desde (Maio)*	desh-de (maa-yoo)
until (June)	*até (Junho)*	a-*te* (zhoo-nyoo)

last ...		
night	*a noite passada*	a *noy*-te pa-*saa*-da
week	*a semana passada*	a se-*ma*-na pa-*saa*-da
month	*o mês passado*	oo mesh pa-*saa*-doo
year	*o ano passado*	oo *a*-noo pa-*saa*-doo

next ...		
week	*na próxima semana*	na *pro*-see-ma se-*ma*-na
month	*no próximo mês*	noo *pro*-see-moo mesh
year	*no próximo ano*	noo *pro*-see-moo *a*-noo

yesterday/tomorrow ...	*ontem/amanhã ...*	ong-teng/aa-ma-*nyang* ...
morning	*de manhã*	de ma-*nyang*
afternoon	*à tarde*	aa *taar*-de
evening	*à noite*	aa *noy*-te

weather

What's the weather like?	Como está o tempo?	ko·moo shtaa oo teng·poo
It's ...	Está ...	shtaa ...
cloudy	enublado	e·noo·blaa·doo
cold	frio	free·oo
hot	muito quente	mweeng·too keng·te
raining	a chover	a shoo·ver
snowing	a nevar	a ne·vaar
sunny	sol	sol
warm	quente	keng·te
windy	ventoso	veng·to·zoo
spring	primavera f	pree·ma·ve·ra
summer	verão m	ve·rowng
autumn	outono m	oh·to·noo
winter	inverno m	eeng·ver·noo

border crossing

I'm here ...	Estou ...	shtoh ...
in transit	em trânsito	eng trang·zee·too
on business	em negócios	eng ne·go·syoosh
on holiday	de férias	de fe·ree·ash
I'm here for ...	Vou ficar por ...	voh fee·kaar poor ...
(10) days	(dez) dias	(desh) dee·ash
(three) weeks	(três) semanas	(tresh) se·ma·nash
(two) months	(dois) meses	(doysh) me·zesh

I'm going to (Elvas).
Vou para (Elvas).   voh pa·ra (el·vash)

I'm staying at the (Hotel Lisbon).
Estou no (Hotel Lisboa).   shtoh noo (o·tel leezh·bo·a)

I have nothing to declare.
Não tenho nada a declarar.   nowng ta·nyoo naa·da a de·kla·raar

I have something to declare.
Tenho algo a declarar.   ta·nyoo al·goo a de·kla·raar

That's (not) mine.
Isto (não) é meu.   eesh·too (nowng) e me·oo

transport

tickets & luggage

Where can I buy a ticket?
Onde é que eu compro o bilhete?   *ong*·de e ke e·oo *kong*·proo oo bee·*lye*·te

Do I need to book a seat?
Preciso de fazer reserva?   pre·*see*·zoo de fa·*zer* rre·*zer*·va

One ... ticket (to Braga), please.	Um bilhete de ... (para Braga), por favor.	oong bee·*lye*·te de ... (pra *braa*·ga) poor fa·*vor*
one-way	*ida*	*ee*·da
return	*ida e volta*	*ee*·da ee *vol*·ta

I'd like to ... my ticket, please.	Queria ... o bilhete, por favor.	ke·*ree*·a ... oo bee·*lye*·te poor fa·*vor*
cancel	*cancelar*	kang·se·*laar*
change	*trocar*	troo·*kaar*
collect	*cobrar*	koo·*braar*
confirm	*confirmar*	kong·feer·*maar*

I'd like a ... seat, please.	Queria um lugar ... por favor.	ke·*ree*·a oong loo·*gaar* ... poor fa·*vor*
nonsmoking	*de não fumadores*	de nowng foo·ma·*do*·resh
smoking	*para fumadores*	pra foo·ma·*do*·resh

How much is it?
Quanto é?   *kwang*·too e

Is there air conditioning?
Tem ar condicionado?   teng aar kong·dee·syoo·*naa*·doo

Is there a toilet?
Tem casa de banho?   teng *kaa*·za de *ba*·nyoo

How long does the trip take?
Quanto tempo é que leva a viagem?   *kwang*·too *teng*·poo e ke *le*·va a vee·*aa*·zheng

Is it a direct route?
É uma rota directa?   e *oo*·ma *rro*·ta dee·*re*·ta

I'd like a luggage locker.
Queria o depósito de bagagens.   ke·*ree*·a oo de·*po*·zee·too de ba·*gaa*·zhengsh

My luggage	A minha	a *mee*·nya
has been ...	bagagem ...	ba·*gaa*·zheng ...
damaged	foi danificada	foy da·nee·fee·*kaa*·da
lost	perdeu-se	per·*de*·oo·se
stolen	foi roubada	foy rroh·*baa*·da

getting around

Where does flight (TP 615) arrive/depart?

De onde pára/parte o voo   de ong·de *paa*·ra/*paar*·te oo *vo*·oo
(TP 615)?   (te pe saysh·*seng*·toosh e *keeng*·ze)

Where's (the) ...?	Onde é ...?	ong·de e ...
arrivals hall	a porta de chegada	a *por*·ta de she·*gaa*·da
departures hall	a porta de partida	a *por*·ta de par·*tee*·da
duty-free shop	a loja duty-free	a *lo*·zha doo·tee·free
gate (12)	a porta (doze)	a *por*·ta (*do*·ze)

Is this the ...	Este é o ...	*esh*·te e oo ...
to (Lisbon)?	para (Lisboa)?	pra (leezh·*bo*·a)
boat	barco	*baar*·koo
bus	autocarro	ow·to·*kaa*·rroo
plane	avião	a·vee·*owng*
train	comboio	kong·*boy*·oo

What time's	Quando é que sai	*kwang*·doo e ke sai
the ... bus?	o ... autocarro?	oo ... ow·to·*kaa*·rroo
first	primeiro	pree·*may*·roo
last	último	*ool*·tee·moo
next	próximo	*pro*·see·moo

At what time does it arrive/leave?

A que horas chega/sai?   a ke *o*·rash *she*·ga/sai

How long will it be delayed?

Quanto tempo é que   *kwang*·too *teng*·poo e ke
vai chegar atrasado?   vai she·*gaar* a·tra·*zaa*·doo

What station/stop is this?

Qual estação/paragem é este?   kwaal shta·*sowng*/pa·*raa*·zheng e *esh*·te

What's the next station/stop?

Qual é a próxima estação/   kwaal e a *pro*·see·ma shta·*sowng*/
paragem?   pa·*raa*·zheng

Does it stop at (Amarante)?
Pára em (Amarante)? — paa·ra eng (a·ma·rang·te)

Please tell me when we get to (Évora).
Por favor avise-me quando chegarmos a (Évora). — poor fa·vor a·vee·ze·me kwang·doo she·gaar·moosh a (e·voo·ra)

How long do we stop here?
Quanto tempo vamos ficar parados aqui? — kwang·too teng·poo va·moosh fee·kaar pa·raa·doosh a·kee

Is this seat available?
Este lugar está vago? — esh·te loo·gaar shtaa va·goo

That's my seat.
Este é o meu lugar. — esh·te e oo me·oo loo·gaar

I'd like a taxi ...	*Queria chamar um táxi ...*	ke·ree·a sha·maar oong taak·see ...
at (9am)	*para as (nove da manhã)*	pra ash (no·ve da ma·nyang)
now	*agora*	a·go·ra
tomorrow	*amanhã*	aa·ma·nyang

Is this taxi available?
Este táxi está livre? — esh·te taak·see shtaa lee·vre

How much is it to ...?
Quanto custa até ao ...? — kwang·too koosh·ta a·te ow ...

Please put the meter on.
Por favor, ligue o taxímetro. — poor fa·vor lee·ge oo taak·see·me·troo

Please take me to (this address).
Leve-me para (este endereço), por favor. — le·ve·me pa·ra (esh·te eng·de·re·soo) poor fa·vor

Please ...	*Por favor ...*	poor fa·vor ...
slow down	*vá mais devagar*	vaa maish de·va·gaar
stop here	*pare aqui*	paa·re a·kee
wait here	*espere aqui*	shpe·re a·kee

car, motorbike & bicycle hire

I'd like to hire a …	Queria alugar …	ke·ree·a a·loo·gaar …
bicycle	uma bicicleta	oo·ma bee·see·kle·ta
car	um carro	oong kaa·rroo
motorbike	uma mota	oo·ma mo·ta
with …	com …	kong …
a driver	motorista	moo·too·reesh·ta
air conditioning	ar condicionado	aar kong·dee·syoo·naa·doo
How much	Quanto custa para	kwang·too koosh·ta pa·ra
for … hire?	alugar por …?	a·loo·gaar poor …
hourly	hora	o·ra
daily	dia	dee·a
weekly	semana	se·ma·na
air	ar m	aar
oil	óleo m	o·le·oo
petrol	gasolina f	ga·zoo·lee·na
tyres	pneus m pl	pe·ne·oosh

I need a mechanic.
Preciso de um mecânico.   pre·see·zoo de oong me·kaa·nee·koo

I've run out of petrol.
Estou sem gasolina.   shtoh seng ga·zoo·lee·na

I have a flat tyre.
Tenho um furo no pneu.   ta·nyoo oong foo·roo noo pe·ne·oo

directions

Where's the …?	Onde é …?	ong·de e …
bank	o banco	oo bang·koo
city centre	o centro da cidade	oo seng·troo da see·daa·de
hotel	o hotel	oo o·tel
market	o mercado	oo mer·kaa·doo
police station	a esquadra da polícia	a shkwaa·dra da poo·lee·sya
post office	o correio	oo koo·rray·oo
public toilet	a casa de banho pública	a kaa·za de ba·nyoo poo·blee·ka
tourist office	o escritório de turismo	oo shkree·to·ryoo de too·reezh·moo

Is this the road to (Sintra)?
Esta é a estrada para (Sintra)? — esh·ta e a shtraa·da pa·ra (seeng·tra)

Can you show me (on the map)?
Pode-me mostrar (no mapa)? — po·de·me moosh·traar (noo maa·pa)

How far is it?
A que distância fica? — a ke deesh·tang·sya fee·ka

How do I get there?
Como é que eu chego lá? — ko·moo e ke e·oo she·goo laa

Turn ...	*Vire ...*	vee·re ...
at the corner	*na esquina*	na shkee·na
at the traffic lights	*nos semáforos*	noosh se·maa·foo·roosh
left	*à esquerda*	aa shker·da
right	*à direita*	aa dee·ray·ta

It's ...	*É...*	e ...
behind ...	*atrás de ...*	a·traash de ...
far away	*longe*	long·zhe
here	*aqui*	a·kee
in front of ...	*em frente de ...*	eng freng·te de ...
left	*à esquerda*	aa shker·da
near (to ...)	*perto (de ...)*	per·too (de ...)
next to ...	*ao lado de ...*	ow laa·doo de ...
on the corner	*na esquina*	na shkee·na
opposite ...	*do lado oposto ...*	doo laa·doo oo·posh·too ...
right	*à direita*	aa dee·ray·ta
straight ahead	*em frente*	eng freng·te
there	*lá*	laa

by bus	*de autocarro*	de ow·to·kaa·rroo
by taxi	*de táxi*	de taak·see
by train	*de comboio*	de kong·boy·oo
on foot	*a pé*	a pe

north	*norte*	nor·te
south	*sul*	sool
east	*leste*	lesh·te
west	*oeste*	o·esh·te

Entrada/Saída	eng-*traa*-da/sa-*ee*-da	Entrance/Exit
Aberto/Fechado	a-*ber*-too/fe-*shaa*-doo	Open/Closed
Há Vaga	aa *vaa*-ga	Rooms Available
Não Há Vaga	nowng aa *vaa*-ga	No Vacancies
Informação	eeng-for-ma-*sowng*	Information
Esquadra da Polícia	shkwaa-dra da poo-*lee*-sya	Police Station
Proibido	pro-ee-*bee*-doo	Prohibited
Casa de Banho	*kaa*-za de ba-*nyoo*	Toilets
Homens	o-*mengsh*	Men
Mulheres	moo-*lye*-resh	Women
Quente/Frio	*keng*-te/*free*-oo	Hot/Cold

accommodation

finding accommodation

Where's a ...?	*Onde é que há ...?*	*ong*-de e ke aa ...
camping ground	*um parque de campismo*	oong *paar*-ke de kang-*peezh*-moo
guesthouse	*uma casa de hóspedes*	*oo*-ma *kaa*-za de *osh*-pe-desh
hotel	*um hotel*	oong o-*tel*
youth hostel	*uma pousada de juventude*	*oo*-ma poh-*zaa*-da de zhoo-veng-*too*-de
Can you recommend somewhere ...?	*Pode recomendar algum lugar ...?*	*po*-de rre-koo-meng-*daar* aal-*goong* loo-*gaar* ...
cheap	*barato*	ba-*raa*-too
good	*bom*	bong
nearby	*perto daqui*	*per*-too da-*kee*

I'd like to book a room, please.
Eu queria fazer uma reserva, por favor.
e-oo ke-*ree*-a fa-*zer* *oo*-ma rre-*zer*-va poor fa-*vor*

I have a reservation.
Eu tenho uma reserva.
e-oo *ta*-nyoo *oo*-ma rre-*zer*-va

My name's ...
O meu nome é ...
oo *me*-oo *no*-me e ...

Do you have a ... room?　　*Tem um quarto ...?*　　teng oong *kwaar*·too ...

single	*de solteiro*	de sol·*tay*·roo
double	*de casal*	de ka·*zaal*
twin	*duplo*	*doo*·ploo

How much is it per ...?　　*Quanto custa por ...?*　　*kwang*·too *koosh*·ta poor ...

night	*noite*	*noy*·te
person	*pessoa*	pe·*so*·a

Can I pay by ...?　　*Posso pagar com ...?*　　*po*·soo pa·*gaar* kong ...

credit card	*cartão de crédito*	kar·*towng* de kre·dee·too
travellers cheque	*traveller cheque*	*tra*·ve·ler shek

I'd like to stay for (three) nights.
Para (três) noites.　　　　　　　　*pa*·ra (tresh) *noy*·tesh

From (2 July) to (6 July).
De (dois de julho) até　　　　　　de (doysh de *zhoo*·lyoo) a·*te*
(seis de julho).　　　　　　　　　(saysh de *zhoo*·lyoo)

Can I see it?
Posso ver?　　　　　　　　　　　*po*·soo ver

Am I allowed to camp here?
Posso acampar aqui?　　　　　　*po*·soo a·kang·*paar* a·*kee*

Where can I find a camping ground?
Onde é o parque de campismo?　　*ong*·de e oo *par*·ke de kang·*peesh*·moo

requests & queries

When/Where is breakfast served?
Quando/Onde é que servem　　　　*kwang*·doo/*ong*·de e ke *ser*·veng
o pequeno almoço?　　　　　　　oo pe·*ke*·noo aal·*mo*·soo

Please wake me at (seven).
Por favor acorde-me às (sete).　　poor fa·*vor* aa·*kor*·de·me aash (*se*·te)

Could I have my key, please?
Pode-me dar a minha chave,　　　*po*·de·me daar a *mee*·nya *shaa*·ve
por favor?　　　　　　　　　　poor fa·*vor*

Can I get another (blanket)?
Pode-me dar mais um (cobertor)?　*po*·de·me daar maish oong (koo·ber·*tor*)

Is there a/an ...?	Tem ...?	teng ...
elevator	elevador	e·le·va·*dor*
safe	cofre	*ko*·fre

The room is too ...	É demasiado ...	e de·ma·zee·*aa*·doo ...
expensive	caro	*kaa*·roo
noisy	barulhento	ba·roo·*lyeng*·too
small	pequeno	pe·*ke*·noo

The ... doesn't work.	... não funciona.	... nowng foong·see·*o*·na
air conditioner	O ar condicionado	oo aar kong·dee·syoo·*naa*·doo
fan	A ventoínha	a veng·too·*ee*·na
toilet	A sanita	a sa·*nee*·ta

This ... isn't clean.	Esta ... está suja.	esh·ta ... shtaa *soo*·zha
pillow	almofada	aal·moo·*faa*·da
towel	toalha	*twaa*·lya

This sheet isn't clean.	Este lençol está sujo.	esh·te leng·*sol* shtaa *soo*·zho

checking out

What time is checkout?

A que horas é a partida? a ke *o*·rash e a par·*tee*·da

Can I leave my luggage here?

Posso deixar as minhas po·soo day·*shaar* ash *mee*·nyash
malas aqui? *maa*·lash a·*kee*

Could I have	Pode-me devolver	po·de·me de·vol·*ver*
my ..., please?	..., por favor?	... poor fa·*vor*
deposit	o depósito	oo de·*po*·zee·too
passport	o passaporte	oo paa·sa·*por*·te
valuables	os objectos	oosh o·be·*zhe*·toosh
	de valor	de va·*lor*

communications & banking

the internet

Where's the local Internet café?
Onde fica um café da internet   ong·de fee·ka oong ka·fe da eeng·ter·net
nas redondezas?   nash rre·dong·de·zash

How much is it per hour?
Quanto custa por hora?   kwang·too koosh·ta pooro·ra

I'd like to ...	*Queria ...*	ke·ree·a ...
check my email	*ler o meu email*	ler oo me·oo ee·mayl
get Internet access	*ter acesso à internet*	ter a·se·soo aa eeng·ter·net
use a printer	*usar uma*	oo·zaar oo·ma
	impressora	eeng·pre·so·ra
use a scanner	*usar um*	oo·zaar oong
	digitalizador	dee·zhee·ta·lee·za·dor

mobile/cell phone

I'd like a ...	*Queria ...*	ke·ree·a ...
mobile/cell	*alugar um*	a·loo·gaar oong
phone for hire	*telemóvel*	te·le·mo·vel
SIM card for	*cartão SIM*	kar·towng seeng
your network	*para a sua rede*	pa·ra a soo·a rre·de

What are the rates?   *Qual é o valor cobrado?*   kwaal e oo va·lor koo·braa·doo

telephone

What's your phone number?
Qual é o seu número de telefone?   kwaal e oo se·oo noo·me·roo de te·le·fo·ne

The number is ...
O número é ...   oo noo·me·roo e ...

Where's the nearest public phone?
Onde fica o telefone   ong·de fee·ka o te·le·fo·ne
público mais perto?   poo·blee·koo maish per·too

I'd like to buy a phonecard.
Quero comprar um   ke·roo kong·praar oong
cartão telefónico.   kar·towng te·le·fo·nee·koo

I want to ...	Quero ...	ke·roo ...
call (Singapore)	telefonar (para Singapura)	te·le·foo·naar (pa·ra seeng·ga·poo·ra)
make a local call	fazer uma chamada local	fa·zer oo·ma sha·maa·da loo·kaal
reverse the charges	fazer uma chamada a cobrar	fa·zer oo·ma sha·maa·da a koo·braar

How much does ... cost?	Quanto custa ...?	kwang·too koosh·ta ...
a (three)-minute call	uma ligação de (três) minutos	oo·ma lee·ga·sowng de (tresh) mee·noo·toosh
each extra minute	cada minuto extra	kaa·da mee·noo·too aysh·tra

It's (30c) per (30) seconds.
(Trinta cêntimos) por (trinta) segundos.
(treeng·ta seng·tee·moosh) poor (treeng·ta) se·goong·doosh

post office

I want to send a ...	Quero enviar ...	ke·roo eng·vee·aar ...
fax	um fax	oong faks
letter	uma carta	oo·ma kaar·ta
parcel	uma encomenda	oo·ma eng·koo·meng·da
postcard	um postal	oong poosh·taal

I want to buy a/an ...	Quero comprar um ...	ke·roo kong·praar oong ...
envelope	envelope	eng·ve·lo·pe
stamp	selo	se·loo

Please send it (to Australia) by ...	Por favor envie isto (para Australia) por ...	poor fa·vor eng·vee·e eesh·too (pa·ra owsh·traa·lya) poor ...
airmail	via aérea	vee·a a·e·ree·a
express mail	correio azul	koo·rray·oo a·zool
registered mail	registado/a m/f	rre·zheesh·taa·doo/a
surface mail	via terrestre	vee·a te·rresh·tre

Is there any mail for me?
Há alguma correspondência para mim?
aa aal·goo·ma koo·rresh·pong·deng·sya pa·ra meeng

2

bank

English	Portuguese	Pronunciation
Where's a/an ...?	Onde é que há ...?	ong·de e ke aa ...
ATM	um caixa automático	oong kai·sha ow·too·maa·tee·koo
foreign exchange office	um câmbio	oong kang·byoo
I'd like to ...	Queria ...	ke·ree·a ...
Where can I ...?	Onde é que posso ...?	ong·de e ke po·soo ...
arrange a transfer	fazer uma transferencia	faa·zer oo·ma trans·fe·reng·sya
cash a cheque	trocar um cheque	troo·kaar oong she·ke
change a travellers cheque	trocar traveller cheque	troo·kaar tra·ve·ler shek
change money	trocar dinheiro	troo·kaar dee·nyay·roo
get a cash advance	fazer um levantamento adiantado	fa·zer oong le·vang·ta·meng·too a·dee·ang·taa·doo
withdraw money	levantar dinheiro	le·vang·taar dee·nyay·roo
What's the ...?	Qual é ...?	kwaal e ...
commission	a comissão	a koo·mee·sowng
charge for that	o imposto	oo eeng·posh·too
exchange rate	o câmbio do dia	oo kang·byoo doo dee·a
It's ...	É ...	e ...
(12) euros	(doze) euros	(do·ze) e·oo·roosh
free	gratuito	gra·twee·too

What time does the bank open?

A que horas é que abre o banco?   a ke o·rash e ke aa·bre oo bang·koo

Has my money arrived yet?

O meu dinheiro já chegou?   oo me·oo dee·nyay·roo zhaa she·goh

sightseeing

getting in

What time does it open/close?
A que horas abre/fecha?   a ke o·rash *aa*·bre/*fe*·sha

What's the admission charge?
Qual é o preço de entrada?   kwaal e oo *pre*·soo de eng·*traa*·da

Is there a discount for children/students?
Tem desconto para crianças/   teng desh·*kong*·too *pa*·ra kree·*ang*·sash/
estudantes?   shtoo·*dang*·tesh

I'd like a ...	*Queria um ...*	ke·*ree*·a oong ...
catalogue	*catálogo*	ka·*taa*·loo·goo
guide	*guia*	*gee*·a
local map	*mapa local*	*maa*·pa loo·*kaal*

I'd like to see ...	*Eu gostava de ver ...*	e·oo goosh·*taa*·va de ver ...
What's that?	*O que é aquilo?*	oo ke e a·*kee*·loo
Can I take a photo?	*Posso tirar uma*	*po*·soo tee·*raar* oo·ma
	fotografia?	foo·too·gra·*fee*·a

tours

When's the next ...?	*Quando é ...?*	*kwang*·doo e ...
day trip	*o próximo passeio*	oo *pro*·see·moo pa·*say*·oo
tour	*a próxima excursão*	a *pro*·see·ma shkoor·*sowng*

Is ... included?	*Inclui ...?*	eeng·*kloo*·ee ...
accommodation	*hospedagem*	osh·pe·*daa*·zheng
the admission charge	*preço de entrada*	*pre*·soo de eng·*traa*·da
food	*comida*	koo·*mee*·da
transport	*transporte*	trangsh·*por*·te

How long is the tour?
Quanto tempo dura   *kwang*·too teng·poo *doo*·ra
a excursão?   a shkoor·*sowng*

What time should we be back?
A que hora é que devemos   a ke o·ra e ke de·*ve*·moosh
estar de volta?   shtaar de *vol*·ta

sightseeing

castle	*castelo* m	kash·*te*·loo
cathedral	*catedral* f	ka·te·*draal*
church	*igreja* f	ee·*gre*·zha
main square	*praça principal* f	*praa*·sa preeng·see·*paal*
monastery	*mosteiro* m	moosh·*tay*·roo
monument	*monumento* m	moo·noo·*meng*·too
museum	*museu* m	moo·*ze*·oo
old city	*cidade antiga* f	see·*daa*·de ang·*tee*·ga
palace	*palácio* m	pa·*laa*·syoo
ruins	*ruínas* f pl	rroo·*ee*·nash
stadium	*estádio* m	*shtaa*·dyoo
statues	*estátuas* f pl	*shtaa*·too·ash

shopping

enquiries

Where's a ...?	*Onde é ...?*	*ong*·de e ...
bank	*o banco*	oo *bang*·koo
bookshop	*a livraria*	a lee·vra·*ree*·a
department store	*loja de*	*lo*·zha de
	departamentos	de·par·ta·*meng*·toosh
grocery store	*a mercearia*	a mer·see·a·*ree*·a
market	*o mercado*	oo mer·*kaa*·doo
newsagency	*o quiosque*	oo kee·*osh*·ke
supermarket	*o supermercado*	oo soo·per·mer·*kaa*·doo

Where can I buy (a padlock)?
Onde é que posso comprar   *ong*·de e ke *po*·soo kong·*praar*
(um cadeado)?   (oong ka·de·*aa*·doo)

I'm looking for ...
Estou à procura de ...   shtoh aa proo·*koo*·ra de ...

Can I look at it?
Posso ver?   *po*·soo ver

Do you have any others?
Tem outros?   teng *oh*·troosh

Does it have a guarantee?
Tem garantia? — teng ga·rang·*tee*·a

Can I have it sent overseas?
Podem enviar para o — po·deng eng·vee·*aar* pa·ra oo
estrangeiro? — shtrang·*zhay*·roo

Can I have my ... repaired?
Vocês consertam ...? — vo·*sesh* kong·*ser*·tang ...

It's faulty.
Tem defeito. — teng de·*fay*·too

I'd like ..., please. | *Queria ..., por favor.* | ke·*ree*·a ... poor fa·*vor*
a bag | *um saco* | oong *saa*·koo
a refund | *ser reembolsado/a* m/f | ser rre·eng·bol·*saa*·doo/a
to return this | *devolver isto* | de·vol·*ver* eesh·too

paying

How much is it?
Quanto custa? — kwang·too *koosh*·ta

Can you write down the price?
Pode escrever o preço? — po·de shkre·*ver* oo *pre*·soo

That's too expensive.
Está muito caro. — shtaa *mweeng*·too *kaa*·roo

What's your lowest price?
Qual é o seu último preço? — kwaal e oo *se*·oo *ool*·tee·moo *pre*·soo

I'll give you (five) euros.
Dou-lhe (cinco) euros. — doh·lye (*seeng*·koo) e·oo·*roosh*

There's a mistake in the bill.
Há um erro na conta. — aa oong e·rroo na *kong*·ta

Do you accept ...? | *Aceitam ...?* | a·*say*·tang ...
credit cards | *cartão de crédito* | kar·*towng* de kre·dee·too
debit cards | *multibanco* | mool·tee·*bang*·koo
travellers cheques | *travellers cheques* | tra·ve·ler *she*·kesh

I'd like ..., please. | *Queria ..., por favor.* | ke·*ree*·a ... poor fa·*vor*
a receipt | *um recibo* | oong rre·*see*·boo
my change | *o troco* | oo *tro*·koo

clothes & shoes

Can I try it on?	*Posso experimentar?*	po·soo shpree·meng·*taar*
My size is (40).	*O meu número é (quarenta).*	oo me·oo noo·me·roo e (kwa·*reng*·ta)
It doesn't fit.	*Não serve.*	nowng ser·ve
small	*pequeno/pequena* m/f	pe·*ke*·noo/pe·*ke*·na
medium	*meio/meia* m/f	*may*·oo/*may*·a
large	*grande* m&f	*grang*·de

books & music

I'd like a ...	*Queria comprar ...*	ke·*ree*·a kong·*praar* ...
newspaper	*um jornal*	oong zhor·*naal*
(in English)	*(em inglês)*	(eng eeng·*glesh*)
pen	*uma caneta*	oo·ma ka·*ne*·ta

Is there an English-language bookshop?
Há uma livraria de　　　　　　aa oo·ma lee·vra·*ree*·a de
língua inglesa?　　　　　　　leeng·gwa eeng·*gle*·za

I'm looking for something by (Fernando Pessoa).
Estou à procura de qualquer　　shtoh aa proo·*koo*·ra de kwaal·*ker*
coisa do (Fernando Pessoa).　　　koy·za doo (fer·*nang*·doo pe·*so*·a)

Can I listen to this?
Posso ouvir?　　　　　　　　po·soo oh·*veer*

photography

I need a/an ... film for this camera.	*Preciso de filme ... para esta máquina.*	pre·*see*·zoo de *feel*·me ... pa·ra esh·ta maa·kee·na
APS	*sistema APS*	seesh·*te*·ma aa pe e·se
B&W	*a preto e branco*	a *pre*·too e *brang*·koo
colour	*a cores*	a *ko*·resh
slide	*de diapositivos*	de dee·a·po·zee·*tee*·voosh
(200) ASA	*de (duzentos) ASA*	de (doo·*zeng*·toosh) aa·za
When will it be ready?	*Quando fica pronto?*	kwang·doo fee·ka prong·too

Can you ...?	Pode ...?	po·de ...
develop this film	revelar este filme	rre·ve·laar esh·te feel·me
load my film	carregar o filme	kaa·rre·gaar oo feel·me
transfer photos	transferir as	trangsh·fe·reer ash
from my camera	fotografias	foo·too·gra·fee·ash
to CD	da minha máquina	da mee·nya maa·kee·na
	para um CD	pa·ra oong se·de

meeting people

greetings, goodbyes & introductions

Hello/Hi.	Olá.	o·laa
Good night.	Boa noite.	bo·a noy·te
Goodbye/Bye.	Adeus.	a·de·oosh
See you later.	Até logo.	a·te lo·goo
Mr	Senhor	se·nyor
Mrs	Senhora	se·nyo·ra
Ms	Senhorita	se·nyo·ree·ta
How are you?	Como está?	ko·moo shtaa
Fine. And you?	Bem. E você?	beng e vo·se
What's your name?	Qual é o seu nome?	kwaal e oo se·oo no·me
My name is ...	O meu nome é ...	oo me·oo no·me e ...
I'm pleased to	Prazer em conhecê-lo/	pra·zer eng koo·nye·se·lo/
meet you.	conhecê-la. m/f	koo·nye·se·la
This is my ...	Este é o meu ... m	esh·te e oo me·oo ...
	Esta é a minha ... f	esh·ta e a mee·nya ...
brother	irmão	eer·mowng
daughter	filha	fee·lya
father	pai	pai
friend	amigo/a m/f	a·mee·goo/a
husband	marido	ma·ree·doo
mother	mãe	maing
partner (intimate)	companheiro/a m/f	kong·pa·nyay·roo/a
sister	irmã	eer·mang
son	filho	fee·lyoo
wife	esposa	shpo·za

Here's my ...	Aqui está o meu ...	a-kee shtaa oo me-oo ...
What's your ...?	Qual é o seu ...?	kwaal e oo se-oo ...
address	endereço	eng-de-re-soo
email address	email	ee-mayl
fax number	número de fax	noo-me-roo de faaks
phone number	número de telefone	noo-me-roo de te-le-fo-ne

occupations

What's your occupation?
Qual é a sua profissão?   kwaal e a soo-a proo-fee-sowng

I'm a/an ...	Sou ...	soh ...
artist	artista m&f	ar-teesh-ta
business person	homem/mulher de	o-meng/moo-lyer de
	negócios m/f	ne-go-syoosh
farmer	agricultor m&f	a-gree-kool-tor
manual worker	trabalhador m	tra-ba-lya-dor
	trabalhadora f	tra-ba-lya-do-ra
office worker	empregado/a	eng-pre-gaa-doo/a
	de escritório m/f	de shkree-to-ryoo
scientist	cientista m&f	see-eng-teesh-ta
student	estudante m&f	shtoo-dang-te
tradesperson	comerciante m&f	koo-mer-see-aang-te

background

Where are you from?	De onde é?	dong-de e
I'm from ...	Eu sou ...	e-oo soh ...
Australia	da Austrália	da owsh-traa-lya
Canada	do Canadá	doo ka-na-daa
England	da Inglaterra	da eeng-gla-te-rra
New Zealand	da Nova Zelândia	da no-va ze-lang-dya
the USA	dos Estados	doosh shtaa-doosh
	Unidos	oo-nee-doosh
Are you married?	É casado/a? m/f	e ka-zaa-doo/a
I'm ...	Eu sou ...	e-oo soh ...
married	casado/a m/f	ka-zaa-doo/a
single	solteiro/a m/f	sol-tay-roo/a

age

How old ...?	*Quantos anos ...?*	kwang·toosh a·noosh ...
are you	*tem*	teng
is your daughter	*tem a sua filha*	teng a soo·a fee·lya
is your son	*tem o seu filho*	teng oo se·oo fee·lyoo

I'm ... years old.	*Tenho ... anos.*	ta·nyoo ... a·noosh
He/She is ... years old.	*Ele/Ela tem ... anos.*	e·le/e·la teng ... a·noosh

feelings

I'm (not) ...	*(Não) Estou ...*	(nowng) shtoh ...
Are you ...?	*Está ...*	shtaa ...
cold	*com frio*	kong free·oo
happy	*feliz*	fe·leesh
hot	*com calor*	kong ka·lor
hungry	*com fome*	kong fo·me
OK	*bem*	beng
sad	*triste*	treesh·te
thirsty	*com sede*	kong se·de
tired	*cansado/a* m/f	kang·saa·doo/a

entertainment

going out

Where can I find ...?	*Onde é que há ...?*	ong·de e ke aa ...
clubs	*discotecas*	deesh·koo·te·kash
gay/lesbian	*lugares de*	loo·gaa·resh de
venues	*gays/lésbicas*	gaysh/lezh·bee·kash
pubs	*bares*	ba·resh

I feel like	*Está-me a*	shtaa·me a
going to a ...	*apetecer ir a ...*	a·pe·te·ser eer a ...
concert	*um concerto*	oong kong·ser·too
movies	*um filme*	oong feel·me
party	*uma festa*	oo·ma fesh·ta
restaurant	*um restaurante*	oong rresh·tow·rang·te
theatre	*uma peça de teatro*	oo·ma pe·sa de tee·aa·troo

interests

Do you like ...?	Gosta de ...?	gosh·ta de ...
I (don't) like ...	Eu (não) gosto de ...	e·oo (nowng) gosh·too de ...
art	arte	aar·te
cooking	cozinhar	koo·zee·nyaar
movies	ver filmes	ver feel·mesh
reading	ler	ler
sport	fazer desporto	fa·zer desh·por·too
travelling	viajar	vee·a·zhaar
Do you like to ...?	Costuma ...?	koosh·too·ma ...
dance	ir dançar	eer dang·saar
go to concerts	ir a concertos	eer a kong·ser·toosh
listen to music	ouvir música	oh·veer moo·zee·ka

food & drink

finding a place to eat

Can you	Pode-me	po·de·me
recommend a ...?	recomendar um ...?	rre·koo·meng·daar oong ...
bar	bar	bar
café	café	ka·fe
restaurant	restaurante	rresh·tow·rang·te
I'd like ..., please.	Queria uma ..., por favor.	ke·ree·a oo·ma ... poor fa·vor
a table for (five)	mesa para (cinco)	me·za pa·ra (seeng·koo)
the (non)smoking	mesa de (não)	me·za de (nowng)
section	fumador	foo·ma·dor

ordering food

breakfast	pequeno almoço m	pe·ke·noo aal·mo·soo
lunch	almoço m	aal·mo·soo
dinner	jantar m	zhang·taar
snack	lanche m	lang·she

What would you recommend?
O que é que recomenda? oo ke e ke rre·koo·meng·da

I'd like (the) ..., please.	Queria ..., por favor.	ke·ree·a ...poor fa·vor
bill	a conta	a kong·ta
drink list	a lista das bebidas	a leesh·ta dash be·bee·dash
menu	um menu	oong me·noo
that dish	aquele prato	a·ke·le praa·too

drinks

(cup of) coffee ...	(chávena de) café ...	(shaa·ve·na de) ka·fe ...
(cup of) tea ...	(chávena de) chá ...	(shaa·ve·na de) shaa ...
with milk	com leite	kong lay·te
without sugar	sem açúcar	seng a·soo·kar
(orange) juice	sumo (de laranja) m	soo·moo (de la·rang·zha)
soft drink	refrigerante m	rre·free·zhe·rang·te
... water	água ...	aa·gwa ...
hot	quente	keng·te
(sparkling) mineral	mineral (com gás)	mee·ne·raal (kong gaash)

in the bar

I'll have ...	Eu queria ...	e·oo ke·ree·a ...
I'll buy you a drink.	Eu pago-lhe uma	e·oo paa·goo·lye oo·ma
	bebida.	be·bee·da
What would you like?	O que é que quer?	oo ke e ke ker
Cheers!	À nossa!	aa no·sa
brandy	brandy f	brang·dee
cocktail	cocktail m	kok·tayl
a shot of (whisky)	um copinho de	oong koo·pee·nyoo de
	(uísque)	(oo·eesh·kee)
a ... of beer	... de cerveja	... de ser·ve·zha
bottle	uma garrafa	oo·ma ga·rraa·fa
glass	um copo	oong ko·poo
a bottle of ... wine	uma garrafa de vinho ...	oo·ma ga·rraa·fa de vee·nyoo ...
a glass of ... wine	um copo de vinho ...	oong ko·poo de vee·nyoo ...
red	tinto	teeng·too
sparkling	espumante	shpoo·mang·te
white	branco	brang·koo

food & drink – PORTUGUESE

277

self-catering

What's the local speciality?
Qual é a especialidade local? — kwaal e a shpe·see·a·lee·*daa*·de loo·*kaal*

What's that?
O que é aquilo? — oo ke e a·*kee*·loo

How much is (a kilo of cheese)?
Quanto é (um quilo de queijo)? — kwang·too e (oong *kee*·loo de *kay*·zhoo)

I'd like ...	Eu queria ...	e·oo ke·*ree*·a ...
(200) grams	(duzentos) gramas	(doo·*zeng*·toosh) *graa*·mash
(two) kilos	(dois) quilos	(doysh) *kee*·loosh
(three) pieces	(três) peças	(tresh) *pe*·sash
(six) slices	(seis) fatias	(saysh) fa·*tee*·ash

Less.	Menos.	*me*·noosh
Enough.	Chega.	*she*·ga
More.	Mais.	maish

special diets & allergies

Is there a vegetarian restaurant near here?
Há algum restaurante — aa aal·*goong* rresh·tow·*rang*·te
vegetariano perto daqui? — ve·zhe·ta·ree·*aa*·noo per·too da·*kee*

Do you have vegetarian food?
Tem comida vegetariana? — teng koo·*mee*·da ve·zhe·ta·ree·*aa*·na

Could you prepare	Pode preparar	po·de pre·pa·*raar*
a meal without ...?	sem ...?	seng ...
butter	manteiga	mang·*tay*·ga
eggs	ovos	*o*·voosh
meat stock	caldo de carne	*kaal*·doo de *kaar*·ne

I'm allergic to ...	Eu sou alérgico/a	e·oo soh a·*ler*·zhee·koo/a
	a ... m/f	a ...
dairy produce	produtos lácteos	pro·*doo*·toosh *laak*·tee·oosh
gluten	glúten	*gloo*·teng
MSG	MSG	e·me·e·se·*zhe*
nuts	oleaginosas	o·lee·a·zhee·*no*·zash
seafood	marisco	ma·*reesh*·koo

menu reader

açorda f	a-*sor*-da	bread-based thick soup, flavoured with garlic, coriander & olive oil
alheiras f pl	a-*lyay*-rash	bread, garlic, chilli & meat sausage
arroz árabe m	a-*rrosh aa*-ra-be	rice with raisins, nuts & dried fruit
arroz de bacalhau m	a-*rrosh* de ba-ka-*lyow*	rice with shredded salt cod
assado de peixe m	a-*saa*-doo de *pay*-she	mix of roasted or baked fish
bacalhau no borralho m	ba-ka-*lyow* noo boo-*rraa*-lyoo	salt cod steak wrapped in cabbage leaves & bacon
bacalhau roupa-velha m	ba-ka-*lyow* rroh-pa-*ve*-lya	mixture of cabbage, salt cod & potatoes, sautéed in olive oil & garlic
bifana no pão f	bee-*fa*-na noo powng	thin pork steak sandwich
bitoque m	bee-*to*-ke	steak or fillet with a fried egg on top
bolo de mel m	*bo*-loo de mel	rich molasses & spice cake with candied fruit & almonds
borrachões m pl	boo-rra-*shoyngsh*	fried ring-shaped biscuits flavoured with brandy or white wine & cinnamon
caldeirada f	kaal-day-*raa*-da	soup-like stew, usually with fish
chanfana f	shang-*fa*-na	hearty stew with goat or mutton in heavy red wine sauce
chouriço m	shoh-*ree*-soo	garlicky pork sausage flavoured with red pepper paste
coelho à caçador m	koo-e-*lyoo* aa ka-sa-*dor*	rabbit stewed with wine & tomato
cozido à Portuguesa m	koo-*zee*-doo aa poor-too-*ge*-za	hearty meal with chunks of meats & sausages, vegetables, beans & rice
dobrada f	doo-*braa*-da	tripe with white beans & rice
duchesse f	doo-*shes*	puff pastry filled with whipped cream & topped with fruit

2

escabeche m	shka-*be*-she	raw meat or fish pickled in olive oil, vinegar, garlic & bay leaf
favada à Portuguesa f	fa-*vaa*-da aa poor-too-*ge*-za	stew of fava beans, sausage & sometimes poached eggs
feijoada f	fay-*zhwaa*-da	bean stew with sausages or other meat
francesinha f	frang-se-*zee*-nya	ham, sausage & cheese in a tomato-cream sauce, on slices of bread
gaspacho m	gash-*paa*-shoo	chilled tomato & garlic bread soup with olive oil, vinegar & oregano
jesuítas m pl	zhe-zoo-ee-tash	puff pastry with baked meringue icing
manjar branco m	mang-*zhaar* brang-koo	coconut-milk & prunes pudding with syrup poured over the top
migas f pl	mee-gash	a side dish, usually bread flavoured with olive oil, garlic & spices & fried
morgados m pl	mor-*gaa*-doosh	sweetmeats made with almonds & figs
pastéis de feijão m pl	pash-*taysh* de fay-*zhowng*	rich lima bean & almond mixture in flaky pastry shells
pataniscas de bacalhau f pl	pa-ta-*neesh*-kash de ba-ka-*lyow*	seasoned salt cod fritters
prato de grão m	*praa*-too de growng	chickpea stew flavoured with tomato, garlic, bay leaf & cumin
salada de atum f	sa-*laa*-da de a-*toong*	salad of tuna, potato, peas, carrots & eggs in an olive oil & vinegar dressing
salame de chocolate m	sa-*la*-me de shoo-koo-*laa*-te	dense chocolate fudge roll studded with bits of biscuits, served sliced
sopa de pedra f	*so*-pa de *pe*-dra	vegetable soup with red beans, onions, potatoes, pig's ear, bacon & sausages
tecolameco m	te-koo-la-*me*-koo	rich orange & almond cake
tripas à moda do Porto f pl	*tree*-pash aa *mo*-da doo *por*-too	slow-cooked dried beans, trotters, tripe, chicken, vegetables & sausages

emergencies

basics

English	Portuguese	Pronunciation
Help!	Socorro!	soo-ko-rroo
Stop!	Stop!	stop
Go away!	Vá-se embora!	vaa-se eng-bo-ra
Thief!	Ladrão!	la-drowng
Fire!	Fogo!	fo-goo
Watch out!	Cuidado!	kwee-daa-doo

Call ...!	Chame ...!	shaa-me ...
a doctor	um médico	oong me-dee-koo
an ambulance	uma ambulância	oo-ma ang-boo-lang-sya
the police	a polícia	a poo-lee-sya

It's an emergency.
É uma emergência. — e oo-ma ee-mer-zheng-sya

Could you help me, please?
Pode ajudar, por favor? — po-de a-zhoo-daar poor fa-vor

Can I use the telephone?
Posso usar o seu telefone? — po-soo oo-zaar oo se-oo te-le-fo-ne

I'm lost.
Estou perdido/a. m/f — shtoh per-dee-doo/a

Where are the toilets?
Onde é a casa de banho? — ong-de e a kaa-za de ba-nyoo

police

Where's the police station?
Onde é a esquadra da polícia? — ong-de e a shkwaa-dra da poo-lee-sya

I want to report an offence.
Eu quero denunciar um crime. — e-oo ke-roo de-noong-see-aar oong kree-me

I have insurance.
Eu estou coberto/a pelo seguro. m/f — e-oo shtoh koo-ber-too/a pe-loo se-goo-roo

English	Portuguese	Pronunciation
I've been assaulted.	Eu fui agredido/a. m/f	e-oo fwee a-gre-dee-doo/a
I've been raped.	Eu fui violado/a. m/f	e-oo fwee vee-oo-laa-doo/a
I've been robbed.	Eu fui roubado/a. m/f	e-oo fwee rroh-baa-doo/a

emergencies

I've lost my ...	Eu perdi ...	e·oo per·dee
My ... was/were stolen.	Roubaram ...	rroh·baa·rang ...
backpack	a minha mochila	a meeng·nya moo·shee·la
bags	os meus sacos	oosh me·oosh saa·koosh
credit card	o meu cartão de crédito	oo me·oo kar·towng de kre·dee·too
handbag	a minha bolsa	a mee·nya bol·sa
jewellery	as minhas jóias	ash mee·nyash zhoy·ash
money	o meu dinheiro	oo me·oo dee·nyay·roo
passport	o meu passaporte	oo me·oo paa·sa·por·te
travellers cheques	os meus travellers cheques	oosh me·oosh tra·ve·ler she·kesh
wallet	a minha carteira	a mee·nya kar·tay·ra
I want to contact my ...	Eu quero contactar com ...	e·oo ke·roo kong·tak·taar kong ...
consulate	o meu consulado	oo me·oo kong·soo·laa·doo
embassy	a minha embaixada	a mee·nya eng·bai·shaa·da

health

medical needs

Where's the nearest ...?	Qual é ... mais perto?	kwaal e ... maish per·too
dentist	o dentista	oo deng·teesh·ta
doctor	o médico m	oo me·dee·koo
	a médica f	a me·dee·ka
hospital	o hospital	oo osh·pee·taal
(night) pharmacist	a farmácia (de serviço)	a far·maa·sya (de ser·vee·soo)

I need a doctor (who speaks English).
Eu preciso de um médico (que fale inglês).
e·oo pre·see·zoo de oong me·dee·koo (que faa·le eeng·glesh)

Could I see a female doctor?
Posso ser vista por uma médica?
po·soo ser veesh·ta poor oo·ma me·dee·ka

I've run out of my medication.
Os meus medicamentos acabaram.
oosh me·oosh me·dee·ka·meng·toosh a·ka·baa·rowng

symptoms, conditions & allergies

| I'm sick. | Estou doente. | shtoh doo·*eng*·te |
| It hurts here. | Dói-me aqui. | doy·me a·*kee* |

I have (a) ...	Eu tenho ...	e·oo ta·nyoo ...
asthma	asma	*ash*·ma
bronchitis	bronquite	brong·*kee*·te
constipation	prisão de ventre	pree·*zowng* de *veng*·tre
cough	tosse	*to*·se
diarrhoea	diarreia	dee·a·*rray*·a
fever	febre	*fe*·bre
headache	dor de cabeça	dor de ka·*be*·sa
heart condition	problemas cardíacos	proo·*ble*·mash kar·*dee*·a·koosh
nausea	náusea	*now*·zee·a
pain	dor	dor
sore throat	dores de garganta	*do*·resh de gar·*gang*·ta
toothache	uma dor de dentes	*oo*·ma dor de *deng*·tesh

I'm allergic to ...	Eu sou alérgico/a	e·oo soh a·*ler*·zhee·koo/a
	a ... m/f	a ...
antibiotics	antibióticos	ang·tee·bee·*o*·tee·koosh
anti-	anti-	ang·tee·
inflammatories	inflamatórios	eeng·fla·ma·*to*·ryoosh
aspirin	aspirina	ash·pee·*ree*·na
bees	abelhas	a·*be*·lyash
codeine	codeína	ko·de·*ee*·na
penicillin	penicilina	pe·nee·see·*lee*·na

antiseptic	antiséptico m	ang·tee·*se*·tee·koo
bandage	ligadura f	lee·ga·*doo*·ra
condoms	preservativos m pl	pre·zer·va·*tee*·voosh
contraceptives	contraceptivos m pl	kong·tra·se·*tee*·voosh
diarrhoea medicine	remédio para	re·*me*·dyo *pa*·ra
	diarreia m	dee·a·*rray*·a
insect repellent	repelente m	rre·pe·*leng*·te
laxatives	laxantes m pl	la·*shang*·tesh
painkillers	comprimidos	kong·pree·*mee*·doosh
	para as dores m pl	*pa*·ra ash *do*·resh
rehydration salts	sais rehidratantes m pl	saish rre·ee·dra·*tang*·tesh
sleeping tablets	pílulas para	*pee*·loo·laash *pa*·ra
	dormir f pl	door·*meer*

english–portuguese dictionary

Portuguese nouns and adjectives in this dictionary have their gender indicated with ⓜ (masculine) and ⓕ (feminine). If it's a plural noun, you'll also see see pl. Words are also marked as v (verb), n (noun), a (adjective), pl (plural), sg (singular), inf (informal) and pol (polite) where necessary.

A

accident *acidente* ⓜ a-see-*deng*-te
accommodation *hospedagem* ⓕ osh-pe-*daa*-zheng
adaptor *adaptador* ⓜ a-da-pe-ta-*dor*
address *endereço* ⓜ eng-de-*re*-soo
after *depois* de-*poysh*
air conditioned *com ar condicionado* kong aar kong-dee-syoo-*naa*-doo
airplane *avião* ⓜ a-vee-*owng*
airport *aeroporto* ⓜ a-e-ro-*por*-too
alcohol *álcool* ⓜ *al*-ko-ol
all a *todo/a* ⓜ/ⓕ *to*-doo/a
allergy *alergia* ⓕ a-ler-*zhee*-a
ambulance *ambulância* ⓕ ang-boo-*lang*-sya
and *e* e
ankle *tornozelo* ⓜ toor-noo-ze-loo
arm *braço* ⓜ *braa*-soo
ashtray *cinzeiro* ⓜ seeng-*zay*-roo
ATM *caixa automático* ⓜ *kai*-sha ow-too-*maa*-tee-koo

B

baby *bebé* ⓜ&ⓕ be-*be*
back (body) *costas* ⓕ pl *kosh*-tash
backpack *mochila* ⓕ moo-*shee*-la
bad *mau/má* ⓜ/ⓕ *ma*-oo/maa
bag *saco* ⓜ *saa*-koo
baggage claim *balcão de bagagens* ⓜ bal-*kowng* de ba-*gaa*-zhengsh
bank *banco* ⓜ *bang*-koo
bar *bar* ⓜ baar
bathroom *casa de banho* ⓕ *kaa*-za de *ba*-nyoo
battery *pilha* ⓕ *pee*-lya
beautiful *bonito/a* ⓜ/ⓕ boo-*nee*-too/a
bed *cama* ⓕ *ka*-ma
beer *cerveja* ⓕ ser-*ve*-zha
before *antes* ang-*tesh*
behind *atrás* a-*traash*
bicycle *bicicleta* ⓕ bee-see-*kle*-ta
big *grande* ⓜ&ⓕ *grang*-de

bill *conta* ⓕ *kong*-ta
black *preto/a* ⓜ/ⓕ *pre*-too/a
blanket *cobertor* ⓜ koo-ber-*tor*
blood group *grupo sanguíneo* ⓜ *groo*-poo sang-*gwee*-nee-oo
blue *azul* a-*zool*
boat *barco* ⓜ *baar*-koo
book (make a reservation) v *reservar* rre-zer-*vaar*
bottle *garrafa* ⓕ ga-*rraa*-fa
bottle opener *saca-rolhas* ⓜ *saa*-ka-*rro*-lyash
boy *menino* ⓜ me-*nee*-noo
brake (car) *travão* ⓜ tra-*vowng*
breakfast *pequeno almoço* ⓜ pe-*ke*-noo aal-*mo*-soo
broken (faulty) *defeituoso/a* ⓜ/ⓕ de-fay-too-o-*zoo*/a
bus *autocarro* ⓜ ow-to-*kaa*-roo
business *negócios* ⓜ pl ne-*go*-syoosh
buy *comprar* kong-*praar*

C

café *café* ⓜ ka-*fe*
camera *máquina fotográfica* ⓕ *maa*-kee-na foo-too-*graa*-fee-ka
camp site *parque de campismo* ⓜ *paar*-ke de kang-*peezh*-moo
cancel *cancelar* kang-se-*laar*
can opener *abre latas* ⓜ *aa*-bre *laa*-tash
car *carro* ⓜ *kaa*-rroo
cash *dinheiro* ⓜ dee-*nyay*-roo
cash (a cheque) v *levantar (um cheque)* le-vang-*taar* (oong *she*-ke)
cell phone *telemóvel* ⓜ te-le-*mo*-vel
centre *centro* ⓜ *seng*-troo
change (money) v *trocar* troo-*kaar*
cheap *barato/a* ba-*raa*-too/a
check (bill) *conta* ⓕ *kong*-ta
check-in *check-in* ⓜ shek-*eeng*
chest *peito* ⓜ *pay*-too
child *criança* ⓜ&ⓕ kree-*ang*-sa
cigarette *cigarro* ⓜ see-*gaa*-rroo
city *cidade* ⓕ see-*daa*-de
clean a *limpo/a* ⓜ/ⓕ *leeng*-poo/a

closed *fechado/a* ⓜ/ⓕ fe-*shaa*-doo/a
coffee *café* ⓜ ka-*fe*
coins *moedas* ⓕ pl moo-e-dash
cold a *fria/a* ⓜ/ⓕ *free*-oo/a
collect call *ligação a cobrar* ⓕ lee-ga-*sowng* a ko-*braar*
come *vir* veer
computer *computador* ⓜ kong-poo-ta-*dor*
condom *preservativo* ⓜ pre-zer-va-*tee*-voo
contact lenses *lentes de contacto* ⓜ pl
    leng-tesh de kong-*taak*-too
cook v *cozinhar* koo-zee-*nyaar*
cost *preço* ⓜ *pre*-soo
credit card *cartão de crédito* ⓜ kar-*towng* de kre-dee-too
cup *chávena* ⓕ *shaa*-ve-na
currency exchange *câmbio* ⓜ *kang*-byoo
customs (immigration) *alfândega* ⓕ aal-*fang*-de-ga

D

dangerous *perigoso/a* ⓜ/ⓕ pe-ree-*go*-zoo/a
date (time) *data* ⓕ *daa*-ta
day *dia* ⓜ *dee*-a
delay n *atraso* ⓜ a-*traa*-zoo
dentist *dentista* ⓜ&ⓕ deng-*teesh*-ta
depart *partir* par-*teer*
diaper *fralda* ⓕ *fraal*-da
dictionary *dicionário* ⓜ dee-syoo-*naa*-ryoo
dinner *jantar* ⓜ zhang-*taar*
direct *directo/a* ⓜ/ⓕ dee-*re*-too/a
dirty *sujo/a* ⓜ/ⓕ *soo*-zhoo/a
disabled *deficiente* de-fee-see-*eng*-te
discount *desconto* ⓜ desh-*kong*-too
doctor *médico/a* ⓜ/ⓕ *me*-dee-koo/a
double bed *cama de casal* ⓕ *ka*-ma de ka-*zaal*
double room *quarto de casal* ⓜ *kwaar*-too de ka-*zaal*
drink *bebida* ⓕ be-*bee*-da
drive v *conduzir* kong-doo-*zeer*
drivers licence *carta de condução* ⓕ
    kaar-ta de kong-doo-*sowng*
drugs (illicit) *droga* ⓕ *dro*-ga
dummy (pacifier) *chupeta* ⓕ shoo-*pe*-ta

E

ear *orelha* ⓕ o-*re*-lya
east *leste* *lesh*-te
eat *comer* koo-*mer*
economy class *classe económica* ⓕ
    klaa-se ee-koo-no-mee-ka
electricity *electricidade* ⓕ ee-le-tree-see-*daa*-de

elevator *elevador* ⓜ ee-le-va-*dor*
email *email* ⓜ ee-*mayl*
embassy *embaixada* ⓕ eng-bai-*shaa*-da
emergency *emergência* ⓕ ee-mer-*zheng*-sya
English (language) *inglês* ⓜ eeng-*glesh*
entrance *entrada* ⓕ eng-*traa*-da
evening *noite* ⓕ *noy*-te
exchange rate *taxa de câmbio* ⓕ *taa*-sha de *kang*-byoo
exit *saída* ⓕ saa-*ee*-da
expensive *caro/a* ⓜ/ⓕ *kaa*-roo/a
express mail *correio azul* ⓜ koo-*rray*-oo a-*zool*
eye *olho* ⓜ *o*-lyoo

F

far *longe* *long*-zhe
fast *rápido/a* ⓜ/ⓕ *rraa*-pee-doo/a
father *pai* ⓜ pai
film (camera) *filme* ⓜ *feel*-me
finger *dedo* ⓜ *de*-doo
first-aid kit *estojo de primeiros socorros* ⓜ
    shto-zhoo de pree-*may*-roosh so-ko-*rroosh*
first class *primeira classe* ⓕ pree-*may*-ra *klaa*-se
fish *peixe* ⓜ *pay*-she
food *comida* ⓕ koo-*mee*-da
foot *pé* ⓜ pe
fork *garfo* ⓜ *gaar*-foo
free (of charge) *grátis* *graa*-teesh
friend *amigo/a* ⓜ/ⓕ a-*mee*-goo/a
fruit *fruta* ⓕ *froo*-ta
full *cheio/a* ⓜ/ⓕ *shay*-oo/a
funny *engraçado/a* ⓜ/ⓕ eng-gra-*saa*-doo/a

G

gift *presente* ⓜ pre-*zeng*-te
girl *menina* ⓕ me-*nee*-na
glass (drinking) *copo* ⓜ *ko*-poo
glasses *óculos* ⓜ pl *o*-koo-loosh
go *ir* eer
good *bom/boa* ⓜ/ⓕ bong/*bo*-a
green *verde* *ver*-de
guide n *guia* ⓜ *gee*-a

H

half *metade* ⓕ me-*taa*-de
hand *mão* ⓕ mowng
handbag *mala de mão* ⓕ *maa*-la de mowng
happy *feliz* ⓜ&ⓕ fe-*leesh*

D

english–portuguese

28.

have *ter* ter
he *ele* e-le
head *cabeça* ① ka-be-sa
heart *coração* ⑩ koo-ra-sowng
heat *calor* ⑩ ka-lor
heavy *pesado/a* ⑩/① pe-zaa-doo/a
help v *ajudar* a-zhoo-daar
here *aqui* a-kee
high *alto/a* ⑩/① aal-too/a
highway *autoestrada* ① ow-to-shtraa-da
hike v *caminhar* ka-mee-nyaar
holiday *feriado* ⑩ fe-ree-aa-doo
homosexual n&a *homosexual* ⑩&①
o-mo-sek-soo-aal
hospital *hospital* ⑩ osh-pee-taal
hot *quente* keng-te
hotel *hotel* ⑩ o-tel
hungry *faminto/a* ⑩/① fa-meeng-too/a
husband *marido* ⑩ ma-ree-doo

I

I *eu* e-oo
identification (card) *bilhete de identidade* ⑩
bee-lye-te de ee-deng-tee-daa-de
ill *doente* ⑩&① doo-eng-te
important *importante* ⑩&① eeng-por-tang-te
included *incluído/a* ⑩/① eeng-kloo-ee-doo/a
injury *ferimento* ⑩ fe-ree-meng-too
insurance *seguro* ⑩ se-goo-roo
Internet *internet* ① eeng-ter-net
interpreter *intérprete* ⑩&① eeng-ter-pre-te

J

jewellery *ourivesaria* ① oh-ree-ve-za-ree-a
job *emprego* ⑩ eng-pre-goo

K

key *chave* ① shaa-ve
kilogram *quilograma* ① kee-loo-graa-ma
kitchen *cozinha* ① koo-zee-nya
knife *faca* ① faa-ka

L

laundry (place) *lavandaria* ① la-vang-da-ree-a
lawyer *advogado/a* ⑩/① a-de-voo-gaa-doo/a
left (direction) *esquerda* ① shker-da

left-luggage office *perdidos e achados* ⑩ pl
per-dee-doosh ee aa-shaa-doosh
leg *perna* ① per-na
lesbian n&a *lésbica* ① lezh-bee-ka
less *menos* me-noosh
letter (mail) *carta* ① kaar-ta
lift (elevator) *elevador* ⑩ ee-le-va-dor
light *luz* ① loosh
like v *gostar* goosh-taar
lock *tranca* ① trang-ka
long *longo/a* ⑩/① long-goo/a
lost *perdido/a* ⑩/① per-dee-doo/a
lost-property office *gabinete de perdidos e achados* ⑩
gaa-bee-ne-te de per-dee-doosh ee a-shaa-doosh
love v *amar* a-maar
luggage *bagagem* ① ba-gaa-zheng
lunch *almoço* ⑩ aal-mo-soo

M

mail *correio* ⑩ koo-rray-oo
man *homem* ⑩ o-meng
map *mapa* ① maa-pa
market *mercado* ⑩ mer-kaa-doo
matches *fósforos* ⑩ pl fosh-foo-roosh
meat *carne* ① kaar-ne
medicine *medicamentos* ⑩ pl me-dee-ka-meng-toosh
menu *ementa* ① ee-meng-ta
message *mensagem* ① meng-saa-zheng
milk *leite* ⑩ lay-te
minute *minuto* ⑩ mee-noo-too
mobile phone *telemóvel* ⑩ te-le-mo-vel
money *dinheiro* ⑩ dee-nyay-roo
month *mês* ⑩ mesh
morning *manhã* ① ma-nyang
mother *mãe* ① maing
motorcycle *mota* ① mo-ta
motorway *autoestrada* ① ow-to-shtraa-da
mouth *boca* ① bo-ka
music *música* ① moo-zee-ka

N

name *nome* ⑩ no-me
napkin *guardanapo* ⑩ gwar-da-naa-poo
nappy *fralda* ① fraal-da
near *perto* per-too
neck *pescoço* ⑩ pesh-ko-soo
new *novo/a* ⑩/① no-voo/a
news *notícias* ① pl noo-tee-syash

newspaper *jornal* ⓜ zhor-*naal*
night *noite* ⓕ *noy*-te
no *não* nowng
noisy *barulhento/a* ⓜ/ⓕ ba-roo-*lyeng*-too/a
nonsmoking *não-fumador* nowng-foo-ma-*dor*
north *norte* nor-te
nose *nariz* ⓜ na-*reesh*
now *agora* a-*go*-ra
number *número* ⓜ *noo*-me-roo

O

oil (engine) *petróleo* ⓜ pe-*tro*-lyoo
old *velho/a* ⓜ/ⓕ *ve*-lyoo/a
one-way ticket *bilhete de ida* ⓜ bee-*lye*-te de *ee*-da
open a *aberto/a* ⓜ/ⓕ a-*ber*-too/a
outside *fora* fo-ra

P

package *embrulho* ⓜ eng-*broo*-lyoo
paper *papel* ⓜ pa-*pel*
park (car) v *estacionar* shta-syoo-*naar*
passport *passaporte* ⓕ paa-sa-*por*-te
pay *pagar* pa-*gaar*
pen *caneta* ⓕ ka-*ne*-ta
petrol *gasolina* ⓕ ga-zoo-*lee*-na
pharmacy *farmácia* ⓕ far-*maa*-sya
phonecard *cartão telefónico* ⓜ
    kar-*towng* te-le-fo-nee-koo
photo *fotografia* ⓕ foo-too-gra-*fee*-a
plate *prato* ⓜ *praa*-too
police *polícia* ⓕ poo-*lee*-sya
Portugal *Portugal* ⓜ poor-too-*gaal*
Portuguese (language) *português* poor-too-*gesh*
postcard *postal* ⓜ poosh-*taal*
post office *correio* ⓜ koo-*rray*-oo
pregnant *grávida* ⓕ *graa*-vee-da
price *preço* ⓜ *pre*-soo

Q

quiet *calado/a* ⓜ/ⓕ ka-*laa*-doo/a

R

rain *chuva* ⓕ *shoo*-va
razor *gilete* ⓕ zhee-*le*-te
receipt *recibo* ⓜ rre-*see*-boo
red *vermelho/a* ⓜ/ⓕ ver-*me*-lyoo/a

refund *reembolso* ⓜ rre-eng-*bol*-soo
registered mail *correio registado* ⓜ
    koo-*rray*-oo re-zhee-*shtaa*-doo
rent v *alugar* a-loo-*gaar*
repair v *consertar* kong-ser-*taar*
reservation *reserva* ⓕ rre-*zer*-va
restaurant *restaurante* ⓜ rresh-tow-*rang*-te
return v *voltar* vol-*taar*
return ticket *bilhete de ida e volta* ⓜ
    bee-*lye*-te de *ee*-da ee *vol*-ta
right (direction) *direita* ⓕ dee-*ray*-ta
road *estrada* ⓕ *shtraa*-da
room *quarto* ⓜ *kwaar*-too

S

safe a *seguro/a* ⓜ/ⓕ se-*goo*-roo/a
sanitary napkin *penso higiénico* ⓜ
    peng-soo ee-zhee-e-nee-koo
seat *assento* ⓜ a-*seng*-too
send *enviar* eng-vee-*aar*
service station *posto de gasolina* ⓜ
    posh-too de ga-zoo-*lee*-na
sex *sexo* ⓜ *sek*-soo
shampoo *champô* ⓜ shang-*poo*
share (a dorm) *partilhar* par-tee-*lyaar*
shaving cream *creme de barbear* ⓜ
    kre-me de bar-bee-*aar*
she *ela* e-la
sheet (bed) *lençol* ⓜ leng-*sol*
shirt *camisa* ⓕ ka-*mee*-za
shoes *sapatos* ⓜ pl sa-*paa*-toosh
shop n *loja* ⓕ *lo*-zha
short *curto/a* ⓜ/ⓕ *koor*-too/a
shower n *chuveiro* ⓜ shoo-*vay*-roo
single room *quarto de solteiro* ⓜ
    kwaar-too de sol-*tay*-roo
skin *pele* ⓕ *pe*-le
skirt *saia* ⓕ *sai*-a
sleep v *dormir* door-*meer*
slowly *vagarosamente* va-ga-ro-za-*meng*-te
small *pequeno/a* ⓜ/ⓕ pe-ke-*noo*/a
smoke (cigarettes) v *fumar* foo-*maar*
soap *sabonete* ⓜ sa-boo-*ne*-te
some *uns/umas* ⓜ/ⓕ pl oongsh/*oo*-mash
soon *em breve* eng *bre*-ve
south *sul* sool
souvenir shop *loja de lembranças* ⓕ
    lo-zha de leng-*brang*-sash
speak *falar* fa-*laar*

spoon *colher* ① koo-*lyer*
stamp *selo* ⓜ *se*-loo
stand-by ticket *bilhete sem garantia* ⓜ
  bee-*lye*-te seng ga-rang-*tee*-a
station (train) *estação* ① shta-*sowng*
stomach *estômago* ⓜ *shto*-ma-goo
stop v *parar* pa-*raar*
stop (bus) *paragem* ① pa-*raa*-zheng
street *rua* ① *rroo*-a
student *estudante* ⓜ&① shtoo-*dang*-te
sun *sol* ⓜ sol
sunscreen *protecção anti-solar* ①
  proo-te-*sowng* ang-tee-soo-*laar*
swim v *nadar* na-*daar*

T

tampons *tampões* ⓜ pl tang-*powngsh*
taxi *táxi* ⓜ *taak*-see
teaspoon *colher de chá* ① koo-*lyer* de shaa
teeth *dentes* ⓜ pl *deng*-tesh
telephone *telefone* ⓜ te-le-*fo*-ne
television *televisão* ① te-le-vee-*zowng*
temperature (weather) *temperatura* ①
  teng-pe-ra-*too*-ra
tent *tenda* ① *teng*-da
that (one) *aquele/a* ⓜ/① a-*ke*-le/a
they *eles/elas* ⓜ/① *e*-lesh/*e*-lash
thirsty *sedento/a* ⓜ/① se-*deng*-too/a
this (one) *este/a* ⓜ/① *esh*-te/a
throat *garganta* ① gar-*gang*-ta
ticket *bilhete* ⓜ bee-*lye*-te
time *tempo* ⓜ *teng*-poo
tired *cansado/a* ⓜ/① kang-*saa*-doo/a
tissues *lenços de papel* ⓜ pl *leng*-soosh de pa-*pel*
today *hoje* o-zhe
toilet *casa de banho* ① *kaa*-za de *ba*-nyoo
tomorrow *amanhã* aa-ma-*nyang*
tonight *hoje à noite* o-zhe aa *noy*-te
toothbrush *escova de dentes* ① shko-va de *deng*-tesh
toothpaste *pasta de dentes* ① *paash*-ta de *deng*-tesh
torch (flashlight) *lanterna eléctrica* ①
  lang-*ter*-na ee-*le*-tree-ka
tour n *excursão* ① shkoor-*sowng*
tourist office *escritório de turismo* ⓜ
  shkree-*to*-ryoo de too-*reezh*-moo
towel *toalha* ① *twaa*-lya
train *comboio* ⓜ kong-*boy*-oo
translate *traduzir* tra-doo-*zeer*

travel agency *agência de viagens* ①
  a-*zheng*-sya de vee-*aa*-zhengsh
travellers cheque *travellers cheque* ⓜ *tra*-ve-ler shek
trousers *calças* ① pl *kaal*-sash
twin beds *camas gémeas* ① pl *ka*-mash zhe-me-ash
tyre *pneu* ⓜ pe-*ne*-oo

U

underwear *roupa interior* ① *rroh*-pa eeng-te-*ree*-or
urgent *urgente* ⓜ&① oor-*zheng*-te

V

vacant *vago/a* ⓜ/① *vaa*-goo/a
vacation *férias* ① pl *fe*-ree-ash
vegetable *legume* ⓜ le-*goo*-me
vegetarian a *vegetariano/a* ⓜ/① ve-zhe-ta-ree-*a*-noo/a
visa *visto* ⓜ *veesh*-too

W

waiter *criado/a de mesa* ⓜ/① kree-*aa*-doo/a de *me*-za
walk v *caminhar* ka-mee-*nyaar*
wallet *carteira* ① kar-*tay*-ra
warm a *morno/a* ⓜ/① *mor*-noo/a
wash (something) *lavar* la-*vaar*
watch *relógio* ⓜ rre-*lo*-zhyoo
water *água* ① *aa*-gwa
we *nós* nosh
weekend *fim-de-semana* ⓜ feeng-de-se-*ma*-na
west *oeste* o-*esh*-te
wheelchair *cadeira de rodas* ① ka-*day*-ra de *rro*-dash
when *quando* *kwang*-doo
where *onde* *ong*-de
white *branco/a* ⓜ/① *brang*-koo/a
who *quem* keng
why *porquê* poor-*ke*
wife *esposa* ① *shpo*-za
window *janela* ① zha-*ne*-la
wine *vinho* ⓜ *vee*-nyoo
with *com* kong
without *sem* seng
woman *mulher* ① *moo*-lyer
write *escrever* shkre-*ver*

Y

yellow *amarelo/a* ⓜ/① a-ma-re-*loo*/a
yes *sim* seeng
yesterday *ontem* *ong*-teng
you inf sg/pl *tu/vocês* too/vo-*sesh*
you pol sg/pl *você/vós* vo-*se*/vosh

Slovene

slovene alphabet

A a a	*B b* buh	*C c* tsuh	*Č č* chuh	*D d* duh
E e e	*F f* fuh	*G g* guh	*H h* huh	*I i* ee
J j yuh	*K k* kuh	*L l* luh	*M m* muh	*N n* nuh
O o o	*P p* puh	*R r* ruh	*S s* suh	*Š š* shuh
T t tuh	*U u* oo	*V v* vuh	*Z z* zuh	*Ž ž* zhuh

slovene

SLOVENŠČINA

introduction

The language spoken by about 2 million people 'on the sunny side of the Alps', Slovene (*slovenščina* slo-*vensh*-chee-na) is sandwiched between German, Italian and Hungarian, against the backdrop of its wider South Slavic family. Its distinctive geographical position parallels its unique evolution, beginning with Slav settlement in this corner of Europe back in the 6th century, then becoming the official language of Slovenia – first as a part of Yugoslavia and since 1991 an independent republic.

Although Croatian and Serbian are its closest relatives within the South Slavic group, Slovene is nevertheless much closer to Croatia's northwestern and coastal dialects. It also shares some features with the more distant West Slavic languages (through contact with a dialect of Slovak, from which it was later separated by the arrival of the Hungarians to Central Europe in the 9th century). Unlike any other modern Slavic language, it has preserved the archaic Indo-European dual grammatical form, which means, for example, that instead of *pivo pee*-vo (a beer) or *piva pee*-va (beers), you and a friend could simply order *pivi pee*-vee (two beers).

German, Italian and Hungarian words entered Slovene during the centuries of foreign rule (in the Austro-Hungarian Empire or under the control of Venice), as these were the languages of the elite, while the common people spoke one of the Slovene dialects. Croatian and Serbian influence on Slovene was particularly significant during the 20th century when all three countries coexisted within the Yugoslav state.

For a language with a relatively small number of speakers, Slovene abounds in regional variations – eight major dialect groups have been identified, which are further divided into fifty or so regional dialects. Some of these cover the neighbouring areas of Austria, Italy and Hungary. The modern literary language is based largely on the central dialects and was shaped through a gradual process that lasted from the 16th to the 19th century.

Slovenia has been called 'a nation of poets', and what better way to get immersed in that spirit than to plunge into this beautiful language first? While you're soaking up the atmosphere of the capital, Ljubljana (whose central square is graced with a monument in honour of the nation's greatest poet, France Prešeren), remember that its name almost equals 'beloved' (*ljubljena* lyoob-*lye*-na) in Slovene!

introduction – SLOVENE

pronunciation

vowel sounds

The vowels in Slovene can be pronounced differently, depending on whether they're stressed or unstressed, long or short. Don't worry about these distinctions though, as you shouldn't have too much trouble being understood if you follow our coloured pronunciation guides. Note that we've used the symbols oh and ow to help you pronounce vowels followed by the letters *l* and *v* in written Slovene – when they appear at the end of a syllable, these combinations sometimes produce a sound similar to the 'w' in English.

symbol	english equivalent	slovene example	transliteration
a	father	*dan*	dan
ai	aisle	*srajca*	srai·tsa
e	bet	*center*	tsen·ter
ee	see	*riba*	ree·ba
o	pot	*oče*	o·che
oh	oh	*pol, nov*	poh, noh
oo	zoo	*jug*	yoog
ow	how	*ostal, prav*	os·tow, prow
uh	ago	*pes*	puhs

word stress

Slovene has free stress, which means there's no general rule regarding which syllable the stress falls on – it simply has to be learned. You'll be fine if you just follow our coloured pronunciation guides, in which the stressed syllable is always in italics.

consonant sounds

Most Slovene consonant sounds are pronounced more or less as they are in English. Don't be intimidated by the vowel-less words such as *trg* tuhrg (square) or *vrt* vuhrt (garden) – we've put a slight 'uh' sound before the r, which serves as a semi-vowel between the two other consonants.

symbol	english equivalent	slovene example	transliteration
b	bed	*brat*	brat
ch	cheat	*hči*	hchee
d	dog	*datum*	*da*-toom
f	fat	*telefon*	te-le-*fon*
g	go	*grad*	grad
h	hat	*hvala*	*hva*-la
k	kit	*karta*	*kar*-ta
l	lot	*ulica*	oo-*lee*-tsa
m	man	*mož*	mozh
n	not	*naslov*	nas-*loh*
p	pet	*pošta*	*po*-shta
r	run (rolled)	*brez*	brez
s	sun	*sin*	seen
sh	shot	*tuš*	toosh
t	top	*sto*	sto
ts	hats	*cesta*	*tse*-sta
v	very	*vlak*	vlak
y	yes	*jesen*	*ye*-sen
z	zero	*zima*	*zee*-ma
zh	pleasure	*žena*	*zhe*-na
'	a slight y sound	*kašelj, manj*	*ka*-shel', man'

tools

language difficulties

Do you speak English?
Ali govorite angleško? — a·lee go·vo·ree·te ang·lesh·ko

Do you understand?
Ali razumete? — a·lee ra·zoo·me·te

I (don't) understand.
(Ne) Razumem. — (ne) ra·zoo·mem

What does (*danes*) mean?
Kaj pomeni (danes)? — kai po·me·nee (da·nes)

Could you repeat that?
Lahko ponovite? — lah·ko po·no·vee·te

How do you ...? — *Kako se ...?* — ka·ko se ...
  pronounce this word — *izgovori to besedo* — eez·go·vo·ree to be·se·do
  write (*hvala*) — *napiše (hvala)* — na·pee·she (hva·la)

Could you please ...? — *Prosim ...* — pro·seem ...
  speak more slowly — *govorite počasneje* — go·vo·ree·te po·cha·sne·ye
  write it down — *napišite* — na·pee·shee·te

essentials

Yes.	*Da.*	da
No.	*Ne.*	ne
Please.	*Prosim.*	pro·seem
Thank you (very much).	*Hvala (lepa).*	hva·la (le·pa)
You're welcome.	*Ni za kaj.*	nee za kai
Excuse me.	*Dovolite.*	do·vo·lee·te
Sorry.	*Oprostite.*	op·ros·tee·te

numbers

0	*nula*	noo·la	16	*šestnajst*	shest·naist	
1	*en/ena* m/f	en/e·na	17	*sedemnajst*	se·dem·naist	
2	*dva/dve* m/f	dva/dve	18	*osemnajst*	o·sem·naist	
3	*trije/tri* m/f	tree·ye/tree	19	*devetnajst*	de·vet·naist	
4	*štirje* m	shtee·rye	20	*dvajset*	dvai·set	
	štiri f	shtee·ree	21	*enaindvajset*	e·na·een·dvai·set	
5	*pet*	pet	22	*dvaindvajset*	dva·een·dvai·set	
6	*šest*	shest	30	*trideset*	tree·de·set	
7	*sedem*	se·dem	40	*štirideset*	shtee·ree·de·set	
8	*osem*	o·sem		*deset*	de·set	
9	*devet*	de·vet	50	*petdeset*	pet·de·set	
10	*deset*	de·set	60	*šestdeset*	shest·de·set	
11	*enajst*	e·naist	70	*sedemdeset*	se·dem·de·set	
12	*dvanajst*	dva·naist	80	*osemdeset*	o·sem·de·set	
13	*trinajst*	tree·naist	90	*devetdeset*	de·vet·de·set	
14	*štirinajst*	shtee·ree·naist	100	*sto*	sto	
15	*petnajst*	pet·naist	1000	*tisoč*	tee·soch	

time & dates

What time is it?	*Koliko je ura?*	ko·lee·ko ye oo·ra
It's one o'clock.	*Ura je ena.*	oo·ra ye e·na
It's (10) o'clock.	*Ura je (deset).*	oo·ra ye (de·set)
Quarter past (one).	*Četrt čez (ena).*	che·*tuhrt* chez (e·na)
Half past (one).	*Pol (dveh).* (lit: half two)	pol (dveh)
Quarter to (one).	*Petnajst do (enih).*	pet·naist do (e·neeh)
At what time ...?	*Ob kateri uri ...?*	ob ka·*te*·ree oo·ree ...
At ...	*Ob ...*	ob ...
am	*dopoldne*	do·*poh*·dne
pm	*popoldne*	po·*poh*·dne
Monday	*ponedeljek*	po·ne·*del*·yek
Tuesday	*torek*	to·rek
Wednesday	*sreda*	sre·da
Thursday	*četrtek*	che·*tuhr*·tek
Friday	*petek*	pe·tek
Saturday	*sobota*	so·*bo*·ta
Sunday	*nedelja*	ne·*del*·ya

January	januar	ya·noo·ar
February	februar	feb·roo·ar
March	marec	ma·rets
April	april	ap·reel
May	maj	mai
June	junij	yoo·neey
July	julij	yoo·leey
August	avgust	av·goost
September	september	sep·tem·ber
October	oktober	ok·to·ber
November	november	no·vem·ber
December	december	de·tsem·ber

What date is it today?
Katerega smo danes?   ka·te·re·ga smo da·nes

It's (18 October).
Smo (osemnajstega oktobra).   smo (o·sem·nai·ste·ga) ok·tob·ra

| since (May) | od (maja) | od (ma·ya) |
| until (June) | do (junija) | do (yoo·nee·ya) |

last ...		
night	prejšnji večer	preysh·nyee ve·cher
week	prejšnji teden	preysh·nyee te·den
month	prejšnji mesec	preysh·nyee me·sets
year	prejšnje leto	preysh·nye le·to

next ...		
week	naslednji teden	nas·led·nyee te·den
month	naslednji mesec	nas·led·nyee me·sets
year	naslednje leto	nas·led·nye le·to

yesterday/tomorrow ...	včeraj/jutri ...	vche·rai/yoot·ree ...
morning	zjutraj	zyoot·rai
afternoon	popoldne	po·poh·dne
evening	zvečer	zve·cher

weather

What's the weather like?	Kakšno je vreme?	kak-shno ye vre-me
It's raining/snowing.	Dežuje/Sneži.	de-zhoo-ye/sne-zhee
It's	... je.	... ye
cloudy	Oblačno	ob-lach-no
cold	Mrzlo	muhr-zlo
hot	Vroče	vro-che
sunny	Sončno	sonch-no
warm	Toplo	top-lo
windy	Vetrovno	vet-roh-no
spring	pomlad f	pom-lad
summer	poletje n	po-let-ye
autumn	jesen f	ye-sen
winter	zima f	zee-ma

border crossing

I'm here ...	Tu sem ...	too sem ...
on business	poslovno	pos-lov-no
on holiday	na počitnicah	na po-cheet-nee-tsah
I'm here for ...	Ostanem ...	os-ta-nem ...
(10) days	(deset) dni	(de-set) dnee
(two) months	(dva) meseca	(dva) me-se-tsa
(three) weeks	(tri) tedne	(tree) ted-ne

I'm going to ...
Namenjen/Namenjena sem v ... m/f   na-men-yen/na-men-ye-na sem v ...

I'm staying at the (Slon).
Stanujem v (Slonu).   sta-noo-yem v (slo-noo)

I have nothing to declare.
Ničesar nimam za prijaviti.   nee-che-sar nee-mam za pree-ya-vee-tee

I have something to declare.
Nekaj imam za prijaviti.   ne-kai ee-mam za pree-ya-vee-tee

That's mine.
To je moje.   to ye mo-ye

That's not mine.
To ni moje.   to nee mo-ye

transport

tickets & luggage

Where can I buy a ticket?
Kje lahko kupim vozovnico? — kye lah·*ko koo*·peem vo·*zov*·nee·tso

Do I need to book a seat?
Ali moram rezervirati sedež? — a·lee mo·ram re·zer·vee·ra·tee se·dezh

One ... ticket to (Koper), please.	... vozovnico do (Kopra), prosim.	... vo·*zov*·nee·tso do (ko·pra) pro·seem
one-way	Enosmerno	e·no·*smer*·no
return	Povratno	pov·*rat*·no

I'd like to ... my ticket, please.	Želim ... vozovnico, prosim.	zhe·leem ... vo·*zov*·nee·tso pro·seem
cancel	preklicati	prek·*lee*·tsa·tee
change	zamenjati	za·*men*·ya·tee
collect	dvigniti	dveeg·nee·tee
confirm	potrditi	po·tuhr·*dee*·tee

I'd like a ... seat, please.	Želim ... sedež, prosim.	zhe·leem ... se·dezh pro·seem
nonsmoking	nekadilski	ne·ka·*deel*·skee
smoking	kadilski	ka·*deel*·skee

How much is it?
Koliko stane? — ko·lee·ko sta·ne

Is there air conditioning?
Ali ima klimo? — a·lee ee·ma klee·mo

Is there a toilet?
Ali ima stranišče? — a·lee ee·ma stra·*neesh*·che

How long does the trip take?
Kako dolgo traja potovanje? — ka·ko dol·go tra·ya po·to·*van*·ye

Is it a direct route?
Je to direktna proga? — ye to dee·*rekt*·na pro·ga

I'd like a luggage locker.
Želim garderobno omarico. — zhe·leem gar·de·*rob*·no o·*ma*·ree·tso

My luggage has been ...	Moja prtljaga je ...	mo·ya puhrt·lya·ga ye ...
damaged	poškodovana	posh·ko·do·va·na
lost	izgubljena	eez·goob·lye·na
stolen	ukradena	oo·kra·de·na

getting around

Where does flight (AF 46) arrive/depart?
Kje pristane/odleti let — kye pree·sta·ne/od·le·tee let
številka (AF 46)? — shte·veel·ka (a fuh shtee·ree shest)

Where's (the) ...?	Kje je/so ...? sg/pl	kye ye/so ...
arrivals hall	prihodi pl	pree·ho·dee
departures hall	odhodi pl	od·ho·dee
duty-free shop	brezcarinska	brez·tsa·reen·ska
	trgovina sg	tuhr·go·vee·na
gate (12)	izhod (dvanajst) sg	eez·hod (dva·naist)

Is this the ... to (Venice)?	Je to ... za (Benetke)?	ye to ... za (be·net·ke)
boat	ladja	lad·ya
bus	avtobus	av·to·boos
plane	letalo	le·ta·lo
train	vlak	vlak

What time's the ... bus?	Kdaj odpelje ... avtobus?	kdai od·pel·ye ... av·to·boos
first	prvi	puhr·vee
last	zadnji	zad·nyee
next	naslednji	nas·led·nyee

At what time does it arrive/leave?
Kdaj prispe/odpelje? — kdai prees·pe/od·pel·ye

How long will it be delayed?
Koliko je zamujen? — ko·lee·ko ye za·moo·yen

What station is this?
Katera postaja je to? — ka·te·ra pos·ta·ya ye to

What stop is this?
Katero postajališče je to? — ka·te·ro pos·ta·ya·leesh·che ye to

What's the next station?
Katera je naslednja postaja? — ka·te·ra ye nas·led·nya pos·ta·ya

What's the next stop?
Katero je naslednje postajališče? — ka·te·ro ye nas·led·nye pos·ta·ya·leesh·che

Does it stop at (Postojna)?
Ali ustavi v (Postojni)? — a-lee oos-*ta*-vee v (pos-*toy*-nee)

Please tell me when we get to (Kranj).
Prosim povejte mi, — pro-*seem* po-*vey*-te mee
ko prispemo v (Kranj). — ko prees-*pe*-mo v (kran)

How long do we stop here?
Kako dolgo stojimo tu? — ka-*ko dol*-go sto-*yee*-mo too

Is this seat available?
Je ta sedež prost? — ye ta se-dezh prost

That's my seat.
To je moj sedež. — to ye moy se-dezh

I'd like a taxi …	*Želim taksi …*	zhe-*leem* tak-see …
at (9am)	*ob (devetih*	ob (de-*ve*-teeh
	dopoldne)	do-*poh*-dne)
now	*zdaj*	zdai
tomorrow	*jutri*	*yoot*-ree

Is this taxi available?
Je ta taksi prost? — ye ta *tak*-see prost

How much is it to …?
Koliko stane do …? — ko-lee-ko *sta*-ne do …

Please put the meter on.
Prosim, vključite taksimeter. — pro-*seem* vklyoo-chee-te tak-see-me-ter

Please take me to (this address).
Prosim, peljite me na (ta naslov). — pro-*seem* pel-*yee*-te me na (ta nas-*loh*)

Please …	*Prosim …*	pro-*seem* …
slow down	*vozite počasneje*	vo-*zee*-te po-chas-*ne*-ye
stop here	*ustavite tukaj*	oos-*ta*-vee-te *too*-kai
wait here	*počakajte tukaj*	po-*cha*-kai-te *too*-kai

car, motorbike & bicycle hire

I'd like to hire a …	*Želim najeti …*	zhe-*leem* na-*ye*-tee …
bicycle	*kolo*	ko-*lo*
car	*avto*	*av*-to
motorbike	*motor*	mo-*tor*

with ...	s ...	s ...
a driver	*šoferjem*	sho-*fer*-yem
air conditioning	*klimo*	*klee*-mo
antifreeze	*sredstvom proti*	*sreds*-tvom *pro*-tee
	zmrzovanju	zmuhr-zo-*van*-yoo
snow chains	*snežnimi*	*snezh*-nee-mee
	verigami	ve-*ree*-ga-mee
How much for	*Koliko stane najem*	ko-*lee*-ko *sta*-ne na-*yem*
... hire?	*na ...?*	na ...
hourly	*uro*	*oo*-ro
daily	*dan*	dan
weekly	*teden*	*te*-den
air	*zrak* m	zrak
oil	*olje* n	*ol*-ye
petrol	*bencin* m	ben-*tseen*
tyres	*gume* f	*goo*-me

I need a mechanic.
 Potrebujem mehanika. pot-re-*boo*-yem me-*ha*-nee-ka

I've run out of petrol.
 Zmanjkalo mi je bencina. zman'-ka-lo mee ye ben-*tsee*-na

I have a flat tyre.
 Počila mi je guma. po-chee-la mee ye *goo*-ma

directions

Where's the ...?	*Kje je ...?*	kye ye ...
bank	*banka*	*ban*-ka
city centre	*center mesta*	*tsen*-ter *mes*-ta
hotel	*hotel*	ho-*tel*
market	*tržnica*	*tuhrzh*-nee-tsa
police station	*policijska*	po-lee-*tseey*-ska
	postaja	pos-*ta*-ya
post office	*pošta*	*posh*-ta
public toilet	*javno stranišče*	*yav*-no stra-*neesh*-che
tourist office	*turistični*	too-*rees*-teech-nee
	urad	oo-*rad*

Is this the road to (Ptuj)?
Pelje ta cesta do (Ptuja)? — pel·ye ta tses·ta do (ptoo·ya)

Can you show me (on the map)?
Mi lahko pokažete (na zemljevidu)? — mee lah·ko po·ka·zhe·te (na zem·lye·vee·doo)

What's the address?
Na katerem naslovu je? — na ka·te·rem nas·lo·voo ye

How far is it?
Kako daleč je? — ka·ko da·lech ye

How do I get there?
Kako pridem tja? — ka·ko pree·dem tya

Turn ...	Zavijte ...	za·veey·te ...
at the corner	na vogalu	na vo·ga·loo
at the traffic lights	pri semaforju	pree se·ma·for·yoo
left/right	levo/desno	le·vo/des·no

It's ...		
behind ...	Za ...	za ...
far away	Daleč.	da·lech
here	Tukaj.	too·kai
in front of ...	Pred ...	pred ...
left	Levo.	le·vo
near (to ...)	Blizu ...	blee·zoo ...
next to ...	Poleg ...	po·leg ...
on the corner	Na vogalu.	na vo·ga·loo
opposite ...	Nasproti ...	nas·pro·tee ...
right	Desno.	des·no
straight ahead	Naravnost naprej.	na·rav·nost na·prey
there	Tam.	tam

by bus	z avtobusom	z av·to·boo·som
by taxi	s taksijem	s tak·see·yem
by train	z vlakom	z vla·kom
on foot	peš	pesh

north	sever	se·ver
south	jug	yoog
east	vzhod	vzhod
west	zahod	za·hod

signs

Vhod/Izhod	vhod/eez-*hod*	**Entrance/Exit**
Odprto/Zaprto	od-*puhr*-to/za-*puhr*-to	**Open/Closed**
Proste sobe	*pros*-te *so*-be	**Rooms Available**
Ni prostih mest	nee *pros*-teeh mest	**No Vacancies**
Informacije	een-for-*ma*-tsee-ye	**Information**
Policijska postaja	po-lee-*tseey*-ska pos-*ta*-ya	**Police Station**
Prepovedano	pre-po-*ve*-da-no	**Prohibited**
Stranišče	stra-*neesh*-che	**Toilets**
Moški	*mosh*-kee	**Men**
Ženske	*zhen*-ske	**Women**
Vroče/Mrzlo	*vro*-che/*muhr*-zlo	**Hot/Cold**

accommodation

finding accommodation

Where's a ...?	*Kje je ... ?*	kye ye ...
camping ground	*kamp*	kamp
guesthouse	*gostišče*	gos-*teesh*-che
hotel	*hotel*	ho-*tel*
youth hostel	*mladinski hotel*	mla-*deen*-skee ho-*tel*
Can you recommend	*Mi lahko priporočite*	mee lah-*ko* pree-po-ro-*chee*-te
a ... hotel?	*... hotel?*	... ho-*tel*
cheap	*poceni*	po-*tse*-nee
good	*dober*	*do*-ber

Can you recommend a hotel nearby?
Mi lahko priporočite hotel v   mee lah-*ko* pree-po-ro-*chee*-te ho-*tel* oo
bližini?   blee-*zhee*-nee

I'd like to book a room, please.
Želim rezervirati sobo, prosim.   zhe-*leem* re-zer-*vee*-ra-tee *so*-bo *pro*-seem

I have a reservation.
Imam rezervacijo.   ee-*mam* re-zer-*va*-tsee-yo

My name's ...
Ime mi je ...   ee-*me* mee ye ...

Do you have a twin room?
Imate sobo z ločenima posteljama? ee·ma·te so·bo z lo·che·nee·ma pos·tel·ya·ma

Do you have a ... room? *Ali imate ... sobo?* a·lee ee·ma·te ... so·bo
   single   *enoposteljno*   e·no·pos·tel'·no
   double   *dvoposteljno*   dvo·pos·tel'·no

How much is it per ...? *Koliko stane na ...?* ko·lee·ko sta·ne na ...
   night   *noč*   noch
   person   *osebo*   o·se·bo

Can I pay by ...? *Lahko plačam s ...?* lah·ko pla·cham s ...
   credit card   *kreditno kartico*   kre·deet·no kar·tee·tso
   travellers cheque   *potovalnim čekom*   po·to·val·neem che·kom

I'd like to stay for (three) nights.
Rad bi ostal (tri) noči. m   rada bee os·tow (tree) no·chee
Rada bi ostala (tri) noči. f   ra·da bee os·ta·la (tree) no·chee

From (2 July) to (6 July).
Od (drugega julija)   od (droo·ge·ga yoo·lee·ya)
do (šestega julija).   do (shes·te·ga yoo·lee·ya)

Can I see the room?
Lahko vidim sobo?   lah·ko vee·deem so·bo

Am I allowed to camp here?
Smem tu kampirati?   smem too kam·pee·ra·tee

Is there a camp site nearby?
Je v bližini kakšen kamp?   ye v blee·zhee·nee kak·shen kamp

requests & queries

When/Where is breakfast served?
Kdaj/Kje strežete zajtrk?   kdai/kye stre·zhe·te zai·tuhrk

Please wake me at (seven).
Prosim, zbudite me ob (sedmih).   pro·seem zboo·dee·te me ob (sed·meeh)

Could I have my key, please?
Lahko prosim dobim ključ?   lah·ko pro·sim do·beem klyooch

Can I get another (blanket)?
Lahko dobim drugo (odejo)?   lah·ko do·beem droo·go (o·de·yo)

Is there an elevator/a safe?
Imate dvigalo/sef?   ee·ma·te dvee·ga·lo/sef

The room is too...	Soba je ...	so-ba ye ...
expensive	predraga	pre-*dra*-ga
noisy	prehrupna	pre-*hroop*-na
small	premajhna	pre-*mai*-hna

This ... isn't clean.	Ta ... ni čista.	ta ... nee *chees*-ta
pillow	blazina	bla-*zee*-na
sheet	rjuha	*ryoo*-ha
towel	brisača	bree-*sa*-cha

The fan doesn't work.
Ventilator je pokvarjen.   ven-tee-*la*-tor ye pok-*var*-yen

The air conditioning doesn't work.
Klima je pokvarjena.   *klee*-ma ye pok-*var*-ye-na

The toilet doesn't work.
Stranišče je pokvarjeno.   stra-*neesh*-che ye pok-*var*-ye-no

checking out

What time is checkout?
Kdaj se moram odjaviti?   kdai se *mo*-ram od-*ya*-vee-tee

Can I leave my luggage here?
Lahko pustim prtljago tu?   lah-ko poos-*teem* puhrt-*lya*-go too

Could I have my ..., please?	Lahko prosim dobim ...?	lah-ko *pro*-seem do-*beem* ...
deposit	moj polog	moy *po*-log
passport	moj potni list	moy *pot*-nee leest
valuables	moje dragocenosti	*mo*-ye dra-go-*tse*-nos-tee

communications & banking

the internet

Where's the local Internet café?
Kje je najbližja internetna kavarna?   kye ye nai-*bleezh*-ya een-ter-*net*-na ka-*var*-na

How much is it per hour?
Koliko stane ena ura?   ko-lee-ko *sta*-ne *e*-na *oo*-ra

I'd like to ...	Želim ...	zhe-leem ...
check my email	preveriti	pre-ve-ree-tee
	elektronsko pošto	e-lek-tron-sko posh-to
get Internet access	dostop do interneta	dos-top do een-ter-ne-ta
use a printer	uporabiti tiskalnik	oo-po-ra-bee-tee tees-kal-neek
use a scanner	uporabiti optični	oo-po-ra-bee-tee op-teech-nee
	čitalnik	chee-tal-neek

mobile/cell phone

I'd like a ...	Želim ...	zhe-leem ...
mobile/cell phone	najeti mobilni	na-ye-tee mo-beel-nee
for hire	telefon	te-le-fon
SIM card for	SIM kartico za	seem kar-tee-tso za
your network	vaše omrežje	va-she om-rezh-ye

What are the rates?	Kakšne so cene?	kak-shne so tse-ne

telephone

What's your phone number?
Lahko izvem vašo telefonsko   lah-ko eez-vem va-sho te-le-fon-sko
številko?   shte-veel-ko

The number is ...
Številka je ...   shte-veel-ka ye ...

Where's the nearest public phone?
Kje je najbližja govorilnica?   kye ye nai-bleezh-ya go-vo-reel-nee-tsa

I'd like to buy a phonecard.
Želim kupiti telefonsko kartico.   zhe-leem koo-pee-tee te-le-fon-sko kar-tee-tso

I want to ...	Želim ...	zhe-leem ...
call (Singapore)	poklicati (Singapur)	pok-lee-tsa-tee (seen-ga-poor)
make a local call	klicati lokalno	klee-tsa-tee lo-kal-no
reverse the	klicati na stroške	klee-tsa-tee na strosh-ke
charges	klicanega	klee-tsa-ne-ga

How much does	Koliko stane ...?	ko-lee-ko sta-ne ...
... cost?		
a (three)-minute	(tri)minutni klic	(tree-)mee-noot-nee kleets
call		
each extra minute	vsaka dodatna minuta	vsa-ka do-dat-na mee-noo-ta

post office

I want to send a ...	Želim poslati ...	zhe-*leem* pos-*la*-tee ...
letter	pismo	*pees*-mo
parcel	paket	pa-*ket*
postcard	razglednico	raz-*gled*-nee-tso

I want to buy a/an ...	Želim kupiti ...	zhe-*leem* koo-*pee*-tee ...
envelope	kuverto	koo-*ver*-to
stamp	znamko	*znam*-ko

Please send it by ...	Prosim, pošljite ...	*pro*-seem posh-*lyee*-te ...
airmail	z letalsko pošto	z le-*tal*-sko *posh*-to
express mail	s hitro pošto	s *heet*-ro *posh*-to
registered mail	s priporočeno pošto	s pree-po-ro-*che*-no *posh*-to
surface mail	z navadno pošto	z na-*vad*-no *posh*-to

bank

Where's a/an ...?	Kje je ...?	kye ye ...
ATM	bankomat	ban-ko-*mat*
foreign exchange office	menjalnica	men-*yal*-nee-tsa

I'd like to ...	Želim ...	zhe-*leem* ...
Where can I ...?	Kje je mogoče ...?	kye ye mo-*go*-che ...
cash a cheque	unovčiti ček	oo-*nov*-chee-tee chek
change a travellers cheque	zamenjati potovalni ček	za-*men*-ya-tee po-to-*val*-nee chek
change money	zamenjati denar	za-*men*-ya-tee de-*nar*
withdraw money	dvigniti denar	dveeg-nee-tee de-*nar*

What's the ...?	Kakšen/Kakšna je ...? m/f	kak-shen/*kak*-shna ye ...
commission	provizija f	pro-*vee*-zee-ya
exchange rate	menjalni tečaj m	men-*yal*-nee te-*chai*

Can I arrange a transfer of money?
Lahko uredim prenos denarja?   lah-*ko* oo-re-*deem* pre-*nos* de-*nar*-ya

What time does the bank open?
Kdaj se banka odpre?   kdai se *ban*-ka od-*pre*

Has my money arrived yet?
Je moj denar že prispel?   ye moy de-*nar* zhe prees-*pe*-oo

sightseeing

getting in

What time does it open/close?
Kdaj se odpre/zapre? · kdai se od·*pre*/za·*pre*

What's the admission charge?
Koliko stane vstopnica? · ko·lee·ko *sta*·ne *vstop*·nee·tsa

Is there a discount for students/children?
Imate popust za · ee·*ma*·te po·*poost* za
študente/otroke? · shtoo·*den*·te/ot·*ro*·ke

I'd like a ...	*Želim ...*	zhe·*leem* ...
catalogue	*katalog*	ka·ta·*log*
guide	*vodnik*	vod·*neek*
local map	*zemljevid kraja*	zem·lye·*veed* kra·ya

I'd like to see ... · *Želim videti ...* · zhe·*leem* vee·de·tee ...
What's that? · *Kaj je to?* · kai ye to
Can I take a photo? · *Ali lahko fotografiram?* · a·lee lah·ko fo·to·gra·*fee*·ram

tours

When's the next ...?	*Kdaj je naslednji ...?*	kdai ye nas·*led*·nyee ...
boat trip	*izlet s čolnom*	eez·*let* s *choh*·nom
day trip	*dnevni izlet*	*dnev*·nee eez·*let*
tour	*izlet*	eez·*let*

Is ... included?	*Je ... vključena?*	ye ... *vklyoo*·che·na
accommodation	*nastanitev*	nas·ta·*nee*·tev
the admission charge	*vstopnina*	vstop·*nee*·na
food	*hrana*	*hra*·na

Is transport included?
Je prevoz vključen? · ye pre·*voz* vklyoo·chen

How long is the tour?
Koliko časa traja izlet? · ko·lee·ko *cha*·sa *tra*·ya eez·*let*

What time should we be back?
Kdaj naj se vrnemo? · kdai nai se *vuhr*·ne·mo

castle	*grad* m	grad
cathedral	*stolnica* f	*stol*-nee-tsa
church	*cerkev* f	*tser*-kev
main square	*glavni trg* m	*glav*-nee tuhrg
monastery	*samostan* m	sa-mos-*tan*
monument	*spomenik* m	spo-me-*neek*
museum	*muzej* m	moo-*zey*
old city	*staro mesto* n	*sta*-ro *mes*-to
palace	*palača* f	pa-*la*-cha
ruins	*ruševine* f	roo-she-*vee*-ne
stadium	*stadion* m	*sta*-dee-on
statue	*kip* m	keep

shopping

enquiries

Where's a ...?	*Kje je ...?*	kye ye ...
bank	*banka*	*ban*-ka
bookshop	*knjigarna*	knyee-*gar*-na
camera shop	*trgovina s*	tuhr-go-*vee*-na s
	fotografsko opremo	fo-to-*graf*-sko op-*re*-mo
department store	*blagovnica*	bla-*gov*-nee-tsa
grocery store	*trgovina s*	tuhr-go-*vee*-na s
	špecerijo	shpe-tse-*ree*-yo
market	*tržnica*	*tuhrzh*-nee-tsa
newsagency	*kiosk*	*kee*-osk
supermarket	*trgovina*	tuhr-go-*vee*-na

Where can I buy (a padlock)?
Kje lahko kupim (ključavnico)?   kye lah-*ko koo*-peem (klyoo-*chav*-nee-tso)

I'm looking for ...
Iščem ...   *eesh*-chem ...

Can I look at it?
Lahko pogledam?   lah-*ko* pog-*le*-dam

shopping – SLOVENE

309

Do you have any others?
Imate še kakšnega/kakšno? m/f — ee·*ma*·te she *kak*·shne·ga/*kak*·shno

Does it have a guarantee?
Ali ima garancijo? — a·lee ee·*ma* ga·ran·*tsee*·yo

Can I have it sent abroad?
Mi lahko pošljete v tujino? — mee lah·*ko* posh·lye·te v too·*yee*·no

Can I have my ... repaired?
Mi lahko popravite ...? — mee lah·*ko* po·*pra*·vee·te ...

It's faulty.
Ne deluje. — ne de·*loo*·ye

I'd like ..., please.
Želim ..., prosim. — zhe·*leem* ... *pro*·seem
  a bag — *vrečko* — *vrech*·ko
  a refund — *vračilo denarja* — vra·*chee*·lo de·*nar*·ya
  to return this — *vrniti tole* — vr·*nee*·tee *to*·le

paying

How much is this?
Koliko stane? — ko·lee·ko *sta*·ne

Can you write down the price?
Lahko napišete ceno? — lah·ko na·*pee*·she·te *tse*·no

That's too expensive.
To je predrago. — to ye pre·dra·*go*

What's your lowest price?
Povejte vašo najnižjo ceno. — po·*vey*·te *va*·sho nai·*neezh*·yo *tse*·no

I'll give you (five) euros.
Dam vam (pet) evrov. — dam vam (pet) *ev*·roh

There's a mistake in the bill.
Na računu je napaka. — na ra·*choo*·noo ye na·*pa*·ka

Do you accept ...?
Ali sprejemate ...? — a·lee spre·ye·ma·te ...
  credit cards — *kreditne kartice* — kre·*deet*·ne *kar*·tee·tse
  debit cards — *debetne kartice* — de·bet·ne *kar*·tee·tse
  travellers cheques — *potovalne čeke* — po·to·*val*·ne *che*·ke

I'd like ..., please.
Želim ..., prosim. — zhe·*leem* ... *pro*·seem
  a receipt — *račun* — ra·*choon*
  my change — *drobiž* — dro·*beezh*

clothes & shoes

Can I try it on?	Lahko pomerim?	lah·ko po·me·reem
My size is (42).	Nosim številko	no·seem shte·veel·ko
	(dvainštirideset).	(dva·een·shtee·ree·de·set)
It doesn't fit.	Ni mi prav.	nee mee prow
... size	... številka	... shte·veel·ka
small	majhna	mai·hna
medium	srednja	sred·nya
large	velika	ve·lee·ka

books & music

I'd like a ...	Želim ...	zhe·leem ...
newspaper	časopis	cha·so·pees
(in English)	(v angleščini)	(v ang·lesh·chee·nee)
pen	pisalo	pee·sa·lo

I'm looking for an English-language bookshop.
Iščem angleško knjigarno.   eesh·chem ang·lesh·ko knyee·gar·no

I'm looking for a book/music by (Miha Mazzini/Zoran Predin).
Iščem knjigo/glasbo   eesh·chem knyee·go/glaz·bo
(Mihe Mazzinija/Zorana Predina).   (mee·he ma·tsee·nee·ya/zo·ra·na pre·dee·na)

Can I listen to this?
Lahko tole poslušam?   lah·ko to·le pos·loo·sham

photography

Can you ...?	Lahko ...?	lah·ko ...
burn a CD from	zapečete CD z moje	za·pe·che·te tse·de z mo·ye
my memory card	spominske kartice	spo·meen·ske kar·tee·tse
develop this film	razvijete ta film	raz·vee·ye·te ta feelm
load this film	vstavite ta film	vsta·vee·te ta feelm

I need a/an ... film	Potrebujem ... film	pot·re·boo·yem ... feelm
for this camera.	za ta fotoaparat.	za ta fo·to·a·pa·rat
APS	APS	a pe es
B&W	črno-bel	chuhr·no·be·oo
colour	barvni	barv·nee
(200) speed	(dvesto) ASA	(dve·sto) a·sa

I need a slide film for this camera.

Potrebujem film za diapozitive   pot·re·*boo*·yem feelm za dee·a·po·zee·*tee*·ve
za ta fotoaparat.   za ta fo·to·a·pa·*rat*

When will it be ready?

Kdaj bo gotovo?   kdai bo go·*to*·vo

meeting people

greetings, goodbyes & introductions

Hello/Hi.	*Zdravo.*	*zdra*·vo
Good night.	*Lahko noč.*	*lah*·ko noch
Goodbye/Bye.	*Na svidenje/Adijo.*	na *svee*·den·ye/a·*dee*·yo
See you later.	*Se vidiva.*	se *vee*·dee·va
Mr/Mrs	*gospod/gospa*	gos·pod/gos·pa
Miss	*gospodična*	gos·po·*deech*·na
How are you?	*Kako ste/si?* pol/inf	ka·*ko* ste/see
Fine, thanks.	*Dobro, hvala.*	*dob*·ro *hva*·la
And you?	*Pa vi/ti?* pol/inf	pa vee/tee
What's your name?	*Kako vam/ti je ime?* pol/inf	ka·*ko* vam/tee ye ee·*me*
My name is ...	*Ime mi je ...*	ee·*me* mee ye ...
I'm pleased to	*Veseli me, da sem vas*	ve·se·*lee* me da sem vas
meet you.	*spoznal/spoznala.* m/f	spoz·*now*/spoz·*na*·la
This is my ...	*To je moj/moja ...* m/f	to ye moy/*mo*·ya ...
boyfriend	*fant*	fant
brother	*brat*	brat
daughter	*hči*	hchee
father	*oče*	*o*·che
friend	*prijatelj* m	pree·*ya*·tel'
	prijateljica f	pree·*ya*·tel·yee·tsa
girlfriend	*punca*	*poon*·tsa
husband	*mož*	mozh
mother	*mama*	*ma*·ma
partner (intimate)	*partner/partnerka* m/f	*part*·ner/*part*·ner·ka
sister	*sestra*	*ses*·tra
son	*sin*	seen
wife	*žena*	*zhe*·na

Here's my phone number.
Tu je moja telefonska številka.   too ye *mo*·ya te·le·*fon*·ska shte·*veel*·ka

What's your phone number?
Mi poveste vašo telefonsko številko?   mee po·*ves*·te *va*·sho te·le·*fon*·sko shte·*veel*·ko

Here's my …	*Tu je moj/moja …* m/f	too ye moy/*mo*·ya …
What's your …?	*Kakšen je vaš …?* m	*kak*·shen ye vash …
	Kakšna je vaša …? f	*kak*·shna ye *va*·sha …
(email) address	*(elektronski) naslov* m	(e·lek·*tron*·skee) nas·*loh*
fax number	*številka faksa* f	shte·*veel*·ka *fak*·sa

occupations

What's your occupation?	*Kaj ste po poklicu?*	kai ste po pok·*lee*·tsoo
I'm a/an …	*… sem.*	… sem
artist	*Umetnik* m	oo·*met*·neek
	Umetnica f	oo·*met*·nee·tsa
farmer	*Kmet/Kmetica* m/f	kmet/kme·*tee*·tsa
office worker	*Uradnik* m	oo·*rad*·neek
	Uradnica f	oo·*rad*·nee·tsa
scientist	*Znanstvenik* m	znans·tve·neek
	Znanstvenica f	znans·tve·nee·tsa
student	*Študent/Študentka* m/f	shtoo·*dent*/ shtoo·*dent*·ka
tradesperson	*Trgovec/Trgovka* m/f	tuhr·*go*·vets/ tuhr·*gov*·ka

background

Where are you from?	*Od kod ste?*	od kod ste
I'm from …	*Iz … sem.*	eez … sem
Australia	*Avstralije*	av·*stra*·lee·ye
Canada	*Kanade*	*ka*·na·de
England	*Anglije*	*an*·glee·ye
New Zealand	*Nove Zelandije*	*no*·ve ze·*lan*·dee·ye
the USA	*Združenih držav*	zdroo·zhe·neeh dr·*zhav*
Are you married?	*Ste poročeni?*	ste po·ro·*che*·nee
I'm married.	*Poročen/Poročena*	po·ro·*chen*/po·ro·*che*·na
	sem. m/f	sem
I'm single.	*Samski/Samska sem.* m/f	*sam*·skee/*sam*·ska sem

How old ...?	Koliko ...?	ko·lee·ko ...
are you	si star/stara m/f inf	see star/sta·ra
are you	ste stari m&f pol	ste sta·ree
is your daughter	je stara vaša hči	ye sta·ra va·sha hchee
is your son	je star vaš sin	ye star vash seen

| I'm ... years old. | Imam ... let. | ee·mam ... let |
| He/She is ... years old. | ... let ima. | ... let ee·ma |

feelings

I'm ...	... sem.	... sem
hungry	Lačen/Lačna m/f	la·chen/lach·na
thirsty	Žejen/Žejna m/f	zhe·yen/zhey·na
tired	Utrujen m	oot·roo·yen
	Utrujena f	oot·roo·ye·na

I'm not ...	Nisem ...	nee·sem ...
hungry	lačen/lačna m/f	la·chen/lach·na
thirsty	žejen/žejna m/f	zhe·yen/zhey·na
tired	utrujen/utrujena m/f	oot·roo·yen/oot·roo·ye·na

Are you ... ?	Ste ...?	ste ...
hungry	lačni	lach·nee
thirsty	žejni	zhey·nee
tired	utrujeni	oot·roo·ye·nee

I'm ...	... mi je.	... mee ye
hot	Vroče	vro·che
well	Dobro	dob·ro

I'm not ...	Ni mi ...	nee mee ...
Are you ...?	Vam je ...?	vam ye ...
hot	vroče	vro·che
well	dobro	dob·ro

| I'm (not) cold. | (Ne) Zebe me. | ne ze·be me |
| Are you cold? | Vas zebe? | vas ze·be |

entertainment

going out

Where can I find ...?	Kje je kakšen ...?	kye ye *kak*·shen ...
clubs	klub	kloob
gay venues	homoseksualski bar	ho·mo·sek·soo·*al*·skee bar
pubs	bar	bar
I feel like going to a/the ...	Želim iti	zhe·*leem* ee·tee ...
concert	na koncert	na kon·*tsert*
movies	v kino	oo *kee*·no
party	na zabavo	na za·*ba*·vo
restaurant	v restavracijo	oo res·tav·*ra*·tsee·yo
theatre	v gledališče	oo gle·da·*leesh*·che

interests

Do you like ...?	Vam je všeč ...?	vam ye vshech ...
I like ...	Všeč mi je ...	vshech mee ye ...
I don't like ...	Ni mi všeč ...	nee mee vshech ...
art	umetnost	oo·*met*·nost
cooking	kuhanje	koo·*han*·ye
reading	branje	*bran*·ye
shopping	nakupovanje	na·koo·po·*van*·ye
sport	šport	shport
Do you like ...?	So vam všeč ...?	so vam vshech ...
I like ...	Všeč so mi ...	vshech so mee ...
I don't like ...	Niso mi všeč ...	*nee*·so mee vshech ...
movies	filmi	*feel*·mee
nightclubs	nočni bari	*noch*·nee ba·ree
travelling	potovanja	po·to·*van*·ya
Do you like to ...?	Ali radi ...?	a·lee ra·dee ...
dance	plešete	ple·she·te
go to concerts	hodite na koncerte	ho·dee·te na kon·*tser*·te
listen to music	poslušate glasbo	pos·*loo*·sha·te *glas*·bo

food & drink

finding a place to eat

Can you recommend a ...?	Mi lahko priporočite ...?	mee lah·*ko* pree·po·ro·*chee*·te ...
bar	bar	bar
café	kavarno	ka·*var*·no
restaurant	restavracijo	res·tav·*ra*·tsee·yo
I'd like ..., please.	Želim ..., prosim.	zhe·*leem* ... pro·*seem*
a table for (five)	mizo za (pet)	*mee*·zo za (pet)
the (non)smoking section	prostor za (ne)kadilce	*pros*·tor za (ne·)ka·*deel*·tse

ordering food

breakfast	zajtrk m	*zai*·tuhrk
lunch	kosilo n	ko·*see*·lo
dinner	večerja f	ve·*cher*·ya
snack	malica f	*ma*·lee·tsa
today's special	danes nudimo	*da*·nes *noo*·dee·mo
What would you recommend?	Kaj priporočate?	kai pree·po·*ro*·cha·te
I'd like (the) ..., please.	Želim ..., prosim.	zhe·*leem* ... pro·*seem*
bill	račun	ra·*choon*
drink list	meni pijač	me·*nee* pee·*yach*
menu	jedilni list	ye·*deel*·nee leest
that dish	to jed	to yed

drinks

cup of coffee ...	skodelica kave ...	sko·*de*·lee·tsa *ka*·ve ...
cup of tea ...	skodelica čaja ...	sko·*de*·lee·tsa *cha*·ya ...
with milk	z mlekom	z *mle*·kom
without sugar	brez sladkorja	brez slad·*kor*·ya

(orange) juice	*(pomarančni) sok* m	(po-ma-*ranch*-nee) sok
soft drink	*brezalkoholna*	brez-al-ko-*hol*-na
	pijača f	pee-*ya*-cha
... water	*... voda*	*... vo*-da
boiled	*prekuhana*	pre-*koo*-ha-na
(sparkling)	*mineralna*	mee-ne-*ral*-na
mineral	*(gazirana)*	(ga-*zee*-ra-na)

in the bar

I'll have ...
Jaz bom ... yaz bom ...

I'll buy you a drink.
Povabim te na pijačo. inf po-*va*-beem te na pee-*ya*-cho

What would you like?
Kaj boš? inf kai bosh

Cheers!
Na zdravje! na *zdrav*-ye

brandy	*vinjak* m	*veen*-yak
champagne	*šampanjec* m	sham-*pan*-yets
cocktail	*koktajl* m	kok-*tail*
cognac	*konjak* m	*kon*-yak
a shot of (whisky)	*kozarček (viskija)*	ko-*zar*-chek (*vees*-kee-ya)
a ... of beer	*... piva*	*... pee*-va
glass	*kozarec*	ko-*za*-rets
jug	*vrč*	vuhrch
pint	*vrček*	*vuhr*-chek
a bottle/glass	*steklenica/kozarec*	stek-le-*nee*-tsa/ko-*za*-rets
of ... wine	*... vina*	*... vee*-na
red	*rdečega*	*rde*-che-ga
sparkling	*penečega*	pe-*ne*-che-ga
white	*belega*	*be*-le-ga

self-catering

What's the local speciality?
Kaj je lokalna specialiteta? kai ye lo-*kal*-na spe-tsee-a-lee-*te*-ta

What's that?
Kaj je to? kai ye to

How much is (a kilo of cheese)?
Koliko stane (kila sira)? ko-lee-ko *sta*-ne (*kee*-la *see*-ra)

I'd like ...	*Želim ...*	zhe-*leem* ...
(200) grams	*(dvesto) gramov*	(dve-sto) *gra*-mov
(two) kilos	*(dva) kilograma*	(dva) kee-lo-*gra*-ma
(three) pieces	*(tri) kose*	(tree) *ko*-se
(six) slices	*(šest) rezin*	(shest) re-*zeen*

Less.	*Manj.*	man'
Enough.	*Dovolj.*	do-*vol*
More.	*Več.*	vech

special diets & allergies

Is there a vegetarian restaurant near here?
Je tu blizu vegetarijanska ye too *blee*-zoo ve-ge-ta-ree-*yan*-ska
restavracija? res-tav-*ra*-tsee-ya

Do you have vegetarian food?
Ali imate vegetarijansko hrano? a-lee ee-*ma*-te ve-ge-ta-ree-*yan*-sko *hra*-no

Could you prepare	*Lahko pripravite*	lah-ko pree-*pra*-vee-te
a meal without ...?	*obed brez ...?*	o-*bed* brez ...
butter	*masla*	*mas*-la
eggs	*jajc*	yaits
meat stock	*mesne osnove*	mes-ne os-*no*-ve

I'm allergic to ...	*Alergičen/Alergična*	a-*ler*-gee-chen/a-*ler*-geech-na
	sem na ... m/f	sem na ...
dairy produce	*mlečne izdelke*	*mlech*-ne eez-*del*-ke
gluten	*gluten*	gloo-ten
MSG	*MSG*	em es ge
nuts	*oreške*	o-*resh*-ke
seafood	*morsko hrano*	*mor*-sko *hra*-no

menu reader

bograč m	*bog*-rach	*beef goulash*
brancin na maslu m	bran-*tseen* na *mas*-loo	*sea bass in butter*
čebulna bržola f	che-*bool*-na br-*zho*-la	*braised beef with onions*
čevapčiči m	che-*vap*-chee-chee	*spicy beef or pork meatballs*
drobnjakovi štruklji m	drob-*nya*-ko-vee *shtrook*-lyee	*dumplings of cottage cheese & chives*
dunajski zrezek m	doo-nai-skee *zre*-zek	*breaded veal or pork cutlet*
francoska solata f	fran-*tsos*-ka so-*la*-ta	*diced potatoes & vegetables with mayonnaise*
gobova kremna juha f	go-bo-va *krem*-na *yoo*-ha	*creamed mushroom soup*
goveja juha z rezanci f	go-*ve*-ya *yoo*-ha z *re*-zan-tsee	*beef broth with little egg noodles*
jota f	*yo*-ta	*beans, sauerkraut & potatoes or barley cooked with pork*
kisle kumarice f	*kees*-le *koo*-ma-ree-tse	*pickled cucumbers*
kmečka pojedina f	*kmech*-ka po-*ye*-dee-na	*smoked meats with sauerkraut*
kranjska klobasa z gorčico f	*kran'*-ska klo-*ba*-sa z *gor*-chee-tso	*sausage with mustard*
kraški pršut z olivami m	*krash*-kee puhr-*shoot* z o-*lee*-va-mee	*air-dried ham with black olives*
krofi m	*kro*-fee	*jam-filled doughnuts*
kuhana govedina s hrenom f	*koo*-ha-na go-*ve*-dee-na s *hre*-nom	*boiled beef with horseradish*
kuhana postrv f	*koo*-ha-na pos-*tuhrv*	*boiled trout*
kumarična solata f	*koo*-ma-reech-na so-*la*-ta	*cucumber salad*
ljubljanski zrezek m	lyoob-*lyan*-skee *zre*-zek	*breaded cutlet with cheese*

mešano meso na žaru n	*me*·sha·no me·*so* na *zha*·roo	mixed grill
ocvrt oslič m	ots·*vuhrt* os·*leech*	fried cod
ocvrt piščanec m	ots·*vuhrt* peesh·*cha*·nets	fried chicken
orada na žaru f	o·*ra*·da na *zha*·roo	grilled sea bream
palačinke f	pa·la·*cheen*·ke	thin pancakes with marmalade, nuts or chocolate
pečena postrv f	pe·*che*·na pos·*tuhrv*	grilled trout
pečene sardele f	pe·*che*·ne sar·*de*·le	grilled sardines
pleskavica f	*ples*·ka·vee·tsa	spicy meat patties
pariški zrezek m	pa·*reesh*·kee zre·zek	cutlet fried in egg batter
puranov zrezek s šampinjoni m	poo·*ra*·nov zre·zek s sham·peen·*yo*·nee	turkey steak with white mushrooms
ražnjiči m	*razh*·nyee·chee	shish kebab
riba v marinadi f	*ree*·ba v ma·ree·*na*·dee	marinated fish
ričet m	*ree*·chet	barley stew with smoked pork ribs
rižota z gobami f	ree·*zho*·ta z *go*·ba·mee	risotto with mushrooms
sadna kupa f	*sad*·na *koo*·pa	fruit salad with whipped cream
srbska solata f	*suhrb*·ska so·*la*·ta	salad of tomatoes & green peppers with onions & cheese
svinjska pečenka f	sveen'·ska pe·*chen*·ka	roast pork
škampi na žaru m	*shkam*·pee na *zha*·roo	grilled prawns
školjke f	*shkol'*·ke	clams
zelena solata f	ze·*le*·na so·*la*·ta	lettuce salad
zelenjavna juha f	ze·*len*·*yav*·na *yoo*·ha	vegetable soup

emergencies

basics

Help!	Na pomoč!	na po·*moch*
Stop!	Ustavite (se)!	oos·*ta*·vee·te (se)
Go away!	Pojdite stran!	poy·*dee*·te stran
Thief!	Tat!	tat
Fire!	Požar!	po·*zhar*
Watch out!	Pazite!	pa·*zee*·te

Call ...!	Pokličite ...!	pok·*lee*·chee·te ...
a doctor	zdravnika	zdrav·*nee*·ka
an ambulance	rešilca	re·*sheel*·tsa
the police	policijo	po·lee·*tsee*·yo

It's an emergency.
Nujno je.   nooy·no ye

Could you help me, please?
Pomagajte mi, prosim.   po·*ma*·gai·te mee *pro*·seem

I have to use the telephone.
Poklicati moram.   pok·*lee*·tsa·tee *mo*·ram

I'm lost.
Izgubil/Izgubila sem se. m/f   eez·*goo*·beew/eez·goo·*bee*·la sem se

Where are the toilets?
Kje je stranišče?   kye ye stra·*neesh*·che

police

Where's the police station?
Kje je policijska postaja?   kye ye po·lee·*tseey*·ska pos·*ta*·ya

I want to report an offence.
Želim prijaviti prestopek.   zhe·*leem* pree·*ya*·vee·tee pres·*to*·pek

I have insurance.
Zavarovan/Zavarovana sem. m/f   za·va·ro·*van*/za·va·ro·*va*·na sem

I've been ...	... so me.	... so me
assaulted	Napadli	na·*pad*·lee
raped	Posilili	po·*see*·lee·lee
robbed	Oropali	o·*ro*·pa·lee

I've lost my ...	Izgubil/Izgubila sem ... m/f	eez-goo-beew/eez-goo-bee-la sem ...
My ... was/were stolen.	Ukradli so mi ...	ook-rad-lee so mee ...
backpack	nahrbtnik	na-huhrbt-neek
bags	torbe	tor-be
credit card	kreditno kartico	kre-deet-no kar-tee-tso
handbag	ročno torbico	roch-no tor-bee-tso
jewellery	nakit	na-keet
money	denar	de-nar
passport	potni list	pot-nee leest
travellers cheques	potovalne čeke	po-to-val-ne che-ke
wallet	denarnico	de-nar-nee-tso
I want to contact my ...	Želim poklicati ... svoj/svojo ... m/f	zhe-leem pok-lee-tsa-tee ... svoy/svo-yo ...
consulate	konzulat m	kon-zoo-lat
embassy	ambasado f	am-ba-sa-do

health

medical needs

Where's the nearest ...?	Kje je najbližji/ najbližja ... ? m/f	kye ye nai-bleezh-yee/ nai-bleezh-ya ...
dentist	zobozdravnik m	zo-bo-zdrav-neek
doctor	zdravnik m	zdrav-neek
hospital	bolnišnica f	bol-neesh-nee-tsa
(night) pharmacist	(nočna) lekarna f	(noch-na) le-kar-na

I need a doctor (who speaks English).
Potrebujem zdravnika
(ki govori angleško).
pot-re-boo-yem zdrav-nee-ka
(kee go-vo-ree ang-lesh-ko)

Could I see a female doctor?
Bi me lahko pregledala
zdravnica?
bee me lah-ko preg-le-da-la
zdrav-nee-tsa

I've run out of my medication.
Zmanjkalo mi je zdravil.
zman'-ka-lo mee ye zdra-veel

symptoms, conditions & allergies

I'm sick.	*Bolan/Bolna sem.* m/f	bo-*lan*/*boh*-na sem
It hurts here.	*Tu me boli.*	too me bo-*lee*
I have (a) ...	*Imam ...*	ee-*mam* ...
asthma	*astmo*	*ast*-mo
bronchitis	*bronhitis*	bron-*hee*-tees
constipation	*zapeko*	za-*pe*-ko
diarrhoea	*drisko*	*drees*-ko
fever	*vročino*	vro-*chee*-no
headache	*glavobol*	gla-vo-*bol*
heart condition	*srčno bolezen*	*suhr*-chno bo-*le*-zen
toothache	*zobobol*	zo-bo-*bol*
pain	*bolečine*	bo-le-*chee*-ne
I'm nauseous.	*Slabo mi je.*	sla-*bo* mee ye
I'm coughing.	*Kašljam.*	*kash*-lyam
I have a sore throat.	*Boli me grlo.*	bo-*lee* me *guhr*-lo
I'm allergic to ...	*Alergičen/Alergična sem na ...* m/f	a-*ler*-gee-chen/a-*ler*-geech-na sem na ...
antibiotics	*antibiotike*	an-tee-bee-*o*-tee-ke
anti-inflammatories	*protivnetna zdravila*	pro-teev-*net*-na zdra-*vee*-la
aspirin	*aspirin*	as-pee-*reen*
bees	*čebelji pik*	che-*bel*-yee peek
codeine	*kodein*	ko-de-*een*
penicillin	*penicilin*	pe-nee-tsee-*leen*
antiseptic	*razkužilo* n	raz-koo-*zhee*-lo
bandage	*obveza* f	ob-*ve*-za
condoms	*kondomi* m pl	kon-*do*-mee
contraceptives	*kontracepcija* f	kon-tra-*tsep*-tsee-ya
diarrhoea medicine	*zdravilo za drisko* n	zdra-*vee*-lo za *drees*-ko
insect repellent	*sredstvo proti mrčesu* n	*sreds*-tvo *pro*-tee muhr-*che*-soo
laxatives	*odvajala* n pl	od-va-*ya*-la
painkillers	*analgetiki* m pl	a-nal-*ge*-tee-kee
rehydration salts	*sol za rehidracijo* f	sol za re-heed-*ra*-tsee-yo
sleeping tablets	*uspavalne tablete* f pl	oos-pa-*val*-ne tab-*le*-te

english–slovene dictionary

Slovene nouns in this dictionary have their gender indicated by ⓜ (masculine), ⓕ (feminine) or ⓝ (neuter).
If it's a plural noun, you'll also see pl. Adjectives are given in the masculine form only. Words are also marked
as a (adjective), v (verb), sg (singular), pl (plural), inf (informal) or pol (polite) where necessary.

A

accident *nesreča* ⓕ nes-re-cha
accommodation *nastanitev* ⓕ na-sta-*nee*-tev
adaptor *adapter* ⓜ a-*dap*-ter
address *naslov* ⓜ nas-*loh*
after *po* po
air-conditioned *klimatiziran* klee-ma-tee-*zee*-ran
airplane *letalo* ⓝ le-*ta*-lo
airport *letališče* ⓝ le-ta-*leesh*-che
alcohol *alkohol* ⓜ al-ko-*hol*
all *vse* vse
allergy *alergija* ⓕ a-ler-*gee*-ya
ambulance *rešilni avto* ⓜ re-*sheel*-nee *av*-to
and *in* een
ankle *gleženj* ⓜ *gle*-zhen'
arm *roka* ⓕ *ro*-ka
ashtray *pepelnik* ⓜ pe-*pel*-neek
ATM *bankomat* ⓜ ban-ko-*mat*

B

baby *dojenček* ⓜ do-yen-*chek*
back (body) *hrbet* ⓜ *huhr*-bet
backpack *nahrbtnik* ⓜ na-*huhrbt*-neek
bad *slab* slab
bag *torba* ⓕ *tor*-ba
baggage *prtljaga* ⓕ puhrt-*lya*-ga
baggage claim *prevzem prtljage* ⓜ
    prev-*zem* puhrt-*lya*-ge
bank *banka* ⓕ *ban*-ka
bar *bar* ⓜ bar
bathroom *kopalnica* ⓕ ko-*pal*-nee-tsa
battery *baterija* ⓕ ba-te-*ree*-ya
beautiful *lep* lep
bed *postelja* ⓕ *pos*-tel-ya
beer *pivo* ⓝ *pee*-vo
before *prej* prey
behind *zadaj* za-dai
bicycle *bicikel* ⓜ bee-*tsee*-kel
big *velik* ve-*leek*
bill *račun* ⓜ ra-*choon*
black *črn* chuhrn

blanket *odeja* ⓕ o-*de*-ya
blood group *krvna skupina* ⓕ *kuhrv*-na skoo-*pee*-na
blue *moder* mo-der
boat (ship) *ladja* ⓕ *lad*-ya
boat (small) *čoln* ⓜ chohn
book (make a reservation) v *rezervirati*
    re-zer-vee-ra-tee
bottle *steklenica* ⓕ stek-le-*nee*-tsa
bottle opener *odpirač* ⓜ od-pee-*rach*
boy *fant* ⓜ fant
brakes (car) *zavore* ⓕ pl za-*vo*-re
breakfast *zajtrk* ⓜ *zai*-tuhrk
broken (faulty) *pokvarjen* pok-*var*-yen
bus *avtobus* ⓜ av-to-*boos*
business *posel* ⓜ po-se-oo
buy *kupiti* koo-*pee*-tee

C

café *kavarna* ⓕ ka-*var*-na
camera *fotoaparat* ⓜ fo-to-a-pa-*rat*
camera shop *trgovina s fotografsko opremo* ⓕ
    tr-go-*vee*-na s fo-to-*graf*-sko o-*pre*-mo
campsite *kamp* ⓜ kamp
cancel *preklicati* prek-*lee*-tsa-tee
can opener *odpirač za pločevinke* ⓜ
    od-pee-*rach* za plo-che-*veen*-ke
car *avtomobil* ⓜ av-to-mo-*beel*
cash *gotovina* ⓕ go-to-vee-na
cash (a cheque) v *unovčiti (ček)* oo-nov-*chee*-tee (chek)
cell phone *mobilni telefon* ⓜ mo-*beel*-nee te-le-*fon*
centre *center* ⓜ tsen-ter
change (money) v *menjati (denar)* men-ya-tee (de-nar)
cheap *poceni* po-tse-nee
check (bill) *račun* ⓜ ra-*choon*
check-in *prijava za let* ⓕ pree-*ya*-va za let
chest *prsni koš* ⓜ *puhr*-snee kosh
child *otrok* ⓜ ot-rok
cigarette *cigareta* ⓕ tsee-ga-*re*-ta
city *mesto* ⓝ *mes*-to
clean a *čist* cheest
closed *zaprt* za-*puhrt*
coffee *kava* ⓕ *ka*-va
coins *kovanci* ⓜ pl ko-*van*-tsee

cold a *hladen* hla-den
collect call *klic na stroške klicanega* m
   kleets na *strosh*-ke *klee*-tsa-ne-ga
come *priti* pree-tee
computer *računalnik* m ra-choo-nal-neek
condom *kondom* m kon-dom
contact lenses *kontaktne leče* f pl kon-*takt*-ne *le*-che
cook v *kuhati* koo-ha-tee
cost *strošek* m stro-shek
credit card *kreditna kartica* f kre-*deet*-na *kar*-tee-tsa
cup *skodelica* f sko-de-lee-tsa
currency exchange *menjava* f men-ya-va
customs (immigration) *carina* f tsa-ree-na

D

dangerous *nevaren* ne-*va*-ren
date (time) *datum* m da-toom
day *dan* m dan
delay *zamuda* f za-moo-da
dentist *zobozdravnik* m zo-boz-drav-neek
depart *oditi* o-dee-tee
diaper *plenica* f ple-nee-tsa
dictionary *slovar* m slo-var
dinner *večerja* f ve-cher-ya
direct *direkten* dee-rek-ten
dirty *umazan* oo-ma-zan
disabled (person) *invaliden* een-va-lee-den
discount *popust* m po-poost
doctor *zdravnik* m zdrav-neek
double bed *dvojna postelja* f dvoy-na pos-tel-ya
double room *dvoposteljna soba* f
   dvo-pos-tel'-na so-ba
drink *pijača* f pee-ya-cha
drive v *voziti* vo-zee-tee
drivers licence *vozniško dovoljenje* m
   voz-neesh-ko do-vol-yen-ye
drug (illicit) *mamilo* m ma-mee-lo
dummy (pacifier) *duda* f doo-da

E

ear *uho* m oo-ho
east *vzhod* m vzhod
eat *jesti* yes-tee
economy class *turistični razred* m
   too-rees-teech-nee raz-red
electricity *elektrika* f e-lek-tree-ka
elevator *dvigalo* m dvee-ga-lo
email *elektronska pošta* f e-lek-tron-ska posh-ta
embassy *ambasada* f am-ba-sa-da
emergency *nujen primer* m noo-yen pree-mer
English (language) *angleščina* f ang-lesh-chee-na

entrance *vhod* m vhod
evening *večer* m ve-cher
exchange rate *menjalni tečaj* m men-yal-nee te-chai
exit *izhod* m eez-hod
expensive *drag* drag
express mail *hitra pošta* f heet-ra posh-ta
eye *oko* m o-ko

F

far *daleč* da-lech
fast *hitro* heet-ro
father *oče* m o-che
film (camera) *film* m feelm
finger *prst* m puhrst
first-aid kit *komplet za prvo pomoč* m
   kom-plet za puhr-vo po-moch
first class *prvi razred* m puhr-vee raz-red
fish *riba* f ree-ba
food *hrana* f hra-na
foot *stopalo* m sto-pa-lo
fork *vilice* f pl vee-lee-tse
free (of charge) *brezplačen* brez-pla-chen
friend *prijatelj/prijateljica* m/f
   pree-ya-tel/pree-ya-tel-yee-tsa
fruit *sadje* m pl sad-ye
full *poln* poln
funny *smešen* sme-shen

G

gift *darilo* m da-ree-lo
girl *dekle* m dek-le
glass (drinking) *kozarec* m ko-za-rets
glasses *očala* m pl o-cha-la
go *iti* ee-tee
good *dober* do-ber
green *zelen* ze-len
guide *vodnik* m vod-neek

H

half *pol* poh
hand *roka* f ro-ka
handbag *ročna torbica* f roch-na tor-bee-tsa
happy *srečen* sre-chen
have *imeti* ee-me-tee
he *on* m on
head *glava* f gla-va
heart *srce* m suhr-tse
heat *vročina* f vro-chee-na
heavy *težek* te-zhek

help v *pomagati* po-*ma*-ga-tee
here *tukaj* too-kai
high *visok* vee-*sok*
highway *hitra cesta* ① heet-ra tses-ta
(go on a) hike v *iti na pohod* ee-tee na po-*hod*
holidays *počitnice* ① pl po-*cheet*-nee-tse
homosexual *homoseksualec* ⑩ ho-mo-sek-soo-*a*-lets
hospital *bolnišnica* ① bol-*neesh*-nee-tsa
hot *vroč* vroch
hotel *hotel* ⑩ ho-*tel*
hungry *lačen* la-chen
husband *mož* ⑩ mozh

I

I *jaz* yaz
identification (card) *osebna izkaznica* ①
o-*seb*-na eez-*kaz*-nee-tsa
ill *bolan* bo-*lan*
important *pomemben* po-mem-ben
included *vključen* vklyoo-chen
injury *poškodba* ① posh-*kod*-ba
insurance *zavarovanje* ⑩ za-va-ro-*van*-ye
Internet *internet* ⑩ een-ter-net
interpreter *tolmač* ⑩ tol-*mach*

J

jewellery *nakit* ⑩ na-*keet*
job *služba* ① sloozh-ba

K

key *ključ* ⑩ klyooch
kilogram *kilogram* ⑩ kee-lo-*gram*
kitchen *kuhinja* ① koo-heen-ya
knife *nož* ⑩ nozh

L

laundry (place) *pralnica* ① pral-nee-tsa
lawyer *odvetnik* ⑩ od-vet-neek
left (direction) *levo* le-vo
left-luggage office *garderoba* ① gar-de-*ro*-ba
leg *noga* ① no-ga
lesbian *lezbijka* ① lez-beey-ka
less *manj* man'
letter (mail) *pismo* ⑩ pees-mo
lift (elevator) *dvigalo* ⑩ dvee-*ga*-lo
light *svetloba* ① svet-*lo*-ba
like v *všeč biti* vshech bee-tee

lock *ključavnica* ① klyoo-*chav*-nee-tsa
long *dolg* dohg
lost *izgubljen* eez-goob-*lyen*
lost-property office *urad za izgubljene predmete* ⑩
oo-rad za eez-goob-*lye*-ne pred-*me*-te
love v *ljubiti* lyoo-bee-tee
luggage *prtljaga* ① puhrt-*lya*-ga
lunch *kosilo* ⑩ ko-see-lo

M

mail *pošta* ① posh-ta
man *moški* ⑩ mosh-kee
map *zemljevid* ⑩ zem-lye-veed
market *tržnica* ① tuhrzh-nee-tsa
matches *vžigalice* ① pl vzhee-*ga*-lee-tse
meat *meso* ⑩ me-so
medicine *zdravilo* ⑩ zdra-vee-lo
menu *jedilni list* ⑩ ye-deel-nee leest
message *sporočilo* ⑩ spo-ro-chee-lo
milk *mleko* ⑩ mle-ko
minute *minuta* ① mee-noo-ta
mobile phone *mobilni telefon* ⑩ mo-beel-nee te-le-*fon*
money *denar* ⑩ de-nar
month *mesec* ⑩ me-sets
morning *dopoldne* ⑩ do-*pol*-dne
mother *mama* ① ma-ma
motorcycle *motorno kolo* ⑩ mo-tor-no ko-lo
motorway *motorna cesta* ① mo-tor-na tses-ta
mouth *usta* ① oos-ta
music *glasba* ① glaz-ba

N

name *ime* ⑩ ee-me
napkin *prtiček* ⑩ puhr-tee-chek
nappy *plenica* ① ple-nee-tsa
near *blizu* blee-zoo
neck *vrat* ⑩ vrat
new *nov* noh
news *novice* ① pl no-vee-tse
newspaper *časopis* ⑩ cha-so-pees
night *noč* ① noch
no *ne* ne
noisy *hrupen* hroo-pen
nonsmoking *nekadilski* ne-ka-*deel*-skee
north *sever* ⑩ se-ver
nose *nos* ⑩ nos
now *zdaj* zdai
number *število* ⑩ shte-*vee*-lo

O

oil (engine) *olje* ⓝ *ol*·ye
old *star* star
one-way ticket *enosmerna vozovnica* ⓕ
  e·no·*smer*·na vo·zov·nee·tsa
open a *odprt* od·*puhrt*
outside *zunaj* zoo·nai

P

package *paket* ⓜ pa·*ket*
paper *papir* ⓜ pa·*peer*
park (car) v *parkirati* par·*kee*·ra·tee
passport *potni list* ⓜ *pot*·nee leest
pay *plačati* pla·cha·tee
pen *pisalo* ⓝ pe·*sa*·lo
petrol *bencin* ⓜ ben·*tseen*
pharmacy *lekarna* ⓕ le·*kar*·na
phonecard *telefonska kartica* ⓕ
  te·le·*fon*·ska kar·tee·tsa
photo *fotografija* ⓕ fo·to·gra·*fee*·ya
picnic *piknik* ⓜ *peek*·neek
plate *krožnik* ⓜ *krozh*·neek
police *policija* ⓕ po·lee·*tsee*·ya
postcard *razglednica* ⓕ raz·*gled*·nee·tsa
post office *pošta* ⓕ *posh*·ta
pregnant *noseča* no·se·cha
price *cena* ⓕ *tse*·na

Q

quiet *tih* teeh

R

rain *dež* ⓜ dezh
razor *brivnik* ⓜ *breev*·neek
receipt *račun* ⓜ ra·*choon*
red *rdeč* rdech
refund *vračilo denarja* ⓝ vra·chee·lo de·*nar*·ya
registered mail *priporočena pošta* ⓕ
  pree·po·ro·che·na posh·ta
rent v *najeti* na·ye·tee
repair v *popraviti* pop·*ra*·vee·tee
reservation *rezervacija* ⓕ re·zer·*va*·tsee·ya
restaurant *restavracija* ⓕ res·tav·*ra*·tsee·ya
return v *vrniti* vr·nee·tee

return ticket *povratna vozovnica* ⓕ
  pov·*rat*·na vo·zov·nee·tsa
right (direction) *desno* des·no
road *cesta* ⓕ *tses*·ta
room *soba* ⓕ *so*·ba

S

safe a *varen* va·ren
sanitary napkins *damski vložki* ⓜ pl
  dam·skee vlozh·kee
seat *sedež* ⓜ se·dezh
send *poslati* pos·*la*·tee
service station *servis* ⓜ *ser*·vees
sex *seks* ⓜ seks
shampoo *šampon* ⓜ sham·*pon*
share (a dorm) *deliti (sobo)* de·lee·tee (so·bo)
shaving cream *krema za britje* ⓕ *kre*·ma za breet·ye
she *ona* ⓕ o·na
sheet (bed) *rjuha* ⓕ ryoo·ha
shirt *srajca* ⓕ *srai*·tsa
shoes *čevlji* ⓜ pl chev·lyee
shop *trgovina* ⓕ tuhr·go·vee·na
short *kratek* kra·tek
shower *prha* ⓕ puhr·ha
single room *enoposteljna soba* ⓕ
  e·no·pos·tel'·na so·ba
skin *koža* ⓕ ko·zha
skirt *krilo* ⓝ kree·lo
sleep v *spati* spa·tee
Slovenia *Slovenija* ⓕ slo·ve·nee·ya
Slovene (language) *slovenščina* ⓕ slo·vensh·chee·na
Slovene a *slovenski* slo·ven·skee
slowly *počasi* po·cha·see
small *majhen* mai·hen
smoke (cigarettes) v *kaditi* ka·dee·tee
soap *milo* ⓝ *mee*·lo
some *nekaj* ne·kai
soon *kmalu* kma·loo
south *jug* ⓜ yoog
souvenir shop *trgovina s spominki* ⓕ
  tuhr·go·vee·na s spo·meen·kee
speak *govoriti* go·vo·ree·tee
spoon *žlica* ⓕ zhlee·tsa
stamp *znamka* ⓕ *znam*·ka
stand-by ticket *stand-by vozovnica* ⓕ
  stend·bai vo·zov·nee·tsa
station (train) *postaja* ⓕ pos·*ta*·ya
stomach *želodec* ⓜ zhe·lo·dets

stop v *ustaviti* oos-ta-vee-tee
stop (bus) *postajališče* ⓝ pos-ta-ya-leesh-che
street *ulica* ⓕ oo-lee-tsa
student *študent/študentka* ⓜ/ⓕ
  shtoo-dent/shtoo-dent-ka
sun *sonce* ⓝ son-tse
sunscreen *krema za sončenje* ⓝ kre-ma za son-chen-ye
swim v *plavati* pla-va-tee

T

tampons *tamponi* ⓜ pl tam-po-nee
taxi *taksi* ⓜ tak-see
teaspoon *čajna žlička* ⓕ chai-na zhleech-ka
teeth *zobje* ⓜ zob-ye
telephone *telefon* ⓜ te-le-fon
television *televizija* ⓕ te-le-vee-zee-ya
temperature (weather) *temperatura* ⓕ
  tem-pe-ra-too-ra
tent *šotor* ⓜ sho-tor
that (one) *tisti* tees-tee
they *oni/one* ⓜ/ⓕ o-nee/o-ne
thirsty *žejen* zhe-yen
this (one) *ta* ta
throat *grlo* ⓝ guhr-lo
ticket (entrance) *vstopnica* ⓕ vstop-nee-tsa
ticket (travel) *vozovnica* ⓕ vo-zov-nee-tsa
time *čas* ⓜ chas
tired *utrujen* oo-troo-yen
tissues *robčki* ⓜ pl rob-chkee
today *danes* da-nes
toilet *stranišče* ⓝ stra-neesh-che
tomorrow *jutri* yoot-ree
tonight *nocoj* no-tsoy
toothbrush *zobna ščetka* ⓕ zob-na shchet-ka
toothpaste *zobna pasta* ⓕ zob-na pas-ta
torch (flashlight) *baterija* ⓕ ba-te-ree-ya
tour *izlet* ⓜ eez-let
tourist office *turistični urad* ⓜ too-rees-teech-nee oo-rad
towel *brisača* ⓕ bree-sa-cha
train *vlak* ⓜ vlak
translate *prevesti* pre-ves-tee
travel agency *potovalna agencija* ⓕ
  po-to-val-na a-gen-tsee-ya
travellers cheque *potovalni ček* ⓜ po-to-val-nee chek
trousers *hlače* ⓕ pl hla-che
twin beds *ločeni postelji* ⓕ pl lo-che-nee pos-tel-yee
tyre *guma* ⓕ goo-ma

U

underwear *spodnje perilo* ⓝ spod-nye pe-ree-lo
urgent *nujen* noo-yen

V

vacant *prost* prost
vacation *počitnice* ⓕ pl po-cheet-nee-tse
vegetable *zelenjava* ⓕ ze-len-ya-va
vegetarian a *vegetarijanski* ve-ge-ta-ree-yan-skee
visa *viza* ⓕ vee-za

W

waiter *natakar* ⓜ na-ta-kar
walk v *hoditi* ho-dee-tee
wallet *denarnica* ⓕ de-nar-nee-tsa
warm a *topel* to-pe-oo
wash (something) *prati* pra-tee
watch *zapestna ura* ⓕ za-pest-na oo-ra
water *voda* ⓕ vo-da
we *mi* mee
weekend *vikend* ⓜ vee-kend
west *zahod* ⓜ za-hod
wheelchair *invalidski voziček* ⓜ
  een-va-leed-skee vo-zee-chek
when *kdaj* kdai
where *kje* kye
white *bel* be-oo
who *kdo* kdo
why *zakaj* za-kai
wife *žena* ⓕ zhe-na
window *okno* ⓝ ok-no
wine *vino* ⓝ vee-no
with *z/s* z/s
without *brez* brez
woman *ženska* ⓕ zhen-ska
write *pisati* pee-sa-tee

Y

yellow *rumen* roo-men
yes *da* da
yesterday *včeraj* vche-rai
you sg inf/pol *ti/vi* tee/vee
you pl *vi* vee

Spanish

spanish alphabet

A a a	*B b* be	*C c* the	*Ch ch* che	*D d* de
E e e	*F f* e·fe	*G g* khe	*H h* a·che	*I i* ee
J j kho·ta	*K k* ka	*L l* e·le	*LL ll* e·lye	*M m* e·me
N n e·ne	*Ñ ñ* e·nye	*O o* a	*P p* pe	*Q q* koo
R r e·re	*S s* e·se	*T t* te	*U u* oo	*V v* oo·ve
W w oo·ve do·vle	*X x* e·kees	*Y y* ee·grye·ga	*Z z* the·ta	

■ spanish

ESPAÑOL

introduction

The lively and picturesque language of Cervantes' *Don Quijote* and Almodóvar's movies, Spanish (*español* es-pa-*nyol*), or Castilian (*castellano* kas-te-*lya*-no), as it's also called in Spain, has over 390 million speakers worldwide. Outside Spain, it's the language of most of Latin America and the West Indies and is also spoken in the Philippines and Guam, in some areas of the African coast and in the US.

Spanish belongs to the Romance group of languages – the descendents of Latin – together with French, Italian, Portuguese and Romanian. It's derived from Vulgar Latin, which Roman soldiers and merchants brought to the Iberian Peninsula during the period of Roman conquest (3rd to 1st century BC). By 19 BC Spain had become totally Romanised and Latin became the language of the peninsula in the four centuries that followed. Thanks to the Arabic invasion in AD 711 and the Arabs' continuing presence in Spain during the next eight centuries, Spanish has also been strongly influenced by Arabic, although mostly in the vocabulary. Today's Castilian is spoken in the north, centre and south of Spain. Completing the colourful linguistic profile of the country, Basque (*euskera* e-*oos*-ke-ra), Catalan (*catalán* ka-ta-*lan*) and Galician (*gallego* ga-*lye*-go) are also official languages in Spain, though Castilian covers by far the largest territory.

Besides the shared vocabulary of Latin origin that English and Spanish have in common, there's also a large corpus of words from the indigenous American languages that have entered English via Spanish. After Columbus' discovery of the New World in 1492, America's indigenous languages had a considerable impact on Spanish, especially in words to do with flora, fauna and topography (such as *tobacco*, *chocolate*, *coyote*, *canyon*, to name a few).

Even if you're not familiar with the sound of Spanish through, say, the voices of José Carreras or Julio Iglesias, you'll be easily seduced by this melodic language and have fun trying to roll your rr's like the locals. You may have heard the popular legend about one of the Spanish kings having a slight speech impediment which prompted all of Spain to mimic his lisp. Unfortunately, this charming explanation of the lisping 's' is only a myth – it's actually due to the way Spanish evolved from Latin and has nothing to do with lisping monarchs at all. So, when you hear someone say *gracias* gra-thyas, they're no more lisping than when you say 'thank you' in English.

pronunciation

vowel sounds

Vowels are pronounced short and fairly closed. The sound remains level, and each vowel is pronounced as an individual unit. There are, however, a number of cases where two vowel sounds become very closely combined (so-called diphthongs).

symbol	english equivalent	spanish example	transliteration
a	run	*agua*	*a*·gwa
ai	aisle	*bailar*	bai·*lar*
ay	say	*seis*	says
e	bet	*número*	*noo*·me·ro
ee	see	*día*	*dee*·a
o	pot	*ojo*	*o*·kho
oo	zoo	*gusto*	*goo*·sto
ow	how	*autobús*	ow·to·*boos*
oy	toy	*hoy*	oy

word stress

Spanish words have stress, which means you emphasise one syllable of a word over another. Here's a rule of thumb: when a written word ends in *n*, *s* or a vowel, the stress falls on the second-last syllable. Otherwise, the final syllable is stressed. If you see an accent mark over a syllable, it cancels out this rule and you just stress that syllable instead. You needn't worry about this though, as the stressed syllables are always italicised in our pronunciation guides .

consonant sounds

Remember that in Spanish the letter *h* is never pronounced. The Spanish *v* sounds more like a *b*, said with the lips pressed together. When ending a word, *d* is pronounced soft, like a *th*, or it's so slight it doesn't get pronounced at all. Finally, try to roll your *r*'s, especially at the start of a word and in words with *rr*.

ESPAÑOL – pronunciation

symbol	english equivalent	spanish example	transliteration
b	**bed**	*barco*	*bar*·ko
ch	**ch**eat	*chica*	*chee*·ka
d	**d**og	*dinero*	dee·*ne*·ro
f	**f**at	*fiesta*	*fye*·sta
g	**g**o	*gato*	*ga*·to
k	**k**it	*cabeza, queso*	ka·*be*·tha, *ke*·so
kh	lo**ch** (harsh and guttural)	*jardín, gente*	khar·*deen, khen*·te
l	**l**ot	*lago*	*la*·go
ly	mi**lli**on	*llamada*	lya·*ma*·da
m	**m**an	*mañana*	ma·*nya*·na
n	**n**ot	*nuevo*	*nwe*·vo
ny	ca**ny**on	*señora*	se·*nyo*·ra
p	**p**et	*padre*	*pa*·dre
r	like '**tt**' in 'bu**tt**er' said fast	*hora*	*o*·ra
rr	**r**un (but stronger and rolled)	*ritmo, burro*	*rreet*·mo, *boo*·rro
s	**s**un	*semana*	se·*ma*·na
t	**t**op	*tienda*	*tyen*·da
th	**th**in	*Barcelona, manzana*	bar·the·*lo*·na, man·*tha*·na
v	soft 'b', between 'v' and 'b'	*abrir*	a·*vreer*
w	**w**in	*guardia*	*gwar*·dya
y	**y**es	*viaje*	*vya*·khe

tools

language difficulties

Do you speak English?
¿Habla inglés?   *ab*·la een·*gles*

Do you understand?
¿Me entiende?   me en·*tyen*·de

I (don't) understand.
(No) Entiendo.   (no) een·*tyen*·do

What does (cuenta) mean?
¿Qué significa (cuenta)?   ke seeg·nee·*fee*·ka (*kwen*·ta)

How do you ...?	*¿Cómo se ...?*	*ko*·mo se ...
pronounce this	*pronuncia esta*	pro·*noon*·thya es·ta
word	*palabra*	pa·*lab*·ra
write (ciudad)	*escribe (ciudad)*	es·*kree*·be (thee·oo·*da*)

Could you	*¿Puede ...,*	*pwe*·de ...
please ...?	*por favor?*	por fa·*vor*
repeat that	*repetir*	rre·pe·*teer*
speak more slowly	*hablar más despacio*	ab·*lar* mas des·*pa*·thyo
write it down	*escribirlo*	es·kree·*beer*·lo

essentials

Yes.	*Sí.*	see
No.	*No.*	no
Please.	*Por favor.*	por fa·*vor*
Thank you (very much).	*(Muchas) Gracias.*	(*moo*·chas) *gra*·thyas
You're welcome.	*De nada.*	de *na*·da
Excuse me.	*Perdón/Discúlpeme.*	per·*don*/dees·*kool*·pe·me
Sorry.	*Lo siento.*	lo *syen*·to

numbers

0	cero	*the·*ro	16	*dieciséis*	dye-thee-*seys*
1	uno	*oo·*no	17	*diecisiete*	dye-thee-*sye·*te
2	dos	dos	18	*dieciocho*	dye-thee-*o·*cho
3	tres	tres	19	*diecinueve*	dye-thee-*nwe·*ve
4	cuatro	*kwa·*tro	20	*veinte*	*veyn·*te
5	cinco	*theen·*ko	21	*veintiuno*	veyn-tee-*oo·*no
6	seis	seys	22	*veintidós*	veyn-tee-*dos*
7	siete	*sye·*te	30	*treinta*	*treyn·*ta
8	ocho	*o·*cho	40	*cuarenta*	kwa-*ren·*ta
9	nueve	*nwe·*ve	50	*cincuenta*	theen-*kwen·*ta
10	diez	dyeth	60	*sesenta*	se-*sen·*ta
11	once	*on·*the	70	*setenta*	se-*ten·*ta
12	doce	*do·*the	80	*ochenta*	o-*chen·*ta
13	trece	*tre·*the	90	*noventa*	no-*ven·*ta
14	catorce	ka-*tor·*the	100	*cien*	thyen
15	quince	*keen·*the	1000	*mil*	mil

time & dates

What time is it?	*¿Qué hora es?*	ke *o·*ra es
It's one o'clock.	*Es la una.*	es la *oo·*na
It's (10) o'clock.	*Son (las diez).*	son (las dyeth)
Quarter past (one).	*Es (la una) y cuarto.*	es (la *oo·*na) ee *kwar·*to
Half past (one).	*Es (la una) y media.*	es (la *oo·*na) ee *me·*dya
Quarter to (one).	*Es (la una) menos cuarto.*	es (la *oo·*na) *me·*nos *kwar·*to
At what time …?	*¿A qué hora …?*	a ke *o·*ra …
At …	*A las …*	a las …
am	*de la mañana*	de la ma·*nya·*na
pm	*de la tarde*	de la *tar·*de
Monday	*lunes*	*loo·*nes
Tuesday	*martes*	*mar·*tes
Wednesday	*miércoles*	*myer·*ko-les
Thursday	*jueves*	*khwe·*ves
Friday	*viernes*	*vyer·*nes
Saturday	*sábado*	*sa·*ba-do
Sunday	*domingo*	do-*meen·*go

January	enero	e·*ne*·ro
February	febrero	fe·*bre*·ro
March	marzo	*mar*·tho
April	abril	a·*breel*
May	mayo	*ma*·yo
June	junio	*khoo*·nyo
July	julio	*khoo*·lyo
August	agosto	a·*gos*·to
September	septiembre	sep·*tyem*·bre
October	octubre	ok·*too*·bre
November	noviembre	no·*vyem*·bre
December	diciembre	dee·*thyem*·bre

What date is it today?
¿Qué día es hoy? ke *dee*·a es oy

It's (18 October).
Es (el dieciocho de octubre). es (el dye·thee·*o*·cho de ok·*too*·bre)

| since (May) | desde (mayo) | *des*·de (*ma*·yo) |
| until (June) | hasta (junio) | *as*·ta (*khoo*·nyo) |

last ...		
night	anoche	a·*no*·che
week	la semana pasada	la se·*ma*·na pa·*sa*·da
month	el mes pasado	el mes pa·*sa*·do
year	el año pasado	el *a*·nyo pa·*sa*·do

next ...	... que viene	... ke *vye*·ne
week	la semana	la se·*ma*·na
month	el mes	el mes
year	el año	el *a*·nyo

yesterday/tomorrow ...	ayer/mañana por la ...	a·*yer*/ma·*nya*·na por la ...
morning	mañana	ma·*nya*·na
afternoon	tarde	*tar*·de
evening	noche	*no*·che

weather

What's the weather like?	¿Qué tiempo hace?	ke *tyem*·po *a*·the

It's ...
cloudy	Está nublado.	es·ta noo·*bla*·do
cold	Hace frío.	a·the *free*·o
hot	Hace calor.	a·the ka·*lor*
raining	Está lloviendo.	es·ta lyo·*vyen*·do
snowing	Está nevando.	es·ta ne·*van*·do
sunny	Hace sol.	a·the sol
warm	Hace calor.	a·the ka·*lor*
windy	Hace viento.	a·the *vyen*·to

spring	primavera f	pree·ma·*ve*·ra
summer	verano m	ve·*ra*·no
autumn	otoño m	o·*to*·nyo
winter	invierno m	een·*vyer*·no

border crossing

I'm here ...	Estoy aquí ...	es·*toy* a·*kee* ...
in transit	en tránsito	en *tran*·see·to
on business	de negocios	de ne·*go*·thyos
on holiday	de vacaciones	de va·ka·*thyo*·nes

I'm here for ...	Estoy aquí por ...	es·*toy* a·*kee* por ...
(10) days	(diez) días	(dyeth) *dee*·as
(three) weeks	(tres) semanas	(tres) se·*ma*·nas
(two) months	(dos) meses	(dos) *me*·ses

I'm going to (Salamanca).
Voy a (Salamanca).   voy a (sa·la·*man*·ka)

I'm staying at the (Flores Hotel).
Me estoy alojando en (hotel Flores).   me es·*toy* a·lo·*khan*·do en (o·*tel flo*·res)

I have nothing to declare.
No tengo nada que declarar.   no *ten*·go *na*·da ke dek·la·*rar*

I have something to declare.
Quisiera declarar algo.   kee·*sye*·ra dek·la·*rar al*·go

That's (not) mine.
Eso (no) es mío.   eso (no) es *mee*·o

transport

tickets & luggage

Where can I buy a ticket?
¿Dónde puedo comprar un billete?   don-de *pwe*-do kom-*prar* oon bee-*lye*-te

Do I need to book a seat?
¿Tengo que reservar?   ten-go ke rre-ser-*var*

One ... ticket to (Barcelona), please.	*Un billete ... a (Barcelona), por favor.*	oon bee-*lye*-te ... a (bar-the-*lo*-na) por fa-*vor*
one-way	*sencillo*	sen-*thee*-lyo a
return	*de ida y vuelta*	de *ee*-da ee *vwel*-ta

I'd like to ...	*Me gustaría ...*	me goos-ta-*ree*-a ...
my ticket.	*mi billete.*	mee bee-*lye*-te
cancel	*cancelar*	kan-the-*lar*
change	*cambiar*	kam-*byar*
confirm	*confirmar*	kon-feer-*mar*

I'd like a ... seat.	*Quisiera un asiento ...*	kee-*sye*-ra oon a-*syen*-to ...
nonsmoking	*de no fumadores*	de no foo-ma-*do*-res
smoking	*de fumadores*	de foo-ma-*do*-res

How much is it?
¿Cuánto cuesta?   kwan-to *kwes*-ta

Is there air conditioning?
¿Hay aire acondicionado?   ai *ai*-re a-kon-dee-thyo-*na*-do

Is there a toilet?
¿Hay servicios?   ai ser-*vee*-thyos

How long does the trip take?
¿Cuánto se tarda?   kwan-to se *tar*-da

Is it a direct route?
¿Es un viaje directo?   es oon *vya*-khe dee-*rek*-to

I'd like a luggage locker.
Quisiera un casillero de consigna.   kee-*sye*-ra oon ka-see-*lye*-ro de kon-*seeg*-na

My luggage	Mis maletas	mees ma·*le*·tas
has been ...	han sido ...	an *see*·do ...
damaged	dañadas	da·*nya*·das
lost	perdidas	per·*dee*·das
stolen	robadas	rro·*ba*·das

getting around

Where does flight (G10) arrive/depart?
¿Dónde llega/sale el vuelo (G10)?   don·de *lye*·ga/*sa*·le el *vwe*·lo (khe dyeth)

Where's the ...?	¿Dónde está...?	don·de es·*ta* ...
arrivals hall	el hall de partidas	el hol de par·*tee*·das
departures hall	el hall de llegadas	el hol de lye·*ga*·das
duty-free shop	la tienda libre de impuestos	la *tyen*·da *lee*·bre de eem·*pwe*·stos
gate (12)	la puerta (doce)	la *pwer*·ta (*do*·the)

Is this the ...	¿Es el ... para	es el ... *pa*·ra
to (Valencia)?	(Valencia)?	(va·*len*·thya)?
boat	barco	*bar*·ko
bus	autobús	ow·to·*boos*
plane	avión	a·*vyon*
train	tren	tren

What time's	¿A qué hora es el	a ke *o*·ra es el
the ... bus?	... autobús?	... ow·to·*boos*
first	primer	pree·*mer*
last	último	*ool*·tee·mo
next	próximo	*prok*·see·mo

At what time does it arrive/leave?
¿A qué hora llega/sale?   a ke *o*·ra *lye*·ga/*sa*·le

How long will it be delayed?
¿Cuánto tiempo se retrasará?   *kwan*·to *tyem*·po se rre·tra·sa·*ra*

What station/stop is this?
¿Cuál es esta estación/parada?   kwal es *es*·ta es·ta·*thyon*/pa·*ra*·da

What's the next station/stop?
¿Cuál es la próxima estación/parada?   kwal es la *prok*·see·ma es·ta·*thyon*/pa·*ra*·da

Does it stop at (Aranjuez)?
¿Para en (Aranjuez)? pa·ra en (a·ran·khweth)

Please tell me when we get to (Seville).
¿Puede avisarme pwe·de a·vee·sar·me
cuando lleguemos a (Sevilla)? kwan·do lye·ge·mos a (se·vee·lya)

How long do we stop here?
¿Cuánto tiempo vamos a parar aquí? kwan·to tyem·po va·mos a pa·rar a·kee

Is this seat available?
¿Está libre este asiento? es·ta lee·bre es·te a·syen·to

That's my seat.
Ése es mi asiento. e·se es mee a·syen·to

I'd like a taxi ... *Quisiera un taxi ...* kee·sye·ra oon tak·see ...
  at (9am) *a (las nueve* a (las nwe·ve
    de la mañana) de la ma·nya·na)
  now *ahora* a·o·ra
  tomorrow *mañana* ma·nya·na

Is this taxi available?
¿Está libre este taxi? es·ta lee·bre es·te tak·see

How much is it to ...?
¿Cuánto cuesta ir a ...? kwan·to kwes·ta eer a ...

Please put the meter on.
Por favor, ponga el taxímetro. por fa·vor pon·ga el tak·see·me·tro

Please take me to (this address).
Por favor, lléveme a (esta dirección). por fa·vor lye·ve·me a (es·ta dee·rek·thyon)

Please ... *Por favor ...* por fa·vor ...
  slow down *vaya más despacio* va·ya mas des·pa·thyo
  stop here *pare aquí* pa·re a·kee
  wait here *espere aquí* es·pe·re a·kee

car, motorbike & bicycle hire

I'd like to hire a ... *Quisiera alquilar ...* kee·sye·ra al·kee·lar ...
  bicycle *una bicicleta* oo·na bee·thee·kle·ta
  car *un coche* oon ko·che
  motorbike *una moto* oo·na mo·to

with ...	con ...	kon ...
a driver	chófer	cho·fer
air conditioning	aire acondicionado	ai·re a·kon·dee·thyo·na·do
antifreeze	anticongelante	an·tee·kon·khe·lan·te
snow chains	cadenas de nieve	ka·de·nas de nye·ve

How much for	¿Cuánto cuesta	kwan·to kwes·ta
... hire?	el alquiler por ...?	el al·kee·ler por ...
hourly	hora	o·ra
daily	día	dee·a
weekly	semana	se·ma·na

air	aire m	ai·re
oil	aceite m	a·they·te
petrol	gasolina f	ga·so·lee·na
tyres	neumáticos f pl	ne·oo·ma·tee·kos

I need a mechanic.
Necesito un mecánico. ne·the·see·to oon me·ka·nee·ko

I've run out of petrol.
Me he quedado sin gasolina. me e ke·da·do seen ga·so·lee·na

I have a flat tyre.
Tengo un pinchazo. ten·go oon peen·cha·tho

directions

Where's the ...?	¿Dónde está/ están ...? sg/pl	don·de es·ta/ es·tan ...
bank	el banco sg	el ban·ko
city centre	el centro de la ciudad sg	el then·tro de la theew·da
hotel	el hotel sg	el o·tel
market	el mercado sg	el mer·ka·do
police station	la comisaría sg	la ko·mee·sa·ree·a
post office	el correos sg	el ko·rre·os
public toilet	los servicios pl	los ser·vee·thyos
tourist office	la oficina de turismo sg	la o·fee·thee·na de too·rees·mo

Is this the road to (Valladolid)?
¿Se va a (Valladolid) por esta carretera? — se va a (va·lya·do·*lee*) por es·ta ka·rre·*te*·ra

Can you show me (on the map)?
¿Me lo puede indicar (en el mapa)? — me lo *pwe*·de een·dee·*kar* (en el *ma*·pa)

What's the address?
¿Cuál es la dirección? — kwal es la dee·rek·*thyon*

How far is it?
¿A cuánta distancia está? — a *kwan*·ta dees·*tan*·thya es·*ta*

How do I get there?
¿Cómo se llega ahí? — *ko*·mo se *lye*·ga a·*ee*

Turn ...	Doble ...	do·ble ...
at the corner	en la esquina	en la es·*kee*·na
at the traffic lights	en el semáforo	en el se·*ma*·fo·ro
left	a la izquierda	a la eeth·*kyer*·da
right	a la iderecha	a la de·*re*·cha

It's ...	Está ...	es·*ta* ...
behind ...	detrás de ...	de·*tras* de ...
far away	lejos	*le*·khos
here	aquí	a·*kee*
in front of ...	enfrente de ...	en·*fren*·te de ...
left	por la izquierda	por la eeth·*kyer*·da
near (to ...)	cerca (de ...)	*ther*·ka (de ...)
next to ...	al lado de ...	al *la*·do de ...
opposite ...	frente a ...	*fren*·te a ...
right	por la derecha	por la de·*re*·cha
straight ahead	todo recto	*to*·do *rrek*·to
there	ahí	a·*ee*

by bus	por autobús	por ow·to·boos
by taxi	por taxi	por *tak*·see
by train	por tren	por tren
on foot	a pie	a pye

north	norte m	*nor*·te
south	sur m	soor
east	este m	es·te
west	oeste m	o·es·te

signs

Acceso/Salida	ak-the-so/sa-lee-da	Entrance/Exit
Abierto/Cerrado	a-byer-to/the-rra-do	Open/Closed
Hay Lugar	ai loo-gar	Rooms Available
No Hay Lugar	no ai loo-gar	No Vacancies
Información	een-for-ma-thyon	Information
Comisaría	ko-mee-sa-ree-a	Police Station
de Policía	de po-lee-thee-a	
Prohibido	pro-ee-bee-do	Prohibited
Servicios	ser-vee-thyos	Toilets
Caballeros	ka-ba-lye-ros	Men
Señoras	se-nyo-ras	Women
Caliente/Frío	ka-lyen-te/free-o	Hot/Cold

accommodation

finding accommodation

Where's a ...?	¿Dónde hay ...?	don-de ai ...
camping ground	un terreno de cámping	oon te-rre-no de kam-peeng
guesthouse	una pensión	oo-na pen-syon
hotel	un hotel	oon o-tel
youth hostel	un albergue juvenil	oon al-ber-ge khoo-ve-neel

Can you recommend	¿Puede recomendar	pwe-de rre-ko-men-dar
somewhere ...?	algún sitio ...?	al-goon see-tio ...
cheap	barato	ba-ra-to
good	bueno	bwe-no
nearby	cercano	ther-ka-no

I'd like to book a room, please.
Quisiera reservar una habitación.   kee-sye-ra rre-ser-var oo-na a-bee-ta-thyon

I have a reservation.
He hecho una reserva.   e e-cho oo-na rre-ser-va

My name's ...
Me llamo ...   me lya-mo ...

Do you have a ... room?	¿Tiene una habitación ...?	tye·ne oo·na a·bee·ta·thyon ...
single	individual	een·dee·vee·dwal
double	doble	do·ble
twin	con dos camas	kon dos ka·mas

How much is it per ...?	¿Cuánto cuesta por ...?	kwan·to kwes·ta por ...
night	noche	no·che
person	persona	per·so·na

Can I pay by ...?	¿Puedo pagar con ...?	pwe·do pa·gar con ...
credit card	tarjeta de crédito	tar·khe·ta de kre·dee·to
travellers cheque	cheque de viajero	che·ke de vya·khe·ro

I'd like to stay for (three) nights/weeks.
Quisiera quedarme por (tres)   kee·sye·ra ke·dar·me por (tres)
noches/semanas.   no·ches/se·ma·nas

From (July 2) to (July 6).
Desde (el dos de julio)   des·de (el dos de khoo·lyo)
hasta (el seis de julio).   as·ta (el seys de khoo·lyo)

Can I see it?
¿Puedo verla?   pwe·do ver·la

Am I allowed to camp here?
¿Se puede acampar aquí?   se pwe·de a·kam·par a·kee

Is there a camp site nearby?
¿Hay un terreno de cámping   ai oon te·rre·no de kam·peeng
cercano?   ther·ka·no

requests & queries

When/Where's breakfast served?
¿Cuándo/Dónde se sirve el desayuno?   kwan·do/don·de se seer·ve el de·sa·yoo·no

Please wake me at (seven).
Por favor, despiérteme a (las siete).   por fa·vor des·pyer·te·me a (las sye·te)

Could I have my key, please?
¿Me puede dar la llave, por favor?   me pwe·de dar la lya·ve por fa·vor

Can I get another (blanket)?
¿Puede darme otra (manta)?   pwe·de dar·me ot·ra (man·ta)

Is there a/an ...?	¿Hay ...?	ai ...
elevator	ascensor	as·then·sor
safe	una caja fuerte	oo·na ka·kha fwer·te

The room is too ...	Es demasiado ...	es de·ma·sya·do ...
expensive	cara	ka·ra
noisy	ruidosa	rrwee·do·sa
small	pequeña	pe·ke·nya

The ... doesn't work.	No funciona ...	no foon·thyo·na ...
air conditioning	el aire	el ai·re
	acondicionado	a·kon·dee·thyo·na·do
fan	el ventilador	el ven·tee·la·dor
toilet	el retrete	el rre·tre·te

This ... isn't clean.	Esta ... no está limpia.	es·ta ... no es·ta leem·pya
pillow	almohada	al·mwa·da
sheet	sábana	sa·ba·na
towel	toalla	to·a·lya

checking out

What time is checkout?
¿A qué hora hay que dejar   a ke o·ra ai ke de·khar
libre la habitación?   lee·bre la a·bee·ta·thyon

Can I leave my luggage here?
¿Puedo dejar las maletas aquí?   pwe·do de·khar las ma·le·tas a·kee

Could I have ..., please?	¿Me puede dar ..., por favor?	me pwe·de dar ... por fa·vor
my deposit	mi depósito	mee de·po·see·to
my passport	mi pasaporte	mee pa·sa·por·te
my valuables	mis objetos de valor	mees ob·khe·tos de va·lor

communications & banking

the internet

Where's the local Internet café?
  ¿Dónde hay un cibercafé cercano?   *don*·de ai oon thee·ber·ka·*fe* ther·*ka*·no

How much is it per hour?
  ¿Cuánto cuesta por hora?   kwan·to *kwes*·ta por o·ra

I'd like to ...	Quisiera ...	kee·*sye*·ra ...
check my email	revisar mi correo electrónico	rre·vee·*sar* mee ko·*re*·o e·lek·*tro*·nee·ko
get Internet access	usar el Internet	oo·*sar* el *een*·ter·net
use a printer	usar una impresora	oo·*sar* oo·na eem·pre·*so*·ra
use a scanner	usar un escáner	oo·*sar* oon es·*ka*·ner

mobile/cell phone

I'd like a ...	Quisiera ...	kee·*sye*·ra ...
mobile/cell phone for hire	un móvil para alquilar	oon *mo*·veel *pa*·ra al·kee·*lar*
SIM card for your network	una tarjeta SIM para su red	*oo*·na tar·*khe*·ta seem *pa*·ra soo rred

What are the rates?   ¿Cuál es la tarifa?   kwal es la ta·*ree*·fa

telephone

What's your phone number?
  ¿Cuál es su/tu número   kwal es soo/too *noo*·me·ro
  de teléfono? pol/inf   de te·*le*·fo·no

The number is ...
  El número es ...   el *noo*·me·ro es ...

Where's the nearest public phone?
  ¿Dónde hay una cabina telefónica?   *don*·de ai *oo*·na ka·*bee*·na te·le·*fo*·nee·ka

I'd like to buy a phonecard.
  Quiero comprar una   *kye*·ro kom·*prar* oo·na
  tarjeta telefónica.   tar·*khe*·ta te·le·*fo*·nee·ka

I want to ...	Quiero ...	kye·ro ...
call (Singapore)	hacer una llamada (a Singapur)	a·ther oo·na lya·ma·da (a seen·ga·poor)
make a local call	hacer una llamada local	a·ther oo·na lya·ma·da lo·kal
reverse the charges	hacer una llamada a cobro revertido	a·ther oo·na lya·ma·da a ko·bro rre·ver·tee·do

How much does ... cost?	¿Cuánto cuesta ...?	kwan·to kwes·ta ...
a (three)-minute call	una llamada de (tres) minutos	oo·na lya·ma·da de (tres) mee·noo·tos
each extra minute	cada minuto extra	ka·da mee·noo·to ek·stra

It's (one euro) per (minute).
(Un euro) por (un minuto).   (oon e·oo·ro) por (oon mee·noo·to)

post office

I want to send a ...	Quisiera enviar ...	kee·sye·ra en·vee·ar ...
fax	un fax	oon faks
letter	una carta	oo·na kar·ta
parcel	un paquete	oon pa·ke·te
postcard	una postal	oo·na pos·tal

I want to buy ...	Quisiera comprar ...	kee·sye·ra kom·prar ...
an envelope	un sobre	oon so·bre
stamps	sellos	se·lyos

Please send it (to Australia) by ...	Por favor, mándelo (a Australia) por ...	por fa·vor man·de·lo (a ows·tra·lya) por ...
airmail	vía aérea	vee·a a·e·re·a
express mail	correo urgente	ko·rre·o oor·khen·te
registered mail	correo certificado	ko·rre·o ther·tee·fee·ka·do
surface mail	vía terrestre	vee·a te·rres·tre

Is there any mail for me?
¿Hay alguna carta para mí?   ai al·goo·na kar·ta pa·ra mee

bank

Where's a/an ...?	¿Dónde hay ...?	don-de ai ...
ATM	un cajero automático	oon ka-khe-ro ow-to-ma-tee-ko o
foreign exchange office	una oficina de cambio	oo-na o-fee-thee-na de kam-byo

I'd like to ...	Me gustaría ...	me goos-ta-ree-a ...
cash a cheque	cambiar un cheque	kam-byar oon che-ke
change a travellers cheque	cobrar un cheque de viajero	ko-brar oon che-ke de vee-a-khe-ro
change money	cambiar dinero	kam-byar dee-ne-ro
get a cash advance	obtener un adelanto	ob-te-ner oon a-de-lan-to
withdraw money	sacar dinero	sa-kar dee-ne-ro

What's the ...?	¿Cuál es ...?	kwal es ...
commission	la comisión	la ko-mee-syon
exchange rate	el tipo de cambio	el tee-po de kam-byo

It's (12) euros.	Es (doce) euros.	es (do-the) e-oo-ros
It's free.	Es gratis.	es gra-tees

What's the charge for that?
¿Cuánto hay que pagar por eso?   kwan-to ai ke pa-gar por e-so

What time does the bank open?
¿A qué hora abre el banco?   a ke o-ra a-bre el ban-ko

Has my money arrived yet?
¿Ya ha llegado mi dinero?   ya a lye-ga-do mee dee-ne-ro

sightseeing

getting in

What time does it open/close?
¿A qué hora abren/cierran?   a ke o-ra ab-ren/thye-rran

What's the admission charge?
¿Cuánto cuesta la entrada?   kwan-to kwes-ta la en-tra-da

Is there a discount for children/students?
¿Hay descuentos para niños/estudiantes?   ai des-kwen-tos pa-ra nee-nyos/es-too-dyan-tes

I'd like a ...	Quisiera ...	kee-*sye*-ra ...
catalogue	un catálogo	oon ka-*ta*-lo-go
guide	una guía	*oo*-na gee-a
(local) map	un mapa (de la zona)	oon *ma*-pa (de la *tho*-na)

I'd like to see ...	Me gustaría ver ...	me goos-ta-*ree*-a ver ...
What's that?	¿Qué es eso?	ke es *e*-so
Can I take a photo?	¿Puedo tomar un foto?	*pwe*-do to-*mar* un *fo*-to

tours

When's the next day trip?

| ¿Cuándo es la próxima | *kwan*-do es la *prok*-see-ma |
| excursión de un día? | eks-koor-*syon* de oon *dee*-a |

When's the next tour?

| ¿Cuándo es el próximo recorrido? | *kwan*-do es ela *prok*-see-mo rre-ko-*rree*-do |

Is ... included?	¿Incluye ...?	een-*kloo*-ye ...
accommodation	alojamiento	a-lo-kha-*myen*-to
the admission charge	entrada	en-*tra*-da
food	comida	ko-*mee*-da
transport	transporte	trans-*por*-te

How long is the tour?

| ¿Cuánto dura el recorrido? | *kwan*-to *doo*-ra el rre-ko-*rree*-do |

What time should we be back?

| ¿A qué hora tenemos que volver? | a ke *o*-ra te-*ne*-mos ke vol-*ver* |

sightseeing

castle	castillo m	kas-*tee*-lyo
cathedral	catedral f	ka-te-*dral*
church	iglesia f	ee-*gle*-sya
main square	plaza mayor f	*pla*-tha ma-*yor*
monastery	monasterio m	mo-na-*ste*-ryo
monument	monumento m	mo-noo-*men*-to
museum	museo m	moo-*se*-o
old city	casco antiguo m	*kas*-ko an-*tee*-gwo
palace	palacio m	pa-*la*-thyo
ruins	ruinas f pl	*rrwee*-nas
stadium	estadio m	es-*ta*-dyo
statues	estatuas f pl	es-*ta*-twas

shopping

enquiries

Where's a ...?	¿Dónde está ...?	don·de es·ta ...
bank	el banco	el ban·ko
bookshop	la librería	la lee·bre·ree·a
camera shop	la tienda de fotografía	la tyen·da de fo·to·gra·fee·a
department store	el centro comercial	el then·tro ko·mer·thyal
grocery store	la tienda de comestibles	la tyen·da de ko·mes·tee·bles
market	el mercado	el mer·ka·do
newsagency	el quiosco	el kyos·ko
supermarket	el supermercado	el soo·per·mer·ka·do

Where can I buy (a padlock)?
¿Dónde puedo comprar (un candado)?
don·de pwe·do kom·prar (oon kan·da·do)

I'm looking for ...
Estoy buscando ...
es·toy boos·kan·do ...

Can I look at it?
¿Puedo verlo?
pwe·do ver·lo

Do you have any others?
¿Tiene otros?
tye·ne o·tros

Does it have a guarantee?
¿Tiene garantía?
tye·ne ga·ran·tee·a

Can I have it sent overseas?
¿Pueden enviarlo por correo a otro país?
pwe·den en·vee·ar·lo por ko·rre·o a o·tro pa·ees

Can I have my ... repaired?
¿Puede reparar mi ... aquí?
pwe·de rre·pa·rar mee ... a·kee

It's faulty.
Es defectuoso.
es de·fek·too·o·so

I'd like …, please.	Quisiera …, por favor.	kee-*sye*-ra … por fa-*vor*
a bag	una bolsa	oo-na bol-sa
a refund	que me devuelva	ke me de-*vwel*-va
	el dinero	el dee-*ne*-ro
to return this	devolver esto	de-vol-*ver* es-to

paying

How much is it?
¿Cuánto cuesta esto?   kwan-to kwes-ta es-to

Can you write down the price?
¿Puede escribir el precio?   pwe-de es-kree-*beer* el *pre*-thyo

That's too expensive.
Es muy caro.   es mooy *ka*-ro

What's your lowest price?
¿Cuál es su precio más bajo?   kwal es soo *pre*-thyo mas *ba*-kho

I'll give you (five) euros.
Te daré (cinco) euros.   te da-*re* (*theen*-ko) e-oo-ros

There's a mistake in the bill.
Hay un error en la cuenta.   ai oon e-*rror* en la *kwen*-ta

Do you accept …?	¿Aceptan …?	a-*thep*-tan …
credit cards	tarjetas de crédito	tar-*khe*-tas de kre-dee-to
debit cards	tarjetas de débito	tar-*khe*-tas de *de*-bee-to
travellers cheques	cheques de viajero	che-kes de vya-*khe*-ro

I'd like …, please.	Quisiera …, por favor.	kee-*sye*-ra … por fa-*vor*
a receipt	un recibo	oon rre-*thee*-bo
my change	mi cambio	mee *kam*-byo

clothes & shoes

Can I try it on?	¿Me lo puedo probar?	me lo *pwe*-do pro-bar
My size is (40).	Uso la talla (cuarenta).	oo-so la *ta*-lya (kwa-*ren*-ta)
It doesn't fit.	No me queda bien.	no me *ke*-da byen

small	pequeño/a m/f	pe-*ke*-nyo/a
medium	mediano/a m/f	me-*dya*-no/a
large	grande m&f	gran-de

books & music

I'd like a ...	Quisiera un ...	kee-sye-ra oon ...
newspaper	periódico	pe-ryo-dee-ko
(in English)	(en inglés)	(en een-gles)
pen	bolígrafo	bo-lee-gra-fo

Is there an English-language bookshop?
¿Hay alguna librería en inglés?   ai al-goo-na lee-bre-ree-a en een-gles

I'm looking for something by (Enrique Iglesias).
Estoy buscando algo de   es-toy boos-kan-do al-go de
(Enrique Iglesias).   (en-ree-ke ee-gle-syas)

Can I listen to this?
¿Puedo escuchar esto aquí?   pwe-do es-koo-char es-to a-kee

photography

Can you ...?	¿Puede usted ...?	pwe-de oos-ted ...
burn a CD from	copiar un disco	ko-pyar oon dees-ko
my memory card	compacto de esta	kom-pak-to de es-ta
	tarjeta de memoria	tar-khe-ta de me-mo-rya
develop this film	revelar este carrete	rre-ve-lar es-te ka-rre-te
load my film	cargar el carrete	kar-gar el ka-rre-te

I need a ... film	Necesito película ...	ne-the-see-to pe-lee-koo-la ...
for this camera.	para esta cámara.	pa-ra es-ta ka-ma-ra
APS	APS	a pe e-se
B&W	en blanco y negro	en blan-ko y ne-gro
colour	en color	en ko-lor
slide	para diapositivas	pa-ra dya-po-see-tee-vas
(200) speed	de sensibilidad	de sen-see-bee-lee-da
	(doscientos)	(dos-thyen-tos)

When will it be ready?
¿Cuándo estará listo?   kwan-do es-ta-ra lees-to

meeting people

greetings, goodbyes & introductions

Hello/Hi.	*Hola.*	*o·la*
Good night.	*Buenas noches.*	*bwe·nas no·ches*
Goodbye/Bye.	*Adiós.*	*a·dyos*
See you later.	*Hasta luego.*	*as·ta lwe·go*
Mr	*Señor*	*se·nyor*
Mrs	*Señora*	*se·nyo·ra*
Miss	*Señorita*	*se·nyo·ree·ta*
How are you?	*¿Qué tal?*	*ke tal*
Fine, thanks.	*Bien, gracias.*	*byen gra·thyas*
And you?	*¿Y Usted/tú?* pol/inf	*ee oos·te/too*
What's your name?	*¿Cómo se llama Usted?* pol	*ko·mo se lya·ma oos·te*
	¿Cómo te llamas? inf	*ko·mo te lya·mas*
My name is …	*Me llamo …*	*me lya·mo …*
I'm pleased to meet you.	*Mucho gusto.*	*moo·cho goos·to*
This is my …	*Éste/Ésta es mi …* m/f	*es·te/a es mee …*
boyfriend	*novio*	*no·vyo*
brother	*hermano*	*er·ma·no*
daughter	*hija*	*ee·kho*
father	*padre*	*pa·dre*
friend	*amigo/a* m/f	*a·mee·go/a*
girlfriend	*novia*	*no·vya*
husband	*marido*	*ma·ree·do*
mother	*madre*	*ma·dre*
partner (intimate)	*pareja*	*pa·re·kha*
sister	*hermana*	*er·ma·na*
son	*hijo*	*ee·kho*
wife	*esposa*	*es·po·sa*
Here's my …	*Éste/Ésta es mi …* m/f	*es·te/a es mee …*
What's your …?	*¿Cuál es su/tu …?* pol/inf	*kwal es soo/too …*
address	*dirección* f	*dee·rek·thyon*
email address	*dirección de email* f	*dee·rek·thyon de ee·mayl*
fax number	*número de fax* m	*noo·me·ro de faks*
phone number	*número de teléfono* m	*noo·me·ro de te·le·fo·no*

occupations

What's your occupation?	¿A qué se dedica Usted? pol	a ke se de·*dee*·ka oos·*te*
	¿A qué te dedicas? inf	a ke te de·*dee*·kas
I'm a/an ...	Soy un/una ... m/f	soy oon/*oo*·na ...
artist	artista m&f	ar·*tees*·ta
business person	comerciante m&f	ko·mer·*thyan*·te
farmer	agricultor m	a·gree·kool·*tor*
	agricultora f	a·gree·kool·*to*·ra
manual worker	obrero/a m/f	o·*bre*·ro/a
office worker	oficinista m&f	o·fee·thee·*nees*·ta
scientist	científico/a m/f	thyen·*tee*·fee·ko/a
student	estudiante m&f	es·too·*dyan*·te
tradesperson	artesano/a m/f	ar·te·*sa*·no/a

background

Where are you from?	¿De dónde es Usted? pol	de *don*·de es oos·*te*
	¿De dónde eres? inf	de *don*·de e·res
I'm from ...	Soy de ...	soy de ...
Australia	Australia	ow·*stra*·lya
Canada	Canadá	ka·na·*da*
England	Inglaterra	een·gla·*te*·rra
New Zealand	Nueva Zelanda	*nwe*·va the·*lan*·da
the USA	los Estados Unidos	los es·*ta*·dos oo·*nee*·dos
Are you married?	¿Estás casado/a? m/f	es·*tas* ka·*sa*·do/a
I'm married.	Estoy casado/a. m/f	es·*toy* ka·*sa*·do/a
I'm single.	Soy soltero/a. m/f	soy sol·*te*·ro/a

age

How old ...?	¿Cuántos años ...?	*kwan*·tos *a*·nyos ...
are you	tienes inf	*tye*·nes
is your daughter	tiene su hija pol	*tye*·ne soo *ee*·kha
is your son	tiene su hijo pol	*tye*·ne soo *ee*·kho
I'm ... years old.	Tengo ... años.	*ten*·go ... *a*·nyos
He/She is ... years old.	Tiene ... años.	*tye*·ne ... *a*·nyos

feelings

I'm (not) ...	(No) Tengo ...	(no) ten·go ...
Are you ...?	¿Tiene Usted ...? pol	tye·ne oos·te ...
	¿Tienes ...? inf	tye·nes ...
cold	frío	free·o
hot	calor	ka·lor
hungry	hambre	am·bre
thirsty	sed	se
I'm (not) ...	(No) Estoy ...	(no) es·toy ...
Are you ...?	¿Está Usted ...? pol	es·ta oos·te ...
	¿Estás ...? inf	es·tas ...
happy	feliz m&f	fe·leeth
OK	bien m&f	byen
sad	triste m&f	trees·te
tired	cansado/a m/f	kan·sa·do/a

entertainment

going out

Where can I find ...?	¿Dónde hay ...?	don·de ai ...
clubs	clubs nocturnos	kloobs nok·toor·nos
gay venues	lugares gay	loo·ga·res gai
pubs	bares	ba·res
I feel like going to a/the ...	Tengo ganas de ir ...	ten·go ga·nas de eer ...
concert	a un concierto	a oon kon·thyer·to
movies	al cine	al thee·ne
party	a una fiesta	a oo·na fyes·ta
restaurant	a un restaurante	a oon rres·tow·ran·te
theatre	al teatro	al te·a·tro

interests

Do you like ...	¿Le/Te gusta ...? pol/inf	le/te *goos*·ta ...
I (don't) like ...	(No) Me gusta ...	(no) me *goos*·ta ...
art	el arte	el *ar*·te
movies	el cine	el *thee*·ne
reading	leer	le·er
sport	el deporte	el de·*por*·te
travelling	viajar	vya·*khar*
Do you like to ...?	¿Le/Te gusta ...? pol/inf	le/te *goos*·ta ...
dance	ir a bailar	eer a bai·*lar*
go to concerts	ir a conciertos	eer a kon·*thyer*·tos
listen to music	escuchar música	es·koo·*char* moo·see·ka

food & drink

finding a place to eat

Can you recommend a ...?	¿Puede recomendar un ...?	*pwe*·de rre·ko·men·*dar* oon ...
bar	bar	bar
café	café	ka·*fe*
restaurant	restaurante	rres·tow·*ran*·te
I'd like ..., please.	Quisiera ..., por favor.	kee·*sye*·ra ... por fa·*vor*
a table for (two)	una mesa para (dos)	*oo*·na *me*·sa *pa*·ra (dos)
the (non)smoking section	(no) fumadores	(no) foo·ma·*do*·res

ordering food

breakfast	desayuno m	de·sa·*yoo*·no
lunch	comida f	ko·*mee*·da
dinner	almuerzo m	al·*mwer*·tho
snack	tentempié m	ten·tem·*pye*

What would you recommend?
¿Qué recomienda?   ke rre·ko·*myen*·da

I'd like (the) ...	Quisiera ..., por favor.	kee·sye·ra ... por fa·vor
bill	la cuenta	la kwen·ta
drink list	la lista de bebidas	la lees·ta de be·bee·das
menu	el menú	el me·noo
that dish	ese plato	e·se pla·to

drinks

(cup of) coffee ...	(taza de) café ...	(ta·tha de) ka·fe ...
(cup of) tea ...	(taza de) té ...	(ta·tha de) te ...
with milk	con leche	kon le·che
without sugar	sin azúcar	seen a·thoo·kar
(orange) juice	zumo de (naranja) m	zoo·mo de (na·ran·kha)
soft drink	refresco m	rre·fres·ko
... water	agua ...	a·gwa ...
boiled	hervida	er·vee·da
(sparkling) mineral	mineral (con gas)	mee·ne·ral (kon gas)

in the bar

I'll have ...	Para mí ...	pa·ra mee ...
I'll buy you a drink.	Te invito a una copa. inf	le/te een·vee·to a oo·na ko·pa
What would you like?	¿Qué quieres tomar? inf	ke kye·res to·mar
Cheers!	¡Salud!	sa·loo
brandy	coñac m	ko·nyak
cocktail	combinado m	kom·bee·na·do
red-wine punch	sangría f	san·gree·a
a shot of (whisky)	chupito de (güisqui)	choo·pee·to de (gwees·kee)
a ... of beer	una ... de cerveza	oo·na ... de ther·ve·tha
bottle	botella	bo·te·lya
glass	caña	ka·nya
a bottle/glass of	una botella/copa	oo·na bo·te·lya/ko·pa
... wine	de vino ...	de vee·no ...
red	tinto	teen·to
sparkling	espumoso	es·poo·mo·so
white	blanco	blan·ko

self-catering

What's the local speciality?
  ¿Cuál es la especialidad de la zona?   kwal es la es·pe·thya·lee·*da* de la *tho*·na

What's that?
  ¿Qué es eso?   ke es *e*·so

How much is (a kilo of cheese)?
  ¿Cuánto vale (un kilo de queso)?   *kwan*·to *va*·le (oon *kee*·lo de *ke*·so)

I'd like ...	*Póngame ...*	*pon*·ga·me ...
(200) grams	*(doscientos) gramos*	(dos·*thyen*·tos) *gra*·mos
(two) kilos	*(dos) kilos*	(dos) *kee*·los
(three) pieces	*(tres) piezas*	(tres) *pye*·thas
(six) slices	*(seis) lonchas*	(seys) *lon*·chas

Less.	*Menos.*	*me*·nos
Enough.	*Basta.*	*ba*·sta
More.	*Más.*	mas

special diets & allergies

Is there a vegetarian restaurant near here?
  ¿Hay un restaurante   ai oon rres·tow·*ran*·te
  vegetariano por aquí?   ve·khe·ta·*rya*·no por a·*kee*

Do you have vegetarian food?
  ¿Tienen comida vegetariana?   *tye*·nen ko·*mee*·da ve·khe·ta·*rya*·na

Could you prepare a	¿Me puede preparar	me *pwe*·de pre·pa·*rar*
meal without ...?	una comida sin ...?	oo·na ko·*mee*·da seen ...
butter	*mantequilla*	man·te·*kee*·lya
eggs	*huevos*	*we*·vos
meat stock	*caldo de carne*	*kal*·do de *kar*·ne

I'm allergic to ...	Soy alérgico/a ... m/f	soy a·*ler*·khee·ko/a ...
dairy produce	*a los productos*	a los pro·*dook*·tos
	lácteos	*lak*·te·os
gluten	*al gluten*	al *gloo*·ten
MSG	*al glutamato*	al gloo·ta·*ma*·to
	monosódico	mo·no·*so*·dee·ko
nuts	*a las nueces*	a las *nwe*·thes
seafood	*a los mariscos*	a los ma·*rees*·kos

menu reader

aceitunas rellenas f pl	a·they·*too*·nas rre·*lye*·nas	*stuffed olives*
albóndigas f pl	al·*bon*·dee·gas	*meatballs*
almejas f pl	al·*me*·khas	*clams*
arroz con leche m	a·*rroth* kon *le*·che	*rice pudding*
atún m	a·*toon*	*tuna*
bacalao m	ba·ka·*low*	*salted cod*
beicon con queso m	*bey*·kon kon *ke*·so	*cold bacon with cheese*
berberechos m pl	ber·be·re·chos	*cockles*
boquerones fritos m pl	bo·ke·*ro*·nes *free*·tos	*fried anchovies*
butifarra f	boo·tee·*fa*·rra	*thick sausage*
calamares m pl	ka·la·*ma*·res	*squid*
camarón m	ka·ma·*ron*	*shrimp • small prawn*
cangrejo m	kan·*gre*·kho	*crab*
caracol m	ka·ra·*kol*	*snail*
cazuela f	ka·*thwe*·la	*casserole*
champiñones m pl	cham·pee·*nyo*·nes	*mushrooms*
charcutería f	char·koo·te·*ree*·a	*cured pork meats*
chorizo m	cho·*ree*·tho	*spicy red or white sausage*
churrasco m	choo·*rras*·ko	*grilled meat in a tangy sauce*
churro m	*choo*·rro	*long, deep-fried doughnut*
cocido m	ko·*thee*·do	*stew of chickpeas, pork & chorizo*
cuajada f	kwa·*kha*·da	*milk junket with honey*
ensaladilla f	en·sa·la·*dee*·lya	*vegetable salad*
escabeche m	es·ka·*be*·che	*pickled or marinated fish*
estofado m	es·to·*fa*·do	*stew*

fideos m pl	fee-*de*-os	*thin pasta noodles with sauce*
flan m	flan	*crème caramel*
gachos m pl	*ga*-chos	*type of porridge*
gazpacho m	gath-*pa*-cho	*cold soup with garlic, tomato & vegetables*
helado m	e-*la*-do	*ice cream*
jamón m	kha-*mon*	*ham*
langosta f	lan-*gos*-ta	*spiny lobster*
langostino m	lan-gos-*tee*-no	*large prawn*
lomo m	*lo*-mo	*pork loin • sausage*
longaniza f	lon-ga-*nee*-tha	*dark pork sausage*
magdalena f	mag-da-*le*-na	*fairy cake (often dunked in coffee)*
mejillones m pl	me-khee-*lyo*-nes	*mussels*
natillas f pl	na-*tee*-lyas	*creamy milk dessert*
ostras f pl	*os*-tras	*oysters*
paella f	pa-e-*lya*	*rice & seafood dish (sometimes with meat)*
peregrina f	pe-re-*gree*-na	*scallop*
pescaíto frito m	pes-*kai*-to *free*-to	*tiny fried fish*
picadillo m	pee-ka-*dee*-lyo	*minced meat*
pinchitos m pl	peen-*chee*-tos	*Moroccan-style kebabs*
pulpo m	*pool*-po	*octopus*
salchicha f	sal-*chee*-cha	*fresh pork sausage*
sobrasada f	so-bra-*sa*-da	*soft pork sausage*
tortilla española f	tor-*tee*-lya es-pa-*nyo*-la	*potato omelette*
trucha f	*troo*-cha	*trout*
zarzuela f	thar-*thwe*-la	*fish stew*

emergencies

basics

Help!	¡Socorro!	so-*ko*-ro
Stop!	¡Pare!	*pa*-re
Go away!	¡Váyase!	*va*-ya-se
Thief!	¡Ladrón!	lad-*ron*
Fire! ¡	¡Fuego!	*fwe*-go
Watch out!	¡Cuidado!	kwee-*da*-do
Call ...!	¡Llame a ...!	*lya*-me a ...
a doctor	un médico	oon *me*-dee-ko
an ambulance	una ambulancia	*oo*-na am-boo-*lan*-thya
the police	la policía	la po-lee-*thee*-a

It's an emergency.
Es una emergencia.   es *oo*-na e-mer-*khen*-thya

Could you help me, please?
¿Me puede ayudar, por favor?   me *pwe*-de a-yoo-*dar* por fa-*vor*

I have to use the telephone.
Necesito usar el teléfono.   ne-the-*see*-to oo-*sar* el te-*le*-fo-no

I'm lost.
Estoy perdido/a. m/f   es-*toy* per-*dee*-do/a

Where are the toilets?
¿Dónde están los servicios?   *don*-de es-*tan* los ser-*vee*-thyos

police

Where's the police station?
¿Dónde está la comisaría?   *don*-de es-*ta* la ko-mee-sa-*ree*-a

I want to report an offence.
Quiero denunciar un delito.   *kye*-ro de-noon-*thyar* oon de-*lee*-to

I have insurance.
Tengo seguro.   *ten*-go se-*goo*-ro

I've been assaulted.	He sido asaltado/a. m/f	e *see*-do a-sal-*ta*-do/a
I've been raped.	He sido violado/a. m/f	e *see*-do vee-o-*la*-do/a
I've been robbed.	Me han robado.	me an rro-*ba*-do

I've lost my ...	He perdido ...	e per-*dee*-do ...
backpack	mi mochila	mee mo-*chee*-la
bags	mis maletas	mees ma-*le*-tas
credit card	mi tarjeta de crédito	mee tar-*khe*-ta de *kre*-dee-to
handbag	mi bolso	mee *bol*-so
jewellery	mis joyas	mees *kho*-yas
money	mi dinero	mee dee-*ne*-ro
passport	mi pasaporte	mee pa-sa-*por*-te
travellers cheques	mis cheques de viajero	mees *che*-kes de vya-*khe*-ro
wallet	mi cartera	mee kar-*te*-ra

I want to contact my ...	Quiero ponerme en contacto con mi ...	*kye*-ro po-*ner*-me en kon-*tak*-to kon mee ...
consulate	consulado	kon-soo-*la*-do
embassy	embajada	em-ba-*kha*-da

health

medical needs

Where's the nearest ...?	¿Dónde está el ... más cercano?	*don*-de es-*ta* el ... mas ther-*ka*-no
dentist	dentista	den-*tees*-ta
doctor	médico	*me*-dee-ko
hospital	hospital	os-pee-*tal*

Where's the nearest (night) pharmacist?
¿Dónde está la farmacia
(de guardia) más cercana?
don-de es-*ta* la far-*ma*-thya
(de *gwar*-dya) mas ther-*ka*-na

I need a doctor (who speaks English).
Necesito un médico
(que hable inglés).
ne-the-*see*-to oon *me*-dee-ko
(ke *a*-ble een-*gles*)

Could I see a female doctor?
¿Puede examinarme una
médica?
pwe-de ek-sa-mee-*nar*-me *oo*-na
me-dee-ka

I've run out of my medication.
Se me terminaron los
medicamentos.
se me ter-mee-*na*-ron los
me-dee-ka-*men*-tos

symptoms, conditions & allergies

| I'm sick. | *Estoy enfermo/a.* m/f | es·*toy* en·*fer*·mo/a |
| It hurts here. | *Me duele aquí.* | me *dwe*·le a·*kee* |

I have (a) ...	*Tengo...*	*ten*·go ...
asthma	*asma*	*as*·ma
bronchitis	*bronquitis*	bron·*kee*·tees
constipation	*estreñimiento*	es·tre·nyee·*myen*·to
cough	*tos*	tos
diarrhoea	*diarrea*	dya·*rre*·a
fever	*fiebre*	*fye*·bre
headache	*dolor de cabeza*	do·*lor* de ka·*be*·tha
heart condition	*una condición cardíaca*	*oo*·na kon·dee·*thyon* kar·*dee*·a·ka
nausea	*náusea*	*now*·se·a
pain	*dolor*	do·*lor*
sore throat	*dolor de garganta*	do·*lor* de gar·*gan*·ta
toothache	*dolor de muelas*	do·*lor* de *mwe*·las

I'm allergic to ...	*Soy alérgico/a a ...* m/f	soy a·*ler*·khee·ko/a a ...
antibiotics	*los antibióticos*	los an·tee·*byo*·tee·kos
anti-inflammatories	*los anti-inflamatorios*	los *an*·tee·een·fla·ma·*to*·ryos
aspirin	*la aspirina*	la as·pee·*ree*·na
bees	*las abejas*	las a·*be*·khas
codeine	*la codeína*	la ko·de·*ee*·na
penicillin	*la penicilina*	la pe·nee·thee·*lee*·na

antiseptic	*antiséptico* m	an·tee·*sep*·tee·ko
bandage	*vendaje* m	ven·*da*·khe
condoms	*condones* m pl	kon·*do*·nes
contraceptives	*anticonceptivos* m pl	an·tee·kon·thep·*tee*·vos
diarrhoea medicine	*medicina para diarrea* f	me·dee·*thee*·na *pa*·ra dya·*rre*·a
insect repellent	*repelente de insectos* m	re·pe·*len*·te de een·*sek*·tos
laxatives	*laxantes* m pl	lak·*san*·tes
painkillers	*analgésicos* m pl	a·nal·*khe*·see·kos
rehydration salts	*sales rehidratantes* f pl	*sa*·les re·eed·ra·*tan*·tes
sleeping tablets	*pastillas para dormir* f pl	pas·*tee*·lyas *pa*·ra dor·*meer*

english–spanish dictionary

Spanish nouns in this dictionary, and adjectives affected by gender, have their gender indicated by ⓜ (masculine) or ⓕ (feminine). If it's a plural noun, you'll also see pl. Words are also marked as v (verb), n (noun), a (adjective), pl (plural), sg (singular), inf (informal) and pol (polite) where necessary.

A

accident *accidente* ⓜ ak-thee-*den*-te
accommodation *alojamiento* ⓜ a-lo-kha-*myen*-to
adaptor *adaptador* ⓜ a-dap-ta-*dor*
address *dirección* ⓕ dee-rek-*thyon*
after *después* de des-*pwes* de
air-conditioned *con aire acondicionado*
  kon *ai*-re a-kon-dee-thyo-*na*-do
airplane *avión* ⓜ a-*vyon*
airport *aeropuerto* ⓜ ay-ro-*pwer*-to
alcohol *alcohol* ⓜ al-*col*
all a *todo/a* *to*-do/a
allergy *alergia* ⓕ a-*ler*-khya
ambulance *ambulancia* ⓕ am-boo-*lan*-thya
ankle *tobillo* ⓜ to-*bee*-lyo
and *y* ee
arm *brazo* ⓜ *bra*-tho
ashtray *cenicero* ⓜ the-nee-*the*-ro
ATM *cajero automático* ka-*khe*-ro ow-to-*ma*-tee-ko

B

baby *bebé* ⓜ be-*be*
back (body) *espalda* ⓕ es-*pal*-da
backpack *mochila* ⓕ mo-*chee*-la
bad *malo/a* ⓜ/ⓕ *ma*-lo/a
bag *bolso* ⓜ *bol*-so
baggage claim *recogida de equipajes* ⓕ
  rre-ko-*khee*-da de e-kee-*pa*-khes
bank *banco* ⓜ *ban*-ko
bar *bar* ⓜ bar
bathroom *baño* ⓜ *ba*-nyo
battery (general) *pila* ⓕ *pee*-la
battery (car) *batería* ⓕ ba-te-*ree*-a
beautiful *hermoso/a* ⓜ/ⓕ er-*mo*-so/a
bed *cama* ⓕ *ka*-ma
beer *cerveza* ⓕ ther-*ve*-tha
before *antes* *an*-tes
behind *detrás de* de-*tras* de
bicycle *bicicleta* ⓕ bee-thee-*kle*-ta

big *grande* *gran*-de
bill *cuenta* ⓕ *kwen*-ta
black *negro/a* ⓜ/ⓕ *ne*-gro/a
blanket *manta* ⓕ *man*-ta
blood group *grupo sanguíneo* ⓜ *groo*-po san-*gee*-neo
blue *azul* a-*thool*
boat *barco* ⓜ *bar*-ko
book (make a reservation) v *reservar* rre-ser-*var*
bottle *botella* ⓕ bo-*te*-lya
bottle opener *abrebotellas* ⓜ a-bre-bo-*te*-lyas
boy *chico* ⓜ *chee*-ko
brakes (car) *frenos* ⓜ pl *fre*-nos
breakfast *desayuno* ⓜ des-a-*yoo*-no
broken (faulty) *roto/a* ⓜ/ⓕ *ro*-to/a
bus *autobús* ⓜ ow-to-*boos*
business *negocios* ⓜ pl ne-*go*-thyos
buy *comprar* kom-*prar*

C

café *café* ⓜ ka-*fe*
camera *cámara (fotográfica)* ⓕ
  ka-ma-ra (fo-to-*gra*-fee-ka)
camp site *cámping* ⓜ *kam*-peen
cancel *cancelar* kan-the-*lar*
can opener *abrelatas* ⓜ a-bre-*la*-tas
car *coche* ⓜ *ko*-che
cash *dinero en efectivo* ⓜ dee-*ne*-ro en e-fek-*tee*-vo
cash (a cheque) v *cambiar (un cheque)*
  kam-*byar* (oon *che*-ke)
cell phone *teléfono móvil* ⓜ te-*le*-fo-no *mo*-veel
centre *centro* ⓜ *then*-tro
change (money) v *cambiar* kam-*byar*
cheap *barato/a* ⓜ/ⓕ ba-*ra*-to/a
check (bill) *cuenta* ⓕ *kwen*-ta
check-in *facturación de equipajes* ⓕ
  fak-too-ra-*thyon* de e-kee-*pa*-khes
chest *pecho* ⓜ *pe*-cho
child *niño/a* ⓜ/ⓕ *nee*-nyo/a
cigarette *cigarillo* ⓜ thee-ga-*ree*-lyo
city *ciudad* ⓕ theew-*da*
clean a *limpio/a* ⓜ/ⓕ *leem*-pyo/a

closed *cerrado/a* ⓜ/ⓕ the-rra-do/a
coffee *café* ⓜ ka-fe
coins *monedas* ⓕ pl mo-ne-das
cold a *frío/a* ⓜ/ⓕ free-o/a
collect call *llamada a cobro revertido* ⓕ
   lya-ma-da a ko-bro re-ver-tee-do
come *venir* ve-neer
computer *ordenador* ⓜ or-de-na-dor
condom *condones* ⓜ pl kon-do-nes
contact lenses *lentes de contacto* ⓜ pl
   len-tes de kon-tak-to
cook v *cocinar* ko-thee-nar
cost *precio* ⓜ pre-thyo
credit card *tarjeta de crédito* ⓕ
   tar-khe-ta de kre-dee-to
cup *taza* ⓕ ta-tha
currency exchange *cambio de dinero* ⓜ
   kam-byo de dee-ne-ro
customs (immigration) *aduana* ⓕ a-dwa-na

D

dangerous *peligroso/a* ⓜ/ⓕ pe-lee-gro-so/a
date (time) *fecha* ⓕ fe-cha
day *día* ⓜ dee-a
delay *demora* ⓕ de-mo-ra
dentist *dentista* ⓜ/ⓕ den-tees-ta
depart *salir* de sa-leer de
diaper *pañal* ⓜ pa-nyal
dictionary *diccionario* ⓜ deek-thyo-na-ryo
dinner *cena* ⓕ the-na
direct *directo/a* ⓜ/ⓕ dee-rek-to/a
dirty *sucio/a* ⓜ/ⓕ soo-thyo/a
disabled *minusválido/a* ⓜ/ⓕ mee-noos-va-lee-do/a
discount *descuento* ⓜ des-kwen-to
doctor *doctor/doctora* ⓜ/ⓕ dok-tor/dok-to-ra
double bed *cama de matrimonio* ⓕ
   ka-ma de ma-tree-mo-nyo
double room *habitación doble* ⓕ a-bee-ta-thyon do-ble
drink *bebida* ⓕ be-bee-da
drive v *conducir* kon-doo-theer
drivers licence *carnet de conducir* ⓜ
   kar-ne de kon-doo-theer
drugs (illicit) *droga* ⓕ dro-ga
dummy (pacifier) *chupete* ⓜ choo-pe-te

E

ear *oreja* ⓕ o-re-kha
east *este* es-te
eat *comer* ko-mer

economy class *clase turística* ⓕ kla-se too-rees-tee-ka
electricity *electricidad* ⓕ e-lek-tree-thee-da
elevator *ascensor* ⓜ as-then-sor
email *correo electrónico* ⓜ ko-rre-o e-lek-tro-nee-ko
embassy *embajada* ⓕ em-ba-kha-da
emergency *emergencia* ⓕ e-mer-khen-thya
English (language) *inglés* ⓜ een-gles
entrance *entrada* ⓕ en-tra-da
evening *noche* ⓕ no-che
exchange rate *tipo de cambio* ⓜ tee-po de kam-byo
exit *salida* ⓕ sa-lee-da
expensive *caro/a* ⓜ/ⓕ ka-ro/a
express mail *correo urgente* ⓜ ko-rre-o oor-khen-te
eye *ojo* ⓜ o-kho

F

far *lejos* le-khos
fast *rápido/a* ⓜ/ⓕ rra-pee-do/a
father *padre* ⓜ pa-dre
film (camera) *carrete* ⓜ ka-rre-te
finger *dedo* ⓜ de-do
first-aid kit *maletín de primeros auxilios* ⓜ
   ma-le-teen de pree-me-ros ow-ksee-lyos
first class *de primera clase* de pree-me-ra kla-se
fish *pez* ⓜ peth
food *comida* ⓕ ko-mee-da
foot *pie* ⓜ pye
fork *tenedor* ⓜ te-ne-dor
free (of charge) *gratis* gra-tees
friend *amigo/a* ⓜ/ⓕ a-mee-go/a
fruit *fruta* ⓕ froo-ta
full *lleno/a* ⓜ/ⓕ lye-no/a
funny *graciosa/a* ⓜ/ⓕ gra-thyo-so/a

G

gift *regalo* ⓜ rre-ga-lo
girl *chica* ⓕ chee-ka
glass (drinking) *vaso* ⓜ va-so
glasses *gafas* ⓕ pl ga-fas
go *ir* eer
good *bueno/a* ⓜ/ⓕ bwe-no/a
green *verde* ver-de
guide n *guía* ⓕ gee-a

H

half *mitad* ⓕ mee-tad
hand *mano* ⓕ ma-no
handbag *bolsa* ⓜ bol-so

happy *feliz* fe-*leeth*

have *tener* te-*ner*

he *él* el

head *cabeza* ① ka-*be*-tha

heart *corazón* ⓜ ko-ra-*thon*

heat *calor* ⓜ ka-*lor*

heavy *pesado/a* ⓜ/① pe-*sa*-do/a

help v *ayudar* a-yoo-*dar*

here *aquí* a-*kee*

high *alto/a* ⓜ/① *al*-to/a

highway *autovía* ① ow-to-*vee*-a

hike v *ir de excursión* eer de eks-koor-*syon*

holiday *vacaciones* ① pl va-ka-*thyo*-nes

homosexual *homosexual* ⓜ/① o-mo-se-*kswal*

hospital *hospital* ⓜ os-pee-*tal*

hot *caliente* ka-*lyen*-te

hotel *hotel* ⓜ o-*tel*

hungry *hambriento/a* ⓜ/① am-bree-*en*-to/a

husband *marido* ⓜ ma-*ree*-do

I

I *yo* yo

identification (card) *carnet de identidad* ⓜ kar-*net* de ee-den-tee-*da*

ill *enfermo/a* ⓜ/① en-*fer*-mo/a

important *importante* eem-por-*tan*-te

included *incluido* een-kloo-*ee*-do

injury *herida* ① e-*ree*-da

insurance *seguro* ⓜ se-*goo*-ro

Internet *Internet* ⓜ een-ter-*net*

interpreter *intérprete* ⓜ/① een-*ter*-pre-te

J

jewellery *joyas* ① pl *kho*-yas

job *trabajo* ⓜ tra-*ba*-kho

K

key *llave* ① *lya*-ve

kilogram *kilogramo* ⓜ kee-lo-*gra*-mo

kitchen *cocina* ① ko-*thee*-na

knife *cuchillo* ⓜ koo-*chee*-lyo

L

laundry (place) *lavadero* ⓜ la-va-*de*-ro

lawyer *abogado/a* ⓜ/① a-bo-*ga*-do/a

left (direction) *izquierda* ① eeth-*kyer*-da

left-luggage office *consigna* ① kon-*seeg*-na

leg *pierna* ① *pyer*-na

lesbian *lesbiana* ① les-bee-*a*-na

less *menos* me-nos

letter (mail) *carta* ① *kar*-ta

lift (elevator) *ascensor* ⓜ as-then-*sor*

light *luz* ① looth

like v *gustar* goos-*tar*

lock *cerradura* ① the-rra-*doo*-ra

long *largo/a* ⓜ/① *lar*-go/a

lost *perdido/a* ⓜ/① per-*dee*-do/a

lost-property office *oficina de objetos perdidos* ① o-fee-*thee*-na de ob-*khe*-tos per-*dee*-dos

love v *querer* ke-*rer*

luggage *equipaje* ⓜ e-kee-*pa*-khe

lunch *almuerzo* ⓜ al-*mwer*-tho

M

mail *correo* ⓜ ko-*rre*-o

man *hombre* ⓜ *om*-bre

map *mapa* ⓜ *ma*-pa

market *mercado* ⓜ mer-*ka*-do

matches *cerillas* ① pl the-*ree*-lyas

meat *carne* ① *kar*-ne

medicine *medicina* ① me-dee-*thee*-na

menu *menú* ⓜ me-*noo*

message *mensaje* ⓜ men-*sa*-khe

milk *leche* ① *le*-che

minute *minuto* ⓜ mee-*noo*-to

mobile phone *teléfono móvil* ⓜ te-*le*-fo-no *mo*-veel

money *dinero* ⓜ dee-*ne*-ro

month *mes* ⓜ mes

morning *mañana* ① ma-*nya*-na

mother *madre* ① *ma*-dre

motorcycle *motocicleta* ① mo-to-thee-*kle*-ta

motorway *autovía* ① ow-to-*vee*-a

mouth *boca* ① *bo*-ka

music *música* ① *moo*-see-ka

N

name *nombre* ⓜ *nom*-bre

napkin *servilleta* ① ser-vee-*lye*-ta

nappy *pañal* ⓜ pa-*nyal*

near *cerca* *ther*-ka

neck *cuello* ⓜ *kwe*-lyo

new *nuevo/a* ⓜ/① *nwe*-vo/a

news *noticias* ① pl no-*tee*-thyas

newspaper *periódico* ⓜ pe-*ryo*-dee-ko

night *noche* ① no-che

no *no* no

noisy *ruidoso/a* ⑩/① rrwee-do-so/a

nonsmoking *no fumadores* no foo-ma-*do*-res

north *norte* ⑩ nor-te

nose *nariz* ① na-*reeth*

now *ahora* a-o-ra

number *número* ⑩ *noo*-me-ro

O

oil (engine) *aceite* ⑩ a-*they*-te

old *viejo/a* ⑩/① *vye*-kho/a

one-way ticket *billete sencillo* ⑩ bee-*lye*-te sen-*thee*-lyo

open a *abierto/a* ⑩/① a-*byer*-to/a

outside *exterior* ⑩ eks-te-*ryor*

P

package *paquete* ⑩ pa-*ke*-te

paper *papel* ⑩ pa-*pel*

park (car) v *estacionar* es-ta-thyo-*nar*

passport *pasaporte* ⑩ pa-sa-*por*-te

pay *pagar* pa-*gar*

pen *bolígrafo* ⑩ bo-*lee*-gra-fo

petrol *gasolina* ① ga-so-*lee*-na

pharmacy *farmacia* ① far-*ma*-thya

phonecard *tarjeta de teléfono* ① tar-*khe*-ta de te-*le*-fo-no

photo *foto* ① *fo*-to

plate *plato* ⑩ *pla*-to

police *policía* ① po-lee-*thee*-a

postcard *postal* ① pos-*tal*

post office *correos* ⑩ ko-*rre*-os

pregnant *embarazada* ① em-ba-ra-*tha*-da

price *precio* ⑩ *pre*-thyo

Q

quiet *tranquilo/a* ⑩/① tran-*kee*-lo/a

R

rain *lluvia* ① *lyoo*-vya

razor *afeitadora* ① a-fey-ta-*do*-ra

receipt *recibo* ① rre-*thee*-bo

red *rojo/a* ⑩/① *rro*-kho/a

refund *reembolso* ① rre-em-*bol*-so

registered mail *correo certificado* ⑩ ko-*rre*-o ther-tee-fee-*ka*-do

rent v *alquilar* al-kee-*lar*

repair v *reparar* rre-pa-*rar*

reservation *reserva* ① rre-*ser*-va

restaurant *restaurante* ⑩ rres-tow-*ran*-te

return v *volver* vol-*ver*

return ticket *billete de ida y vuelta* ⑩ bee-*lye*-te de ee-da ee *vwel*-ta

right (direction) *derecha* de-*re*-cha

road *carretera* ① ka-rre-*te*-ra

room *habitación* ① a-bee-ta-*thyon*

S

safe a *seguro/a* ⑩/① se-*goo*-ro/a

sanitary napkin *compresas* ① pl kom-*pre*-sas

seat *asiento* ⑩ a-*syen*-to

send *enviar* en-vee-*ar*

service station *gasolinera* ① ga-so-lee-*ne*-ra

sex *sexo* ⑩ *se*-kso

shampoo *champú* ⑩ cham-*poo*

share (a dorm) *compartir* kom-par-*teer*

shaving cream *espuma de afeitar* ① es-*poo*-ma de a-fey-*tar*

she *ella* ① *e*-lya

sheet (bed) *sábana* ① *sa*-ba-na

shirt *camisa* ① ka-*mee*-sa

shoes *zapatos* ⑩ pl tha-*pa*-tos

shop *tienda* ① *tyen*-da

short *corto/a* ⑩/① *kor*-to/a

shower *ducha* ① *doo*-cha

single room *habitación individual* ① a-bee-ta-*thyon* een-dee-vee-*dwal*

skin *piel* ① pyel

skirt *falda* ① *fal*-da

sleep v *dormir* dor-*meer*

slowly *despacio* des-*pa*-thyo

small *pequeño/a* ⑩/① pe-*ke*-nyo/a

smoke (cigarettes) v *fumar* foo-*mar*

soap *jabón* ① kha-*bon*

some *alguno/a* ⑩/① al-*goo*-no/a

soon *pronto* pron-to

south *sur* ⑩ soor

souvenir shop *tienda de recuerdos* ① *tyen*-da de re-*kwer*-dos

Spain *España* ① es-*pa*-nya

Spanish (language) *español/castellano* ⑩ es-pa-*nyol*/kas-te-*lya*-no

speak *hablar* a-*blar*

spoon *cuchara* ① koo-*cha*-ra

stamp *sello* ⑩ *se*-lyo

stand-by ticket *billete de lista de espera* m
bee-*lye*-te de *lees*-ta de es-*pe*-ra
station (train) *estación* f es-ta-*thyon*
stomach *estómago* m es-to-ma-go
stop v *parar* pa-*rar*
stop (bus) *parada* f pa-*ra*-da
street *calle* f *ka*-lye
student *estudiante* m/f es-too-*dyan*-te
sun *sol* m sol
sunscreen *crema solar* f *kre*-ma so-*lar*
swim v *nadar* na-*dar*

T

tampons *tampones* m pl tam-*po*-nes
taxi *taxi* m *tak*-see
teaspoon *cucharita* f koo-cha-*ree*-ta
teeth *dientes* m pl *dyen*-tes
telephone *teléfono* m te-*le*-fo-no
television *televisión* f te-le-vee-*syon*
temperature (weather) *temperatura* f
tem-pe-ra-*too*-ra
tent *tienda (de campaña)* f *tyen*-da (de kam-*pa*-nya)
that (one) *ése/a* m/f *e*-se/a
they *ellos/ellas* m/f *e*-lyos/*e*-lyas
thirsty *sediento/a* m/f se-dee-*en*-to/a
this (one) *éste/a* m/f *es*-te/a
throat *garganta* f gar-*gan*-ta
ticket *billete* m bee-*lye*-te
time *tiempo* m *tyem*-po
tired *cansado/a* m/f kan-*sa*-do/a
tissues *pañuelos de papel* m pl pa-*nywe*-los de pa-*pel*
today *hoy* oy
toilet *servicio* m ser-*vee*-thyo
tomorrow *mañana* ma-*nya*-na
tonight *esta noche* es-ta *no*-che
toothbrush *cepillo de dientes* m the-*pee*-lyo de *dyen*-tes
toothpaste *pasta dentífrica* f *pas*-ta den-*tee*-free-ka
torch (flashlight) *linterna* f leen-*ter*-na
tour *excursión* f eks-koor-*syon*
tourist office *oficina de turismo* f
o-fee-*thee*-na de too-*rees*-mo
towel *toalla* f to-*a*-lya
train *tren* m tren
translate *traducir* tra-doo-*theer*
travel agency *agencia de viajes* f
a-*khen*-thya de *vya*-khes
travellers cheque *cheque de viajero* m
che-ke de vya-*khe*-ro
trousers *pantalones* m pl pan-ta-*lo*-nes

twin beds *dos camas* f pl dos *ka*-mas
tyre *neumático* m ne-oo-*ma*-tee-ko

U

underwear *ropa interior* f *rro*-pa een-te-*ryor*
urgent *urgente* oor-*khen*-te

V

vacant *vacante* va-*kan*-te
vacation *vacaciones* f va-ka-*thyo*-nes
vegetable *verdura* f ver-*doo*-ra
vegetarian a *vegetariano/a* m/f ve-khe-ta-*rya*-no/a
visa *visado* m vee-*sa*-do

W

waiter *camarero/a* m/f ka-ma-*re*-ro/a
walk v *caminar* ka-mee-*nar*
wallet *cartera* f kar-*te*-ra
warm a *templado/a* m/f tem-*pla*-do/a
wash (something) *lavar* la-*var*
watch *reloj de pulsera* m rre-*lokh* de pool-*se*-ra
water *agua* f *a*-gwa
we *nosotros/nosotras* m/f no-*so*-tros/ no-*so*-tras
weekend *fin de semana* m feen de se-*ma*-na
west *oeste* m o-*es*-te
wheelchair *silla de ruedas* f *see*-lya de *rrwe*-das
when *cuando* *kwan*-do
where *donde* *don*-de
white *blanco/a* m/f *blan*-ko/a
who *quien* kyen
why *por qué* por ke
wife *esposa* f es-*po*-sa
window *ventana* f ven-*ta*-na
wine *vino* m *vee*-no
with *con* kon
without *sin* seen
woman *mujer* f moo-*kher*
write *escribir* es-kree-*beer*

Y

yellow *amarillo/a* m/f a-ma-*ree*-lyo/a
yes *sí* see
yesterday *ayer* a-*yer*
you sg inf/pol *tú/Usted* too/oos-*te*
you pl *vosotros/vosotras* m/f vo-*so*-tros/vo-*so*-tras

Turkish

turkish alphabet				
A a a	*B b* be	*C c* je	*Ç ç* che	*D d* de
E e e	*F f* fe	*G g* ge	*Ğ ğ* yu-*moo*-shak ge	*H h* he
I ı uh	*İ i* ee	*J j* zhe	*K k* ke	*L l* le
M m me	*N n* ne	*O o* o	*Ö ö* er	*P p* pe
R r re	*S s* se	*Ş ş* she	*T t* te	*U u* oo
Ü ü ew	*V v* ve	*Y y* ye	*Z z* ze	

turkish

introduction

Turkish (*Türkçe* tewrk·che) – the language which traces its roots as far back as 3500 BC, has travelled through Central Asia, Persia, North Africa and Europe and been written in both Arabic and Latin script – has left us words like *yogurt*, *horde*, *sequin* and *bridge* (the game) along the way. But how did it transform itself from a nomad's tongue spoken in Mongolia into the language of modern Turkey, with a prestigious interlude as the diplomatic language of the Ottoman Empire?

The first evidence of the Turkish language, which is a member of the Ural-Altaic language family, was found on stone monuments from the 8th century BC, in what's now Outer Mongolia. In the 11th century, the Seljuq clan invaded Asia Minor (Anatolia) and imposed their language on the peoples they ruled. Over time, Arabic and Persian vocabulary was adopted to express artistic and philosophical concepts and Arabic script began to be used. By the 14th century, another clan – the Ottomans – was busy establishing the empire that was to control Eurasia for centuries. In their wake, they left the Turkish language. There were then two levels of Turkish – ornate Ottoman Turkish, with flowery Persian phrases and Arabic honorifics (words showing respect), used for diplomacy, business and art, and the language of the common Turks, which still used 'native' Turkish vocabulary and structures.

When the Ottoman Empire fell in 1922, the military hero, amateur linguist and historian Kemal Atatürk came to power and led the new Republic of Turkey. With the backing of a strong language reform movement, he devised a phonetic Latin script that reflected Turkish sounds more accurately than Arabic script. On 1 November 1928, the new writing system was unveiled: within two months, it was illegal to write Turkish in the old script. In 1932 Atatürk created the *Türk Dil Kurumu* (Turkish Language Society) and gave it the brief of simplifying the Turkish language to its 'pure' form of centuries before. The vocabulary and structure was completely overhauled. As a consequence, Turkish has changed so drastically that even Atatürk's own speeches are barely comprehensible to today's speakers of *öztürkçe* ('pure Turkish').

With 70 million speakers worldwide, Turkish is the official language of Turkey and the Turkish Republic of Northern Cyprus (recognised as a nation only by the Turkish government). Elsewhere, the language is also called *Osmanlı* os·man-luh, and is spoken by large populations in Germany, Bulgaria, Macedonia, Greece and the '-stans' of Central Asia. So start practising and you might soon be complimented with *Ağzına sağlık!* a·zuh·na sa·luhk (lit: health to your mouth) – 'Well said!'

pronunciation

vowel sounds

Most Turkish vowel sounds can be found in English, although in Turkish they're generally shorter and slightly harsher. When you see a double vowel, such as *saat* sa·*at* (hour), you need to pronounce both vowels.

symbol	english equivalent	turkish example	transliteration
a	run	*abide*	a·bee·*de*
ai	aisle	*hayvan*	hai·*van*
ay	say	*ney*	nay
e	bet	*ekmek*	ek·*mek*
ee	see	*ile*	ee·le
eu	nurse	*özel*	eu·*zel*
ew	ee pronounced with rounded lips	*üye*	ew·*ye*
o	pot	*oda*	o·*da*
oo	zoo	*uçak*	oo·*chak*
uh	ago	*ıslak*	uhs·*lak*

word stress

In Turkish, the stress generally falls on the last syllable of the word. Most two-syllable placenames, however, are stressed on the first syllable (eg *Kıbrıs kuhb*·ruhs), and in three-syllable placenames the stress is usually on the second syllable (eg *İstanbul* ees·*tan*·bool). Another common exception occurs when a verb has a form of the negative marker *me* (*me* me, *ma* ma, *mı* muh, *mi* mee, *mu* moo, or *mü* mew) added to it. In those cases, the stress goes onto the syllable before the marker – eg *gelmiyorlar* gel·mee·yor·lar (they're not coming). You don't need to worry too much about this, as the stressed syllable is always in italics in our coloured pronunciation guides.

consonant sounds

Most Turkish consonants sound the same as in English, so they're straightforward to pronounce. The exception is the Turkish r, which is always rolled. Note also that ğ is a silent letter which extends the vowel before it – it acts like the 'gh' combination in 'weigh', and is never pronounced.

symbol	english equivalent	turkish example	transliteration
b	bed	*bira*	*bee·ra*
ch	cheat	*çanta*	*chan·ta*
d	dog	*deniz*	*de·neez*
f	fat	*fabrika*	*fab·ree·ka*
g	go	*gar*	*gar*
h	hat	*hala*	*ha·la*
j	joke	*cadde*	*jad·de*
k	kit	*kadın*	*ka·duhn*
l	lot	*lider*	*lee·der*
m	man	*maç*	*mach*
n	not	*nefis*	*ne·fees*
p	pet	*paket*	*pa·ket*
r	red (rolled)	*rehber*	*reh·ber*
s	sun	*saat*	*sa·at*
sh	shot	*şarkı*	*shar·kuh*
t	top	*tas*	*tas*
v	van (but softer, between 'v' and 'w')	*vadi*	*va·dee*
y	yes	*yarım*	*ya·ruhm*
z	zero	*zarf*	*zarf*
zh	pleasure	*jambon*	*zham·bon*

tools

language difficulties

Do you speak English?
İngilizce konuşuyor musunuz?
een-gee-*leez*-je ko-noo-*shoo*-yor moo-soo-*nooz*

Do you understand?
Anlıyor musun?
an-*luh*-yor moo-*soon*

I understand.
Anlıyorum.
an-*luh*-yo-room

I don't understand.
Anlamıyorum.
an-*la*-muh-yo-room

What does (*kitap*) mean?
(Kitap) ne demektir?
(kee-*tap*) ne de-*mek*-teer

How do you pronounce this?
Bunu nasıl telaffuz edersiniz?
boo-*noo* na-suhl te-laf-*fooz* e-*der*-see-neez

How do you write (*yabancı*)?
(Yabancı) kelimesini
nasıl yazarsınız?
(ya-ban-*juh*) ke-lee-me-see-*nee*
na-suhl ya-*zar*-suh-nuhz

Could you please ...? | *Lütfen ...?* | *lewt*-fen ...
repeat that | *tekrarlar mısınız* | tek-*rar*-lar muh-suh-*nuhz*
speak more | *daha yavaş* | da-*ha* ya-*vash*
 slowly | *konuşur musunuz* | ko-noo-*shoor* moo-soo-*nooz*
write it down | *yazar mısınız* | ya-*zar* muh-suh-*nuhz*

---

essentials

Yes. | *Evet.* | e-*vet*
No. | *Hayır.* | ha-*yuhr*
Please. | *Lütfen.* | *lewt*-fen
Thank you | *(Çok) Teşekkür* | (chok) te-shek-*kewr*
 (very much). pol | *ederim.* | e-*de*-reem
Thanks. inf | *Teşekkürler.* | te-shek-kewr-*ler*
You're welcome. | *Birşey değil.* | beer-*shay* de-*eel*
Excuse me. | *Bakar mısınız?* | ba-*kar* muh-suh-*nuhz*
Sorry. | *Özür dilerim.* | eu-zewr dee-*le*-reem

numbers

0	sıfır	suh·fuhr	16	onaltı	on·al·tuh
1	bir	beer	17	onyedi	on·ye·dee
2	iki	ee·kee	18	onsekiz	on·se·keez
3	üç	ewch	19	ondokuz	on·do·kooz
4	dört	deurt	20	yirmi	yeer·mee
5	beş	besh	21	yirmibir	yeer·mee·beer
6	altı	al·tuh	22	yirmiiki	yeer·mee·ee·kee
7	yedi	ye·dee	30	otuz	o·tooz
8	sekiz	se·keez	40	kırk	kuhrk
9	dokuz	do·kooz	50	elli	el·lee
10	on	on	60	altmış	alt·muhsh
11	onbir	on·beer	70	yetmiş	yet·meesh
12	oniki	on·ee·kee	80	seksen	sek·sen
13	onüç	on·ewch	90	doksan	dok·san
14	ondört	on·deurt	100	yüz	yewz
15	onbeş	on·besh	1000	bin	been

time & dates

What time is it?	Saat kaç?	sa·at kach
It's one o'clock.	Saat bir.	sa·at beer
It's (10) o'clock.	Saat (on).	sa·at (on)
Quarter past (10).	(Onu) çeyrek geçiyor.	(o·noo) chay·rek ge·chee·yor
Half past (10).	(On) buçuk.	(on) boo·chook
Quarter to (11).	(Onbire) çeyrek var.	(on·bee·re) chay·rek var
At what time ...?	Saat kaçta ...?	sa·at kach·ta ...
At ...	Saat ...	sa·at ...
am (morning)	sabah	sa·bah
pm (afternoon)	öğleden sonra	er·le·den son·ra
pm (evening)	gece	ge·je
Monday	Pazartesi	pa·zar·te·see
Tuesday	Salı	sa·luh
Wednesday	Çarşamba	char·sham·ba
Thursday	Perşembe	per·shem·be
Friday	Cuma	joo·ma
Saturday	Cumartesi	joo·mar·te·see
Sunday	Pazar	pa·zar

January	*Ocak*	o·*jak*
February	*Şubat*	shoo·*bat*
March	*Mart*	mart
April	*Nisan*	nee·*san*
May	*Mayıs*	ma·*yuhs*
June	*Haziran*	ha·zee·*ran*
July	*Temmuz*	tem·*mooz*
August	*Ağustos*	a·oos·*tos*
September	*Eylül*	ay·*lewl*
October	*Ekim*	e·*keem*
November	*Kasım*	ka·*suhm*
December	*Aralık*	a·ra·*luhk*

What date is it today?
   Bugün ayın kaçı?   boo·gewn a·*yuhn* ka·chuh

It's (18 October).
   (Onsekiz Ekim).   (on·se·*keez* e·*keem*)

since (May)	*(Mayıs'tan) beri*	(ma·yuhs·*tan*) be·*ree*
until (June)	*(Haziran'a) kadar*	(ha·zee·ra·*na*) ka·*dar*
yesterday	*dün*	dewn
today	*bugün*	boo·*gewn*
tonight	*bu gece*	boo ge·*je*
tomorrow	*yarın*	*ya*·ruhn
last/next ...	*geçen/gelecek ...*	ge·*chen*/ge·le·*jek* ...
night	*gece*	ge·*je*
week	*hafta*	haf·*ta*
month	*ay*	ai
year	*yıl*	yuhl
yesterday/tomorrow ...	*dün/yarın ...*	dewn/*ya*·ruhn ...
morning	*sabah*	sa·*bah*
afternoon	*öğleden sonra*	eu·le·*den* son·ra
evening	*akşam*	ak·*sham*

weather

What's the weather like?	Hava nasıl?	ha·va na·suhl
It's ...	Hava ...	ha·va ...
cloudy	bulutlu	boo·loot·loo
cold	soğuk	so·ook
hot	sıcak	suh·jak
raining	yağmurlu	ya·moor·loo
snowing	kar yağışlı	kar ya·uhsh·luh
sunny	güneşli	gew·nesh·lee
warm	ılık	uh·luhk
windy	rüzgarlı	rewz·gar·luh
spring	ilkbahar	eelk·ba·har
summer	yaz	yaz
autumn	sonbahar	son·ba·har
winter	kış	kuhsh

border crossing

I'm here ...	Ben ...	ben ...
in transit	transit yolcuyum	tran·seet yol·joo·yoom
on business	iş gezisindeyim	eesh ge·zee·seen·de·yeem
on holiday	tatildeyim	ta·teel·de·yeem
I'm here for ...	Ben ... buradayım.	ben ... boo·ra·da·yuhm
(10) days	(on) günlüğüne	(on) gewn·lew·ew·ne
(three) weeks	(üç) haftalığına	(ewch) haf·ta·luh·uh·na
(two) months	(iki) aylığına	(ee·kee) ai·luh·uh·na

I'm going to (Sarıyer).
(Sarıyer'e) gidiyorum.   (sa·ruh·ye·re) gee·dee·yo·room

I'm staying at the (Divan).
(Divan'da) kalıyorum.   (dee·van·da) ka·luh·yo·room

I have nothing to declare.
Beyan edecek hiçbir şeyim yok.   be·yan e·de·jek heech·beer she·yeem yok

I have something to declare.
Beyan edecek bir şeyim var.   be·yan e·de·jek beer she·yeem var

That's (not) mine.
Bu benim (değil).   boo be·neem (de·eel)

transport

tickets & luggage

Where can I buy a ticket?
Nereden bilet alabilirim? ne·re·den bee·*let* a·*la*·bee·lee·reem

Do I need to book a seat?
Yer ayırtmam gerekli mi? yer a·yuhrt·*mam* ge·rek·*lee* mee

One ... ticket to	*(Bostancı'ya) ...*	(bos·*tan*·juh·ya) ...
(Bostancı), please.	*lütfen.*	lewt·fen
one-way	*bir gidiş bileti*	beer gee·*deesh* bee·le·*tee*
return	*gidiş-dönüş*	gee·deesh-deu·*newsh*
	bir bilet	beer bee·*let*

I'd like to ... my	*Biletimi ...*	bee·le·tee·*mee* ...
ticket, please.	*istiyorum.*	ees·*tee*·yo·room
cancel	*iptal ettirmek*	eep·*tal* et·teer·*mek*
change	*değiştirmek*	de·eesh·teer·*mek*
collect	*almak*	al·*mak*
confirm	*onaylatmak*	o·nai·lat·*mak*

I'd like a ... seat,	*... bir yer istiyorum.*	... beer yer ees·*tee*·yo·room
please.		
nonsmoking	*Sigara içilmeyen*	see·*ga*·ra ee·*cheel*·me·yen
	kısımda	kuh·suhm·*da*
smoking	*Sigara içilen*	see·*ga*·ra ee·*chee*·len
	kısımda	kuh·suhm·*da*

How much is it?
Şu ne kadar? shoo ne ka·*dar*

Is there air conditioning?
Klima var mı? klee·ma var muh

Is there a toilet?
Tuvalet var mı? too·va·*let* var muh

How long does the trip take?
Yolculuk ne kadar sürer? yol·joo·*look* ne ka·*dar* sew·rer

Is it a direct route?
Direk güzergah mı? dee·*rek* gew·zer·*gah* muh

Where's the luggage locker?
Emanet dolabı nerede? e·ma·*net* do·la·*buh* ne·re·de

My luggage has been ...	Bagajım ...	ba·ga·zhuhm ...
damaged	zarar gördü	za·rar geu·dew
lost	kayboldu	kai·bol·doo
stolen	çalındı	cha·luhn·duh

getting around

Where does flight (TK0060) arrive?
(TK0060) sefer sayılı uçak nereye iniyor?
(te·ka suh·fuhr suh·fuhr alt·muhsh) se·fer sa·yuh·luh oo·chak ne·re·ye ee·nee·yor

Where does flight (TK0060) depart?
(TK0060) sefer sayılı uçak nereden kalkıyor?
(te·ka suh·fuhr suh·fuhr alt·muhsh) se·fer sa·yuh·luh oo·chak ne·re·den kal·kuh·yor

Where's (the) ...?	... nerede?	... ne·re·de
arrivals hall	Gelen yolcu bölümü	ge·len yol·joo beu·lew·mew
departures hall	Giden yolcu bölümü	gee·den yol·joo beu·lew·mew
duty-free shop	Gümrüksüz satış mağazası	gewm·rewk·sewz sa·tuhsh ma·a·za·suh
gate (12)	(Oniki) numaralı kapı	(on·ee·kee) noo·ma·ra·luh ka·puh

Is this the ... to (Sirkeci)?	(Sirkeci'ye) giden ... bu mu?	(seer·ke·jee·ye) gee·den ... boo moo
boat	vapur	va·poor
bus	otobüs	o·to·bews
plane	uçak	oo·chak
train	tren	tren

What time's the ... bus?	... otobüs ne zaman?	... o·to·bews ne za·man
first	İlk	eelk
last	Son	son
next	Sonraki	son·ra·kee

At what time does it arrive/leave?
Ne zaman varır/kalkacak?
ne za·man va·ruhr/kal·ka·jak

How long will it be delayed?
Ne kadar gecikecek?
ne ka·dar ge·jee·ke·jek

What station/stop is this?
Bu hangi istasyon/durak?   boo *han*·gee ees·tas·*yon*/doo·*rak*

What's the next station/stop?
Sonraki istasyon/durak hangisi?   son·ra·*kee* ees·tas·*yon*/doo·*rak* han·gee·see

Does it stop at (Kadıköy)?
(Kadıköy'de) durur mu?   (ka·*duh*·kay·de) doo·*roor* moo

Please tell me when we get to (Beşiktaş).
(Beşiktaş'a) vardığımızda   (be·*sheek*·ta·sha) var·duh·uh·muhz·*da*
lütfen bana söyleyin.   *lewt*·fen ba·*na* say·*le*·yeen

How long do we stop here?
Burada ne kadar duracağız?   boo·ra·*da* ne ka·*dar* doo·ra·*ja*·uhz

Is this seat available?
Bu koltuk boş mu?   boo kol·*took* bosh moo

That's my seat.
Burası benim yerim.   boo·ra·*suh* be·*neem* ye·*reem*

I'd like a taxi ...   ... *bir taksi istiyorum.*   ... beer tak·*see* ees·*tee*·yo·room
   at (9am)   *(Sabah dokuzda)*   (sa·*bah* do·kooz·*da*)
   now   *Hemen*   *he*·men
   tomorrow   *Yarın*   *ya*·ruhn

Is this taxi available?
Bu taksi boş mu?   boo tak·*see* bosh moo

How much is it to ...?
... *ne kadar?*   ... ne ka·*dar*

Please put the meter on.
Lütfen taksimetreyi   *lewt*·fen tak·*see*·met·re·yee
çalıştırın.   cha·luhsh·*tuh*·ruhn

Please take me to (this address).
Lütfen beni (bu adrese) götürün.   *lewt*·fen be·*nee* (boo ad·re·*se*) geu·*tew*·rewn

Please ...   *Lütfen ...*   *lewt*·fen ...
   slow down   *yavaşlayın*   ya·vash·*la*·yuhn
   stop here   *burada durun*   boo·ra·*da* doo·roon
   wait here   *burada bekleyin*   boo·ra·*da* bek·*le*·yeen

car, motorbike & bicycle hire

I'd like to	Bir ... kiralamak	beer ... kee-ra-la-*mak*
hire a ...	istiyorum.	ees-*tee*-yo-room
bicycle	bisiklet	bee-seek-*let*
car	araba	a-ra-*ba*
motorbike	motosiklet	mo-to-seek-*let*
with ...		
a driver	şoförlü	sho-feur-*lew*
air conditioning	klimalı	klee-ma-*luh*
How much	... kirası ne	... kee-ra-*suh* ne
for ... hire?	kadar?	ka-*dar*
hourly	Saatlık	sa-at-*luhk*
daily	Günlük	gewn-*lewk*
weekly	Haftalık	haf-ta-*luhk*
air	hava	ha-*va*
oil	yağ	ya
petrol	benzin	ben-*zeen*
tyres	lastikler	las-teek-*ler*

I need a mechanic.
   Tamirciye ihtiyacım var.   ta-meer-jee-*ye* eeh-tee-ya-*juhm* var

I've run out of petrol.
   Benzinim bitti.   ben-zee-*neem* beet-*tee*

I have a flat tyre.
   Lastiğim patladı.   las-tee-*eem* pat-la-*duh*

directions

Where's the ...?	... nerede?	... ne-re-de
bank	Banka	*ban*-ka
city centre	Şehir merkezi	she-*heer* mer-ke-*zee*
hotel	Otel	o-*tel*
market	Pazar yeri	pa-*zar* ye-*ree*
police station	Polis karakolu	po-*lees* ka-ra-ko-*loo*
post office	Postane	pos-*ta*-ne
public toilet	Umumi tuvalet	oo-moo-*mee* too-va-*let*
tourist office	Turizm bürosu	too-*reezm* bew-ro-*soo*

Is this the road to (Taksim)?
(Taksim'e) giden yol bu mu? — (tak·see·me) gee·*den* yol boo moo

Can you show me (on the map)?
Bana (haritada) — ba·*na* (ha·ree·ta·*da*)
gösterebilir misiniz? — geus·te·re·bee·leer mee·seen·*neez*

What's the address?
Adresi nedir? — ad·re·*see* ne·deer

How far is it?
Ne kadar uzakta? — ne ka·*dar* oo·zak·*ta*

How do I get there?
Oraya nasıl gidebilirim? — o·ra·*ya* na·suhl gee·*de*·bee·lee·reem

Turn ...	... dön.	... deun
at the corner	Köşeden	keu·she·*den*
at the traffic lights	Trafik	tra·*feek*
	ışıklarından	uh·shuhk·la·ruhn·*dan*
left/right	Sola/Sağa	so·*la*/sa·*a*

It's ...		
behind ...	... arkasında.	... ar·ka·suhn·*da*
far away	Uzak.	oo·*zak*
here	Burada.	boo·ra·*da*
in front of ...	... önünde.	... eu·newn·*de*
left	Solda.	sol·*da*
near ...	... yakınında.	... ya·kuh·nuhn·*da*
next to ...	... yanında.	... ya·nuhn·*da*
on the corner	Köşede.	keu·she·*de*
opposite ...	... karşısında.	... kar·shuh·suhn·*da*
right	Sağda.	sa·*da*
straight ahead	Tam karşıda.	tam kar·shuh·*da*
there	Şurada.	shoo·ra·*da*

by bus	otobüslü	o·to·bews·*lew*
by taxi	taksili	tak·see·*lee*
by train	trenli	tren·*lee*
on foot	yürüyerek	yew·rew·ye·*rek*

north	kuzey	koo·*zay*
south	güney	gew·*nay*
east	doğu	do·*oo*
west	batı	ba·*tuh*

Giriş/Çıkış	gee-reesh/chuh-kuhsh	Entrance/Exit
Açık/Kapalı	a-chuhk/ka-pa-luh	Open/Closed
Boş Oda	bosh o-da	Rooms Available
Boş Yer Yok	bosh yer yok	No Vacancies
Danışma	da-nuhsh-ma	Information
Polis Karakolu	po-lees ka-ra-ko-loo	Police Station
Yasak	ya-sak	Prohibited
Tuvaletler	too-va-let-ler	Toilets
Erkek	er-kek	Men
Kadın	ka-duhn	Women
Sıcak/Soğuk	suh-jak/so-ook	Hot/Cold

accommodation

finding accommodation

Where's a ...?	Buralarda nerede ... var?	boo-ra-lar-da ne-re-de ... var
camping ground	kamp yeri	kamp ye-ree
guesthouse	misafirhane	mee-sa-feer-ha-ne
hotel	otel	o-tel
youth hostel	gençlik hosteli	gench-leek hos-te-lee

Can you recommend somewhere ...?	... bir yer tavsiye edebilir misiniz?	... beer yer tav-see-ye e-de-bee-leer mee-see-neez
cheap	Ucuz	oo-jooz
good	İyi	ee-yee
nearby	Yakın	ya-kuhn

I'd like to book a room, please.
Bir oda ayırtmak
istiyorum lütfen.

beer o-da a-yuhrt-mak
ees-tee-yo-room lewt-fen

I have a reservation.
Rezervasyonum var.

re-zer-vas-yo-noom var

My name's ...
Benim ismim ...

be-neem ees-meem ...

Do you have a … room?	… odanız var mı?	… o-da-nuhz var muh
single	Tek kişilik	tek kee-shee-leek
double	İki kişilik	ee-kee kee-shee-leek
twin	Çift yataklı	cheeft ya-tak-luh

How much is it per …?	… ne kadar?	… ne ka-dar
night	Geceliği	ge-je-lee-ee
person	Kişi başına	kee-shee ba-shuh-na

Can I pay by …?	… ile ödeyebilir miyim?	… ee-le eu-de-ye-bee-leer mee-yeem
credit card	Kredi kartı	kre-dee kar-tuh
travellers cheque	Seyahat çeki	se-ya-hat che-kee

I'd like to stay for (three) nights.
Kalmak istiyorum (üç) geceliğine. kal-mak ees-tee-yo-room (ewch) ge-je-lee-ee-ne

From (2 July) to (6 July).
(İki Temmuz'dan) (ee-kee tem-mooz-dan)
(altı Temmuz'a) kadar. (al-tuh tem-moo-za) ka-dar

Can I see it?
Görebilir miyim. geu-re-bee-leer mee-yeem

Am I allowed to camp here?
Burada kamp yapabilir miyim? boo-ra-da kamp ya-pa-bee-leer mee-yeem

Where can I find a camping ground?
Kamp alanı nerede? kamp a-la-nuh ne-re-de

requests & queries

When/Where is breakfast served?
Kahvaltı ne zaman/ kah-val-tuh ne za-man/
nerede veriliyor? ne-re-de ve-ree-lee-yor

Please wake me at (seven).
Lütfen beni (yedide) kaldırın. lewt-fen be-nee (ye-dee-de) kal-duh-ruhn

Could I have my key, please?
Anahtarımı alabilir miyim? a-nah-ta-ruh-muh a-la-bee-leer mee-yeem

Can I get another (blanket)?
Başka bir (battaniye) bash-ka beer (bat-ta-nee-ye)
alabilir miyim? a-la-bee-leer mee-yeem

Is there an elevator/a safe?
Asansör/Kasanız var mı? a-san-seur/ka-sa-nuhz var muh

The room is too …	Çok …	chok …
expensive	pahalı	pa·ha·luh
noisy	gürültülü	gew·rewl·tew·lew
small	küçük	kew·chewk

The … doesn't work.	… çalışmıyor.	… cha·luhsh·muh·yor
air conditioning	Klima	klee·ma
fan	Fan	fan
toilet	Tuvalet	too·va·let

This … isn't clean.	Bu … temiz değil.	boo … te·meez de·eel
pillow	yastık	yas·tuhk
sheet	çarşaf	char·shaf
towel	havlu	hav·loo

checking out

What time is checkout?
Çıkış ne zaman? · chuh·kuhsh ne za·man

Can I leave my luggage here?
Eşyalarımı burada bırakabilir miyim? · esh·ya·la·ruh·muh boo·ra·da buh·ra·ka·bee·leer mee·yeem

Could I have my …, please?	… alabilir miyim lütfen?	… a·la·bee·leer mee·yeem lewt·fen
deposit	Depozitomu	de·po·zee·to·moo
passport	Pasaportumu	pa·sa·por·too·moo
valuables	Değerli eşyalarımı	de·er·lee esh·ya·la·ruh·muh

communications & banking

the internet

Where's the local Internet café?
En yakın internet kafe nerede? · en ya·kuhn een·ter·net ka·fe ne·re·de

How much is it per hour?
Saati ne kadar? · sa·a·tee ne ka·dar

I'd like to ...	... istiyorum.	... ees·tee·yo·room
check my email	E-postama bakmak	e·pos·ta·ma bak·mak
get Internet access	İnternete girmek	een·ter·ne·te geer·mek
use a printer	Printeri kullanmak	preen·te·ree kool·lan·mak
use a scanner	Tarayıcıyı	ta·ra·yuh·juh·yuh

mobile/cell phone

I'd like a ...	... istiyorum.	... ees·tee·yo·room
mobile/cell	Cep telefonu	jep te·le·fo·noo
phone for hire	kiralamak	kee·ra·la·mak
SIM card for	Buradaki şebeke	boo·ra·da·kee she·be·ke
your network	için SİM kart	ee·cheen seem kart

What are the rates?	Ücret tarifesi nedir?	ewj·ret ta·ree·fe·see ne·deer

telephone

What's your phone number?
Telefon numaranız nedir? — te·le·fon noo·ma·ra·nuhz ne·deer

The number is ...
Telefon numarası ... — te·le·fon noo·ma·ra·suh ...

Where's the nearest public phone?
En yakın telefon
kulübesi nerede? — en ya·kuhn te·le·fon koo·lew·be·see ne·re·de

I'd like to buy a phonecard.
Telefon kartı almak istiyorum. — te·le·fon kar·tuh al·mak ees·tee·yo·room

I want to ...	... istiyorum.	... ees·tee·yo·room
call (Singapore)	(Singapur'u)	(seen·ga·poo·roo)
	aramak	a·ra·mak
make a local	Yerel bir görüşme	ye·rel beer geu·rewsh·me
call	yapmak	yap·mak
reverse the	Ödemeli görüşme	eu·de·me·lee ger·rewsh·me
charges	yapmak	yap·mak

How much does ... cost?	... ne kadar eder?	... ne ka·dar e·der
a (three)-minute call	(Üç) dakikalık konuşma	(ewch) da·kee·ka·luhk ko·noosh·ma
each extra minute	Her ekstra dakika	her eks·tra da·kee·ka

It's (10) *yeni kuruş* per minute.
Bir dakikası (on) yeni kuruş.   beer da·kee·ka·*suh* (on) ye·*nee* koo·*roosh*

post office

I want to send a ...	Bir ... göndermek istiyorum.	beer ... geun·der·mek ees·tee·yo·room
fax	faks	faks
letter	mektup	mek·*toop*
parcel	paket	pa·*ket*
postcard	kartpostal	kart·pos·*tal*

I want to buy a/an ...	... satın almak istiyorum.	... sa·tuhn al·mak ees·tee·yo·room
envelope	Zarf	zarf
stamp	Pul	pool

Please send it (to Australia) by ...	Lütfen ... (Avustralya'ya) gönderin.	lewt·fen ... (a·voos·tral·ya·ya) geun·de·reen
airmail	hava yoluyla	ha·va yo·looy·la
express mail	ekspres posta	eks·pres pos·ta
registered mail	taahhütlü posta	ta·ah·hewt·lew pos·ta
surface mail	deniz yoluyla	de·neez yo·looy·la

Is there any mail for me?	Bana posta var mı?	ba·na pos·ta var muh

bank

Where's a/an ...?	... nerede var?	... ne·re·de var
ATM	Bankamatik	ban·ka·ma·teek
foreign exchange office	Döviz bürosu	deu·veez bew·ro·soo

I'd like to ...	... istiyorum.	... ees·tee·yo·room
cash a cheque	Çek bozdurmak	chek boz·door·mak
change a travellers cheque	Seyahat çeki bozdurmak	se·ya·hat che·kee boz·door·mak
change money	Para bozdurmak	pa·ra boz·door·mak
get a cash advance	Avans çekmek	a·vans chek·mek
withdraw money	Para çekmek	pa·ra chek·mek

What's the ...?	... nedir?	... ne·deer
charge for that	Ücreti	ewj·re·tee
commission	Komisyon	ko·mees·yon
exchange rate	Döviz kuru	deu·veez koo·roo

It's ...		
(12) euros	(Oniki) euro.	(on·ee·kee) yoo·ro
(25) lira	(Yirmibeş) lira.	(yeer·mee·besh) lee·ra
free	Ücretsiz.	ewj·ret·seez

What time does the bank open?

Banka ne zaman açılıyor?　　　ban·ka ne za·man a·chuh·luh·yor

Has my money arrived yet?

Param geldi mi?　　　pa·ram gel·dee mee

sightseeing

getting in

What time does it open/close?

Saat kaçta açılır/kapanır?　　　sa·at kach·ta a·chuh·luhr/ka·pa·nuhr

What's the admission charge?

Giriş ücreti nedir?　　　gee·reesh ewj·re·tee ne·deer

Is there a discount for children/students?

Çocuk/Öğrenci indirimi var mı?　　　cho·jook/eu·ren·jee een·dee·ree·mee var muh

I'd like a ...	... istiyorum.	... ees·tee·yo·room
catalogue	Katalog	ka·ta·log
guide	Rehber	reh·ber
local map	Yerel Harita	ye·rel ha·ree·ta

I'd like to see ...	... görmek istiyorum.	... geur·mek ees·tee·yo·room
What's that?	Bu nedir?	boo ne·deer
Can I take a photo?	Bir fotoğrafınızı çekebilir miyim?	beer fo·to·ra·fuh·nuh·zuh che·ke·bee·leer mee·yeem

tours

When's the next ...?	Sonraki ... ne zaman?	son·ra·kee ... ne za·man
day trip	gündüz turu	gewn·dewz too·roo
tour	tur	toor
Is ... included?	... dahil mi?	... da·heel mee
accommodation	Kalacak yer	ka·la·jak yer
the admission charge	Giriş	gee·reesh
food	Yemek	ye·mek
transport	Ulaşım	oo·la·shuhm

How long is the tour?
Tur ne kadar sürer?   toor ne ka·dar sew·rer

What time should we be back?
Saat kaçta dönmeliyiz?   sa·at kach·ta deun·me·lee·yeez

sightseeing

castle	kale	ka·le
church	kilise	kee·lee·se
main square	meydan	may·dan
monument	anıt	a·nuht
mosque	cami	ja·mee
museum	müze	mew·ze
old city	eski şehir	es·kee she·heer
palace	saray	sa·rai
ruins	harabeler	ha·ra·be·ler
stadium	stadyum	stad·yoom
statue	heykel	hay·kel
Turkish bath	hamam	ha·mam

shopping

enquiries

Where's a ...?	... nerede?	... ne·re·de
bank	Banka	ban·ka
bookshop	Kitapçı	kee·tap·chuh
camera shop	Fotoğrafçı	fo·to·raf·chuh
department store	Büyük mağaza	bew·yewk ma·a·za
grocery store	Bakkal	bak·kal
market	Pazar yeri	pa·zar ye·ree
newsagency	Gazete bayii	ga·ze·te ba·yee·ee
supermarket	Süpermarket	sew·per·mar·ket

Where can I buy (a padlock)?
Nereden (asma kilit)
alabilirim?
ne·re·den (as·ma kee·leet)
a·la·bee·lee·reem

I'm looking for ...
... istiyorum.
... ees·tee·yo·room

Can I look at it?
Bakabilir miyim?
ba·ka·bee·leer mee·yeem

Do you have any others?
Başka var mı?
bash·ka var muh

Does it have a guarantee?
Garantisi var mı?
ga·ran·tee·see var muh

Can I have it sent overseas?
Yurt dışına gönderebilir
misiniz?
yoort duh·shuh·na geun·de·re·bee·leer
mee·see·neez

Can I have my ... repaired?
... burada tamir ettirebilir
miyim?
... boo·ra·da ta·meer et·tee·re·bee·leer
mee·yeem

It's faulty.
Arızalı.
a·ruh·za·luh

I'd like ..., please.	... istiyorum lütfen.	... ees·tee·yo·room lewt·fen
a bag	Çanta	chan·ta
a refund	Para iadesi	pa·ra ee·a·de·see
to return this	Bunu iade etmek	boo·noo ee·a·de et·mek

paying

How much is it?
Ne kadar?
ne ka-*dar*

Can you write down the price?
Fiyatı yazabilir misiniz?
fee-ya-*tuh* ya-*za*-bee-leer mee-see-*neez*

That's too expensive.
Bu çok pahalı.
boo chok pa-ha-*luh*

Is that your lowest price?
Son fiyatınız bu mu?
son fee-ya-tuh-*nuhz* boo moo

I'll give you (30) lira.
(Otuz) lira veririm.
(o-*tooz*) lee-*ra* ve-ree-*reem*

There's a mistake in the bill.
Hesapta bir yanlışlık var.
he-sap-*ta* beer yan-luhsh-*luhk* var

Do you accept …?
… kabul ediyor musunuz?
… ka-bool e-*dee*-yor moo-soo-*nooz*

credit cards	*Kredi kartı*	*kre*-dee kar-*tuh*
debit cards	*Banka kartı*	*ban*-ka kar-*tuh*
travellers cheques	*Seyahat çeki*	se-ya-*hat* che-*kee*

I'd like …, please.
… istiyorum lütfen.
… ees-tee-yo-room *lewt*-fen

a receipt	*Makbuz*	mak-*booz*
my change	*Paramın üstünü*	pa-ra-*muhn* ews-tew-*new*

clothes & shoes

Can I try it on?
Deneyebilir miyim?
de-ne-*ye*-bee-leer mee-*yeem*

My size is (42).
(Kırkiki) beden giyiyorum.
(kuhrk-ee-*kee*) be-*den* gee-*yee*-yo-room

It doesn't fit.
Olmuyor.
ol-moo-yor

small	*küçük*	kew-*chewk*
medium	*orta*	or-*ta*
large	*büyük*	bew-*yewk*

books & music

I'd like a ...	... istiyorum.	... ees·*tee*·yo·room
newspaper	*(İngilizce)*	(een·gee·*leez*·je)
(in English)	*bir gazete*	beer ga·*ze*·te
pen	*Tükenmez kalem*	tew·ken·*mez* ka·*lem*

Is there an English-language bookshop?
İngilizce yayın satan   een·gee·*leez*·je ya·*yuhn* sa·*tan*
bir dükkan var mı?   beer dewk·*kan* var muh

I'm looking for something by (Yaşar Kemal).
(Yaşar Kemal'in) albümlerine   (ya·*shar* ke·mal·*een*) al·bewm·le·ree·ne
bakmak istiyorum.   bak·*mak* ees·*tee*·yo·room

Can I listen to this?
Bunu dinleyebilir miyim?   boo·*noo* deen·le·ye·bee·leer mee·*yeem*

photography

Can you ...?	... misiniz?	... mee·see·*neez*
develop this film	*Bu filmi basabilir*	boo feel·*mee* ba·*sa*·bee·leer
load my film	*Filmi makineye*	feel·*mee* ma·kee·ne·ye
	takabilir	ta·*ka*·bee·leer
transfer photos	*Kameramdaki*	ka·me·ram·da·*kee*
from my	*fotoğrafları*	fo·to·raf·la·*ruh*
camera to CD	*CD'ye aktarabilir*	see·dee·ye ak·ta·*ra*·bee·leer

I need a/an ... film	*Bu kamera için ...*	boo ka·me·ra ee·*cheen* ...
for this camera.	*film istiyorum.*	feelm ees·*tee*·yo·room
APS	*APS*	a·pe·*se*
B&W	*siyah-beyaz*	see·*yah*·be·yaz
colour	*renkli*	renk·*lee*
slide	*slayt*	slayt
(200) speed	*(ikiyüz) hızlı*	(ee·*kee*·yewz) huhz·*luh*

When will it be ready?   *Ne zaman hazır olur?*   ne za·*man* ha·*zuhr* o·*loor*

meeting people

greetings, goodbyes & introductions

Hello.	*Merhaba.*	mer·ha·ba
Hi.	*Selam.*	se·*lam*
Good night.	*İyi geceler.*	ee·*yee* ge·je·*ler*
Goodbye.	*Hoşçakal.* inf	hosh·*cha*·kal
(by person leaving)	*Hoşçakalın.* pol	hosh·*cha*·ka·luhn
Goodbye.	*Güle güle.*	gew·*le* gew·*le*
(by person staying)		
See you later.	*Sonra görüşürüz.*	*son*·ra ger·rew·*shew*·rewz
Mr	*Bay*	bai
Mrs/Miss	*Bayan*	ba·*yan*
How are you?	*Nasılsın?* inf	na·suhl·suhn
	Nasılsınız? pol	na·suhl·suh·nuhz
Fine. And you?	*İyiyim. Ya sen/siz?* inf/pol	ee·*yee*·yeem ya sen/seez
What's your name?	*Adınız ne?* inf	a·duh·*nuhz* ne
	Adınız nedir? pol	a·duh·*nuhz* ne·deer
My name is ...	*Benim adım ...*	be·*neem* a·*duhm* ...
I'm pleased to	*Tanıştığımıza*	ta·nuhsh·tuh·uh·muh·*za*
meet you.	*sevindim.*	se·veen·*deem*
This is my ...	*Bu benim ...*	boo be·*neem* ...
brother	*kardeşim*	kar·de·*sheem*
daughter	*kızım*	kuh·*zuhm*
father	*babayım*	ba·ba·*yuhm*
friend	*arkadaşım*	ar·ka·da·*shuhm*
husband	*kocam*	ko·*jam*
mother	*anneyim*	an·ne·*yeem*
partner (intimate)	*partnerim*	part·ne·*reem*
sister	*kız kardeşim*	kuhz kar·de·*sheem*
son	*oğlum*	o·*loom*
wife	*karım*	ka·*ruhm*
Here's my ...	*İşte benim ...*	eesh·*te* be·*neem* ...
(email) address	*(e-posta) adresiniz*	(e·pos·ta) ad·re·see·*neez*
fax number	*faks numaram*	faks noo·ma·*ram*
phone number	*telefon numaram*	te·le·*fon* noo·ma·*ram*

What's your ...?	Sizin ... nedir?	see·zeen ... ne·deer
(email) address	(e-posta) adresiniz	(e-pos·ta) ad·re·see·neez
fax number	faks numaranız	faks noo·ma·ra·nuhz
phone number	telefon numaranız	te·le·fon noo·ma·ra·nuhz

occupations

What's your occupation?	Mesleğiniz nedir? pol	mes·le·ee·neez ne·deer
	Mesleğin nedir? inf	mes·le·een ne·deer
I'm a/an ...	Ben ...	ben ...
artist	sanatçıyım m&f	sa·nat·chuh·yuhm
business person	iş adamıyım m	ish a·da·muh·yuhm
	kadınıyım f	ka·duh·nuh·yuhm
farmer	çiftçiyim m&f	cheeft·chee·yeem
manual worker	işçiyim m&f	eesh·chee·yeem
office worker	memurum m&f	me·moo·room
scientist	bilim adamıyım m&f	bee·leem a·da·muh·yuhm

background

Where are you from?	Nerelisiniz? pol	ne·re·lee·see·neez
	Nerelisin? inf	ne·re·lee·seen
I'm from ...	Ben ...	ben ...
Australia	Avustralya'lıyım	a·voos·tral·ya·luh·yuhm
Canada	Kanada'lıyım	ka·na·da·luh·yuhm
England	İngiltere'liyim	een·geel·te·re·lee·yeem
the USA	Amerika'lıyım	a·me·ree·ka·luh·yuhm
Are you married?	Evli misiniz?	ev·lee mee·see·neez
I'm married/single.	Ben evliyim/bekarım.	ben ev·lee·yeem/be·ka·ruhm

age

How old ...?	Kaç ...?	kach ...
are you	yaşındasın inf	ya·shuhn·da·suhn
is your son	yaşında oğlunuz	ya·shuhn·da o·loo·nooz
is your daughter	yaşında kızınız	ya·shuhn·da kuh·zuh·nuhz
I'm ... years old.	Ben ... yaşındayım.	ben ... ya·shuhn·da·yuhm
He/She is ... years old.	O ... yaşında.	o ... ya·shuhn·da

feelings

I'm/I'm not ...		
cold	Üşüdüm./	ew·shew·*dewm*/
	Üşümedim.	ew·*shew*·me·deem
happy	Mutluyum./	moot·*loo*·yoom/
	Mutlu değilim.	moot·*loo* de·ee·leem
hot	Sıcakladım./	suh·jak·la·*duhm*/
	Sıcaklamadım.	suh·jak·*la*·ma·duhm
hungry	Acım./Aç değilim.	a·chuhm/ach de·ee·leem
sad	Üzgünüm./	ewz·gew·*newm*/
	Üzgün değilim.	ewz·*gewn* de·ee·leem
thirsty	Susadım./Susamadım.	soo·sa·*duhm*/soo·*sa*·ma·duhm
tired	Yorgunum./	yor·*goo*·noom/
	Yorgun değilim.	yor·*goon* de·ee·leem

Are you ...?		
cold	Üşüdün mü?	ew·shew·*dewn* mew
happy	Mutlu musun?	moot·*loo* moo·*soon*
hot	Sıcakladın mı?	suh·jak·la·*duhn* muh
hungry	Aç mısın?	ach muh·*suhn*
sad	Üzgün musun?	ewz·*gewn* moo·*soon*
thirsty	Susadın mı?	soo·sa·*duhn* muh
tired	Yorgun musun?	yor·*goon* moo·*soon*

entertainment

going out

Where can I find ...?	Buranın ... nerede?	boo·ra·*nuhn* ... *ne*·re·de
clubs	kulüpleri	koo·lewp·le·*ree*
gay venues	gey kulüpleri	gay koo·lewp·le·*ree*
pubs	birahaneleri	bee·ra·ha·ne·le·*ree*

I feel like going to a/the ...	... gitmek istiyor.	... geet·*mek* ees·*tee*·yor
concert	Konsere	kon·se·*re*
movies	Sinemaya	see·ne·ma·*ya*
party	Partiye	par·tee·*ye*
restaurant	Restorana	res·to·ra·*na*
theatre	Oyuna	o·yoo·*na*

interests

Do you like ...?	... sever misin?	... se·ver mee·seen
I like ...	... seviyorum.	... se·vee·yo·room
I don't like ...	... sevmiyorum.	... sev·mee·yo·room
art	Sanat	sa·nat
movies	Sinemaya gitmeyi	see·ne·ma·ya geet·me·yee
reading	Okumayı	o·koo·ma·yuh
sport	Sporu	spo·roo
travelling	Seyahat etmeyi	se·ya·hat et·me·yee
Do you ...?	... misin/misiniz? inf/pol	... mee·seen/mee·see·neez
dance	Dans eder	dans e·der
go to concerts	Konserlere gider	kon·ser·le·re gee·der
listen to music	Müzik dinler	mew·zeek deen·ler

food & drink

finding a place to eat

Can you	İyi bir ... tavsiye	ee·yee beer ... tav·see·ye
recommend a ...?	edebilir misiniz?	e·de·bee·leer mee·see·neez
bar	bar	bar
café	kafe	ka·fe
restaurant	restoran	res·to·ran
I'd like ..., please.	... istiyorum.	... ees·tee·yo·room
a table for (five)	(Beş) kişilik	(besh) kee·shee·leek
	bir masa	beer ma·sa
the nonsmoking	Sigara içilmeyen	see·ga·ra ee·cheel·me·yen
section	bir yer	beer yer
the smoking	Sigara içilen	see·ga·ra ee·chee·len
section	bir yer	beer yer

ordering food

breakfast	kahvaltı	kah·val·tuh
lunch	öğle yemeği	eu·le ye·me·ee
dinner	akşam yemeği	ak·sham ye·me·ee
snack	hafif yemek	ha·feef ye·mek

What would you recommend?
Ne tavsiye edersiniz?   ne tav·see·ye e·der·see·neez

I'd like (a/the)...	... istiyorum.	... ees·tee·yo·room
bill	Hesabı	he·sa·buh
drink list	İçecek listesini	ee·che·jek lees·te·see·nee
menu	Menüyü	me·new·yew
that dish	Şu yemeği	shoo ye·me·ee

drinks

(cup of) coffee ...	(fincan) kahve ...	(feen·jan) kah·ve ...
(cup of) tea ...	(fincan) çay ...	(feen·jan) chai ...
with milk	sütlü	sewt·lew
without sugar	şekersiz	she·ker·seez
(orange) juice	(portakal) suyu	(por·ta·kal) soo·yoo
soft drink	alkolsüz içecek	al·kol·sewz ee·che·jek
sparkling mineral water	maden sodası	ma·den so·da·suh
still mineral water	maden suyu	ma·den soo·yoo
(hot) water	(sıcak) su	(suh·jak) soo

in the bar

I'll have ...	... alayım.	... a·la·yuhm
I'll buy you a drink.	Sana içecek alayım.	sa·na ee·che·jek a·la·yuhm
What would you like?	Ne alırsınız?	ne a·luhr·suh·nuhz
Cheers!	Şerefe!	she·re·fe
brandy	brendi	bren·dee
cocktail	kokteyl	kok·tayl
cognac	konyak	kon·yak
a shot of (whisky)	bir tek (viski)	beer tek (vees·kee)
a bottle/glass of beer	bir şişe/bardak bira	beer shee·she/bar·dak bee·ra
a bottle/glass	bir şişe/bardak	beer shee·she/bar·dak
of ... wine	... şarap	... sha·rap
red	kırmızı	kuhr·muh·zuh
sparkling	köpüklü	keu·pewk·lew
white	beyaz	be·yaz

self-catering

What's the local speciality?
Bu yöreye has yiyecekler neler?   boo yeu·re·*ye* has yee·ye·jek·*ler* ne·ler

What's that?
Bu nedir?   boo *ne*·deer

How much (is a kilo of cheese)?
(Bir kilo peynir) Ne kadar?   (beer kee·*lo* pay·*neer*) ne ka·*dar*

I'd like ...	... istiyorum.	... ees·*tee*·yo·room
(200) grams	*(İkiyüz) gram*	(ee·*kee*·yewz) gram
(two) kilos	*(İki) kilo*	(ee·*kee*) kee·*lo*
(three) pieces	*(Üç) parça*	(ewch) par·*cha*
(six) slices	*(Altı) dilim*	(al·*tuh*) dee·*leem*

Less.	*Daha az.*	da·*ha* az
Enough.	*Yeterli.*	ye·ter·*lee*
More.	*Daha fazla.*	da·*ha* faz·*la*

special diets & allergies

Where's a vegetarian restaurant?
Buralarda vejeteryan restoran   boo·ra·lar·*da* ve·zhe·ter·*yan* res·to·*ran*
var mı?   var muh

Do you have vegetarian food?
Vejeteryan yiyecekleriniz   ve·zhe·ter·*yan* yee·ye·jek·le·ree·*neez*
var mı?   var muh

Is it cooked with ...?	*İçinde ... var mı?*	ee·cheen·*de* ... var muh
butter	*tereyağ*	te·re·*ya*
eggs	*yumurta*	yoo·moor·*ta*
meat stock	*et suyu*	et soo·*yoo*

I'm allergic to ...	... alerjim var.	... a·ler·*zheem* var
dairy produce	*Süt ürünlerine*	sewt ew·rewn·le·ree·*ne*
gluten	*Glutene*	gloo·te·*ne*
MSG	*Mono sodyum*	mo·*no* sod·*yoom*
	glutamata	gloo·ta·ma·*ta*
nuts	*Çerezlere*	che·rez·le·*re*
seafood	*Deniz ürünlerine*	de·*neez* ew·rewn·le·ree·*ne*

menu reader

asma yaprağında sardalya	as·*ma* yap·ra·uhn·*da* sar·*dal*·ya	*sardines in vine leaves*
baklava	bak·la·*va*	*pastry stuffed with pistachio & walnuts*
biber dolması	bee·*ber* dol·ma·*suh*	*stuffed capsicum*
börek	beu·*rek*	*sweet or savoury dishes with a thin crispy pastry*
bumbar	boom·*bar*	*sausage made of rice & meat stuffed in a large sheep or lamb gut*
cacık	ja·*juhk*	*yogurt, mint & cucumber mix*
cevizli bat	je·veez·*lee* bat	*salad of bulgur, lentils, tomato paste & walnuts*
çevirme	che·veer·*me*	*eggplant, chicken, rice & pistachio dish*
çoban salatası	cho·*ban* sa·la·ta·*suh*	*tomato, cucumber & capsicum salad*
çökertme	cheu·kert·*me*	*steak on potatoes with yogurt*
dolma	dol·*ma*	*vine or cabbage leaves stuffed with rice*
erik aşı	e·reek a·*shuh*	*plum dish with prunes, rice & sugar*
gökkuşağı salatası	geuk·koo·sha·uh sa·la·ta·*suh*	*salad of macaroni, capsicum, mushrooms, pickles & salami*
gül tatlısı	gewl tat·luh·*suh*	*fried pastry in lemon sherbet*
halim aşı	ha·*leem* a·*shuh*	*soup of chickpeas, meaty bones, wheat & tomato*
hamsi tava	ham·*see* ta·*va*	*fried, corn-breaded anchovies with onion & lemon*
höşmerim	heush·me·*reem*	*walnut & pistachio pudding*
humus	hoo·*moos*	*mashed chickpeas with sesame oil, lemon & spices*
imam bayıldı	ee·*mam* ba·yuhl·duh	*eggplant, tomato & onion dish*

kadayıf	ka·da·*yuhf*	*dessert of dough soaked in syrup with a layer of sour cream*
kapuska	ka·poos·*ka*	*cold dish of onion, tomato paste & cabbage*
karaş	ka·*rash*	*berry, grape & nut pudding*
kebab/kebap	ke·*bab*/ke·*bap*	*skewered meat & vegetables cooked on an open fire*
keşkül	kesh·*kewl*	*almond, coconut & milk pudding*
köfte	keuf·*te*	*mincemeat or bulgur balls*
kulak çorbası	koo·*lak* chor·ba·*suh*	*meat dumplings boiled in stock*
lokum	lo·*koom*	*Turkish delight*
musakka	moo·sak·*ka*	*vegetable & meat pie*
pastırma	pas·tuhr·*ma*	*pressed beef preserved in spices*
paşa pilavı	pa·*sha* pee·la·*vuh*	*potato, egg & capsicum salad*
patlıcan karnıyarık	pat·luh·*jan* kar·nuh·ya·ruhk	*eggplant stuffed with minced meat*
pirpirim çorbası	peer·pee·reem chor·ba·suh	*chickpea, bean & lentil soup*
pişmaniye	peesh·*ma*·nee·ye	*dessert of sugar, flour & soapwort*
revani	re·*va*·nee	*semolina, vanilla & cream cake*
soğuk çorba	so·*ook* chor·ba	*cold soup of yogurt, rice & capsicum*
sucuk	soo·*jook*	*spicy sausage*
susamlı şeker	soo·sam·*luh* she·*ker*	*sugar-coated peanuts & almonds*
sütlaç	sewt·*lach*	*rice pudding*
şiş kebab	sheesh ke·*bab*	*meat skewered on an open fire*
tarhana	tar·ha·*na*	*yogurt, onion, flour & chilli mix*
topik	to·*peek*	*chickpeas, pistachios, flour & currants topped with sesame sauce*
tulumba tatlısı	too·*loom*·ba tat·luh·*suh*	*fluted fritters served in sweet syrup*
yuvarlama	yoo·var·la·*ma*	*chickpea & mince dumpling soup*

emergencies

basics

Help!	İmdat!	eem-dat
Stop!	Dur!	door
Go away!	Git burdan!	geet boor-dan
Thief!	Hırsız var!	huhr-suhz var
Fire!	Yangın var!	yan-guhn var
Watch out!	Dikkat et!	deek-kat et

Call ...!	... çağırın!	... cha-uh-ruhn
a doctor	Doktor	dok-tor
an ambulance	Ambulans	am-boo-lans
the police	Polis	po-lees

It's an emergency!
Bu acil bir durum.   boo a-jeel beer doo-room

Could you help me, please?
Yardım edebilir misiniz lütfen?   yar-duhm e-de-bee-leer mee-see-neez lewt-fen

Can I use your phone?
Telefonunuzu kullanabilir miyim?   te-le-fe-noo-noo-zoo kool-la-na-bee-leer mee-yeem

I'm lost.
Kayboldum.   kai-bol-doom

Where are the toilets?
Tuvaletler nerede?   too-va-let-ler ne-re-de

police

Where's the police station?
Polis karakolu nerede?   po-lees ka-ra-ko-loo ne-re-de

I want to report an offence.
Şikayette bulunmak istiyorum.   shee-ka-yet-te boo-loon-mak ees-tee-yo-room

I have insurance.
Sigortam var.   see-gor-tam var

4

I've been ...	Ben ...	ben ...
assaulted	saldırıya uğradım	sal·duh·ruh·ya oo·ra·duhm
raped	tecavüze uğradım	te·ja·vew·ze oo·ra·duhm
robbed	soyuldum	so·yool·doom

I've lost my ...	... kayıp.	... ka·yuhp
My ... was/were stolen.	... çalındı.	... cha·luhn·duh
backpack	Sırt çantası	suhrt chan·ta·suh
bags	Çantalar	chan·ta·lar
credit card	Kredi kartı	kre·dee kar·tuh
handbag	El çantası	el chan·ta·suh
jewellery	Mücevherler	mew·jev·her·ler
money	Para	pa·ra
passport	Pasaport	pa·sa·port
travellers cheques	Seyahat çekleri	se·ya·hat chek·le·ree
wallet	Cüzdan	jewz·dan

I want to contact my ...	... görüşmek istiyorum.	... geu·rewsh·mek ees·tee·yo·room
consulate	Konsoloslukla	kon·so·los·look·la
embassy	Elçilikle	el·chee·leek·le

health

medical needs

Where's the nearest ...?	En yakın ... nerede?	en ya·kuhn ... ne·re·de
dentist	dişçi	deesh·chee
doctor	doktor	dok·tor
hospital	hastane	has·ta·ne
(night) pharmacist	(nöbetçi) eczane	(neu·bet·chee) ej·za·ne

I need a doctor (who speaks English).
(İngilizce konuşan) (een·gee·leez·je ko·noo·shan)
Bir doktora ihtiyacım var. beer dok·to·ra eeh·tee·ya·juhm var

Could I see a female doctor?
Bayan doktora ba·yan dok·to·ra
görünebilir miyim? geu·rew·ne·bee·leer mee·yeem

I've run out of my medication.
İlacım bitti. ee·la·juhm beet·tee

symptoms, conditions & allergies

I'm sick.	Hastayım.	has·ta·yuhm
It hurts here.	Burası ağrıyor.	boo·ra·suh a·ruh·yor
I have a toothache.	Dişim ağrıyor.	dee·sheem a·ruh·yor
I have (a) ...	Bende ... var.	ben·de ... var

asthma	astım	as·tuhm
bronchitis	bronşit	bron·sheet
constipation	kabızlık	ka·buhz·luhk
cough	öksürük	euk·sew·rewk
diarrhoea	ishal	ees·hal
fever	ateş	a·tesh
headache	baş ağrısı	bash a·ruh·suh
heart condition	kalp rahatsızlığı	kalp ra·hat·suhz·luh·uh
nausea	bulantı	boo·lan·tuh
pain	ağrı	a·ruh
sore throat	boğaz ağrısı	bo·az a·ruh·suh

I'm allergic to ...	... alerjim var.	... a·ler·zheem var
antibiotics	Antibiyotiklere	an·tee·bee·yo·teek·le·re
anti-inflammatories	Anti-emflamatuarlara	an·tee·em·fla·ma·too·ar·la·ra
aspirin	Aspirine	as·pee·ree·ne
bees	Arılara	a·ruh·la·ra
codeine	Kodeine	ko·de·ee·ne
penicillin	Penisiline	pe·nee·see·lee·ne

antiseptic	antiseptik	an·tee·sep·teek
bandage	bandaj	ban·dazh
condoms	prezervatifler	pre·zer·va·teef·ler
contraceptives	doğum kontrol hapı	do·oom kon·trol ha·puh
diarrhoea medicine	ishal ilacı	ees·hal ee·la·juh
insect repellent	sinek kovucu	see·nek ko·voo·joo
laxatives	müsil ilacı	mew·seel ee·la·juh
painkillers	ağrı kesici	a·ruh ke·see·jee
rehydration salts	rehidrasyon tuzları	re·heed·ras·yon tooz·la·ruh
sleeping tablets	uyku hapı	ooy·koo ha·puh

english–turkish dictionary

Words in this dictionary are marked as a (adjective), n (noun), v (verb), sg (singular), pl (plural), inf (informal) and pol (polite) where necessary.

A

accident *kaza* ka-*za*
accommodation *kalacak yer* ka-la-*jak* yer
adaptor *adaptör* a-dap-*teur*
address n *adres* ad-*res*
after *sonra* son-*ra*
air conditioning *klima* klee-ma
airplane *uçak* oo-*chak*
airport *havaalanı* ha-va-a-la-*nuh*
alcohol *alkol* al-*kol*
all *hepsi* hep-*see*
allergy *alerji* a-ler-*zhee*
ambulance *ambulans* am-boo-*lans*
and *ve* ve
ankle *ayak bileği* a-yak bee-le-*ee*
arm *kol* kol
ashtray *kül tablası* kewl tab-la-*suh*
ATM *bankamatik* ban-ka-ma-*teek*

B

baby *bebek* be-*bek*
back (body) *sırt* suhrt
backpack *sırt çantası* suhrt chan-ta-*suh*
bad *kötü* keu-*tew*
bag *çanta* chan-ta
baggage claim *bagaj konveyörü*
  ba-*gazh* kon-ve-yeu-*rew*
bank *banka* ban-ka
bar *bar* bar
bathroom *banyo* ban-yo
battery *pil* peel
beautiful *güzel* gew-*zel*
bed *yatak* ya-*tak*
beer *bira* bee-ra
before *önce* eun-je
behind *arkasında* ar-ka-suhn-*da*
bicycle *bisiklet* bee-seek-*let*
big *büyük* bew-*yewk*
bill *hesap* he-*sap*
black *siyah* see-*yah*
blanket *battaniye* bat-*ta*-nee-ye

blood group *kan gurubu* kan goo-roo-*boo*
blue *mavi* ma-vee
boat *vapur* va-*poor*
book (make a reservation) v *yer ayırtmak*
  yer a-*yuhrt*-mak
bottle *şişe* shee-*she*
bottle opener *şişe açacağı* shee-*she* a-cha-ja-*uh*
boy *oğlan* o-lan
brakes (car) *fren* fren
breakfast *kahvaltı* kah-val-*tuh*
broken (faulty) *bozuk* bo-*zook*
bus *otobüs* o-to-*bews*
business *iş* eesh
buy *satın almak* sa-tuhn al-*mak*

C

café *kafe* ka-*fe*
camera *kamera* ka-me-ra
camp site *kamp yeri* kamp ye-*ree*
cancel *iptal etmek* eep-*tal* et-*mek*
can opener *konserve açacağı* kon-ser-*ve* a-cha-ja-*uh*
car *araba* a-ra-ba
cash n *nakit* na-*keet*
cash (a cheque) v *(çek) bozdurmak*
  (chek) boz-door-*mak*
cell phone *cep telefonu* jep te-le-fo-*noo*
centre n *merkez* mer-*kez*
change (money) v *bozdurmak* boz-door-*mak*
cheap *ucuz* oo-*jooz*
check (bill) *fatura* fa-too-ra
check-in n *giriş* gee-*reesh*
chest *göğüs* geu-*ews*
child *çocuk* cho-*jook*
cigarette *sigara* see-*ga*-ra
city *şehir* she-*heer*
clean a *temiz* te-*meez*
closed *kapalı* ka-pa-*luh*
coffee *kahve* kah-ve
coins *madeni para* ma-de-*nee* pa-*ra*
cold a *soğuk* so-*ook*
collect call *ödemeli telefon* eu-de-me-*lee* te-le-fon
come *gelmek* gel-*mek*

computer *bilgisayar* beel-gee-sa-yar
condom *prezervatif* pre-zer-va-teef
contact lenses *kontak lens* kon-tak lens
cook v *pişirmek* pee-sheer-mek
cost n *fiyat* fee-yat
credit card *kredi kartı* kre-dee kar-tuh
cup *fincan* feen-jan
currency exchange *döviz kuru* deu-veez koo-roo
customs (immigration) *gümrük* gewm-rewk

D

dangerous *tehlikeli* teh-lee-ke-lee
date (time) *tarih* ta-reeh
day *gün* gewn
delay n *gecikme* ge-jeek-me
dentist *dişçi* deesh-chee
depart *ayrılmak* ai-ruhl-mak
diaper *bebek bezi* be-bek be-zee
dictionary *sözlük* seuz-lewk
dinner *akşam yemeği* ak-sham ye-me-ee
direct *direk* dee-rek
dirty *kirli* keer-lee
disabled *özürlü* eu-zewr-lew
discount n *indirim* een-dee-reem
doctor *doktor* dok-tor
double bed *iki kişilik yatak* ee-kee kee-shee-leek ya-tak
double room *iki kişilik oda* ee-kee kee-shee-leek o-da
drink n *içecek* ee-che-jek
drive v *sürmek* sewr-mek
drivers licence *ehliyet* eh-lee-yet
drugs (illicit) *uyuşturucu* oo-yoosh-too-roo-joo
dummy (pacifier) *emzik* em-zeek

E

ear *kulak* koo-lak
east *doğu* do-oo
eat *yemek* ye-mek
economy class *ekonomi sınıfı* e-ko-no-mee suh-nuh-fuh
electricity *elektrik* e-lek-treek
elevator *asansör* a-san-seur
email *e-posta* e-pos-ta
embassy *elçilik* el-chee-leek
emergency *acil durum* a-jeel doo-room
English (language) *İngilizce* een-gee-leez-je
entrance *giriş* gee-reesh
evening *akşam* ak-sham
exchange rate *döviz kuru* deu-veez koo-roo
exit *çıkış* chuh-kuhsh

expensive *pahalı* pa-ha-luh
express mail *ekspres posta* eks-pres pos-ta
eye *göz* geuz

F

far *uzak* oo-zak
fast *hızlı* huhz-luh
father *baba* ba-ba
film (camera) *film* feelm
finger *parmak* par-mak
first-aid kit *ilk yardım çantası* eelk yar-duhm chan-ta-suh
first class *birinci sınıf* bee-reen-jee suh-nuhf
fish n *balık* ba-luhk
food *yiyecek* yee-ye-jek
foot *ayak* a-yak
fork *çatal* cha-tal
free (of charge) *ücretsiz* ewj-ret-seez
friend *arkadaş* ar-ka-dash
fruit *meyve* may-ve
full *dolu* do-loo
funny *komik* ko-meek

G

gift *hediye* he-dee-ye
girl *kız* kuhz
glass (drinking) *bardak* bar-dak
glasses *gözlük* geuz-lewk
go *gitmek* geet-mek
good *iyi* ee-yee
green *yeşil* ye-sheel
guide n *rehber* reh-ber

H

half n *yarım* ya-ruhm
hand *el* el
handbag *el çantası* el chan-ta-suh
happy *mutlu* moot-loo
have *sahip olmak* sa-heep ol-mak
he *o* o
head *baş* bash
heart *kalp* kalp
heat n *ısı* uh-suh
heavy *ağır* a-uhr
help v *yardım etmek* yar-duhm et-mek
here *burada* boo-ra-da
high *yüksek* yewk-sek

highway *otoyol* o-to-yol
hike v *uzun yürüyüşe çıkmak*
   oo-zoon yew-rew-yew-she chukh-mak
holiday *tatil* ta-teel
homosexual *homoseksüel* ho-mo-sek-sew-el
hospital *hastane* has-ta-ne
hot *sıcak* suh-jak
hotel *otel* o-tel
hungry *aç* ach
husband *koca* ko-ja

I

I *ben* ben
identification (card) *kimlik kartı* keem-leek kar-tuh
ill *hasta* has-ta
important *önemli* eu-nem-lee
included *dahil* da-heel
injury *yara* ya-ra
insurance *sigorta* see-gor-ta
Internet *internet* een-ter-net
interpreter *tercüman* ter-jew-man

J

jewellery *mücevherler* mew-jev-her-ler
job *meslek* mes-lek

K

key *anahtar* a-nah-tar
kilogram *kilogram* kee-log-ram
kitchen *mutfak* moot-fak
knife *bıçak* buh-chak

L

laundry (place) *çamaşırlık* cha-ma-shuhr-luhk
lawyer *avukat* a-voo-kat
left (direction) *sol* sol
left-luggage office *emanet bürosu* e-ma-net bew-ro-soo
leg *bacak* ba-jak
lesbian *lezbiyen* lez-bee-yen
less *daha az* da-ha az
letter (mail) *mektup* mek-toop
lift (elevator) *asansör* a-san-seur
light n *ışık* uh-shuhk
like v *sevmek* sev-mek
lock n *kilit* kee-leet
long *uzun* oo-zoon

lost *kayıp* ka-yuhp
lost-property office *kayıp eşya bürosu*
   ka-yuhp esh-ya bew-ro-soo
love v *âşık olmak* a-shuhk ol-mak
luggage *bagaj* ba-gazh
lunch *öğle yemeği* eu-le ye-me-ee

M

mail n *mektup* mek-toop
man *adam* a-dam
map *harita* ha-ree-ta
market *pazar* pa-zar
matches *kibrit* keeb-reet
meat *et* et
medicine *ilaç* ee-lach
menu *yemek listesi* ye-mek lees-te-see
message *mesaj* me-sazh
milk *süt* sewt
minute *dakika* da-kee-ka
mobile phone *cep telefonu* jep te-le-fo-noo
money *para* pa-ra
month *ay* ai
morning *sabah* sa-bah
mother *anne* an-ne
motorcycle *motosiklet* mo-to-seek-let
motorway *paralı yol* pa-ra-luh yol
mouth *ağız* a-uhz
music *müzik* mew-zeek

N

name *ad* ad
napkin *peçete* pe-che-te
nappy *bebek bezi* be-bek be-zee
near *yakında* ya-kuhn-da
neck *boyun* bo-yoon
new *yeni* ye-nee
news *haberler* ha-ber-ler
newspaper *gazete* ga-ze-te
night *gece* ge-je
no *hayır* ha-yuhr
noisy *gürültülü* gew-rewl-tew-lew
nonsmoking *sigara içilmeyen* see-ga-ra ee-cheel-me-yen
north *kuzey* koo-zay
nose *burun* boo-roon
now *şimdi* sheem-dee
number *sayı* sa-yuh

O

oil (engine) *yağ* ya

old (object/person) *eski/yaşlı* es-kee/yash-luh

one-way ticket *gidiş bilet* gee-deesh bee-let

open a *açık* a-chuhk

outside *dışarıda* duh-sha-ruh-da

P

package *ambalaj* am-ba-lazh

paper *kağıt* ka-uht

park (car) v *park etmek* park et-mek

passport *pasaport* pa-sa-port

pay *ödemek* eu-de-mek

pen *tükenmez kalem* tew-ken-mez ka-lem

petrol *benzin* ben-zeen

pharmacy *eczane* ej-za-ne

phonecard *telefon kartı* te-le-fon kar-tuh

photo *fotoğraf* fo-to-raf

plate *tabak* ta-bak

police *polis* po-lees

postcard *kartpostal* kart-pos-tal

post office *postane* pos-ta-ne

pregnant *hamile* ha-mee-le

price *fiyat* fee-yat

Q

quiet *sakin* sa-keen

R

rain n *yağmur* ya-moor

razor *traş makinesi* trash ma-kee-ne-see

receipt n *makbuz* mak-booz

red *kırmızı* kuhr-muh-zuh

refund n *para iadesi* pa-ra ee-a-de-see

registered mail *taahhütlü posta* ta-ah-hewt-lew pos-ta

rent v *kiralamak* kee-ra-la-mak

repair v *tamir etmek* ta-meer et-mek

reservation *rezervasyon* re-zer-vas-yon

restaurant *restoran* res-to-ran

return v *geri dönmek* ge-ree deun-mek

return ticket *gidiş-dönüş bilet* gee-deesh-deu-newsh bee-let

right (direction) *doğru* yön do-roo yeun

road *yol* yol

room *oda* o-da

S

safe a *emniyetli* em-nee-yet-lee

sanitary napkin *hijyenik kadın bağı* heezh-ye-neek ka-duhn ba-uh

seat *yer* yer

send *göndermek* geun-der-mek

service station *benzin istasyonu* ben-zeen ees-tas-yo-noo

sex *seks* seks

shampoo *şampuan* sham-poo-an

share (a dorm) *paylaşmak* pai-lash-mak

shaving cream *tıraş kremi* tuh-rash kre-mee

she o o

sheet (bed) *çarşaf* char-shaf

shirt *gömlek* geum-lek

shoes *ayakkabılar* a-yak-ka-buh-lar

shop n *dükkan* dewk-kan

short *kısa* kuh-sa

shower n *duş* doosh

single room *tek kişilik oda* tek kee-shee-leek o-da

skin *cilt* jeelt

skirt *etek* e-tek

sleep v *uyumak* oo-yoo-mak

slowly *yavaşça* ya-vash-cha

small *küçük* kew-chewk

smoke (cigarettes) v *sigara içmek* see-ga-ra eech-mek

soap *sabun* sa-boon

some *biraz* bee-raz

soon *yakında* ya-kuhn-da

south *güney* gew-nay

souvenir shop *hediyelik eşya dükkanı* he-dee-ye-leek esh-ya dewk-ka-nuh

speak *konuşmak* ko-noosh-mak

spoon *kaşık* ka-shuhk

stamp *pul* pool

stand-by ticket *açık bilet* a-chuhk bee-let

station (train) *istasyon* ees-tas-yon

stomach *mide* mee-de

stop v *durmak* door-mak

stop (bus) n *durağı* doo-ra-uh

street *sokak* so-kak

student *öğrenci* eu-ren-jee

sun *güneş* gew-nesh

sunscreen *güneşten koruma kremi* gew-nesh-*ten* ko-roo-ma kre-*mee*
swim v *yüzmek* yewz-*mek*

T

tampons *tamponlar* tam-pon-*lar*
taxi *taksi* tak-*see*
teaspoon *çay kaşığı* chai ka-shuh-*uh*
teeth *dişler* deesh-*ler*
telephone n *telefon* te-le-*fon*
television *televizyon* te-le-veez-*yon*
temperature (weather) *derece* de-re-*je*
tent *çadır* cha-*duhr*
that (one) *şunu/onu* shoo-*noo*/o-*noo*
they *onlar* on-*lar*
thirsty *susamış* soo-sa-*muhsh*
this (one) *bunu* boo-*noo*
throat *boğaz* bo-*oz*
ticket *bilet* bee-*let*
time *zaman* za-*man*
tired *yorgun* yor-*goon*
tissues *kağıt mendil* ka-*uht* men-*deel*
today *bugün* boo-*gewn*
toilet *tuvalet* too-va-*let*
tomorrow *yarın* ya-*ruhn*
tonight *bu gece* boo ge-*je*
toothbrush *diş fırçası* deesh fuhr-cha-*suh*
toothpaste *diş macunu* deesh ma-joo-*noo*
torch (flashlight) *el feneri* el fe-ne-*ree*
tour n *tur* toor
tourist office *turizm bürosu* too-reezm bew-ro-*soo*
towel *havlu* hav-*loo*
train *tren* tren
translate *çevirmek* che-veer-*mek*
travel agency *seyahat acentesi* seya-*hat* a-jen-te-*see*
travellers cheque *seyahat çeki* se-ya-hat che-*kee*
trousers *pantolon* pan-to-*lon*
Turkey *Türkiye* tewr-kee-*ye*
Turkish (language) *Türkçe* tewrk-*che*
Turkish Republic of Northern Cyprus (TRNC) *Kuzey Kıbrıs Türk Cumhuriyeti (KKTC)* koo-*zay* kuhb-*ruhs* tewrk joom-hoo-ree-ye-*tee* (ka-ka-te-*je*)
twin beds *çift yatak* cheeft ya-*tak*
tyre *lastik* las-*teek*

U

underwear *iç çamaşırı* eech cha-ma-shuh-*ruh*
urgent *acil* a-*jeel*

V

vacant *boş* bosh
vacation *tatil* ta-*teel*
vegetable n *sebze* seb-*ze*
vegetarian a *vejeteryan* ve-zhe-ter-*yan*
visa *vize* vee-*ze*

W

waiter *garson* gar-*son*
walk v *yürümek* yew-rew-*mek*
wallet *cüzdan* jewz-*dan*
warm a *ılık* uh-*luhk*
wash (something) *yıkamak* yuh-ka-*mak*
watch n *saat* sa-*at*
water *su* soo
we *biz* beez
weekend *hafta sonu* haf-*ta* so-*noo*
west *batı* ba-*tuh*
wheelchair *tekerlekli sandalye* te-ker-lek-*lee* san-dal-*ye*
when *ne zaman* ne za-*man*
where *nerede* ne-re-*de*
white *beyaz* be-*yaz*
who *kim* keem
why *neden* ne-*den*
wife *karı* ka-*ruh*
window *pencere* pen-je-*re*
wine *şarap* sha-*rap*
with *ile* ee-*le*
without *-sız/-siz/-suz/-süz* -*suhz*/-*seez*/-*sooz*/-*sewz*
woman *kadın* ka-*duhn*
write *yazı yazmak* ya-*zuh* yaz-*mak*

Y

yellow *sarı* sa-*ruh*
yes *evet* e-*vet*
yesterday *dün* dewn
you sg inf *sen* sen
you sg pol & pl *siz* seez

INDEX

413

festivals in mediterranean europe

The Tirana International Film Festival in December is the first and only short film festival in **Albania**. Gjirokastra is the home of the Albanian Folklore Festival, usually held in September every four years to celebrate the national traditions, folk music and dance.

In July and August, a programme of theatre, concerts and dance is presented on open-air stages at the prestigious Dubrovnik Summer Festival in **Croatia**. The Rijeka Carnival in February is a week of partying with plenty of parades and street dances.

The Cannes Film Festival in May is the world's most glitzy cinema event and a feast for the paparazzi. Another spectacle is the *Tour de France*, the famous bicycle race through **France** and the neighbouring countries, which ends in Paris in July.

The Hellenic Festival in Athens, the major summer arts festival in **Greece**, features international music, dance and theatre. Το φεστιβάλ κρασιού (the wine festival) is held in early September in Dafni, west of Athens, to celebrate the grape harvest.

The San Remo Music Festival in March has been running in **Italy** since 1951 and was the inspiration for the Eurovision Song Contest. The Italian Gran Prix, organised in September at Monza, is one of the oldest circuits in Formula One.

In July, a village in **Macedonia** hosts very popular and wildly romantic traditional weddings during the Galichnik Wedding Festival. Poets from around 50 countries take part at the Struga Poetry Evenings in August, complete with food and drink in the streets.

Festas das Cruzes (Festival of the Crosses), held in May in Barcelos, **Portugal**, is known for processions, folk music and regional handicrafts. In June, Santarém hosts the *Feira Nacional da Agricultura* (National Agricultural Fair) with bullfighting and folk music.

Kurentovanje, a rite of spring celebrated in February, is the most extravagant folklore event in **Slovenia**, held in Ptuj. Maribor hosts both the International Puppet Festival in July and August and a renowned theatre festival in the second half of October.

In June, Pamplona combines the *San Fermíne* festivities with macho posturing and running bulls, drawing TV crews from all over the world to **Spain**. *Semana Santa* (Holy Week) in April brings parades of holy images and huge crowds, notably in Seville.

Şeker Bayramı (Sweets Festival) is a three-day festival in **Turkey** at the end of the Muslim lunar month of Ramadan. *Kurban Bayramı* (Sacrifice Festival), two months after Ramadan, lasts for four days during which people make animal sacrifices.

What kind of traveller are you?

A. You're eating chicken for dinner *again* because it's the only word you know.

B. When no one understands what you say, you step closer and shout louder.

C. When the barman doesn't understand your order, you point frantically at the beer.

D. You're surrounded by locals, swapping jokes, email addresses and experiences – other travellers want to borrow your phrasebook or audio guide.

If you answered A, B, or C, you NEED Lonely Planet's language products …

- **Lonely Planet Phrasebooks** – for every phrase you need in every language you want
- **Lonely Planet Language & Culture** – get behind the scenes of English as it's spoken around the world – learn and laugh
- **Lonely Planet Fast Talk & Fast Talk Audio** – essential phrases for short trips and weekends away – read, listen and talk like a local
- **Lonely Planet Small Talk** – 10 essential languages for city breaks
- **Lonely Planet Real Talk** – downloadable language audio guides from lonelyplanet.com to your MP3 player

… and this is why

- **Talk to everyone everywhere**
  Over 120 languages, more than any other publisher
- **The right words at the right time**
  Quick-reference colour sections, two-way dictionary, easy pronunciation, every possible subject – and audio to support it

Lonely Planet Offices

Australia
90 Maribyrnong St, Footscray,
Victoria 3011
☎ 03 8379 8000
fax 03 8379 8111
✉ talk2us@lonelyplanet.com.au

USA
150 Linden St, Oakland,
CA 94607
☎ 510 893 8555
fax 510 893 8572
✉ info@lonelyplanet.com

UK
72-82 Rosebery Ave,
London EC1R 4RW
☎ 020 7841 9000
fax 020 7841 9001
✉ go@lonelyplanet.co.uk

lonelyplanet.com